Life and Death in Early Modern Philosophy

Life and Death in Early Modern Philosophy

Edited by
SUSAN JAMES

UNIVERSITY PRESS

Great Clarendon Street, Oxford, OX2 6DP,
United Kingdom

Oxford University Press is a department of the University of Oxford.
It furthers the University's objective of excellence in research, scholarship,
and education by publishing worldwide. Oxford is a registered trade mark of
Oxford University Press in the UK and in certain other countries

© the several contributors 2021

The moral rights of the authors have been asserted

First Edition published in 2021

Impression: 1

All rights reserved. No part of this publication may be reproduced, stored in
a retrieval system, or transmitted, in any form or by any means, without the
prior permission in writing of Oxford University Press, or as expressly permitted
by law, by licence or under terms agreed with the appropriate reprographics
rights organization. Enquiries concerning reproduction outside the scope of the
above should be sent to the Rights Department, Oxford University Press, at the
address above

You must not circulate this work in any other form
and you must impose this same condition on any acquirer

Published in the United States of America by Oxford University Press
198 Madison Avenue, New York, NY 10016, United States of America

British Library Cataloguing in Publication Data

Data available

Library of Congress Control Number: 2021943458

ISBN 978–0–19–284361–6

DOI: 10.1093/oso/9780192843616.001.0001

Printed and bound by
CPI Group (UK) Ltd, Croydon, CR0 4YY

Links to third party websites are provided by Oxford in good faith and
for information only. Oxford disclaims any responsibility for the materials
contained in any third party website referenced in this work.

Contents

Acknowledgements	vii
Notes on Contributors	ix
Introduction: Approaches to Living and Dying *Susan James*	1

PART I. FEELING ALIVE

1. The Consciousness of Being Alive as a Source of Knowledge *Ursula Renz*	19

PART II. IMMORTALITY

2. 'The Thought of Death Changes all our Ideas and Condemns our Plans': Early Modern Christian Philosophical Perspectives on Death *Michael Moriarty*	39
3. The Banishment of Death: Leibniz's Scandalous Immortalism *Matteo Favaretti Camposampiero*	64

PART III. LEARNING TO LIVE

4. Human Life as a State of Mediocrity in John Locke *Giuliana Di Biase*	85
5. Learning to Live a Human Life *Lisa Shapiro*	106
6. Spinozan Meditations on Life and Death *Julie R. Klein*	125

PART IV. LEARNING TO DIE

7. '*Meditatio Mortis*': Post-Cartesian Conceptions of Life and the Conjunction of Mind and Body *Michael Jaworzyn*	157

vi CONTENTS

8. Living Well, Dying Well: Life and Death in Spinoza's Philosophy
   and Biography   181
   Piet Steenbakkers

9. Prevailing over Death: Democritus and the Myth of a
   Philosophical Death   197
   Piero Schiavo

PART V. SUICIDE

10. When the Manner of Death Disagrees with the Status of Life:
    The Intricate Question of Suicide in Early Modern Philosophy   211
    Sarah Tropper

11. David Hume's Philosophical Approach to Suicide   227
    Teresa Tato Lima

12. Less than Zero: Kant's Opposition to Suicide   239
    John J. Callanan

PART VI. INANIMATE AND ANIMATE

13. 'Everyone Knows What Life is': Life as an Irreducible in and
    outside of Descartes's Metaphysics and Biology   263
    Barnaby R. Hutchins

14. Affect and Effect: Spinoza on Life   277
    Steph Marston

15. Vitalism and the Metaphysics of Life: the Discreet Charm
    of Eighteenth-Century Vitalism   292
    Charles T. Wolfe

Bibliography   315
Index   339

Acknowledgements

This volume arose out of a conference held in London at Birkbeck College and King's College, where versions of each chapter were first presented. The event was made possible by the generous support of the European Society for the History of Philosophy, The British Society for the History of Philosophy, the Philosophy Department of Birkbeck College London, Kings College London, and the Wellcome Foundation. I am extremely grateful to all these benefactors.

It is also a pleasure to thank Charlotte Knowles for her invaluable help with organizing the conference, Laurencia Saenz Benavides for taking charge of the conference poster, and Noemi Magnani for compiling the Bibliography of this volume. Thanks, too, to Professor Maria Rosa Antognazza for enabling us to hold some conference sessions at King's College, and to Birkbeck College for help with translation costs. Without the care and support of Oxford University Press's copyeditors, the editor Henry Clarke, and above all Peter Momtchiloff, there would be no book to read. I am grateful to them all. Finally, my warmest thanks go to the contributors, who have been a pleasure to work with.

S.J.

Notes on Contributors

Giuliana Di Biase is an Associate Professor of Moral Philosophy at the University of Chieti-Pescara 'G. d'Annunzio', Italy. She holds a master's degree in Modern Literature and Philosophy, and received her PhD in History and Foundations of Ethics and Anthropology from the University of Salento in 2002, under the supervision of Professor Eugenio Lecaldano. Di Biase has authored six books and made over seventy contributions devoted to contemporary and early modern moral philosophy. Her recent publications focus mainly on Locke's moral thought and she is the founding editor-in-chief of *Studi lockiani. Ricerche sull'età moderna*, Pisa (2020).

Matteo Favaretti Camposampiero is Associate Professor at the Department of Philosophy and Cultural Heritage of the Ca' Foscari University of Venice. His research is devoted to early modern philosophy from Descartes to Kant. His publications include two books, six co-edited volumes, and several articles on Leibniz, Wolff, their sources, and their influence. Among his recent articles are 'Machines of Nature and Machines of Art: Christian Wolff's Reception of Leibniz', *Rivista di Storia della Filosofia* (2019); 'Mereology and Mathematics: Christian Wolff's Foundational Programme', *British Journal for the History of Philosophy* (2019); 'Infinite Regress: Wolff's Cosmology and the Background of Kant's Antinomies', *Kant-Studien* (forthcoming).

Barnaby R. Hutchins is a research fellow at Ghent University, Belgium. His main areas of research are early modern metaphysics and early modern biology. Among his publications are 'Descartes, Corpuscles and Reductionism: Mechanism and Systems in Descartes' Physiology', *Philosophical Quarterly* (2015), and 'Descartes and the Dissolution of Life', *Southern Journal of Philosophy* (2016).

Susan James is a professor of Philosophy at Birkbeck College London. Her main areas of interest are early modern philosophy, feminist philosophy, political philosophy, and the philosophy of art. Among her publications are *Passion and Action: The Emotions in Early-Modern Philosophy*, Oxford (1997); *Spinoza on Philosophy Religion and Politics: the Theological-Political Treatise*, Oxford (2012); and *Spinoza on Learning to Live Together*, Oxford (2020). She is a Fellow of the British Academy.

Michael Jaworzyn received his doctorate in philosophy at KU Leuven. He is a fellow on the Panentheism and Religious Life project (a research collaboration between King's College London and Johns Hopkins University), and a visiting fellow at the Warburg Institute. He is the author of articles on the early reception and transformation of Descartes' thought, and is particularly interested in the work and legacy of Arnold Geulincx. His publications include: 'Caspar Langenhert's Parisian "School of Egoists" and the Reception of Geulincx's Physics, from Occasionalism to Solipsism', *History of Universities* XXXIII/2 (2021) and '"The mind is more like matter, the body more like the form": Geulincx against Descartes

X NOTES ON CONTRIBUTORS

(and the scholastics) on the sources of difference in minds', in *Differences in Identity in Philosophy and Religion*, S. Flavel and R. Manning, eds. (2020).

Julie R. Klein is Associate Professor of Philosophy at Villanova University. She works in medieval and early modern philosophy and is the author of articles on Gersonides, Spinoza, and Descartes. Her current project on Spinozan pedagogy considers the epistemic, affective, and socio-political dimensions of three kinds of knowing from a developmental perspective. Her other interests include critical theory, queer theory, and psychoanalysis.

Steph Marston is Associate Research Fellow in the Department of Philosophy at Birkbeck, University of London. Her main research interests are in the history of philosophy, feminist philosophy, and political philosophy.

Michael Moriarty is Drapers Professor of French at the University of Cambridge, and a Fellow of Peterhouse. His publications include *Taste and Ideology in Seventeenth-Century France*, Cambridge University Press (1988), *Roland Barthes*, Polity Press (1991), *Early Modern French Thought: The Age of Suspicion*, Oxford University Press (2003), *Fallen Nature, Fallen Selves: Early Modern French Thought II*, Oxford University Press (2006), *Disguised Vices: Theories of Virtue in Early Modern French Thought*, Oxford University Press (2011), and *Pascal: Reasoning and Belief*, Oxford University Press (2020). He is joint editor of *The Cambridge History of French Thought*, Cambridge University Press (2019). He is a Fellow of the British Academy and a Chevalier dans l'Ordre des Palmes Académiques.

Ursula Renz is Professor of Philosophy at the University of Graz, Austria, where she is Speaker of the working unit History of Philosophy and Chair of the Alexius Meinong Institute. Her research focus is the intersection of theoretical philosophy (metaphysics, epistemology) and history of philosophy (in particular, Early Modern Philosophy, nineteenth- and twentieth-century German-written philosophy). Her publications include the monographs *Die Rationalität der Kultur* (2002) and *The Explainability of Experience* (2018; original publication in German 2010), and *Was denn bitte ist kulturelle Identität?* (2019), several edited volumes including *Self-Knowledge. A History*, Oxford University Press (2017) as well as numerous articles.

Piero Schiavo is Professor in a secondary school in Rome and collaborates with the Department of Philosophy and Communication, University of Bologna. He has worked at the universities of Bologna and Barcelona and has been visiting researcher at the ENS in Paris. He is writing a monograph on the reception of Democritus in French culture between the sixteenth and eighteenth centuries. His recent publications include 'Immagini di Democrito nelle edizioni delle *Vite* di Diogene Laerzio dal XV al XVIII secolo', *Bruniana & Campanelliana* XXIV, 2 (2018); 'La maschera di Democrito nella letteratura francese tra XVI e XVIII secolo', *Intersezioni* 3 (2019); 'Démocrite dans les histoire de la philosophie à l'aube des Lumières', in *Historia philosophica* 18 (2020).

Lisa Shapiro is Professor of Philosophy at Simon Fraser University. She is translator and editor of *The Correspondence of Princess Elisabeth of Bohemia and René Descartes*, Chicago (2007), co-editor (with Martin Pickavé) of *Emotion and Cognitive Life in Medieval and Early Modern Philosophy*. Oxford University Press (2012), and editor of *Pleasure: A History*. Oxford University Press (2018). Her research has examined the philosophy of Descartes and Spinoza through their accounts of the passions, and has recovered the philosophical works of early modern women. She is currently interested in how seventeenth-century philosophers developed a Cartesian philosophy of mind in their arguments for women's education.

Piet Steenbakkers studied English and Philosophy in Groningen. His PhD, University of Groningen (1994) was on *Spinoza's Ethica from Manuscript to Print*. Until his retirement he was Senior Lecturer in the History of Modern Philosophy in the Department of Philosophy and Religious Studies at Utrecht University, and holder of the chair of Spinoza Studies at Erasmus University Rotterdam. He is an active researcher at Utrecht University, and in the international *Groupe de Recherches Spinozistes*. Together with Fokke Akkerman and Pierre-François Moreau he produced the critical edition of Spinoza's *Ethica*, Paris, Presses Universitaires de France (2020).

Teresa Tato Lima is a PhD student in Philosophy and a Research Assistant at the Humanities Center (CHAM) at the Universidade Nova de Lisboa. Her research interests span the philosophy of nature, anthropology, epistemology, and ethics, focusing on the modern and contemporary periods. Among her publications are 'The Original Contract and the Institution of Political Society in David Hume' in *Nature, Causality and Forms of Corporeality, Humus* (2017) and 'The human self and the apprehension of harmony in Leibniz Monadology', *Philosophica* (2011).

Sarah Tropper is a University Assistant at the University of Graz, Austria. She received her PhD from King's College London and has published on Leibniz and Spinoza. Her current research focuses on early modern rationalism and its relation to medieval scholasticism.

Charles T. Wolfe is Professor in the Department of Philosophy, Université Toulouse II – Jean Jaurès. He works primarily in history and philosophy of the early modern life sciences, with a particular interest in materialism and vitalism. He is the author of *Materialism: A Historico-Philosophical Introduction*, Springer (2016); *La philosophie de la biologie: une histoire du vitalisme*, Classiques Garnier (2019); *Lire le matérialisme*. ENS Editions (2020). He is editor of *Vitalism and the scientific image in post-Enlightenment life-science* (2013); *Brain Theory* (2014); *Physique de l'esprit* (2018), and *Philosophy of Biology before Biology* (2019). Among his current projects is the *Encyclopedia of Early Modern Philosophy and the Sciences* (edited with D. Jalobeanu). He is co-editor of the book series 'History, Philosophy and Theory of the Life Sciences' (Springer).

Introduction: Approaches to Living and Dying

Susan James

'If nature has sense and reason then she has self motion; and if nature has self motion, then none of her parts can be called inanimate or soulless; for motion is the life and soul of nature and of all her parts, . . . there being no part of the animate body of nature that can be dead.'[1] Margaret Cavendish, the author of these lines, belonged to the eclectic assemblage of early modern philosophers who argued that everything in nature is alive—minerals as well as plants, snow as well as human beings. Writing in the 1660s, she dismissed the everyday assumption of an ontological division between living and non-living things and portrayed a world teeming with life and knowledge. Cavendish's vision provided rich materials for the fantasies she developed in her fictional works, where animal-men converse learnedly with human beings.[2] But her argument also belongs to a wide-ranging philosophical controversy about the extent of life, which runs through European philosophy of the early modern period and finds expression in two persistent questions. How much of nature is alive? And is life bounded by birth and death?

In a culture saturated by Christian theology and policed by the demands of religious orthodoxy, the notion of a lifespan was unavoidably ambiguous. Most living things, it was widely though not universally agreed, are born, live, and die, and when they die they cease to exist. For human beings, however, death is not the end of being; the soul survives and will be reunited with the body after Judgement Day. As the Apostolic Creed has it, 'I believe . . . in the resurrection of the body, and the life everlasting.' Birth, which marks the start of our earthly lifespan, has its double in rebirth, the transition to eternal life. Equally, death is both an end and a beginning; before we can be reborn we must die, but dying is a step towards renewed life. For many authors working within a Christian framework, this narrative constrained what it was acceptable to say and even to think; any credible philosophical system had to accommodate the New Testament's promise of eternal life. It comes as no surprise, however, that this very constraint was also a source of philosophical trouble and creativity. The polysemic conceptions of life

---

[1] Cavendish 2001, I. xvi, 72.
[2] See 'The Description of a New Word called the Blazing World', in Cavendish 2003.

Susan James, *Introduction: Approaches to Living and Dying* In: *Life and Death in Early Modern Philosophy*. Edited by: Susan James, Oxford University Press. © Susan James 2021. DOI: 10.1093/oso/9780192843616.003.0001

2 INTRODUCTION: APPROACHES TO LIVING AND DYING

and death inherited from Christianity, and indeed from other traditions, not only provoked a host of difficult questions, but seem to have served as a catalyst for far-reaching and inventive answers. Perhaps automata are alive, as Descartes seems to imply; perhaps everything is alive, as Cavendish proposes; perhaps death is unreal, as Leibniz claims; perhaps we remain embodied after death, as Malebranche speculates; perhaps, as Conway argues, animals as well as humans are eligible for redemption; and perhaps, as many writers suggest, it is incumbent on us to live as full a human life as we can. Problems relating to life and death arise across the whole of early modern philosophy and call out for attention.

This book aims to convey the breadth of these philosophical concerns. It ranges over debates in metaphysics, the life sciences (as we call them), epistemology, the philosophy of mathematics, philosophical psychology, the philosophy of religion, the philosophy of education, and ethics. At the same time, it aims to illuminate the interconnectedness of the problems explored under these headings. The contents of one category spill over into others as authors examine the metaphysical implications of their ethical commitments or wonder about the epistemological basis of their educational programmes. Needless to say, many of these interconnections have older roots, and the desire to relate one problem with another is amply prefigured in classical, medieval, and renaissance philosophies. What changes, however, is the intellectual and cultural environment within which philosophers find themselves working, and the shifts in ideas to which this gives rise. In some cases, altered conditions generate new questions, a phenomenon illustrated, for example, in Parts I and VI; in others, they suggest new approaches to existing puzzles, as Parts II, III, IV, and V variously show; and alongside them, as we see throughout the book, old problems persist. But regardless of the trajectory of any individual issue, intercommunication between one topic and another gives rise to fresh outlooks and emphases. Much of the fascination of early modern discussions of life and death lies precisely in their complex ramifications—in the way apparently disparate commitments merge into comprehensive philosophical outlooks that frequently challenge our own.

In recent years there has been a wave of interest in the place of the life sciences within early modern natural philosophy. How did the writers of this era view living organisms, and how did they account for their operations? Eminent scholars have studied these issues in relation to individual figures such as Descartes,[3] Leibniz,[4] Buffon and Kant,[5] and have examined the overarching theories within which organisms were studied.[6] In doing so, they have been unavoidably drawn into metaphysical controversies, for example about substance, individuation, causation, or infinity, each with its own theological dimensions. The resulting theologico-metaphysical-biological nexus constitutes one of the

---

[3] Detlefsen 2016, 141–172; Brown and Normore 2019.   [4] Smith 2011.
[5] Wilson 2017a, 53–68; Wilson 2017b, 256–274.   [6] Nachtomy and Smith 2014.

leading areas of current research on life and death, and forms part of the subject matter under discussion here. But this book has a further ambition: to link the predominantly theoretical preoccupations associated with the study of organisms to the practical aspect of philosophy by bringing them into conversation with a range of broadly ethical questions about life and death. Rather than giving priority to themes that anticipate the preoccupations of modern science, the organization of the volume aims to remind us that philosophy, as our early modern predecessors construed it, was also about learning how to live and die.[7] Questions about our nature as living things were explored in the shadow, as it were, of questions about how to conduct and end our own lives. The six parts of the book are therefore roughly divided between theoretical and practical themes. Parts I, II, and VI deal for the most part with metaphysical, theological, and epistemological problems and trace some of their psychological and biological implications. Parts III, IV, and V focus mainly on ethical issues, and follow out some of their consequences for psychology, education, and philosophizing itself. The rest of this Introduction takes these sections one by one and summarizes the topics examined in each of them.

1 Feeling alive

What is it to know that we are alive? This question is not often examined by early modern philosophers, nor by their current commentators; but as Ursula Renz argues in Chapter 1, changes in philosophical language during the course of the seventeenth century make it possible to formulate the problem in new terms. The crucial linguistic shift is in the meaning of 'consciousness'. In Latin, an old sense of *conscientia* to mean 'conscience' comes to be complemented by a novel use, made familiar, for example, by Descartes: 'I use the term "thought" (*cogitatio*) to include everything that is within us in such a way that we are immediately aware (*conscius*) of it. Thus, all the operations of the will, the intellect, the imagination and the senses are thoughts.'[8] To be conscious of something is to be immediately aware of it, and for Descartes the objects of consciousness are our thoughts. Both in Latin and other languages, this modern sense of the term took some time to get established, so that its appearances in seventeenth-century texts need careful interpretation. As it gained hold, however, it became possible to ask whether

---

[7] Hadot 1995; Jones 2006; James 2020.

[8] '*Cogitationis nomine complector illud omne quod sic in nobis est, ut ejus immediate conscii simus. Ita omnes voluntatis, intellectus, imaginationis & sensuum operationes sunt cogitationes.*' René Descartes, *Second Set of Replies*, AT VII.160; CSM II.113. (I use the standard abbreviations of Descartes' *Œuvres* ed. Charles Adam and Paul Tannery, and *The Philosophical Writings of Descartes* ed. and trans. John Cottingham, Robert Stoothof, Dugald Murdoch and Anthony Kenny.)

4 INTRODUCTION: APPROACHES TO LIVING AND DYING

we are conscious of being alive, and what kind of knowledge this consciousness amounts to.

Taking this question as one of the legacies bequeathed by Descartes, Renz traces the way it is taken up in the next generation by a dedicated Cartesian, Louis de la Forge, and by Spinoza. Even the issue at stake, she suggests, is hard to discern. After all, we usually only ask whether we are alive in exceptional circumstances such as out-of-body experiences, and otherwise take living for granted. But la Forge and Spinoza are among the philosophers who recognize the need to explain our feeling of being alive, and their answers tend in a metaphysical direction. For Spinoza, in particular, the feeling gives us immediate access to our being and yields knowledge of what we most fundamentally are.

The metaphysical arguments on which Renz concentrates analyse the knowledge of being alive in general terms, and stand back from its phenomenology. Here, though, philosophical enquiry merges with a range of theologically and poetically inspired attempts to articulate what it feels like to be alive. The theological aspect of this project crops up in Part II; but the genre in which the feeling of being alive is perhaps most deeply explored is poetry. Writing about this development in the English case, Timothy Harrison suggests that seventeenth-century prose lacked the resources to portray the first-person phenomenology of consciousness, and only poetry could rise to the challenge.[9] Some philosophers were inclined to agree. Descartes, for example, resorts to a simile to express the gulf between prosaic philosophical language and poetry's ability to mimic the immediacy of consciousness. 'It seems amazing', he observes, 'what profound thoughts are in the writings of the poets, more so than in those of the philosophers. The reason is that poets write through enthusiasm and the strength of the imagination, for there are sparks of knowledge within us, as in a flint: where philosophers extract them through reason, poets force them out through the imagination and they shine more brightly.'[10]

One way to isolate the feeling of being alive in its purest form is to imagine the dawning of individual consciousness—the first moment at which individuals become aware of themselves. Condillac would later try to reconstruct this moment in prose,[11] but in the seventeenth century it was the poets who captured it most vividly. As Harrison reminds us, Milton's Adam describes his first awakening: 'Straight towards heaven my wondering eyes I turned/ And gazed awhile the ample sky, till raised/By quick instinctive motion, up I sprung/ and thitherwood endeavouring, and upright/ Stood on my feet.'[12] Still more speculatively, Thomas Traherne claims to remember his experiences as a foetus 'shut up in the Narrow

---

[9] Harrison 2020, 24–25.
[10] 'Cogitationes privatae', AT X. 217; CSM I.4. Quoted in Jones 2006, 27–28.
[11] de Condillac 1984.
[12] John Milton 1991, 'Paradise Lost' (VIII. 257–261) in Orgel and Goldberg, eds, 1991; Harrison 2020, 107.

Closet of his Mothers Womb'.[13] 'Those pure and virgin apprehensions I had from the womb, and that divine light wherewith I was born, are the best unto this day, wherein I can see the universe. By the gift of God they attended me into the world, and by his special favor I remember them till now. Verily they seem the greatest gifts his wisdom could bestow, for without them all other gifts had been dead and vain.... All appeared new, and strange, at the first, inexpressibly rare, and delightful, and beautiful.'[14]

For Milton, Adam's first experiences of being alive are a feeling of wonder at his surroundings, but also of his body in motion. He stands upright on his feet. For Traherne, consciousness begins with a sense of beauty and delight. When early modern philosophers examined our knowledge of being alive, they took up the poets' emphasis on feeling, along with its connotations of embodiment. In their own idiom, they contributed to a broader cultural preoccupation, shaped by the emergence of a new conception of consciousness.

2 Immortality

The feeling of being alive as we have so far encountered it is a feature of our mortal, embodied life, bounded by birth and death. But for the majority of the authors discussed in this book, there is a parallel question to be asked about our *post mortem* existence. When Spinoza affirms, for example, that 'we feel and know by experience that we are eternal',[15] he prompts us to consider how the knowledge that we exist eternally relates to the knowledge that we exist here and now. Is there a difference between the embodied feeling of being a living but mortal creature and the feeling that one exists eternally, and can we somehow articulate it? Admittedly, Spinoza's formulation of the problem rides roughshod over the theological narrative that conventionally frames Christian discussions of eternal life: when death destroys our bodies, our souls enter a new phase of existence in which they no longer experience bodily sensations or perceptions. But Christian authors also worried about the nature of *post mortem* consciousness.

As Michael Moriarty shows in Chapter 2, Scholastic Aristotelians and Cartesians were among the philosophers who struggled to conceive the alien life of the disembodied soul, and to confront the anxiety that a life without sensory pleasure would be disastrously diminished. Acknowledging that there is a risk involved in exchanging the mortal pleasures we know for an existence we cannot imagine, Descartes responds with characteristic caution by assessing the balance of probabilities. Natural reason 'teaches that though we should not seriously fear

---

[13] Traherne 2005–2018, 3.436.41–42. Quoted in Harrison 2020, 152.
[14] Traherne 2005–2018, 5.93.3.1–2. Quoted in Harrison 2020, 199.   [15] Spinoza 1985, V P23s.

6 INTRODUCTION: APPROACHES TO LIVING AND DYING

death, we should equally never seek it'.[16] But the need to allay the suspicion that the afterlife is nothing to look forward to also motivated authors to narrow the gap between embodied and disembodied experience by embodying the soul. Henry More, for example, equips souls that are no longer joined to a human body with aerial bodies or vehicles.[17] In this volume Moriarty's discussion of French defences of the pleasures of the afterlife culminates in Malebranche's view that the inter-action between our souls and our material bodies, and thus our sensory experi-ence, is mediated by an immaterial body that can in principle survive death. As long as the soul remains united with this subtle body, a life that is no longer physically embodied is nevertheless capable of sensory pleasure.

Although the strategy of investing the life of the disembodied soul with an analogue of sensory satisfactions was in some ways philosophically tendentious (how can a soul have a body?), it held out a comforting image of life after death. Some philosophers, however, expressed a deeper resistance to Christian concep-tions of mortality by insisting that we are not only eternal, but that we are eternally embodied. While we are born and die in the everyday sense, these events do not mark the beginning and end of our corporeal existence. In relation to birth, this conviction is expressed in theories of preformation. Malebranche is one of a range of theorists who hold that each living thing, human or otherwise, is formed by God at the Creation and exists in miniature form as a seed until, in accordance with mechanical principles, it grows in its mother's womb.[18] Any living being is as old as the world. In relation to death, so-called immortalists defended the claim that living things never die. 'All animals', Leibniz writes, 'are free from extinction, for they are simply transformed by generation and death.'[19]

Immortalism, as Matteo Favaretti Camposampiero explains in Chapter 3, was not uncommon; when Leibniz espoused it, he joined a string of writers, ancient and modern, who had defended immortalist positions. Nevertheless, the commit-ment remained deeply problematic, partly because it demanded a radical rethink-ing of individual identity. If we burn an insect and are left with a pile of ash, one of Leibniz's critics asks, in what sense does the insect survive? Leibniz's response, as Camposampiero reconstructs it, is pleasingly symmetrical: just as an animal's body unfolds at the start of its mortal life, so it folds up again when that life comes to an end. Throughout these transformations it remains embodied and retains its numerical identity. But even if Leibniz's contemporaries had found his view persuasive, which they emphatically did not, immortalism faced a further difficulty. By denying that death is real, it opened up a disconcerting divide between metaphysics and a Christian theology in which dying is the price of

---

[16] Descartes, Letter to Princess Elisabeth, 3 November 1645. AT IV.333; CSM III. 277.
[17] More 1987, II. 15.161.
[18] Malebranche 1997, I. 6. 1; Last Elucidation, 38–41. Detlefsen 2014, 137–156.
[19] Leibniz to Wolff, 9 November 1705. Quoted by Favaretti Camposampiero in this volume, Chapter 3, C3P2.

redemption. At this point, as at many others, theology imposes constraints, not on the metaphysical imagination, but on the extent to which non-orthodox metaphysical views can become regular subjects of philosophical conversation and enter the philosophical curriculum.

3 Learning to live

Immortalism is perhaps the most extreme of the attempts to defy death that are so prominent in early modern philosophy, and its effects on metaphysics are profound. So too, as Part III reveals, are its implications for the ethical dimensions of human life. If, for example, we are immortal, what bearing does this have on how we should live? Does it render what we usually call death morally irrelevant? Or is our so-called *post mortem* existence still shaped by the moral quality of our mortal lives? Problems such as these tend to be addressed in the context of a debate about what we can and should aspire to be. As human beings, located in a divinely ordained universe and in particular historical societies, what is the best kind of life we can lead? The philosophers discussed in this section agree that living well is a matter of knowing what virtues are required of us and having the ability to put them into practice. To become virtuous, we need to cultivate both our understanding of the good and our power to live as this understanding prescribes. However, their diverse approaches to this project reflect their individual temperaments as well as their philosophical commitments and range from the relatively modest to the transformatively ambitious.

At the modest end of the spectrum, Locke emphasizes the importance of acknowledging what he calls our mediocrity: the fact that our capacities lie somewhere between imperfection and perfection. We need to accept, for example, that there are many things about which our knowledge will always be uncertain, and many talents we do not possess. Overweening ambition in any sphere, whether financial, philosophical, or political, leads to perplexity, melancholy, and other forms of unhappiness, and is unsuited to our human station. In Chapter 4, Giuliana di Biase traces Locke's account of mediocrity as it develops from his early notebooks to his *Essay concerning Human Understanding* and relates it to the classical and early Christian traditions on which he drew. When he first discusses mediocrity, Locke urges us to be contented with what we are; but by the time he revises the *Essay*, he is concerned about an inherent restlessness in human nature—the uneasiness that accompanies all our desires, moves the will, and generates new aspirations. How can uneasiness and a steady sense of our mediocrity be reconciled? For Locke, di Biase shows, uneasiness is yet another manifestation of mediocrity. Part of our imperfection lies in our need to learn to direct our uneasiness, so that we become able to refrain from acting on imprudent

8 INTRODUCTION: APPROACHES TO LIVING AND DYING

and otherwise destructive desires.[20] As mediocre beings, this skill does not come easily. We have to work at it, and we make more progress if we are lucky enough to be well educated. In principle, however, learning to live well in relation to our human purposes lies within our grasp.

Locke's emphasis on learning to refrain from acting on one's desires plays a crucial part in Chapter 5, which focuses on the moral role of volition. Lisa Shapiro begins with Descartes, in some respects a more optimist theorist than Locke insofar as he grounds our moral capacities on the untrammelled freedom of the will. But Cartesianism is also alive to our mediocrity. Understanding how to live well is difficult, and we are liable to make mistakes about it. Fortunately, however, we are always free to act on our clearest and most determinate judgements, and this is as much as we should ask of ourselves. As long as we consistently do what we sincerely judge to be best, we are beyond reproach. Descartes recognizes, of course, that we are not born with this capacity; learning to use the will properly is a skill we have to develop. But while he acknowledges this fact, he barely pauses to investigate it. Shapiro argues that it is mainly the next generation of philosophical writers who begin to enquire more carefully into the kinds of training that can equip us to use the will to control our desires.

These explorations draw on earlier educational treatises which extol the benefits of gentleness. Teachers, Pierre Charron warns, 'should proceed not after an austere, rude and severe manner, but sweetly, mildly and cheerfully',[21] using conversation to engage their pupils' interest. By these means, education can strengthen a student's spirit of enquiry and 'open the way at their own will'.[22] Precepts of this kind were still circulating in the latter half of the seventeenth century and were echoed in Locke's reflections on education.[23] By then, however, as Shapiro shows, they were being subjected to fresh forms of criticism. Writers concerned with women's education began to point to the way our capacity to make and act on clear and determinate judgements can be blocked by social prejudices that are reinforced rather than dispelled by educational practice. As Poulain de la Barre points out, an entrenched belief in the inequality of the sexes is a case in point. A widespread belief in women's inferior abilities can undermine women's faith in their own understanding and stunt their ability to freely exercise the will. Taking up this problem, Mary Astell struggles with the question of how women can be trained to abandon the bad habit of submissiveness and exercise their judgement for themselves.

In the work of Locke, Poulain de la Barre, and Astell, moral virtue is closely linked to theological and social values; we manifest our virtue in our links with

---

[20] Hume later mounted a further spirited defence of mediocrity: 'we may also remark of the middle station of life that it is the more favourable to the acquiring of Wisdom and Ability as well as of Virtu'. Hume 1985, 545–551.

[21] Charron 1601, III. 2. xiv, 443.   [22] Charron 1601, 455.   [23] Locke 1989.

God and the people around us, and in order to sustain these relationships we must learn exercise our wills appropriately. But for Descartes, social and religious values flow explicitly from a prior commitment to philosophical understanding. The more we acquire and act on clear and distinct ideas, the more powerful we become, to the point where 'we can control our passions with such skill that the evils which they cause are quite bearable, and even become a source of joy'.[24] As we progress towards this somewhat Stoic goal, the phenomenology of our lives alters. Instead of being preoccupied by our feelings of vulnerability and mediocrity, we turn our attention to their causes and take pleasure in controlling them. Living well in the sense of learning to act on our best judgements brings with it a life of increasingly uninterrupted satisfaction.

Virtue, thus conceived, dramatically alters the moral quality of our lives; but a yet more ambitious account of the transformative effects of understanding is discussed in Chapter 6, in which Julie Klein examines Spinoza's account of eternal life. As we extend our understanding, Spinoza argues, we become better able to control our passions, and in doing so become able to live more virtuously. We become more interested in controlling than merely submitting to our affects, more concerned with manipulating their causes to promote joyfulness than in experiencing the affects themselves. However, this shift of attention away from our own states to our relationships with the things that affect us is only part of the transformation that knowledge brings. As the kind of knowledge Spinoza calls reasoning blends into the kind he describes as intuiting, our minds focus less on our relationships with other finite individuals and more on the eternal structure of nature of which God is the immanent cause. We come to recognize that we are not merely finite beings who are born and die, but also modes of God whose existence is eternal. The change Spinoza describes here is a gradual but ultimately massive shift of attention; as we become more absorbed by our place in nature as a whole, the ready-to-hand alterations that generally preoccupy us become less interesting. Integral to this process, however, is a change in our understanding of how to improve the experienced quality of our lives. Instead of worrying about our own deaths, the prospect of dying ceases to trouble us, and we become progressively more skilful at acting on our knowledge to promote joyfulness. Here Klein takes up a theme also alluded to in Shapiro's title—the project of learning to live a fully human life. A life organized around intuition, she shows, is for Spinoza the pinnacle of virtue. The more our knowledge empowers us, the more vital or alive we become. As well as transforming the quality of life, intuition transforms life itself.

Klein's analysis of these ideas brings us back to the theme of immortality construed as resistance to death. Like some of the philosophers discussed in

---

[24] Descartes, 'Passions of the Soul', AT 11.488; CSM I.404.

10   INTRODUCTION: APPROACHES TO LIVING AND DYING

Part II, Spinoza regards death as a transition in which one kind of thing turns into other kinds of things, but the eternal essence of the mind remains. There is, then, no death in the sense of annihilation. His defence of this view is marked, however, by a complete absence of Christian anxieties about bodily resurrection or the place of pleasure in the afterlife. As the final part of Klein's essay reveals, Spinoza's exceptionally fluid conception of an individual allows these worries to be set aside.

4 Learning to die

Not many philosophers shared Spinoza's view that a preoccupation with death and dying reveals a lack of understanding. According to a more common outlook, dying well is part of living well, and it is part of our moral task to learn to die. If, as Cicero had claimed, a philosopher's life is a preparation for death, death is of central philosophical concern to the living.[25] One consequence of this belief was the emergence of a set of practices known as *meditatio mortis*, meditation on death, which sometimes amounted to nothing less than practising dying. In prophetic states, in transports of love, in some forms of insanity, and in profound philosophical meditation the soul was held to separate temporarily from the body, thus enabling the meditator to experience incorporeality. As Michael Jaworzyn explains in Chapter 7, Dutch Cartesians were both seduced and alarmed by this possibility. While Descartes himself had allowed that the mind becomes less alert to the promptings of the body during philosophical meditation, he was careful to insist that it never withdraws completely; although a meditator may forget to eat, for example, she will remain sensitive to intense pain.[26] But the Dutch Cartesian Johannes Clauberg was less circumspect. In states of deep contemplation, he argued, the connection between body and mind dissolves and the mind experiences a form of ecstasy akin to the pleasures of the afterlife.

Clauberg's suggestion that meditation enables us to mimic dying and get a foretaste of immortality represents another early modern effort to tame the power of death by bringing it under human control. Those with the ability can practise dying as and when they will. However, Jaworzyn shows, this was a difficult position to elucidate and a dangerous one to hold. Clauberg had to work hard to explain the sense in which a meditator can be said to die and yet return to life when their meditation ends. How can the bond between mind and body be broken and then mended? How can the mind-body composite cease to exist and be reconstituted? At the same time Clauberg was assailed by other criticisms. His view smacked of Pelagianism, construed as the heretical doctrine that salvation lies within our own power, and he was implicitly accused of violating the carefully

---

[25] Cicero 1927, 75.   [26] Descartes, Letter to Arnauld, 29 July 1648, AT V.219; CSM III 356.

articulated division of labour between philosophy and theology within the Dutch universities. The suggestion that philosophical understanding might match poetry by endowing its practitioners with the power to move back and forth between life and death, and gain knowledge of what it is like to be a disembodied mind, was profoundly tantalizing. But it was also threatening.

Metaphysically and theologically, early modern writers defended many views of death, and thus many views of what a dying individual confronts. But dying is also a human process, subject to ordinary values such as dignity and cheerfulness. Dying well, as early modern authors conceive of it, embraces both these aspects, epistemological and ethical; but in the case of philosophers, the importance of dying as one's beliefs dictate is accorded a special significance. Piet Steenbakkers illustrates this point in Chapter 8, where he shows how bystanders watched to see whether Spinoza, a philosopher accused of atheism, would recant on his deathbed. Would his professed attitude to death hold up as his own end approached? Would he manage to conform to the model of the free man portrayed in his philosophy? Drawing on new documentary evidence, Steenbakkers traces some of the gossip that circulated in the days after Spinoza died. The rumours Steenbakkers discusses were probably false; but they illuminate the slightly prurient interest that the deaths of philosophers aroused, and in this case convey a mixture of suspicion and grudging admiration. Spinoza, they imply, did not trust himself to die in the company of other people; but it has to be admitted that he probably did not repent. He died more on his own terms than his opponents would have wished.

The image of a good death was partly shaped by an individual philosopher's beliefs, but also conformed to a pattern spelled out in exemplary cases. From Socrates onwards, a good philosophical death was epitomized by particular figures and elaborated in quasi-historical narratives. Running through this tradition is the underlying thought that facing death calmly may be hardest for those who view it as a final annihilation and are convinced that it gives us nothing to hope for. Indeed, this may partly explain why the figure of Democritus continued to excite the early modern imagination, as Piero Schiavo shows in Chapter 9. Democritus's view that death is merely a rearrangement of atoms and should be 'nothing to us' held out a tempting if atheistical release from fears about the afterlife that were endemic to Christianity and Judaism.[27] But there was—and is—something unsettling about his reputation for mocking everyone and everything. His reasons for dismissing death were also grounds for scorning life.

Schiavo explores a sequence of early modern readings of the legend of Democritus's death, most influentially transmitted to us by Diogenes Laertius. Democritus, the story claims, managed to use his knowledge to delay his death so that his sister could enjoy an annual festival. Once again, the anecdote links

---

[27] On seventeenth-century Jewish debates about the afterlife see Nadler 2004.

12   INTRODUCTION: APPROACHES TO LIVING AND DYING

philosophical wisdom with the capacity to defy death, a theme reiterated, as Schiavo reveals, in speculations about the powers of the so-called English Democritus, Robert Burton. Although Burton did not delay his death, he was held to have predicted when it would occur. But the story about Democritus is also taken up in a more sceptical spirit by Bayle, who uses it to illustrate how the historical record gets distorted. Is it likely, Bayle asks, that Democritus defied death in the manner the legend describes? Does it not rather show how imagination and the desires that drive it shape the history that comes down to us? As well as encouraging a more robustly critical appraisal of narratives about the deaths of individual sages, Bayle's discussion is part of a movement in which biography became increasingly marginal to philosophical practice.[28] While this process took some time, it made space for the view (embraced by Steenbakkers but alien to many early modern thinkers) that the way a philosopher dies does not convey a deeper message about the validity of his or her ideas.

5 Suicide

Among the accounts of exemplary deaths inherited by the early modern world were many descriptions of suicide; the ends of Lucretia, Seneca, and Brutus, for example, were repeatedly portrayed by poets, dramatists, and painters, and raised questions about many of the themes discussed so far. If the moral quality of one's life is reflected in the way one dies, the exercise of virtue may require us to take death into our own hands. In fact, controlling the timing and nature of one's death by killing oneself may be what virtue demands. This view continues to be sympathetically discussed by renaissance authors who, as Sarah Tropper points out in Chapter 10, often explore it in fictional settings such as Montaigne's Island of Cea or Thomas More's Utopia. But there is a sharp contrast between their evocations of resolute deaths assisted by supportive onlookers and a Christian image of suicide as a culpable rejection of one's duties to God, oneself, and the communities to which one belongs. While both conceptions are in play in Part V, the latter dominates, as it did in early modern Europe.

Chapters 10 and 11 reflect on Hume's defence of the moral permissibility of suicide, nowadays a key text, but only published in an unofficial French translation during his lifetime.[29] Tropper asks which critics of suicide Hume was opposing and challenges the claim that he was responding to arguments defended by Aquinas. Hume's case, she shows, is directed against his seventeenth-century

---

[28]   Levitin 2015.

[29]   Hume sent the essay to his publisher in 1755 for inclusion in a volume to be called 'Five Dissertations', but withdrew it for fear of condemnation or prosecution. Although an unofficial French translation appeared in 1770, the essay was only published in English in 1777, after Hume's death. See Hume 1985, 577–578.

predecessors, including Descartes, Leibniz, Locke, and Malebranche, who turn their backs on the neo-classical discussions of Montaigne and Erasmus, and instead develop new defences of broadly Thomist conclusions. With different emphases, they all represent suicide as an irrational failure to understand the divinely ordained and benevolent order of which we are a part, along with the laws that govern it, and it is their arguments that Hume contests. Where they insist that suicide violates the natural order, he replies that violating it is impossible; where Malebranche holds that suicide contravenes our duty to the communities in which we live, Hume disagrees.

While Tropper locates Hume's argument in its early modern context, Teresa Tato Lima considers the scope of its ambitions. What does Hume think a philosophical discussion of the morality of suicide can achieve, and how far can it help to 'restore our native liberty'? Tato Lima's argument in Chapter 11 is framed by her view that this liberty is the freedom to act on our natural as opposed to our artificial duties. Insofar as we are persuaded to refrain from suicide by socially imposed duties to God or the communities in which we live, we are subject to artificial constraints that make us unfree. Here, however, philosophy can help to liberate us. It can lead us to alter our beliefs, for example by emancipating us from false superstitions that reinforce religious or social taboos surrounding suicide. It can also help us to refine our moral sentiments by improving our grasp of the pains and pleasures to which objects or courses of action give rise. By these means, we can reassess the reasons normally given for thinking that suicide is incompatible with our religious and civil duties. When Hume comes to the claim that suicide does not violate our natural duties to ourselves, his tone changes and he concedes that philosophy loses its grip. Since reason is relatively powerless against our passions, it cannot hope to resist the authentic desires that drive people to suicide, or interfere with this expression of their natural liberty.

Tato Lima's conclusion draws attention to an aspect of suicide that is strikingly absent from seventeenth-century philosophical discussions of the topic: the despair and isolation often suffered by people who go on to kill themselves. As John Callanan reminds us, such feelings are more fully acknowledged in late eighteenth-century culture, where the lovelorn hero who puts an end to his life becomes a common literary trope, and the popularity of works such as Goethe's *Sorrows of Young Werther* seems to have provoked a rash of romantically motivated suicides. This phenomenon, Callanan argues, not only caused social and political disquiet, but gave rise to philosophical efforts to delegitimize suicide. Chapter 12 traces the evolution of Kant's thinking about this problem through his engagement with Maupertuis and Rousseau, who are, Callanan contends, the true targets of the argument against suicide in the *Groundwork*. One of Kant's reasons for devising an alternative to a mathematically grounded moral theory such as Maupertius' calculus, and also to sentimentalism, was the inability of either stance

14 INTRODUCTION: APPROACHES TO LIVING AND DYING

to rule out the acceptability of suicide. The urgency of this issue is highlighted in the *Groundwork*, where Kant chooses the case of suicide to illustrate his universalization principle. The maxim 'from self-love I make it my principle to shorten my life if, when protracted any longer, it threatens more ill than it promises agreeableness' cannot, he tells us, be universalized without contradiction. Most commentators have dismissed this argument as a failure, but Callanan sets out to vindicate it by offering a new interpretation. If we take account of the intellectual context to which Kant is responding, he shows, we can understand Kant's claim and appreciate its coherence.

Taken as a whole, Part V underlines the breadth and persistence of debate about suicide within early modern philosophy. As the most unequivocal of our efforts to take control of the transition from life to death, it embodied a troubling aspiration to usurp the role of God, while also casting doubt on the value of human life. Perhaps, as Maupertuis was not the first to suggest, total pleasure never outweighs total pain over the course of one's life, and the rational response is to end it. But for most philosophers this was an entirely unacceptable conclusion.

6 Alive or not?

Bound up with the themes so far surveyed was the distinction between animate and inanimate things. At one level, people shared an unproblematic, though historically variable grasp of the boundary between the two and could position items on either side of it. Minerals and corpses are inanimate while plants and animals are animate. It is striking, however, that many early modern philosophers did not seem to feel the need to harmonize their metaphysical outlooks with this everyday point of view. On the contrary, they often drew the line between the animate and inanimate in unexpected places, or even refused to draw it at all. Providing a philosophical account of whatever we are appealing to when, in everyday practice, we distinguish the two categories was peripheral to their concerns. To us this may seem strange. How could such a central feature of our experience fail to be philosophically important? Nevertheless, as Barnaby Hutchins and Steph Marston show in Chapters 13 and 14, respectively, writers of the stature of Descartes and Spinoza say surprisingly little about our common or garden sense of what it is to be animated or alive. In Chapter 15, Charles Wolfe suggests that early modern debate about the distinctive features of living things emerged in medical circles and intensified throughout the eighteenth century. The pressure to make theoretical sense of our everyday conception of life grew stronger as practitioners of the emerging life sciences tried, with only partial success, to separate their enquiries from philosophy by explaining life in what they conceived as non-metaphysical terms.

Between them, the chapters in Part VI illustrate this historical transition. For Descartes, as Hutchins points out, locating our ordinary sense of life within his philosophical system seems an urgent problem. On the one hand, the Cartesian view that living bodies operate on the same mechanical principles as automata such as clocks or pumps seems to imply either that clocks and pumps are alive or that which we regard as living bodies are dead. On the other hand, Descartes continues to distinguish living from non-living bodies in everyday terms, without conveying any sense that the division is problematic. How is this tension to be resolved? Contributing to a lively debate, Hutchins argues that, in biological contexts, Descartes concentrates exclusively on explaining the operations of animal and human bodies, and shows no interest in the issue of what makes them alive. In doing so, however, he tacitly acknowledges the ontological category of living things and cannot completely ignore it. Since the category cannot be conceived in terms of either of the two Cartesian substances, mind or extended matter, it is not easy to see how to accommodate it. But the primitive notion of mind-body union suggests a solution. For Descartes, Hutchins proposes, life is also a primitive notion. Although we do not need to appeal to life to explain how organisms function, we have a metaphysical grasp of what it is to be alive and can appeal to it in non-biological domains.

Spinoza's rejection of the everyday opposition between living and non-living things, examined in Chapter 14, seems yet more uncompromising: there are, he claims, no inanimate things in nature.[30] In Marston's view, however, Spinoza not only recognizes the everyday distinction between living and non-living things, but has the resources to give a metaphysical account of it. Within his philosophical system, organisms such as plants can be systematically distinguished from non-living entities such as crystals. The crucial difference between the two categories lies in the roles they play within the nexus of causes and effects through which individual modes interact. All bodies have what Marston calls transitive effects; they are subject to laws of motion and are continually moving and being moved. But living things also have what she describes as transformative effects; their survival depends on their capacity to transform both other bodies and themselves. Unless a plant transforms oxygen into other products, for example, it will not only fail to grow, but will die.

Spinoza, then, can elucidate the distinction between living and non-living things in his own metaphysical terms. But neither he nor Descartes make their conceptions of our everyday notion of life explicit, and neither seems to find it relevant to do so. For a direct attempt to theorize our colloquial grasp of what makes a thing alive, we need to look, so Wolfe suggests in Chapter 15, to a tradition of 'immanent vitalism' that developed during the eighteenth century as

---

[30] Spinoza 1985, E2p13s.

16 INTRODUCTION: APPROACHES TO LIVING AND DYING

physiologists and other life scientists focused on precisely this problem. Particularly in the Medical Faculty at Montpellier, immanent vitalists debated the pros and cons of three approaches to the operations of living things: explaining them mechanically; explaining them by appeal to the soul; or (their preferred stance) explaining them in terms of an independent life-giving principle. In developing this third approach, the members of the Montpellier School aimed to distance themselves from metaphysics—from any appeal to substances, including souls. Some continued to locate life in a distinctive force, construed as an experimental hypothesis rather than a real thing. Others worked with the idea that life is an emergent feature of the structure of living organisms. Although, as Wolfe points out, metaphysics continued to dog their footsteps, they nevertheless began to establish a more empirical explanatory idiom with which to address the question of what makes a thing alive. In doing so, they definitively left behind the cosmological vitalism of Cavendish or Spinoza, for whom everything is alive or animated, and established a quite different kind of research programme focused on an everyday conception of a living organism.

The vitalists of the Montpellier School embody a somewhat modern aspiration to make the distinction between life and death manageable. In rejecting metaphysics, they were rejecting a series of philosophical worldviews that had spawned a wild variety of highly speculative ideas about the extent of life and downgraded so-called common sense. One of their aspirations, perhaps, was to sideline positions such as immortalism or pan-animation, along with the contentious and sometimes dangerous disputes that arose in their wake. At the same time, their approach introduced a separation between the principally physiological issue of what made a thing alive, and the moral aspects of life and death discussed in this book. To work out what is involved in living and dying well, one must, it seems, take account of whatever we can know about our place in nature. If everything is alive, for example, we need to consider what duties we have to things of other kinds. If the key to living well lies in controlling the will, we need to find out what obstacles we have to learn to deal with? Again, these questions can mainly be fenced off from a more or less scientific explanation of the everyday difference between living and non-living things. It is enough to try to say what makes a thing alive without branching out into the realms of either practical or theoretical philosophy. The gains associated with this transition are balanced by its losses. The holistic early modern approach to life and death discussed throughout this volume is exceptionally rich from a philosophical point of view, and refuses to lose sight of the interconnections between one form of enquiry and another. Perhaps we might even say that the disciplinary separation anticipated, for instance, by the Montpellier School, has in some ways impoverished our explorations of life and death.

PART I
FEELING ALIVE

1

The Consciousness of Being Alive as a Source of Knowledge

Ursula Renz

1 Introduction

The concepts of life and of death lurk in the background of many philosophical debates. There is, first, the metaphysical problem of defining life as a property of certain types of things. Next, there is the discussion on the notion or the existence of some sort of afterlife. In ethics or moral philosophy, furthermore, the notion of life is related with both the conception of a good life, whereas on the other hand there is the issue of death, or also violent death and suicide, as (absolute) evils. From a history of science perspective, finally, there is the question of the (conceptual) prerequisites of life sciences and their role in promoting or preventing scientific naturalism. In this chapter, I shall suggest yet another approach to the issue of life. My question is this: could our consciousness of being alive constitute a source of knowledge, and if so how?

At first glance, this question may look somewhat odd. Many people may feel unsure whether there really is such a thing as a consciousness of being alive. This is not surprising. What I refer to as the consciousness of being alive is often mentioned in the context of other discussions and described in other terms. However, once one begins to pay attention to the idea of there being such a phenomenon, one encounters references to it in many, otherwise diverse philosophers such as la Forge, Spinoza, Shaftesbury, Leibniz, Diderot, and Rousseau, to mention only the most important. Nevertheless, since our consciousness of being alive is mainly articulated indirectly in the course of other debates, it is not easy to see where interest in it originated within early modern philosophy. Nor is it easy to trace its significance for philosophical reflection on life and death.

I concentrate on the rise of this idea as it occurs in two diametrically opposed reactions to Descartes' approach, which I consider as exemplary: one developed by the Cartesian, Louis de La Forge, in his *Treatise of the Human Mind*; the other put forward by the young Spinoza in his early *Treatise on the Emendation of the Intellect*. My question will be how these two philosophers tried to overcome a disquieting problem that arises from Descartes' approach, namely whether, when reflecting on the contents of our minds, we can be sure of being alive, and if so

Ursula Renz, *The Consciousness of Being Alive as a Source of Knowledge* In: *Life and Death in Early Modern Philosophy*. Edited by: Susan James, Oxford University Press. © Ursula Renz 2021. DOI: 10.1093/oso/9780192843616.003.0002

20 THE CONSCIOUSNESS OF BEING ALIVE AS A SOURCE OF KNOWLEDGE

why. One of my claims will be that, once this problem had been solved or discarded, the idea of our consciousness of being alive came to be viewed as a source of both metaphysical and moral knowledge.

2 Consciousness as an epistemic self-relation

How can the relation between the fact of our being alive and our mental constitution as subjects of consciousness be comprehended? A natural way to answer this question would be to say that being alive is a precondition of having conscious mental states. More precisely, a thing's being subject to conscious mental states is a sufficient, but not necessary condition for its being alive. There is thus a conceptual relation between the notion of an entity's being alive and its having consciousness, to the effect that we consider any subject of consciousness as alive. At the same time, however, we also assume that people are alive when asleep or unconscious, and usually tend to think that some natural things are alive without having consciousness.

More interesting than these conceptual interdependencies is another issue. Is there—in addition to the conceptual or metaphysical connection between being conscious and being alive—an epistemic or cognitive relation? Surely, like most of our features, the notion of being alive is potentially an object of a subject's knowledge. But how, or in what sense, are we related in our thought to this feature in ordinary awareness? How does the assumption of such an epistemic relation contribute to our understanding of our basic mental constitution? And how does it contribute to reflection on our moral or ethical condition?

Before we can address these questions, we need to take a look at the way the notion of consciousness developed in early modern philosophy. As scholars have pointed out, the Latin word 'consciousness', or 'conscientia' underwent significant terminological changes in the early modern era; moreover, conceptions of consciousness were seldom analysed or accounted for within the context of theories of consciousness. This lack of explicit discussion characterizes even those approaches in which the idea of consciousness plays a crucial role. As Udo Thiel states, for example, '[i]t was not until the 1720s that consciousness became an object of enquiry in its own right'.[1] Not surprisingly, therefore, texts in which the term 'consciousness' is used are notoriously subject to interpretive debate. Equally, early modern philosophers discussed what we now describe as consciousness in other terms...[2]

---

[1] Thiel 2011, 6.

[2] Alternative terminologies were dependent on the context. In Descartes, as I shall argue, the notion of 'cogitatio' entails the feature of consciousness, Spinoza refers to the phenomenon of consciousness also when employing the verb 'sentire' or its derivatives, and there is also the rise of the terminology of 'apperception', to mention just a few examples.

Despite this diversity, it is possible to make some general statements about consciousness. To emphasize a point that is particularly crucial for our concerns, a common assumption underlying early modern references to the idea of consciousness is that the latter consists in or expresses an *epistemic self-relation*.[3] This assumption is relevant to any early modern theorizing about consciousness though, being very vague and at the same time very specific, it raises several problems. First, it leaves it open what part, aspect, or property of a subject is related by means of its consciousness to what other part, aspect, or property of the same subject. At this point we encounter a great variety of early modern views. Some philosophers locate consciousness in the mind's acquaintance with the body as a whole,[4] while others take it to consist in the subject's relation to its mental operations[5] or bodily actions.[6] In some theories, consciousness is assumed to establish a relationship between a person and her moral motivations,[7] or her intellectual and moral dispositions;[8] in others it seems to be equivalent to the relation between the mind and the contents of its thoughts.[9]

Second, the notion that consciousness is an epistemic self-relation leaves it open *how*, i.e. by what kind of mental act or what property of mental acts, this relation is created. In particular, early modern philosophers (as well as their present-day interpreters) disagree about whether or not consciousness requires a previous act of reflection.[10] Third, we can ask whether the self-relation that constitutes consciousness is to be considered in terms of an object's epistemic accessibility, or in terms of a subject's epistemic capacity to access an object. Is it in virtue of the subject's mental capacities or of some property of the object that consciousness may arise?

Notwithstanding these open questions, the notion of consciousness being an epistemic self-relation is telling: it suggests that early modern philosophers tended to ascribe an *epistemic* status or function to conscious experience.[11] In other

---

[3] Alison Simmons 2013 advocated this view in an unpublished paper she gave in November 2013 at the NYU at *History of Consciousness Conference*. I found this quite instructive. In elaborating on it, I largely rely on evidence other than the one she invoked to put her claim forward.

[4] This is roughly how I reconstruct Spinoza's usage of the term. See also Renz 2018, 161–167.

[5] This is how I understand Locke's view. Here I follow Thiel 2011, 109–120.

[6] This view underlies those approaches that conceptualize consciousness as an internal force of moral accountability.

[7] Shaftesbury 1999, 209f.

[8] This can be derived from Antoine Arnauld's non-technical usage of the term in the *Fourth Objections* to Descartes' *Meditations* where he writes: '[S]i quid mihi tribuis amplius quam deceat, [non] sequitur ut ego meae tenuitatis conscius non sim'. AT VII, 197; for the English translation, see CMS II, 138.

[9] This is the rationale behind Descartes' position who, in the first two definitions to the appendix to the second set of replies, equates thought with consciousness, and forms of thought, or ideas, with objects of consciousness. Cf. also Chapter 2.

[10] This question is discussed in Thiel 2011 with respect to Locke. Underlying Thiel's account are positions belonging to the Heidelberg School, for an English written defence, see Zahavi 2007.

[11] Strikingly, this is often missed in reconstructions of early modern conceptions of consciousness. The reason for this omission could be that in contemporary discussion, consciousness is not considered as an epistemic, but only as a mental feature; i.e. its function of constituting or at least contributing to some sort of knowledge is not thematized in epistemology.

words, consciousness was regarded as a source of knowledge, or even a form of knowledge. This is not a derivative feature. For even if, as some philosophers contended, reflection is required to *establish* consciousness, it is not necessary in order to *entertain* a previously established relation of consciousness. Once the relation called 'consciousness' is created, it requires no intermediary.[12]

To summarize, we can say that the common rationale of the otherwise polysemic employment of the idea of consciousness in early modern philosophy is that it is seen as contributing to a subject's *knowledge* of itself or of some part or feature of itself. That is, even if consciousness is perhaps not sufficient to constitute self-knowledge, it is viewed as an experience by which the subject may feel, sense, or grasp its own presence, or the presence of some of its own features.

As I shall show in the rest of this chapter, this understanding of consciousness as consisting in an immediate epistemic self-relation was also used to vindicate the subject's existence, and this with quite surprising consequences. Arguing against the sceptical challenges raised by Descartes' *First Meditation*, some early modern philosophers assumed that our own existence or our being alive is something to which we have special epistemic access. That we exist and are alive, they thought, is not known by any kind of inference, nor is it simply presupposed by the fact of our own thinking. Rather, our existence or being alive is felt or sensed whenever we pay attention to it. It is something we cannot doubt, since it is integral to our conscious experience.

3 The implications of Descartes' usage of 'conscientia' in the definition of 'thought'

In the appendix to his second set of *Replies*, Descartes provides an exposition *more geometrico* of his arguments for God's existence and for the distinction between the body and soul. There, he defines 'thought' as follows:

> By the term thought [in Latin *cogitationes* in the plural], I comprehend everything which is in us in such a way that we are immediately aware [*conscius*] of it. Thus all operations of the will, the intellect, the imagination and the senses are thoughts [*cogitationes*]. I say 'immediately' in order to exclude what follows from

---

[12] Arguably, therefore, both Locke's 1975 '*Intuitive Knowledge of our own Existence*', in *Essay* book IV, chap. 9, § 3; p. 618; and Leibniz' 'apperception immediate de nostre Existence' (*Nouveaux Essais*, livre IV, chap. 9, § 2; Leibniz 1996, Bd. 3.2., p. 432) are good candidates for cases of consciousness. This is also why the polemic attack in the otherwise insightful essay by Daniel Heller-Roazen 2007, against the over-intellectualistic idea of consciousness is, philosophically considered, beyond the point.

this such as a voluntary movement which has a certain thought [*cogitatio*] as its origin, but is not itself thought [*cogitatio*].[13]

This definition shows, probably better than any other passage, that Descartes equates thoughts with objects of consciousness. It alleges that all thought is conscious, an assumption that is controversial both in the light of Descartes' own views as well as in relation to (recent) empirical findings.[14] What is important for us, however, is a structural point: Descartes' emphasis that we are *immediately* aware of our thoughts. This notion of immediacy corroborates my claim that to be aware (in Latin *conscius*) of an object is to be in its presence and to know its presence. This, of course, does not rule out the possibility that we may still err about its nature or essence; it is just the presence of some object that we know in being conscious of it.[15]

Another point also deserves attention. Given that thoughts or *cogitationes* are modifications of our own being as thinking things, consciousness is in fact the experience of the presence of something which is a part or a feature of ourselves. For Descartes, such experience is possible only with respect to things of a certain kind, a view underscored by the last sentence of the passage quoted above: while we are immediately aware of things that are themselves thought, i.e. that belong to the domain of the thinking thing, we lack consciousness of things that are only caused by thought. For example, we are immediately aware or conscious of the intentions that express our will, but not of the bodily actions they cause.

These commitments generate a fundamental problem with respect to our being alive. Descartes famously claims that man only possesses the property of life in virtue of having a body. Here, for example, is what he writes to Henry More, who was dissatisfied with his account of animals as machines:

> Please note that I am speaking of [the] thought, and not of [the] life or sensation [of animals]. I do not deny life to animals, since I regard it as consisting simply in the heat of the heart; . . .[16]

In this passage, life is reduced to a quality of the heart, which can be accounted for in terms of a mechanist physics. One might of course wonder how serious

---

[13] 'Cogitationis nomine complector illud omne quod sic in nobis est, ut ejus immediate conscii simus. Ita omnes voluntatis, intellectus, imaginationis & sensuum operationes sunt cogitationes. Sed addidi immediate, ad excludenda ea quae ex iis consequuntur, ut motus voluntaries cogitationem quidem pro principio habet, sed ipese tamen non est cogitatio.' AT VII, 160; Translation mine; but see also CMS II, 113.

[14] See Simmons, 2012, for more detailed discussion.

[15] For a more detailed elaboration on the structural features of consciousness in Descartes, see also Barth 2011.

[16] 'Velim tamen notari me loqui de cogitatione, non de vita, vel sensu: vitam enim nulli animali denego, utpote quam in solo cordis calore consistere statuo.' AT V, 278f. see CMSK III, 366, for the English translation.

24 THE CONSCIOUSNESS OF BEING ALIVE AS A SOURCE OF KNOWLEDGE

Descartes really was about this.[17] Was he a reductionist about life?[18] Be that as it may, the view he expresses to More implies that we cannot know by means of conscious experience that we ourselves are alive.

Within the context of Descartes' own philosophy, this conclusion is not surprising. It simply points to an implication of two fundamental characteristics of his thought: the already-mentioned idea that consciousness extends to thought alone; and the way his substance dualism divides the Aristotelian soul into separate parts. And yet, considered in itself, it is a puzzling claim, and casts a critical light on Descartes' so-called *cogito* argument. For however convincing this argument may be in other respects, is it not strange that the meditating 'I' must *argue* for its own existence?

Since I am not concerned here with the question of how the *cogito* works, I am not interested in the debate, initiated by Hobbes and still going on today, as to whether the *cogito* is really an argument. What I find puzzling is something different, which immediately relates to our being alive. When Descartes sets out the problem the *cogito* is meant to solve, he presupposes that our existence is something that can, in principle, be in need of proof. To be sure, this is only a *felt* need. As the *cogito* indicates, doubts about our own existence can easily be dispelled. Still, that such a need might even be felt, and thus that some proof might be called for, remains remarkable.

How does this shed light on Descartes' view concerning one's consciousness of being alive? To see what is at stake, two things have to be kept in mind. First, we must be clear that we do not usually regard 'existence' and 'being alive' as two entirely separate features. In fact, they are hardly ever predicated separately of one and the same object. This is because, according to our ordinary concepts, 'live' and 'being alive' describe a particular mode of existing—the very mode of existing as a living being. One could also say that living is an adverbial, yet essential qualification of the existence of certain types of entities. Second, it is important to recall the distinction between the two problems I mentioned at the beginning of Section 2: it is one thing to posit it as a conceptual fact that a thing's being subject to conscious mental states is a sufficient condition of its being alive, but another to ask how we are epistemically related to our being alive.

Most likely, Descartes would not deny the conceptual point that 'being alive' and 'existence' can never really fall apart. (I say 'most likely' rather than 'certainly' because he lacks the means to accommodate this point.) But he does abstain from

---

[17] This relates to the question of the status of the animal-machine in Cartesian physiology: are, on Descartes' view, living beings literally machines, or is the idea of machine rather a model that is to compensate for the lack of a theory of life? That the Cartesian animal-machine is a theoretical hypothesis and his mechanist physiology a model of the living is emphasized by Duchesneau 1998, 53–72, 68.

[18] This view maintained by MacKenzie 1975, Ablondi 1998, and Detlefsen 2016, has recently been criticized by Hutchins 2016a, who, however, proposes an even more radical, viz. dissolutionist view to the effect that there is just 'nothing in Descartes' ontology for life to be reduced to' (p. 172).

treating our being alive as something of which we might be immediately aware.[19] In consequence, he takes the mind's notion of its own existence to be a rather abstract kind of knowledge. Our being alive is not something to which we have first-person access. This is remarkable, I think, as it conflicts with our ordinary experience. That we are alive is something we are immediately aware of; it is not something we have to find out through self-observation. In this crucial respect, Cartesian dualist metaphysics is therefore at odds with the phenomenology of our ordinary experience, according to which our existence or being alive can simply be taken for granted. It is presumably against this background assumption that Descartes insists in the *cogito* that we must painstakingly distinguish the things we can know by means of our conscious experience from those we cannot. In his view, our existence as living beings belongs to the latter category.

How should we assess this move? For the sake of his argument, Descartes invites us to doubt many ordinary certainties. Nevertheless, the demand that we should doubt whether we exist or are alive may strike many of his readers as a step too far. How can we, at any given moment of our life, doubt that we are alive? Is our own life not something we must take for granted, epistemically as well as pragmatically, even when we are in engaged in sceptical doubt? To be sure, this is not a pressing problem for Descartes. After all, the radical doubts we encounter in the *First Meditation* are explicitly declared to be necessary only 'once in the course of my life', *semel in vita*. Furthermore, taking the *Sixth Meditation* into account, Descartes assumes that once we have pursued the exercise demonstrated in the *Meditations* to its conclusion, we no longer need to be worried about whether we are alive. We not only know indubitably that we exist as thinking things. We also know with moral certainty that our body—including its features—exists. And yet Descartes' view remains troubling, precisely because it radically challenges the certainties of our ordinary experience. It is questionable whether one can consistently affirm one's existence as a thinking thing and at the same time doubt that, considered as a living being, one exists.

4 Louis de La Forge's appeal to the Augustinian notion of the life of the soul

The problem raised in the previous section did not pass unnoticed among Descartes' contemporaries. On the contrary, both defenders and critics of

---

[19] Some might wonder how this is coherent with Descartes' views on the notion of the mind-body union. Simmons 2017, for example, convincingly argues that while Descartes denies that the mind-body union is understood by the intellect, we can nonetheless sense it (2). I do not deny this. I made a similar point in Renz, 2003. But this does not undermine my actual concern. First, even if Descartes embraces the view that we can feel or sense our body and thus allows for a rich phenomenology of bodily awareness, this is not a source of knowledge, but at most of moral certainty.

26   THE CONSCIOUSNESS OF BEING ALIVE AS A SOURCE OF KNOWLEDGE

Cartesian dualism reacted to it. Within the camp of Cartesian dualists, we find a response in Louis de La Forge's *Treatise on the Human Mind* (*THM*) where la Forge subjects Descartes' theory of the mind to greater and more detailed scrutiny than Descartes himself ever did. In the process, la Forge not only develops Descartes' idea of a union between mind and body. He also advocates a reading of Cartesian dualism that, as Desmond Clarke has rightly underlined, sharpens 'the distinction between body and mind and, correspondingly, the distinction between the type of description and explanation which is appropriate for bodily phenomena compared with those which are appropriate for mental phenomena'.[20]

Against the background of a dualism more rigid than Descartes' own, how does la Forge deal with the phenomenon of our consciousness of being alive? To address this question, I shall look closely at some key passages from the Preface of the *THM*, where the question of how we know we are alive is explicitly discussed. This preface, which is pretty long compared to the individual chapters of the main text, compares Descartes with Augustine in order to show 'the agreement between Saint Augustine's teaching concerning the nature of the soul and the views of Mr Descartes'.[21] La Forge begins his comparison by quoting a passage from the second book of Augustine's *De libero arbitrio*—the very same passage Arnauld had cited to highlight the parallels between Descartes' *cogito* and Augustine's principles.[22] However, as we shall see, Arnauld and la Forge draw different conclusions from it.

In the passage in question, Augustine has his alter ego Alipsius ask his student Evodius:

> First, to take as our starting point what is most evident, I ask you to tell me whether you yourself exist. Or are you perhaps afraid of making a mistake in your answer, given that, if you did not exist, it would be quite impossible for you to make a mistake?

Arnauld takes this speech to show that Descartes' approach is grounded on 'the same principle as that laid down by St. Augustine'.[23] At the same time, Arnauld also pointed to several problems he finds in Descartes.[24] Particularly, he doubted the validity of the inference from the indubitable '*ego cogito, ego sum*' to the assumption of substance dualism. Read against this background, Arnauld's

---

[20] Clarke 1997, xvii.   [21] La Forge 1997, 5. See La Forge 1974, for the French text.

[22] Cf. AT VII, 197, where Arnauld writes: 'The first thing that I find remarkable is that our distinguished author has laid down as the basis for his entire philosophy exactly the same principle as that laid down by St Augustine—a man of the sharpest intellect and a remarkable thinker....'

[23] Ibid.

[24] In the entry to the Internet Encyclopedia to Philosophy, Eric Stencil 2013 succinctly describes Arnauld's attitude when saying: '[U]nlike the objections of Hobbes and Gassendi, Arnauld's objections to the *Meditations* are not objections to Descartes' system, but objections internal to Descartes' system'.

quotation from Augustine has a somewhat ironical undertone. Although he identifies an Augustinian thought in Descartes, he does not seem convinced that this thought corroborates Cartesian dualism.

Not so with la Forge. Echoing Arnauld, he affirms that Augustine had already employed the method of doubt that Descartes would later take up. Unlike Arnauld, however, he appeals to this quotation not to challenge but to defend Cartesian doubt. And this is only one of several similarities between Augustine and Descartes to which la Forge draws attention. For our purposes, the. most instructive appeals to a passage from *De Trinitate*, which la Forge renders as follows:

> What does the human mind contain which it knows better than its own life? For it cannot exist without living; and since it is a totality [whose parts are insepar-able, or, more accurately, which has no parts] whenever it lives it lives as a whole. It is aware of the fact that it lives [because, being a thing which thinks, it cannot act without being aware of it].[25]

By contrast, Augustine's original text says:

> What does the human mind contain which it knows better than its own life? It cannot be a mind and not live. But it also has something more, viz. that it understands. For the souls of animals live, but they do not understand. As, therefore, the mind is a whole mind, it also lives as a whole. But it knows that it lives; therefore, it knows itself as a whole.[26]

La Forge's quotation departs in several respects from the Augustinian original. First and most significantly, it replaces a whole sentence of the original passage dealing with the difference between human and animal minds with the tenet that the mind is a whole which has no parts. In the suppressed sentence, Augustine underlines that it is not life, but intellection by which the human mind supersedes the souls of animals, for brutes, too, have living souls.

Another difference between the texts is also worth mentioning. In the final sentence, Augustine claims that, because the mind knows that it lives, it also knows itself as a whole. La Forge reverses the direction of inference, arguing in a more Cartesian spirit that the mind knows it is alive because, as a thinking thing, it cannot act without noticing it. La Forge's point, in other words, is that we know we are alive because we know we are thinking things, rather than that, in virtue of our

---

[25] La Forge 1997, 9. The brackets are added in Clarke's edition to exhibit the additions by La Forge.
[26] In Latin: *quid ejus ei tam notum est quam se vivere? [4.6] non potest autem et mens esse et non vivere quando habet etiam amplius ut intelligat, nam et animae bestiarum vivunt sed non intellegunt. sicut ergo mens tota es, sic tota vivit. novit autem vivere se; totam se igitur novit.* Augustinus 2001, 102. The translation in the main text is mine.

28 THE CONSCIOUSNESS OF BEING ALIVE AS A SOURCE OF KNOWLEDGE

awareness of being alive, we know ourselves to exist as wholes. As this suggests, there is a sort of 'Cartesian drift' in la Forge's use of Augustine.

At the same time, however, la Forge's rendering of Augustine overplays his similarity with Descartes. Descartes' thinker comes to see his existence as necessary by noticing his own thinking. Augustine, by contrast, underlines the mind's necessary (and immediate) awareness[27] of being alive. *Life*, rather than *thought* is taken to constitute the immediate object of the mind's conscious activity.

However, the way la Forge explains this consciousness invokes Descartes' outlook rather than Augustine's. According to la Forge, one's immediate awareness of one's own life is just a characteristic of human thought; but the Augustinian original points in a slightly different direction. In the sentence la Forge suppresses, Augustine claims that even brutes have living souls. On Augustine's view, being alive is a feature of souls, not of bodies, or, if this feature is attached to bodies, then it is so in virtue of the fact that bodies and souls together constitute wholes. Now this holds also with respect to the human mind: even though the human excels the animal mind by its capacity of intellection, it constitutes a whole. Augustine's approach thus comes surprising close to a hylomorphic concept of the mind. And this is also why, on his account, human minds are conscious of their being alive: because this is a feature of the soul or of the embodied mind, and not of the body alone, the mind can know this feature immediately: being a feature of the soul or the embodied mind, it is always, and necessarily, present to the mind.

What does this all show with respect to the issue of our consciousness of being alive? As I said in the preceding section, it is questionable whether one can consistently affirm one's existence as a thinking thing and at the same time doubt that one exists as a living being. La Forge, I suggest is reacting to this problem. When he reinterprets Descartes' notion of 'thought' in line with the Augustinian idea of the life of the soul, he seeks to avoid the impression that, within Cartesianism, epistemic certainty is restricted to the notion of our existence as thinking things. Instead, he argues that, by knowing that we are thinking, we also know we are alive. The question remains whether la Forge's proposal really solves the problem. Does his argument convincingly undermine the view that we cannot separate the knowledge of our existence as thinking things from the consciousness of being alive that our ordinary experience provides?

If la Forge's proposal provides a solution to this problem, it comes at a cost one may not be willing to pay. By importing an Augustinian idea of the life of the mind or soul into a Cartesian framework, la Forge introduces a concept of life that is marked by a striking ambiguity. In the preface to *THM*, he explicitly distinguishes the life of the human mind from the vegetative life of plants,[28] and in Chapter 7 of

---

[27] The French term here is 's'appercevoir'.
[28] See the clarification he adds in brackets to another quote from Augustine in La Forge 1997, 18.

the main text, which is concerned with the immortality of the soul, he differentiates three meanings of the term 'life': life as existence; life as existence accompanied by action; and life as co-existence with an accident perfecting the substance.[29] La Forge clearly had a differentiated vocabulary at his disposal. However, when it comes to the life of the human mind, he wavers, as we have seen, between understanding it in terms of the Cartesian notion of thought, and grasping it in terms of the more hylomorphic Augustinian idea of the soul's being alive. Nor is this wavering accidental; it results from the fact that la Forge employs the idea of the life of the soul to address two different concerns. The broadly Augustinian notion of the soul's being alive is, on the one hand, used to suggest that Descartes' approach is consistent with a hylomorphic picture of the mind. On the other hand, the interpretation of the life of the mind as equivalent to Cartesian thought is invoked to corroborate the claim that substance dualism entails the immortality of the soul. While it is a controversial question whether or not this claim is actually endorsed by Descartes,[30] La Forge leaves no doubt about his view. In fact, he concludes the seventh chapter of *THM* by asserting that, since the mind is entirely distinct from the body and is a simple thing that could perish only by a total annihilation, 'it should never cease to live'.[31]

Let me conclude this section by summarizing where we have got to. In Section 3, I pointed out that Descartes' position implies that our knowledge of our existence as a thinking thing and our knowledge of our being alive can in principle fall apart. This, I argued, challenges our ordinary experience, which entails that, as living things, we are always immediately aware of being alive. In this section, I have examined how la Forge, a fervent advocate of Cartesian dualism, reacts to this challenge in his *THM*. While he appears to see the problem, I have argued that his attempt to solve it by reinterpreting Descartes' concept of thought in terms of the Augustinian notion of the life of mind is a failure. In the next section I shall show how the young Spinoza, who was strongly influenced by Descartes' epistemology but did not embrace his mind-body-dualism, found another way to deal with the problem.

5 Spinoza's response in his early philosophy

Although Spinoza does not directly react to the problem raised by Descartes' *Meditations*, his works suggest he was aware of it. However, this is not obvious

---

[29] La Forge 1997, 62.

[30] As it has already been observed in the second set of objections stemming from Mersenne and his and his friends, Descartes says 'not one word' about this issue (AT VII, 127f.; CMS II, 91) and this even though in the dedicatory letter to the Sorbonne (AT VII, 2; CMS II, 3), as well as in synopsis following it, he promises to give a demonstrative proof of it.

[31] La Forge 1997, 66.

30 THE CONSCIOUSNESS OF BEING ALIVE AS A SOURCE OF KNOWLEDGE

from all his texts. Consider, for example, the passage of his *Descartes' 'Principles of Philosophy*, in which he glosses Descartes' view that only the mind's existence is immediately known. 'The proposition that *I*, insofar as I am a thing consisting of a body, *am*, is not the first thing known, nor is it known through itself.'[32] Spinoza proves this claim by demonstrating that, given the axioms he ascribes to Descartes, 'we shall not arrive at certainty [of the existence of our body] except through the knowledge and certainty of another thing, which is prior in knowledge and certainty'.[33] Here, Spinoza treats Descartes' invitation to doubt the existence of our bodies as defensible, at least within a Cartesian framework. In fact, since he reports Descartes' doubts from a third-personal stance,[34] he can faithfully present them, without himself adopting the attitude of doubt.

More illuminating for our concerns is the way Spinoza elaborates the problem in the *Treatise on the Emendation of the Intellect* (*TEI*). Formally, this text is a first-personal reflection on the narrator's earlier life, a characteristic it shares with the *Meditations*.[35] Like Descartes, Spinoza sets out to develop a method by which the epistemic balance of our cognitions, or what he calls the intellect, can be emended. Nonetheless, there are important differences between his approach and that of Descartes.

First, even in this early text, Spinoza's operates with a view of the relation between body and soul that is at odds with Descartes' dualism. Consider for instance the examples he employs to illustrate the difference between the second and third of his four kinds of perception. In § 21, he explains the second kind of perception as follows:

> But we infer [one thing] from another in this way: after we clearly perceive that we feel such a body, and no other, then I say, we infer clearly that the soul is united to the body, which union is the cause of such a sensation; but we cannot understand absolutely from this what that sensation and union are.

At first glance, Spinoza seems to support Descartes' view that, despite the fact that our daily experience suggests a union between mind and body, there is an incontrovertible case for metaphysical dualism. However, if we turn to Spinoza's evaluative classification of four kinds of cognition, we can see that this is not a promising interpretation. Inferences based on mere experience, such as the experience of mind-body union, are far from reliable. They are certainly less reliable than the knowledge we derive from the third kind of perception, where we draw conclusions from our existing knowledge of the essence of things. To

---

[32] I.P3. Cf. Spinoza 1985, 241.   [33] Ibid.   [34] Cf. Spinoza 1985, 231ff., in particular, 233.
[35] For a general exposition of the epistemological programme underlying this text and the way in which it addresses scepticism, see the first section of my paper on 'Spinoza's epistemology' forthcoming in the second edition of the Cambridge Companion.

illustrate this latter kind of perception Spinoza gives the following example: 'from the fact that I know the essence of the soul, I know that it is united to the body'.[36] Clearly, if these examples are to be taken seriously, they are meant to reject rather than to affirm Cartesian dualism.

Second, and more significantly for our concerns, Spinoza departs from Descartes in adopting a wholly dismissive attitude towards the usefulness of sceptical doubt. Unlike Descartes, who assumes that epistemic certainty can only be achieved if we engage at least once in our life in a radically sceptical exercise, the method proposed in the *TEI* is meant to undermine scepticism from the very start. Even the sort of methodological scepticism we encounter in Descartes is condemned as futile and silly. This last point can be illustrated by a look at paragraph §47. There, having established that his method consists in reflection on existing ideas, guided by the notion of a true idea given in paragraph §§ 38–42, and having defended this approach against several objections (§§ 43–46), Spinoza writes:

> [P]erhaps,...some Skeptic would still doubt both the first truth itself and everything we shall deduce according to the standard of first truth. If so, then either he speaks contrary to his consciousness [*conscientia*], or we shall confess that there are men whose minds are completely blinded, either from birth, or from prejudices, i.e., because of some external chance. For they are not even aware of themselves [*Nam neque seipsos sentient*]. If they affirm or doubt something, they do not know that they affirm or doubt. They say that they know nothing, and that they do not even know that they know nothing. And even this they do not say absolutely. For they are afraid to confess that they exist, so long as they know nothing. In the end, they must be speechless, lest by change they assume something that might smell of truth.

In this striking passage, Spinoza does not even pretend to take the sceptic seriously as an interlocutor; on the contrary he denies him any rationality and thus discredits him once and for all. The sceptic does not even know when he affirms or doubts. However, Spinoza provides good reasons for his dismissive attitude. The Sceptic, he contends, does not just fall prey to fallacies deriving from prejudice, but has so comprehensively ruined his judgement that his mind is 'completely blinded'. Clearly, this is not simply a metaphor, but derives from an elaborated understanding of the source and nature of the mental blindness at issue. Spinoza's problem is not that the Sceptic operates on mistaken presuppositions, but rather that he lacks self-knowledge of his attitude towards any given

---

[36] Spinoza 1985, 14.

32 THE CONSCIOUSNESS OF BEING ALIVE AS A SOURCE OF KNOWLEDGE

proposition. To put it in contemporary terms, one could say that the Sceptic is trapped in a situation that has striking similarities with Moore's paradox.

No less insightful is the way the Sceptic's predicament is explained. The blindness affecting his mind results from a lack of 'self-awareness', or in Spinoza's words, sceptics do not even *feel* themselves—*nam neque seipsos sentient*. To comprehend what is at stake here, we have to consider how Spinoza employs the words 'sentire' and 'sensatio' in the *TEI*. Generally, two different usages may be distinguished. On the one hand, these terms denote a phenomenon we have already encountered in Spinoza's example of the second kind of perception, where the sensation or feeling of one's body is invoked as the experience from which one may infer that our soul and body are united. On the other hand, the same terminology is employed to describe the sense of certainty accompanying all our ideas, a feeling we may best discern by contemplating any given idea, regardless of its particular content.[37] According to this second usage, sensation describes the experience of thought considered from a subjective point of view.

These observations suggest two interesting conclusions. First, they indicate that Spinoza uses the verb '*sentire*' as an equivalent for Descartes' *conscius esse*. For Descartes, to have a thought, *cogitatio*, or idea, is an instance of consciousness, whereas for Spinoza it is to have a sensation. Note, however, that although they serve as functional equivalents, these terms have different connotations. At least in a Cartesian context, to be conscious of a thought is a pretty neutral affair. It consists in a registering of one's mental states whereas, by contrast, the terminology of sensing or sensation suggests the existence of an irreducibly qualitative aspect. Thus, by replacing Cartesian 'consciousness' with 'sensation', Spinoza presents himself as a defender of some kind of 'cognitive qualia'. This is a crucial point, as it undergirds the very project of *TEI* (and, in another form, of the *Ethics*), which is to search for a eudemonistic good by means of an improvement of the epistemic balance of our cognition.

Second, Spinoza's sensation is unlike Cartesian consciousness in having a determinate content, namely the body.[38] Here Spinoza does not just diverge from Descartes' view that consciousness relates the mind to its own thoughts or ideas. As indicated by his claim that we sense a qualified body, *talis corpus*, Spinoza assumes that a particular body recommends itself as the object of our sensation, and seems to do so in an immediate way. This view also underpins his expectation that sensation equips us with reasons for discrediting the Sceptic in the manner suggested in § 47. To have a sensation, Spinoza thinks, precludes any doubt about our own existence. Moreover, given that the privileged object of

---

[37] Cf., for instance, § 35, Spinoza 1985, 18, or § 78, Spinoza 1985, 34.
[38] For parallels in the *Ethics*, see on the one hand, 2ax4 and its usage in 2p13dem, and on the other, the concept of imagination as developed in 2p16 to 2p18. I have dealt with this at some length in Renz 2018, 161–167, and Renz 2019.

sensation is our own body, our sense of our existence is not restricted to our being a thinking thing, but extends to the body with which our mind is united.

Some commentators may hesitate to follow Spinoza here. Why, after all, should we take our own body, rather than, say, some perceptible properties of external things, as the privileged object of our sensations? And did not Spinoza himself leave room for doubt when he assumed that our sensation of our own body is only the source of perceptions of the second kind? I agree that Spinoza's early epistemology is far from providing him with any conclusive argument to rule out scepticism regarding our existence as bodies. Still, the passage we have been focusing on indicates that our body plays an ineliminable epistemological role in constituting an immediate content of cognition or sensation.

To make progress with the question of what qualifies our body as the privileged object of sensation it is helpful to consider the concept of life as it is introduced in chapter six of part two of the *Appendix Containing Metaphysical Thoughts*. Under the heading of *God's Life*, Spinoza here makes a suggestion of ground-breaking novelty. Instead of adapting inherited ideas of life to his needs, he proposes to rethink the issue from a strictly ontological viewpoint, by adopting a stance appropriate to a general metaphysics. (Whether this move also underlies Spinoza's later metaphysics is open to question; after all, life does not appear in the first book of the *Ethics*. But it illuminates, at least in a genetic perspective, some of the most striking tenets of his mature philosophy of mind.)

Roughly, the argument consists of three steps. Having initially alluded to Aristotle's claim that life consists in 'the persistence of the nutritive soul with heat', Spinoza points out in the first step that, given this conception, an additional definition is required.[39] He finds this definition in the Aristotelian idea that life is 'the actuality of the intellect'.[40] Without this, he explains, we (or Aristotle) could not do justice to the idea that minds and God have life. According to Spinoza, then, Aristotle faces a problem similar to the one we have identified in la Forge.

In the second step, Spinoza next goes on to discuss the extension of the concept life. He leaves us in no doubt that he does not share the Aristotelian view of the tripartite soul. But this alone does not eliminate the issue of the mind's or God's life, since, following common usage, life qualifies both our being as thinking subjects and our being as corporeal entities. We should therefore not restrict the attribution of the term 'life' to bodies that are united with souls. Instead, life must be conceptualized in such a way as to allow for its ascription to 'corporeal things not united to minds and to minds separated from the body'.[41] Against this background, Spinoza takes the third step of defining life in terms of 'the force through which things persevere in their being'. He explains this definition by saying that 'because that force is different from the things themselves, we say

---

[39] Spinoza 1985, 325.   [40] Ibid.   [41] Ibid. 325f.

properly that the things themselves have life,'[42] thus distinguishing God, who is life, from things that merely have life.

This is a remarkably fresh definition, the implications of which can hardly be overemphasized. Spinoza not only departs from the Aristotelian and Cartesian conceptions, but suggests a wholly new take on the issue of life. In a nutshell, his innovation is this: rather than considering life as a physiological or psychological feature of a thing, he takes it as a metaphysical property that characterizes any particular being insofar as it is. Thus, if we observe certain things to be alive, this is not because they possess a specific form. On the contrary, it is because they exhibit a force that is connected in some way or other with being itself.

Obviously, this conception of life is a precursor of Spinoza's later view of the conatus, which is defined in terms of a thing's striving 'to persevere in its being'.[43] Famously, this definition applies to any and each particular thing, that is to say, it qualifies entities insofar as they exist as individuated beings.[44] Moreover, as the second step of Spinoza's argument indicates, this interpretation of life lays the ground for the doctrine of panpsychism, according to which all individuals are 'though in different degrees... animate'.[45] Note that Spinoza does not ascribe life to all individual *minds*, as often reported, but *animation*.

There is thus much continuity between Spinoza's early views and the later doctrines for which his philosophy has become famous. Yet, in interpreting these doctrines, we have to be careful not to miss the point of Spinoza's metaphysical stance. If life is a property that goes along with any and each being, this is *not* because all things resemble vital organisms, but on the contrary because being itself consists in a proclivity towards continuance rather than interruption. Equating being with life, Spinoza contends that being itself is not neutral with respect to its continuance. Any existing thing adopts, so to speak, a pro-attitude toward its existence, and if a thing's pro-attitude is not grounded in its very essence, it is established as soon as the thing begins to actually exist.

I presume that this view also underlies the notion that the body recommends itself as the privileged object of sensation. What qualifies the body for this role is that the proclivity toward its own existence that it has in virtue of its being can be felt immediately, not just inferred from previous sensations. Thus, there is in Spinoza a way to know immediately, and as it were to sense that we are alive and exist. This is also why, by virtue of providing us with the consciousness that we are alive, any sensation conveys deep metaphysical insight, both into the very nature of being, and into the fact there is something rather than nothing.

---

[42] Spinoza 1985, 326.   [43] Spinoza 1985, 499.
[44] For this ontological dimension of the conatus, see Renz 2018, 211–214.
[45] Spinoza 1985, 458.

6 Our consciousness of being alive as a source of knowledge

In the previous section I have presented Spinoza's outlook as a turning point in early modern philosophy's search for our consciousness of being alive. But one might wonder whether one could not just as well tell another story—a different narrative about the process through which this idea was articulated. This is possible; yet in one respect competing narratives may yield similar outcomes. If there is some immediate knowledge of our body and of its being alive, then, while this knowledge may not rule out various sceptical attacks inspired by body-mind-dualism, it is nevertheless such that we may rely on it, in life and in philosophical inquiry. 'I take my own being upon trust,' writes Shaftesbury in *The Moralists*, reacting to Descartes' *cogito* and to Locke's notion that personal identity rests on consciousness.[46] We arrive at a similar point when Spinoza asserts in the *Ethics* that, however insecure and distorted our imaginative ideas may be, they nonetheless provide us with information that may rightly be considered knowledge. Like the sensations of the early *TEI*, imagination, including imaginative experience of our bodies, gives us insight into the nature of being, as well as into the fact that there is necessarily something rather than nothing.

For Spinoza, then, our consciousness of being alive is a source of knowledge. By telling us that we are alive, it yields reliable cognition of something that is true about us. Moreover, if we were not alive, we would not have any consciousness of being so, nor consciousness of any other thing. In the terms of contemporary epistemology, we could say that our consciousness of being alive precludes epistemic luck. To reframe the point in Spinoza's terms, our consciousness of being alive provides our most basic common notion, viz. the notion of being, or more specifically of being as that feature in virtue of which any and each thing not just exists, but also embraces its existence.

Spinoza's view has some fascinating implications. First, it deviates, perhaps somewhat surprisingly, from contemporary epistemology, which, so far as I know, has never considered any instance of consciousness as even a candidate for a source of knowledge. There is a reason for this difference. Within contemporary approaches to the philosophy of mind, consciousness is not always conceptualized in terms of a *self*-relation that a subject entertains towards herself or some of her features. But this structural presumption is essential to the notion that our consciousness of being alive is a source of knowledge.

Second, Spinoza regards our consciousness of being alive as more than a source of *self*-knowledge. It is also the basis of our knowledge of some of our most fundamental metaphysical insights. I find this particularly intriguing, as it shows that metaphysical issues do not only concern the most abstract features of reality.

---

[46] Shaftesbury 1999, 421.

They can also be utterly concrete. Given our sensation of being alive, and given that life is a feature of all existent things, we are, in any sensation, immediately acquainted with the pervasiveness of being. While this may sound a bit speculative, it is exciting to see that our knowledge of being and thus of one the most fundamental of metaphysical concepts, may derive from our sensory experiences.

Third, if we accept Spinoza's metaphysical conception of life, our consciousness of being alive casts light on why, and in what sense, we value life. Through our own conscious experience of being alive we are brought into contact with being's own proclivity for continuance. Taking this experience at face value, we can learn that life is inherently desirable. We learn this, however, without considering any *particular* reason for living. It is rather a matter of learning by doing or existing, and by being intimately aware of this. In other words, our consciousness of being alive reveals to us the existential value of life, without reducing this value to any presumptive moral or instrumental usefulness.

Certainly, the insight that life is inherently desirable may be overruled, and sadly enough it often is. Sometimes, we are just too swamped to attend to the lessons that our consciousness of being alive can teach us. Sometimes, we are unduly influenced by considerations which tell us that unless life is good for something it is good for nothing. But the fact that such moments are part of the reality of human life reaffirms Spinoza's point. That we are affected by considerations of this kind is not just a side effect of the way our sensory apparatus is organized. On the contrary, it is a source of knowledge, and a very valuable one.

PART II
IMMORTALITY

2

'The Thought of Death Changes all our Ideas and Condemns all our Plans'

Early Modern Christian Philosophical Perspectives on Death

Michael Moriarty

The title of this chapter speaks of 'Christian philosophical perspectives' and the first term is not otiose. For, leaving aside philosophers who certainly or probably rejected Christianity, there were many early modern Christians who philosophized more or less independently of their Christian beliefs. Montaigne's 1992 chapter on philosophy as a preparation for death contains noble passages of Epicurean and Stoic inspiration, but none indebted to Christian theism.[1] In II.6, 'On practising', he discusses death in the light of his own experience of being knocked unconscious in an accident, possibly put onto that track by a remark of Seneca's about the experience of fainting.[2] His experience confirms him in the idea that the dying may not be experiencing the pain that, from their groans and movements, we infer they are in. Elsewhere he expresses his preference for a gradual slipping into death, a 'molle et douce'('soft and gentle') way to die (III.9, 983). In another late chapter, breaking with the Stoic notion of mentally preparing oneself for death, he cites with approval the example of the peasants he knows, who think of death only when it is actually upon them (III.12, 1052); for a philosophical expression of this attitude, he turns to the Socrates of the *Apology* (1052–1053). The term that informs his thinking about death is 'nature' rather than God (I.20, 96; III.12, 1052): he mentions with apparent approval 'les efforts que la philosophie et la religion produisent, aspres et exemplaires' ('the efforts produced by philosophy and religion, painful and exemplary'), but he has no wish to imitate them: he prefers the approach of Petronius and Tigellinus, compelled to commit suicide, who slotted their death, so to speak, into their

---

[1] Montaigne 1992, I.20, 81–96; see especially 92–96. Further references are by book and chapter numbers, with the page number in this edition. Volume numbers are omitted since these correspond to those of the books. There is a brief reference to contempt for life as the surest human foundation of 'our religion' (91).

[2] Montaigne 1992, II.6, 372. Cf. Seneca 1917–1925, 77.9.

Michael Moriarty, *'The Thought of Death Changes all our Ideas and Condemns all our Plans': Early Modern Christian Philosophical Perspectives on Death* In: *Life and Death in Early Modern Philosophy.* Edited by: Susan James, Oxford University Press. © Michael Moriarty 2021. DOI: 10.1093/oso/9780192843616.003.0003

usual hedonistic pastimes (III.9, 984). So, one can hardly call Montaigne's approach a Christian one.

Belief in an afterlife with rewards and punishments is central to Christianity; but we can ask how an early modern Christian would have approached the belief philosophically.[3] I begin by briefly considering the proofs of immortality as they appear in the work of the early modern scholastic philosopher whose work Descartes considered the best of its kind, namely the Cistercian Eustache de Saint-Paul (1575–1640).[4] I proceed to consider two writers, Leonard Lessius and Jean de Silhon whose approach differs from that of Eustache in two respects: (1) they are responding to a specific anti-religious discourse that denounces the belief in immortality; (2) they particularly emphasize the connection between belief in immortality and belief in divine providence and in the purposiveness exhibited in nature. I then consider Descartes, who is disinclined to consider nature along teleological lines, but believes that, though the immortality of the soul cannot be strictly proved, its capacity for immortality can be. Even more emphatically, Pascal argues that the universe as a whole exhibits no signs of purpose to the unbeliever. For him, the question of immortality is absolutely central; but it cannot be satisfactorily approached with metaphysical arguments. I conclude with a discussion of Malebranche's remarkably original approach to the meta-physics of immortality.

1 Eustache de Saint-Paul

Eustache argues that, although, for Christians, the Scriptures, the decrees of Councils, and the authority of the Fathers put the spirituality and immortality of the soul beyond all possible doubt, it is none the less worthwhile proving those doctrines by natural reasons in order to glorify the faith and subdue heretics and pagans. The first step, then, is to demonstrate the soul's spirituality, from which its immortality can be readily inferred. This he does by a syllogism. The nature of a thing corresponds to its operation since operation follows from being ('operatio sequitur esse'). But the operations of the rational soul transcend the nature of body or matter. Therefore, the rational soul is not material and corporeal but spiritual. The minor premise is proved in relation both to the intellect and to the will. As to

---

[3] There is a very good presentation of the issue in the broader context of theories of the human mind in Clarke 2016, ch. 5, 126–56 (published in Oxford Scholarship Online: March 2016; DOI: 10.1093/acprof:oso/9780198749578.001.0001). Clarke discusses authors such as La Mothe, Le Vayer, and Gassendi who are sceptical of the possibility of philosophical proofs of immortality.

[4] Descartes to Mersenne, 11 November 1640, in *Œuvres*, ed. Charles Adam and Paul Tannery, 11 vols, rev. edn. (Paris: Vrin/CNRS, 1996) [hereafter AT], III, 232. In fact, Descartes thought at one time of publishing his *Principles of Philosophy* alongside a scholastic textbook, so as to highlight the differences of his approach, and it was Eustache's he thought of using for this purpose (to Mersenne, December 1640, AT III, 259–260.

the intellect: it perceives common natures abstracted from particular matter, and then forms the concept of immaterial entities such as God; and it perceives such objects without any dimensions, shape, colour, or any other modification of corporeal matter. But these concepts are not material, therefore they arise from an immaterial faculty and form, which is the rational soul. As to the will: for the sake purely of moral virtue it can overcome and command the sensitive appetite, it can will freely, and exercise acts of virtue and religion; these acts are above sensation and appetite and thus far above body and matter; hence the will, and the soul of which it is a faculty, are of a different order from body and matter: they are immaterial and spiritual. But what is spiritual is immortal and incorruptible. Being independent of matter, it can subsist separately from matter; not consisting of parts, it is not subject to dissolution or corruption. More briefly: the desire for immortality is naturally instilled in us, and so cannot be vain; when the body ages, the soul does not, indeed reason grows stronger with age; besides, the belief in immortality is common to all people, and upheld by the wisest philosophers.[5]

Eustache's main line of argument is familiar from Aquinas.[6] Moreover, he does not identify particular adversaries, except by such general terms as 'heretics' and 'pagans'. Perhaps this is because he is writing a textbook, not a polemic; but perhaps also he is not aware of any specific contemporary challenge to the notion of immortality (or if he is aware, thinks best to ignore it). This is not the case with the next two writers I discuss.

2 'Against atheists and politicians'

Though both are writing in the Aristotelian tradition, the Flemish Jesuit Leonardus Lessius (1554–1623) and the French layman Jean de Silhon (1596–1667) might otherwise seem, on the face of it, to have little in common. Lessius was an academic theologian at the University of Louvain, who produced important works on the theology of grace and on the moral dimension of economic activity. Silhon was a distinguished man of letters, a protégé of Cardinal Richelieu; he was to become a founder-member of the Académie Française in 1635. Later still, when working for Richelieu's successor as chief minister, Cardinal Mazarin, he was instrumental in obtaining a pension for Descartes, who expressed his gratitude in a letter discussed below.[7] But the title of Silhon's two-part work is very close to that of Lessius's, and it is very likely that

---

[5] de Saint-Paul 1609, vol. II, Part III, *De rebus naturalibus*, Part III, treatise IV, disp. 1, q. 2, 414–415.
[6] On the immateriality of the human soul, proved by its knowledge, see Aquinas 1988, Ia, q. 75, a. 2; on its incorruptibility, and its natural desire for eternal existence, see Ia, q. 75, a. 6.
[7] Descartes to Silhon, March/April 1648, AT V, 134–139. See the biographical note on Silhon in Descartes 2009, 2951.

42 THE THOUGHT OF DEATH CHANGES ALL OUR IDEAS

he had read Lessius's work. He certainly declares that he has not scrupled to use arguments already advanced by others, though in the treatise on immortality he has contributed more of his own.[8] Moreover, both authors are engaging with a specific contemporary challenge to the belief in immortality. They are both explicitly countering the claim that immortality is a fictitious notion propagated so as to uphold the social order: in Silhon's words:

> un artifice de police pour tenir les peuples en bride par la crainte des peines de l'autre vie, et par l'espoir de la recompense.   (II.1, 125)
>
> a political contrivance to keep populations under control through the fear of punishment in the afterlife, and the hope of reward.[9]

Hence Lessius's subtitle: he is writing 'adversus Atheos et politicos'.[10] By 'politicos' he means those writers who consider all religions from a political point of view, and value them in proportion to their political efficacy. He singles out the Machiavelli of *The Prince* as an exponent of this view (I.3, 4–5).[11] In his dedicatory preface Lessius cites Machiavelli as the chief in modern times of the sect of those who deny the existence of providence and the immortality of souls.[12] If philosophical justification can be provided for the belief in immortality, then it becomes impossible to maintain that religion is *nothing but* a political fiction. Silhon, moreover, targets a particular social constituency, namely, courtiers who think that professing impiety is a part of social refinement (II.2, 138–139).[13]

Both authors emphasize the existential implications of the issue of immortality.

> Si verò deprehensum fuerit hanc [*sc.* animam] esse mortalem in hominibus sicut in brutis, nihil est quòd vereamur in posterum, sed securi futurorum pro arbitrio vivere poterimus. Si verò contrarium ostensum fuerit, meritò convenit nos esse anxios, ne post hac vitam immortalis anima in graves & immortales pœnas incurrat.   (Lessius 1617, Præfatio, [4])
>
> If indeed it were found that [the soul] is mortal in human beings as it is in animals, there is nothing for us to fear for the future, but, unconcerned as to what is to come, we shall be able to live as we please. But if the contrary is proved, we should well and truly be anxious lest after this life our immortal soul fall into severe and immortal punishment.

---

[8] de Silhon 1991, Advertissement, 13–14; Part II, Introduction, 123. Silhon's defence of belief in immortality is discussed in Clarke 2016, 133–136.

[9] This and all other translations here are my own, unless otherwise stated.   [10] Lessius 1617.

[11] See Tarcov 2014, 193–216 (*Project MUSE* muse.jhu.edu/article/543797).

[12] Lessius 1617, Præfatio, [3].

[13] Pascal likewise mentions unbelievers who imagine that to profess unbelief is a sign of aristocratic distinction ('les belles manières du monde'). Pascal 2010, 427 (Lafuma numbering)/681 (Sellier numbering)/398 (Le Guern numbering).

Silhon observes that self-knowledge (in the early modern sense, which focuses on generic rather than individual characteristics) requires a firm conviction as to the state of our souls in the afterlife: again, the existential, not to say social and political, implications are plain:

> Or un des principaux chefs de cette connoissance [sc. *connois toy toy mesme*] consiste en un jugement ou ferme ou presomptif de l'estat de nos ames après cette vie: de là dépend et la conduitte de nos mœurs, et l'establissement de l'ordre et du bien universel du monde.   (Part II. Introduction, 121)

> Now one of the chief heads of this knowledge consists in a firm or presumptive judgement of the state of our souls after this life; on this depend both the government of our own behaviour and the establishment of the order and universal good of the world.

3 Arguments for immortality

Lessius and Silhon's debt to scholastic Aristotelianism appears most clearly in two respects: (1) their emphasis on the purposive nature of natural things; and (2) their conception of the soul. For both writers, the defence of immortality is preceded by and largely based on a defence of belief in God and his providence, since, as they argue, the two issues are closely related; so much so that in the first part of his work Lessius adduces the immortality of the soul as evidence for the existence of providence (I.152, 177–179), though it is not until the second part that he will go into the reasons for thinking the soul immortal.

In establishing the existence of God, Lessius particularly concentrates on the evidence of purpose in the order of the universe and in the structure of animals and plants, though he also cites miracles and prophecies (I.9, 9–10). Silhon adopts a more metaphysical approach, a form of the causal argument: he methodically reviews all categories of being, from prime matter to the angels, and concludes that none of them can be self-existent and that all owe their being to a supreme intelligence:

> Les mesmes raisons qui concluent, qu'il y a beaucoup de choses qui ne tiennent pas leur estre d'elles mesmes, et par consequent qu'il y en a une au-delà de toutes celles-là qui le leur a communiqué, laquelle nous appellons Dieu. Ces mesmes raisons dis-je, concluent que cette cause est intellectuelle et pleine d'une infinie sagesse.   (I.5, 65)

> The same arguments that prove that there are many things that do not derive their being from themselves and that therefore there is one beyond all of them from which they do derive it, which is what we call God—these same arguments, I say, prove that this cause is intelligent and full of infinite wisdom.

44 THE THOUGHT OF DEATH CHANGES ALL OUR IDEAS

But Silhon does not bracket out considerations of purpose; using the celebrated analogy of the watch and the watchmaker, he goes on to argue that whatever clearly acts for a purpose and is not itself rational bespeaks the influence of a rational mind outside it that has formulated the purpose of the entity and designed it accordingly (I.5, 66–67). In fact, the notion of purpose is even more important to his argumentation than to that of Lessius. Both aim to show that the general Aristotelian conception of the soul, to which they adhere, does not imply that the soul is so completely dependent on the body for all its operations that if the organs of the body cease to function the soul must infallibly perish. It is true, Lessius concedes, that the intellect makes use of the imagination, which requires animal spirits for its operation, and a fit disposition of the brain; but the intellect's dependence on the body is not *per se* but *per accidens*; its prime function is to judge, and this does not depend on the imagination. Its current dependence on imagination results from its current function as the form of the body, but will cease once the soul is liberated from the body (II.52–54, 305–307). In other words, the soul's independence from the body is a proof of immortality.

Silhon likewise believes that the immateriality of the soul can be demonstrated from its intellectual operations, but he is not convinced by the standard argument that immateriality entails incorruptibility: he argues that some immaterial forms, such as the habits of the soul produced by grace or by repeated acts, can perish (II.1, 126). (Whether these count as forms in the sense that the soul is a form I am not clear.) So, he inserts the argument for the human soul's immateriality into a more elaborate teleological schema. This has the advantage of showing both that animals' souls perish when the body dies and that human souls do not.

His point of departure is the axiom,

Dieu ne veut pas que rien soit inutile en la nature. (II.1, 130)

God does not will that there should be anything in nature that is purposeless.
God has therefore prescribed ends for all things, for the sake of which they exist; if they cease to be able to fulfil those ends, he ceases to conserve them; but as long as they are capable of fulfilling them, he continues to preserve them in being. To accomplish the operations (vegetative and sensitive) that pertain to their kind of soul, the brute beasts need the assistance of their bodily organs, and when the body ceases to be able to provide that assistance, the soul is thus unable to function: its continued existence would be pointless, and it is therefore annihilated.

The same fate would befall the human soul were it similarly dependent for all its operations on the bodily organs (II.1, 130–132). But various arguments show this not to be the case: for instance, the soul's highest operations concern purely spiritual entities which can neither harm nor benefit the body; indeed, these operations are positively hampered by sensation and imagination (II.2,

135–136). If the human soul can perform its key operations without input from the body, it can still fulfil its purposes when separate from the body and God will therefore preserve it in being (II.1, 132). In fact, the standard conception of the soul as the form of the body is inadequate and an obstacle to the belief in immortality. The soul does indeed function as the form of the body, but that definition does not exhaust its nature. It is not the form of the body insofar as it reasons and conceives intellectual attachments. True, in this life it can exercise its higher functions only when capable of sensation. But when it withdraws into itself and concentrates on its higher part, when it conceives its highest thoughts and penetrates the highest truths, it ceases to be affected by sensation. This is a good indication of what it will be like when the soul has broken its link with the body and no longer has to act as its form (II.5, 169–170). Silhon offers the analogy of a man shut up in a room, who depends on the windows in order to see, and whose sight is affected by the state or colour of the glass. This dependence will cease if the glass is broken or he leaves the room; he will then have unmediated access to the world through his vision. Likewise, in this life, the soul cannot perform the functions of its higher part if the senses and organs (its windows on the world) are disordered, but when liberated by death it will be able to perform those operations deriving from its essence, namely understanding and volition, without impediment (II.5, 171–172).

Notions of purpose are even more essential to other arguments for immortality offered by Lessius and Silhon. Thus, Lessius argues that the world was made for human beings; it is their spacious and well-furnished home, and without them all its beauty, order, and variety would be in vain (I.62–63, 63–64). But since all things were destined for man, he must have a higher destiny, beyond them. The entire order of nature and its workings would be disproportionate if we were to pass a short and unhappy time on this earth and then revert to nothingness (II.23–24, 256–257). Second, all things tend towards perfection and attain that perfection of which they are capable. But human beings cannot attain the perfection of wisdom and virtue in this life, and if there is no afterlife in which they can do so, nature, which otherwise does nothing in vain, must have given them their capacities and their desire to fulfil them to no purpose (II.21, 253–254). The soul's self-knowledge in this life is very obscure, as witness all the disagreements about it among philosophers. If it perished with the body, it would never succeed in knowing itself; but once released from the body it will have a clear and distinct vision of itself and of spiritual realities (II.22, 254–256). Third, God's goal in creation could be simply to manifest his perfections. But if humans are mortal, the world would not display his wisdom, goodness, providence and so forth. Would it be wise to create an eternal universe of which the lord (i.e. man) is mortal? Would it be good to enable everything else to attain its perfection, while man is unable to attain the hundredth part of the good of which he is capable? Would providence abandon the soul to its own lusts, without incentives for virtue and deterrents for

46 THE THOUGHT OF DEATH CHANGES ALL OUR IDEAS

vice, leaving crimes unpunished and good without reward in a world where the wicked dominate and oppress the good?

As Lessius emphasizes, much bitterness is mixed with the sweetness of life, so much so that life as a whole seems bearable only if there is hope of a future sweetness. It is not surprising that the pagans, largely ignorant of retribution after death, accused the gods of cruelty for allowing the good to suffer and the wicked to rule. In other words, from the perspective of this life, God's perfections are invisible rather than manifest. But all these doubts and complaints fade away once we accept the soul's immortality, along with reward and punishment after death (II.43–45, 286–289).

Silhon's arguments follow a similar path and again require a notion of the divine purpose. As soon as we can use our reason, we desire to be happy. This is a natural instinct, as philosophers and the people agree. The philosophers see that God would not have implanted this desire in humanity if it could not be satisfied, since he does nothing in vain. However, the complete satisfaction of the desire is impossible in this life. Therefore, it must come after death. But if the soul can be happy after death, it must be able to exist without the body, and separation is not tantamount to annihilation (II.2, 140–141; cf. II.5, 170).

Moreover, if we compare our condition with that of the animals, we can see that God's goodness would be radically incompatible with the annihilation of the human soul at death. Echoing Lessius's remark about the pagans' sense of the gods' cruelty, Silhon asserts that if this life were all there is, it could be the gift only of malignity. The most pleasurable existence would be blighted by the prospect of annihilation (II.3, 144–145). But pleasure is rarely the lot of human beings. Silhon methodically lists and eloquently denounces the evils of human life, evils from which the animals are exempt. They need not work to survive, they are blessed with good health, they have the pleasure of sex without shame or disease, they are not tormented by the passions or by the tyrannous and false ideal of honour (145–148). We, by contrast, are ravaged by illnesses, for which the remedies are just as bad: at least as many die from medical treatment as are saved by it. We alone not only kill fellow-members of our species, but actually glory in doing so. Silhon was writing only thirty years after the end of thirty years of religious conflict, and the horrors of war were only too fresh in the memories of his countrymen (148–152).

But surely, comes the objection, we have advantages denied to the beasts? We have society. Nevertheless, Silhon replies, even the best form of government, monarchy, is flawed and can degenerate into tyranny. The administration of justice involves punishment more than reward, and the rewards society offers are either imaginary, as in the case of glory, or real but harmful to others, as in the case of wealth. Property is one of the main sources of evil, and the legal system often reinforces the evil it does instead of removing it. Not only, then, are the beasts better off than man; if death were merely annihilation, it would be better if mankind had never existed (152–158). Why, though, should God have made the world as a palace for man, if the occupant of the palace is condemned to a short and miserable life? How could his wisdom grant the beasts a happier life than man, their king and master (II.4, 159–160)?

Moving on to a further argument, Silhon allows that, while God's purpose is apparent in his attachment of pleasure to the acts that are necessary for the preservation of individuals and of the species, the higher operations of the mind have no such attractions. We experience the war within ourselves, the struggle between the passions and reason, as painful, and could never endure this suffering without the prospect of a reward in the afterlife. The intrinsic quality of virtue is not enough to counterbalance its difficulty and the attractions of unvirtuous pleasure, the more so since the rewards of honour and glory are available to few. God has given us a love of truth and has prescribed the moral law so that society can function peaceably. But if we were to discover that there is no life after death, why should we not just pursue pleasure at the expense of virtue? However, there would then be a strange disconnection between the dictates of truth and those of morality. There is certainly no advantage in pursuing virtue in this life when the virtuous are generally unfortunate, and wealth, honour, and pleasure are achieved by wickedness. Since God is utterly self-sufficient, he can have had no reason to create anything other than his own glory. But if human beings are mortal, they have no reason to glorify him. On the contrary, they have every reason to think him a God without goodness, without wisdom, and without justice (II.4, 160–164).

In both Lessius and Silhon, then, we find a radically pessimistic estimate of human life on earth, inflected only by the certainty of a divine purpose that assures us that death is not the end, and that God's wisdom, justice, and goodness will be manifested in the afterlife. But what happens if that sense of purpose disappears? If, to be more precise, we cease to interpret the workings of the physical universe in terms of the ends fulfilled by inanimate objects?

4 Descartes on immortality: bracketing out cosmic purpose

The question is obviously raised by the natural philosophy of Descartes. It is important to recognize, however, that even though Descartes speaks of a tree of knowledge, in which ethics is one of the branches issuing from the trunk of physics, itself rooted in the truths of metaphysics (*Principles*, letter-preface to the French edition, AT IX-2, 14), he nowhere suggests that ethics should be redefined in keeping with the tenets of his physics. Our understanding of human nature, and in particular of the relationship between soul and body, should indeed reflect what we know about souls and bodies. But this does not mean that the content of ethics is dictated by physics. Rather than confusing the two

48 THE THOUGHT OF DEATH CHANGES ALL OUR IDEAS

perspectives, as scholastic Aristotelianism does, we must recognize that they are independently valid and complementary.

When Descartes considers whether we should seek for final causes in nature, he tends to link his discussion to the question whether the world has been created for our sake. Scientifically speaking, the answer to both questions is no.[14] On the other hand, it is a good and pious thought, from a moral point of view ('in *Ethicis*'), to think that God has made everything for our sake (*Principles*, III.3, AT VIII, 81/IX-2, 104). This encourages us to love God and feel grateful to him; what is more, it is true in so far as there is nothing we cannot make use of, since to consider any natural thing affords exercise for the mind and gives us a reason to praise God. Echoing this view in the letter to Hyperaspistes, Descartes concedes that we can say that all things were created for God's glory: this is true in ethics, and in relation to the human species, since we are bound to praise God for all his works.[15] In any case, God's purposive activity is undoubtedly manifest in the creation of the human being as a compound of soul and body. From a mechanical point of view, we can understand the physical aspects of the process of sensation in terms of the stimulation of nerve-filaments connecting the sense-organs to the brain. But we shall not understand the process fully if we do not go further and conclude that the cerebral motions that deliver particular sensations to the mind do so in order to preserve us in being. The senses have been implanted in us by nature for this purpose, and thus assure us of God's power and goodness (*Meditation* VI, AT VII, 87–88/IX, 69–70).[16]

This argument allows us to deduce that God wills to preserve the union of soul and body and enables us to identify at least one aspect of the divine purpose vis-à-vis human beings. However, Descartes's philosophical approach rules out in advance those arguments for the survival of the soul after death that, like those of Lessius or Silhon, depend on our ability to discern God's purposes from the order of the universe as a whole and from the operations of creatures lower in the ontological hierarchy than man. If the thought that God created everything for human beings is, properly speaking, an ethical conception, then, however valid in that context, it cannot be used to establish a metaphysical thesis (that the soul can survive death), since, as the tree metaphor shows, ethics is logically posterior to metaphysics.

This, for Descartes, hardly jeopardizes belief in immortality, but it does mean that the basis of the belief is narrower: it cannot draw on a vision of man's place in the universe. Nevertheless, he regards the basis as perfectly solid. It consists in a clear and distinct perception, guaranteed by God as veridical, of the distinction

---

[14] *Principles*, III.2–3, AT VIII, 80–81/IX-2, 104; to Hyperaspistes, August 1641, §10, AT III, 431–432; *Fifth Replies*, IV.1, AT VII, 374–375.

[15] To Hyperaspistes, § 10, AT III, 431. Cf. also to Chanut, 6 June 1647, AT V, 53–55; *Fifth Replies*, IV.1, AT VII, 375.

[16] I draw here on the discussion in Moriarty 2006, 43–45.

between the soul and the body and in a theory of knowledge based on innate ideas. Unlike his scholastic predecessors, he is therefore not hampered by a conception of the soul as the form of the body, or as dependent for its operations on the input of the senses.

In the Preface to the Sorbonne theologians, Descartes emphasizes the utility of his work: it offers a rational demonstration that God exists and that the soul does not perish with the body. He observes that since in this life greater rewards appear to be available to vice than to virtue, few people would prefer what is right to what is useful unless they were restrained by fear of God or the expectation of an afterlife. It is no use appealing to Scripture to convince unbelievers of these crucial points (AT VII, 1–2/IX, 4–5). Hence the need for a philosophical treatment of them. Again, Descartes takes it for granted that disbelief in immortality is a contemporary cultural fact.

Yet in the seventh of the *Second Objections*, the Objectors express disappointment that Descartes has said nothing of immortality, when he should have refuted those who are so unworthy of immortality as to deny it and perhaps even detest it. (Like Descartes, then, not to mention Lessius and Silhon, the Objectors, led by Mersenne, are aware of immortality as a live issue). Moreover, even supposing (what they doubt) that Descartes has sufficiently proved the distinction between mind and body, he has not established that the mind is incorruptible. He has not ruled out the possibility that God may have limited its duration in keeping with that of the body (AT VII, 128/IX, 101).

Descartes concedes that he cannot refute this last objection; he would not presume to use human reason to determine a matter that depends purely on God's free will. What natural reason can determine, however, is that the soul is distinct from the body, and is a substance. By contrast, since the individual human body is simply an arrangement of its constituents, it can perish by division or by a change in shape. Now there is no argument or example to show that a substance such as the mind could be annihilated by a change of shape, for shape is not a substance but a mode, and a mode of the body, not of the mind. Nor is there any argument or example to show that substances are liable to perish.[17] Together, these points suffice to show that, as far as philosophy can determine, the human mind is immortal. But as for whether God has decided that the soul will cease to exist when the body is destroyed, that is a matter we could know only by revelation. In fact, God has revealed that the soul is not destroyed by the body (AT VII, 153–154/IX, 119–120). Faith, therefore, is here the necessary supplement to philosophy.

Although Descartes implicitly agrees with Lessius and Silhon that failing to believe in an afterlife has harmful moral implications, his claims about immortality

---

[17] The French version is more explicit: 'are liable to be annihilated'.

50   THE THOUGHT OF DEATH CHANGES ALL OUR IDEAS

are more limited than theirs.[18] Nevertheless, he can regard himself as having discredited the unbelievers' claims that the soul perishes with the body. More than that, he regards his philosophy as offering reasons to hope for an afterlife that also enables us better to cope with this one. Thus, to Huygens, grieving for the loss of his brother, he offers a remedy that he finds efficacious both against the pain of bereavement and the fear of one's own death (though he describes himself as 'du nombre de ceux qui aiment le plus la vie' ('among the number of those who most love life')).[19] It consists in reflecting on the nature of our souls,

> que je pense connaître si clairement devoir durer plus que les corps, et être nées pour des plaisirs et des félicités beaucoup plus grandes que celles dont nous jouissons en ce monde, que je ne puis concevoir autre chose de ceux qui meurent, sinon qu'ils passent à une vie plus douce et plus tranquille que la nôtre, et que nous les irons trouver quelque jour, même avec souvenance du passé; car je reconnais en nous une mémoire intellectuelle, qui est assurément indépendante du corps.   (To Huygens, 10 October 1642, AT III, 798)

> which I think I know so clearly must outlast our bodies, and are born for kinds of pleasure and happiness far greater than those we enjoy in this world, that for those who die, I can conceive only that they pass over to a sweeter and more tranquil life than ours, and that we shall go to meet them one day, even with remembrance of the past; for I recognize in ourselves an intellectual memory which is assuredly independent of the body.

Religion, Descartes knows, has much more to say about the afterlife; but he goes on to admit an 'infirmity', which he supposes most people share: that even though they think they firmly believe in the teachings of religion, they find these less convincing than what they learn from 'des raisons naturelles fort évidentes' ('very evident natural reasons') (AT III, 799). In some ways, this is a curious remark. Descartes can claim, on the basis of the *Meditations*, to have shown that the death of the body does not entail that of the soul; and, if the pure intellect operates independently of the body, then he can plausibly claim that there is an intellectual memory independent of the brain. But though he could argue that a soul independent of the body could experience greater bliss than one, in Andrew Marvell's words, 'hung up, as 'twere, in chains/Of nerves, and arteries, and veins', he has himself nowhere established that we can expect it to do so.[20] It is not, then, so clear that his 'natural reasons' are 'very evident'. He must be implicitly appealing to a

---

[18]   To the Dean and Doctors of the Faculty of Theology, AT VII, 2/IX, 4.

[19]   For other letters offering consolation on bereavement see: to Huygens (on the death of his wife), 20 May 1637, AT I, 631–634; to Colvius (on the death of Beeckman), 14 June 1637, AT I, 379–380, and to Elisabeth (on the execution of Charles I), 22 February 1649, AT V, 281–283.

[20]   Andrew Marvell's poem, 'A Dialogue between the Soul and the Body'.

conception of Providence, such as we saw Lessius and Silhon working with. But to infer that natural reason implies that God will reward virtue with bliss in the afterlife might be seen as the kind of presumptuous reasoning about God's free choices that he claims in the Second Replies to have eschewed.

A more accurate statement of the issue is perhaps to be found in a later letter addressed to Elisabeth of Bohemia: philosophy gives reasons to hope of happiness after death:

> Même sans les enseignements de la foi, la seule philosophie naturelle fait espérer à notre âme un état plus heureux, après la mort, que celui où elle est à présent.[21]

> Even without the teaching of faith, mere natural philosophy gives our soul reason to hope for a better state after death than it is currently in.

The prospect of life after death comes up frequently in the correspondence with Elisabeth. Here too the discussion frequently has a therapeutic aim. The letter of 18 May 1645 is a response to the news of Elisabeth's illness, a slow fever which Descartes diagnoses as resulting from an underlying sadness. This can only be overcome if she learns to strengthen herself against misfortune, and Descartes's treatment for this is a kind of cognitive therapy, whereby the great-souled can learn to master their passions.

> D'une part, se considérant comme immortelles et capables de recevoir de très grands contentements, puis, d'autre part, considérant qu'elles sont jointes à des corps mortels et fragiles, qui sont sujets à beaucoup d'infirmités, et qui ne peuvent manquer de périr dans peu d'années, elles font bien tout ce qui est en leur pouvoir pour se rendre la Fortune favorable en cette vie, mais néanmoins elles l'estiment si peu, au regard de l'Éternité, qu'elles n'en considèrent quasi les événements que comme nous faisons ceux des Comédies.[22]
>
> (To Elisabeth, 18 May 1645, AT IV, 202).

> For, on the one hand, they consider themselves as immortal and capable of experiencing the highest bliss, and then, on the other hand, considering that they are joined to a mortal and fragile body, subject to many infirmities, and which must inevitably perish in a few years, they certainly do everything in their power to win the favour of Fortune in this life, but none the less value it so little, that they consider what results from it almost as we consider the events of a play.[23]

This recognition changes the attitude of great-souled people to what are generally regarded as misfortunes, such as bodily pain or the troubles of their friends. The

---

[21] To Elisabeth, 1 September 1645, AT IV, 282.
[22] On the image of life as a play, see also to Elisabeth, January 1646, AT IV, 355.
[23] The translation of the letters to and from Elisabeth is from Descartes 2015.

former gives them the chance to exercise their fortitude; the latter, to help their friends in every possible way. In either case, the satisfaction of doing their best counteracts their physical or mental pain (AT IV, 203). In other words, because belief in immortality changes one's scheme of values for the better, it brings this-worldly satisfactions, quite apart from the bliss one may attain in the afterlife.[24]

Elisabeth herself emphatically endorses the prospect of a better life after death:

> Si on est bien persuadé de l'immortalité de l'âme, il est impossible de douter qu'elle ne sera plus heureuse après la séparation du corps (qui est l'origine de tous les déplaisirs de la vie, comme l'âme des plus grand contentements). [...] Je ne doute nullement, qu'encore que la vie ne soit pas mauvaise de soi, elle doit être abandonnée pour une condition qu'on connaîtra meilleure.
>
> (To Descartes, 28 October 1645, AT IV, 323)

> If one is thoroughly convinced of the soul's immortality, it is impossible to doubt that it will be happier after separation from the body (which is the source of all the discomforts of life, as the soul is that of the greatest satisfactions). [...] I do not in the least doubt that, although life is not bad in itself, it should be abandoned for a condition we shall experience as better.

She dismisses, however, in a part of the paragraph I have omitted, the view of Sir Kenelm Digby that there must be purgatory after death for those whose souls are not fully purified of the passions of this life. Descartes's response seems to indicate a certain anxiety that Elisabeth's pessimism might lead her to despise life excessively (perhaps with pernicious consequences for her health): he therefore emphasizes the uncertainty of the rational grounds for the hope for a better life after death:

> Pour ce qui regarde l'état de notre âme après cette vie, j'en ai bien moins de confiance que M. D'Igby; car, laissant à part ce que la foi nous en enseigne, je confesse que, par la seule raison naturelle, nous pouvons bien faire beaucoup de conjectures à notre avantage et avoir de belles espérances, mais non point aucune assurance. Et parce que la même raison naturelle nous apprend aussi que nous avons toujours beaucoup plus de biens que de maux en cette vie, et que nous ne devons point laisser le certain pour l'incertain, elle me semble nous enseigner que nous ne devons pas véritablement craindre la mort, mais que nous ne devons aussi jamais la rechercher.   (To Elisabeth, 3 November 1645, AT IV, 333)

> As to the state of our soul after this life, I know much less about it than M. d'Igby; for, setting aside what faith teaches us, I confess that, with the aid of natural

---

[24] For a similar line of argument about the benefits of belief in immortality, see Descartes to Elisabeth, 15 September 1645, AT IV, 292.

reason alone, we can make many conjectures in our favour and entertain great hopes, but can gain no certitude. And because this same natural reason also teaches us that we always have more good than evil in this life, and that we should not forfeit the certain for the sake of the uncertain, it seems to me to teach us that, though we should not really fear death, we should never seek it either.

We can think that the good of this life outweighs the evil, because, on the one hand, we can set little store by whatever is outside us and does not therefore depend on our free will, and, on the other, we can always turn whatever does depend upon our will to good (to Elisabeth, January 1646, AT IV, 356). What depends on our will is of course chiefly our judgements, and this position therefore reflects Descartes's indebtedness to Stoicism and perhaps above all to Epictetus. Descartes here dissents by implication from Lessius and Silhon's representation of life as dominated by evil and suffering.

Speaking as a philosopher, Descartes does not speculate about the nature of post-mortem contentment, except as regards the hope of reunion mentioned in the letter to Huygens quoted above. When he speaks of beatitude or supreme happiness, he speaks of it as obtainable in this life and as within our control.[25] When writing to Christina of Sweden about the notion of the Sovereign Good, as employed by the ancient philosophers, he distinguishes an absolute sense of the term, in which it can only apply to God, and a sense relative to us, in which it refers to something 'qui nous appartient en quelque façon, et qui est tel, que c'est perfection pour nous de l'avoir' ('that in some sense belongs to us, and that is such, that it is a perfection for us to possess it') (20 November 1647, AT V, 82). He points out that the ancients, lacking the light of faith, knew nothing of supernatural beatitude; but his own discussion remains within the same frame of reference as theirs, as he goes on to explain that the sovereign good consists in a 'ferme et constante résolution de faire exactement toutes les choses que l'on jugera être les meilleures, et d'employer toutes les forces de son esprit à les bien connaître' (firm and constant resolution to do everything one judges to be best, and to employ all the powers of one's mind in finding out what these are). From his point of view, this is tantamount to the possession of virtue and is the source of 'le plus grand et le plus solide contentement de la vie' ('the greatest and the most solid contentment in life') (AT V, 83).[26]

Descartes does not, therefore, follow Aquinas in arguing, on metaphysical grounds, that only God, as the universal good, can satisfy the human will and that human beatitude can consist only in the vision of the divine essence (*Summa*

---

[25] To Elisabeth, 4 August 1645, AT IV, 275–277; 18 August 1645, AT IV, 281–282; 6 October 1645, AT IV, 304–309; November 1646, AT IV, 528–530.

[26] For similar accounts of the nature of virtue, see to Elisabeth, 18 August 1645, AT IV, 277 and *Les Passions de l'âme*, §§ 148, 153, AT XI, 441–442, 445–446.

theologiae (*ST*) 1–2.2.8; 1–2.3.8). But philosophy can still illuminate this doctrine, as appears from a letter to none other than Silhon:

> Pour votre autre question, vous avez, ce me semble, fort bien répondu vous-même sur la qualité de la connaissance de Dieu dans la béatitude, la distinguant de celle que nous en avons maintenant, en ce qu'elle sera intuitive. [...] La connaissance intuitive est une illustration de l'esprit, par laquelle il voit en la lumière de Dieu les choses qu'il lui plaît lui découvrir par une impression directe de la clarté divine sur notre entendement. [...] Or, que notre esprit, lorsqu'il sera détaché du corps ou que ce corps glorifié ne lui fera plus d'empêchement, ne puisse recevoir de telles illustrations et connaissances directes, en pouvez-vous douter [...]? (To Silhon, March or April 1648, AT V, 136–137)

> As to your other question, it seems to me that you have yourself provided a very good answer, concerning the quality of the knowledge of God in the state of beatitude, when you distinguish it from the knowledge we have in this life, in that it will be intuitive. [...] Intuitive knowledge is an illumination of the mind, by means of which it sees in the light of God those things that he is pleased to reveal to us by a direct impression on our understanding of the divine clarity. [...] Now, when our soul is detached from our body or united to a glorified body that is no encumbrance to it, can you doubt that it will be able receive illuminations and direct knowledge of this kind?

This is, indeed, a confirmation of what Silhon himself has argued about the cognitive capacities of the soul after death.

In a letter to Chanut of 15 June 1646, Descartes explains that he feels he has made more progress in ethics than in medicine; thus, instead of finding means of prolonging life (as he once hoped to do (*Discourse on the Method*, VI, AT VI, 62)) he has found a better way of dealing with death, which is not to fear it (AT IV, 441–442). How we learn not to fear it is explained in another letter, where he discusses the possibility of a natural love of God. When we contemplate the power and majesty of God, the extent of his providence, and the infallibility of his decrees, these thoughts procure us a joy so extreme we feel that we have lived long enough, since God has given us the grace to attain such knowledge; we have thus attained a natural love of God, a willed identification with him, so perfect that we desire only that his will be done. Hence, we no longer fear death, suffering, or misfortune (to Chanut, 1 February 1647, AT IV, 608–609). This is a powerful expression of a kind of, not exactly Christian, but theistic, as distinct from pantheistic, Stoicism.[27]

---

[27] On submission to providence see also to Huygens, 20 May 1637, AT I, 631–634 and to Mersenne, 9 January 1639, AT II, 480.

5 Pascal: apologetics without metaphysics

For Descartes, as he explains in this letter, the thought of the greatness of creation is an index of the all-powerfulness of God, which is diminished by those who imagine the world as finite (AT IV, 608–609). It is well known that Pascal voices a very different reaction (whether his own or that of an imagined non-believer) to the idea of a world without limits: 'Le silence éternel de ces espaces infinis m'effraie' ('The eternal silence of these infinite spaces frightens me') (L 201/S 233/LG 187).[28]

Like Lessius and Silhon, Pascal insists that the question of immortality is of fundamental existential importance.

> Il importe à toute la vie de savoir si l'âme est mortelle ou immortelle.
>
> (L 164/S 197/LG 153)

> It makes a difference to our whole life to know whether the soul is mortal or immortal.

The point is urged at more length in the following passage:

> L'immortalité de l'âme est une chose qui nous importe si fort, qui nous touche si profondément, qu'il faut avoir perdu tout sentiment pour être dans l'indifférence de savoir ce qui en est. Toutes nos actions et nos pensées doivent prendre des routes si différentes, selon qu'il y aura des biens éternels à espérer ou non, qu'il est impossible de faire une démarche avec sens et jugement, qu'en la réglant par la vue de ce point.[29]

> The immortality of the soul is a thing that makes such a difference to us, that affects us so profoundly, that only someone entirely devoid of awareness can not care what the truth of the matter is. All our actions and our thoughts must follow such different paths, depending on whether or not there is hope of eternal happiness, that it is impossible to make a single move with good sense and judgement if we do not regulate it in accordance with our view of this issue.

Again, like Lessius and Silhon, Pascal maintains that if there is no prospect of immortality, this life is fundamentally wretched. He makes the case at length in the sections 'Misère' and 'Souverain Bien' ('Wretchedness' and 'Supreme Good') of the *Pensées*, and sums it up succinctly in one of his longest and most developed fragments.

---

[28] For numbering see n.13. [29] L 427/S 681/LG 398; cf. L 428/S 682/LG 399.

Il ne faut pas avoir l'âme fort élevée pour comprendre qu'il n'y a point ici de satisfaction véritable et solide, que tous nos plaisirs ne sont que vanité, que nos maux sont infinis. [...] La mort [...] nous menace à chaque instant.

(L 427/S 681/LG 398)

One does not need an exceptionally lofty soul to grasp that there is no true and solid satisfaction in this life, that all our pleasures are nothing but futility, that our sufferings are infinite. [...] Death [...] threatens us at every moment.

A third affinity lies in Pascal's assumption that disbelief in immortality is a concrete social fact. Like Silhon in particular, he locates it in a particular community, aristocratic freethinkers who think it a sign of aristocratic refinement to claim that our soul is nothing but a little wind and smoke (L 427/S 681/LG 398).

However, unlike Lessius or Silhon, Pascal does not see nature as furnishing proofs of the existence of God (L 3, 781/S 38, 644/LG 2, 653). He accepts the Cartesian vision of nature as inanimate. A notion like *horror vacui* appears to him absurd; inanimate bodies cannot have passions, fears, aversions, tendencies, aspirations, inclinations (L 958/S 795/LG 744; L 199/S 230/LG 185). In other words, though he does not explicitly say this, it makes no sense to think of them as acting for an end or as seeking perfection. Thus, the human condition cannot be illuminated by parallels with the physical universe.

Like Descartes again, Pascal believes that there are reasons to think the soul immaterial (L 108, 115/S 140, 147/LG 99, 106). But he does not present them as reasons to think it immortal. Survival after death is not a matter for proof; it is an issue on which we must make a decision. This decision can be arrived at along two paths. Following one, we come to a twofold verdict, on the basis of different kinds of evidence. First, we decide, having examined our own and other people's experience of life, that Christianity offers the best diagnosis and explanation of the human condition, and the best remedy for human unhappiness; second, we judge, having studied the Scriptures and history, that it has good claims to be true. In which case, we shall accept immortality as a central Christian doctrine. Taking the other path, we decide, by analysing the potential outcomes of (a) committing to Christianity and (b) refraining from such commitment, that it is in our interest to believe in Christianity, because of its promise of infinite happiness after death to those who believe. This is, of course, the celebrated Wager argument. The relationship, if any, between the two paths is one of the thorniest problems in Pascal studies, and I cannot go into it here.[30] In any case, it will be clear that Pascal does not think that metaphysical considerations are of much assistance in addressing the existential issue of immortality.

---

[30] On all these issues, see Moriarty 2020.

6 Malebranche: the philosopher's two bodies

The title of this chapter comes from the preface to the 1696 edition of Malebranche's *Entretiens sur la métaphysique et la religion*, first published in 1688, and augmented in 1696 by three 'Entretiens sur la mort'. The work takes the form of a dialogue between the 'meditator' Théodore and the seeker Ariste, a person swayed more by his imagination than by his reason. They are later joined by another 'meditator', Théotime, and all three are involved in the dialogues on death. As Malebranche explains, the discussions of death invoke religious as well as philosophical principles;[31] but it is usually clear which set of principles are being mobilized at a given point, and I shall concentrate on the philosophical ones here.

In the preface, Malebranche insists that, given our invincible will to be happy, the thought of the inevitability of death must inflect the choices we make in our pursuit of happiness:

> La mort est inévitable. Elle rompt tous nos desseins. Elle doit donc changer aussi toutes nos vues. (Malebranche 1979–1992, II, 651)
>
> Death is inevitable. It interrupts all our projects. It must therefore change all our ideas.

The thought of death is so unwelcome precisely because it forces us to re-evaluate our values.

> L'homme charnel et insensé se plaît dans l'illusion. S'il dort d'un sommeil doux et agréable; s'il n'a que de plaisants songes, la mort qui le délivre de son assoupissement, est une importune. Il faut que la douceur de son sommeil soit troublée par quelque fantôme terrible, afin qu'il se réveille avec plaisir. (II, 652)
>
> The carnal and senseless man delights in illusion. If he sleeps a pleasant and agreeable sleep; if he has only pleasant dreams, then death, which delivers him from his stupor, is an unwelcome visitor. The sweetness of his sleep must be troubled by some terrible apparition if he is to awake with pleasure.

But there is a rational obligation (and here Malebranche echoes Pascal) to investigate what, if anything, may happen after death:

> Le doute le plus léger touchant l'éternité de notre être, suffit à tout homme raisonnable pour suspendre la plupart de ses desseins, jusqu'à ce qu'il ait bien reconnu ce qui en est. Quelque désagréable que paraisse l'examen de cette importante question, celui qui la néglige est un insensé. (II, 652)

---

[31] Malebranche 1979–1992, II, 653.

The slightest doubt concerning the eternity of our existence is sufficient for any reasonable man to suspend most of his projects until he has well and truly grasped the truth of the matter. However rebarbative the examination of this important question may appear, whoever leaves it to one side is insane.

The stupidity of one whose investigations lead him to the wrong conclusion is less inexcusable than that of the many people whose choices in life are made irrespective of what follows it (II, 652). Malebranche explains this blindness, (which is at first sight hard to reconcile with our self-love (*amour-propre*) considered as the invincible appetite for happiness), by the dominant influence of the senses, which leads us to relegate whatever transcends them to the level of the imaginary (II, 652–653).

Malebranche insists, and here he is reverting to the Stoic attitude rejected by the later Montaigne, that we need to reflect carefully and frequently on death to tame it.[32] One line of reflection we are invited to follow is to perceive death as a liberation from the ignoble subjection of the soul to the body.[33] At death 'l'esprit la plus noble des créatures, est séparé du corps la plus vile des substances' ('the mind, the noblest of creatures, is separated from the body, the vilest of substances') (II, 999).[34] But this rhetoric does not convince Ariste, and his response would have been applauded by Montaigne.

> Je suis fait à cette servitude, et je la trouve assez douce. Je n'ai pas comme Théotime le cœur noble et élevé: je suis content de mon sort.[35]
>
> I am used to this slavery, and I find it pretty bearable. I am not like Théotime, I do not have a noble and lofty heart; I am content with my lot.

So far from welcoming the prospect of death, he fears it.

The interlocutors now agree that we have an innate physical fear of death that we cannot overcome, though we may learn not to be swayed by it.[36] But there are also rational fears to be assuaged. We might fear death for two reasons: (a) if it entails annihilation; (b) if it means we may be worse off than we are now. We might not, on the other hand, fear death if we had (a) certitude of survival, and (b) certitude of being better off than we are now. On the assumption that we do not have certitude of these things, we may still have good reason to hope for them. But if the best we have is hope, then, supposing we are enjoying life on this earth, we might still fear death, on the grounds that it involves losing a certain good for an uncertain, even if superior one.

---

[32] Malebranche 1979–1992, II, 998–999, 1019–20; III, 1039–1040.
[33] Malebranche 1979–1992, II, 977–978; II, 1000.   [34] Malebranche 1979–1992, II, 999.
[35] Malebranche 1979–1992, II, 978.   [36] Malebranche 1979–1992, II, 974; II, 998.

Et si je crains de mourir, [says Ariste] c'est que je sais bien ce que je quitte, et que je ne sais pas ce que j'aurai.[37]

If I am afraid to die, this is because I know very well what I shall be leaving, and do not know what I shall have.

I will go through these various alternatives. In the first place, death cannot entail annihilation.[38] The soul is not the form of the body, but an independent immaterial substance. However, a substance cannot naturally go out of existence (although God could annihilate the soul or any other created substance). So far Malebranche's position is that of Descartes, but he now adds a consideration we also encountered in Silhon: since the soul is not the form of the body and its function is not to preserve the body, we cannot suppose that God will annihilate it on the grounds that it becomes superfluous once the body has died.

Moving on, the interlocutors claim that, in this world, the most virtuous people are the most unhappy, apart from the foretaste of the future happiness for which they hope. The existence of this hope confirms that there is an afterlife in which the divine justice will be manifested and satisfied, since for God to annihilate the noblest of his creatures would be incompatible with our idea of his wisdom and immutability.[39] This kind of argument, too, we have encountered in Lessius and Silhon, and it scarcely needs pointing out that it depends on an idea that the divine purpose is to some extent discoverable by reason.

But even if we are destined to survive death, that does not eliminate fear. First, death may be the gateway to eternal punishment; we can have no certitude of escaping hell. Second, supposing we do escape hell, we do not know what kind of reward we may receive, in particular whether it will be preferable to a life of earthly pleasure. So, the meditators must establish either that earthly pleasures are unreal or unsatisfactory, or that we have good reason to hope for better pleasures in the afterlife, or both. First, then, the fear of hell. God will not condemn those who have faith in Jesus Christ and who are imbued with charity. We can be reasonably sure we have charity if our feeling of love of God is backed up by the reception of grace in the sacraments.[40] Second, the pain of parting with earthly pleasure. The meditators argue, first, that physical pleasures are inferior, being fleeting, plagued by anxiety, and followed by remorse.[41] In particular, they appeal, as we have seen, to an evaluative schema in which the mind, being nobler than the body, should not be subject to it.

Ariste agrees with this in principle. But he argues that even if the pleasures we actually experience are unsatisfying, we cannot conceive pleasure or indeed any kind of feelings without the body, because the occasional cause of our sensations is

---

[37] Malebranche 1979–1992, II, 978.
[38] Malebranche 1979–1992, II, 977–980.
[39] Malebranche 1979–1992, II, 986.
[40] Malebranche 1979–1992, II, 975, 989–992.
[41] Malebranche 1979–1992, II, 976.

traces on the brain, which will have ceased to function. The reply is (a) that our feelings do not always depend on the body; for instance, our knowledge of our moral state may be a source of joy or sadness (1002);[42] and (b), and this is the really difficult point, that separation from the body in death does not preclude bodily experience in the afterlife. This is not simply because Christianity preaches the resurrection of the body at the Last Day, but because there is a sense in which death is not after all the separation of the soul from the body. Ariste finds this a very challenging idea, so Théotime, in one of the oddest moments of the text, begins his demonstration by squeezing his arm very hard until he protests that it is hurting. The point is to get him to accept that pain is experienced as localized, and as my pain. But an amputee could likewise experience pain in an amputated arm. For Théotime, who is never afraid of flouting common sense, this is proof that we have a second set of limbs that, unlike the physical set, are incorruptible. It is in those limbs that amputees feel pain, but our own situation is in reality no different from theirs. Ariste bridles at this, not surprisingly, and replies, very sensibly, that what the amputee feels is a sensation in the soul occasioned by a process in his brain, in accordance with the laws of body-soul union willed by God. Yes, says Théotime, that is what is happening, but it is not what the person feels; what they feel is a pain in *their* finger, just as Ariste felt a pain in *his* arm, though their physical finger is missing. The 'finger' in which they feel the pain is not a material entity, occupying extension, in line with the Cartesian definition of matter. It exists in 'intelligible extension', which in God corresponds to physical space. It is the idea or archetype of physical space, and it is this, not the inert physical world, that acts on our souls.[43] Consequently, although in a sense our soul is united to a physical body from which it will be separated at death, the body we experience, and through which we experience, is a kind of ideal or intelligible double of that body, what we might call the body-for-consciousness.[44] In other words, God could in principle enable us, even when separated from our physical body, to experience pleasant sensations. Of course, the joys of union with God, as revealed in Scripture must

---

[42] Malebranche 1979–1992, II, 1001–1002.

[43] On intelligible extension, cf. Malebranche 1979–1992, II, 811.

[44] This is a particular development of a more general point about perception, made in the first of the *Entretiens sur la métaphysique et la religion*. God could annihilate the physical world and yet produce the same perceptions in our mind as we had when the physical world existed. We would then be occupying not a physical but an intelligible world. But that is the world we do in fact occupy, even though there is a physical world inhabited by, among other things, our body. The beauties we attribute to the physical world are in fact intelligible beauties, rendered sensible (in this life) by the laws of body-soul union (Malebranche 1979–1992, II, 677–679). I am inclined to think that this notion of a non-physical body through which we experience sensations may be inspired by St Paul's exposition of the meaning of the resurrection of the dead: 'It is sown a physical body, it is raised a spiritual body. If there is a physical body, there is also a spiritual body' (I Corinthians, 15.44; translation from the New Revised Standard Version).

be far superior to these sensations; the point is that the fear of being deprived of such sensations is no reason to fear death.[45]

Our everyday experience of the world, or rather our interpretation of it, is challenged again in relation to a particular pleasure that Ariste fears may be terminated by death: that of friendship. He asks how Théotime would feel about being separated from Théodore. Théotime's reply is essentially that we have no more direct acquaintance with other people than we do with physical objects. Again, the argumentation is a remarkable illustration of Malebranche's ability to question the promptings of spontaneous so-called experience:

> Je ne crains point de le dire devant Théodore; je ne l'aime que très imparfaitement. Comment l'aimerais-je autant qu'il mérite d'être aimé, lui que je ne connais pas, et que je n'ai jamais vu? Car ce que je vois de Théodore n'est qu'un certain arrangement de la matière qu'on appelle un visage: mais ce n'est pas là Théodore.[46]

> I do not fear to say this in Théodore's presence: I love him only very imperfectly. How could I love him as much as he deserves to be loved, when I do not know him, and have never seen him? For what I see of Théodore is nothing but a certain arrangement of matter we call a face; but that is not Théodore.

The Christian philosopher's love for his friend is based on moral qualities: love of truth, rationality, piety. But both the qualities themselves and our perception of them are precarious and we may doubt whether the friendship is reciprocal:

> Je ne me connais pas moi-même, comment sonderais-je le cœur de mon cher ami?[47]

> I do not know myself, how could I sound the heart of my dear friend.

Our access to the moral qualities of our friend is channelled through unreliable sensory perceptions:

> Je ne puis discerner, si le Théodore que j'aime, est devant moi, que par les réponses qu'il me fait; et peut-être qu'un faux Théodore contrefait sa voix.[48]

> I can only discover if the Théodore I love is in my presence by his answers to my speech; and perhaps these are coming from a false Théodore, [an impostor] who is imitating his voice.

---

[45] Malebranche 1979–1992, II, 1010–1016; on Scriptural accounts of the joys of union with God, see 1019.
[46] Malebranche 1979–1992, II, 1016–1017. [47] Malebranche 1979–1992, II, 1017.
[48] Malebranche 1979–1992, II, 1017.

62 THE THOUGHT OF DEATH CHANGES ALL OUR IDEAS

In the afterlife we shall see and rejoice in our friends as they are:

> Ah Théodore! que je vous embrasserai avec joie, lorsque je vous verrai en plein jour, lorsque je verrai clairement que c'est vous; lorsque je saurai certainement que notre amitié est réciproque, et que rien ne pourra jamais ni la rompre ni l'affaiblir![49]
>
> Ah Théodore! with what joy I shall embrace you, when I see you in the full light of day, when I see clearly that it is you; when I shall know for certain that our friendship is reciprocal, and that nothing will ever be able to break or weaken it!

In the third of the *Entretiens sur la mort*, the meditators discuss society in the afterlife, comparing it with the inadequate societies of this world. There can be no true society where there is no justice, and the best ruler in the world cannot render to each his or her due, for he cannot render someone happy who deserves to be so. But when Ariste inveighs against the injustices of the world, he is reproved by Théodore, who insists that these injustices are subject to Providence, and qualifies an earlier statement of his own to the effect that in this world virtuous people are the most unhappy (1 Corinthians 15:19). They would be so, Théodore now claims, but for the joy they feel in the firm hope of a future life, which renders them happier even in this life than the wicked with all their pleasures.[50] In other words, Malebranche is unreconciled to the purely negative portrayal of human life on this earth that for Lessius and Silhon contributed so strongly to their defence of immortality. It is necessary to vindicate Providence in this life, even at the risk of inviting empirical refutation. (We might ask, for instance, whether the wicked are less happy than the virtuous.)

I will follow our three discussants no further into their speculations about the nature of the resurrected body and proceed to draw conclusions about the arguments I have traced. We see that Lessius and Silhon's argumentation, though, straining at times against the Aristotelian framework, was still governed by the idea of purpose discernible at all levels of the universe. God and nature do nothing in vain, and the human condition would be vain if we were not immortal. Moreover, the soul does not perish with the body, for its rational operations exceed the capacity of mere matter. Descartes and Malebranche believe that they have only reinforced this last conclusion by breaking with the Aristotelian concept of the soul. If their acknowledgement of purpose in the universe is more circumscribed than that of the earlier writers, since mechanics explains much that would once have been ascribed to final causality, they recognize that in certain areas we are entitled to discern the purposes of God. Descartes stands out from Lessius, Silhon, and Malebranche in his insistence that, though we are indeed

---

[49] Malebranche 1979–1992, II, 1017.   [50] Malebranche 1979–1992, III, 1023–1030.

immortal, we can obtain a certain beatitude in this life. Although, in the *Principles*, he emphasizes the epistemological confusion that derives from the influence of the body over the soul, he does not regard this as ethically perverse, an ignoble servitude, in the manner of Malebranche. (The reason for this is clearly that his thought prescinds from the doctrine of Original Sin, as understood by the seventeenth-century Augustinian writers.) Malebranche, on the contrary, seeks to highlight the unreality of earthly goods and to assuage our fear that in dying we lose the only goods we can conceive. Not content with asserting the happiness of the beatific vision, he investigates the possibility of post-mortem forms of experience (sensations and attachments) that are in some sense continuous with those of this life: they enhance earthly experience rather than utterly transcending it. But it is another Augustinian writer, Pascal, who is the real outlier here, because he is the one who refuses to discern the signs of any divine purpose either in the nature of human beings as they are or in the physical universe they inhabit. Immortality is not a philosophical truth we can deduce: it is known only by a religious revelation we must, by our own choice, commit to, or, at our peril, ignore.

3

The Banishment of Death

Leibniz's Scandalous Immortalism

Matteo Favaretti Camposampiero

1 Introduction

In 2016 scholars commemorated the tercentenary of the death of Gottfried Wilhelm Leibniz, who passed away on 14 November 1716. However, from a truly Leibnizian point of view it might be incorrect to say that Leibniz ever died. In a letter to Christian Wolff of 1705, he presents his position on death as follows:

> I think that the whole of nature is full of organic bodies endowed with souls; that all souls are free from extinction [*interitus esse expertes*]; and that even all animals are free from extinction, for they are simply transformed by generation and death.[1]

Not only all souls *qua* simple substances but also all animals are immune to destruction. Of course, every animal we can observe is subject to a crucial event that seems to terminate its life. For Leibniz, however, this event called death is not in fact the final extinction of the animal but merely a transformation of its body. Formulations of this unusual doctrine appear not only in private writings and correspondences that have long remained unpublished, such as the letters to Wolff or the 1702 letter to Queen Sophie Charlotte and John Toland (see A I, xxi, 717–725), but also in some of Leibniz's works that were best known to his public. Especially in the last twenty years of his life, Leibniz took care to disseminate his original views on death among his contemporaries. The first resounding account of the doctrine was published in 1695 as part of the *New System of the Nature and Communication of Substances*, followed by the *Considerations on Vital Principles* of 1705 and the *Theodicy* of 1710. Soon after Leibniz's death, additional information was provided by posthumous publications like the *Principles of Nature and Grace* (1718), the articles and letters included in the widely read *Recueil* edited by

---

[1] Leibniz to Wolff, 9 November 1705, in Leibniz and Wolff 1963, 44. In footnotes and text, I use the following abbreviations: A = Leibniz 1923ff., cited by series, volume, and page; GP = Leibniz 1978, cited by volume and page.

Matteo Favaretti Camposampiero, *The Banishment of Death: Leibniz's Scandalous Immortalism* In: *Life and Death in Early Modern Philosophy*. Edited by: Susan James, Oxford University Press. © Matteo Favaretti Camposampiero 2021.
DOI: 10.1093/oso/9780192843616.003.0004

Pierre Des Maizeaux (1720b), and the German and Latin translations of the *Monadology* (Leibniz 1720a, 1721). For instance, here is a formulation from the *Theodicy*:

> So I assume . . . , from the conservation of the soul when once it is created, that the animal is also conserved, and that apparent death is only an envelopment, there being no likelihood that in the order of nature souls exist entirely separated from all body, or that what does not begin naturally can cease through natural forces.[2]

The indestructibility traditionally ascribed to the soul in virtue of its simplicity is thus extended by Leibniz to the whole animal, conceived as the union between a soul and an organic body; and since Leibniz maintains that everything is animated and alive, his statement that animals are immortal actually concerns the entire population of the world. In Leibniz's universe, all real beings live forever. At first sight, this doctrine may only seem to increase the number of death-surviving and ever-enduring entities, but in fact it also has momentous consequences for received views on life and death. If death is described in traditional terms as the separation of an imperishable soul from a perishable body, then Leibniz's doctrine entails that there is no real death, for the soul is always united to its body so as to form a living being that can never cease to exist, unless God expressly annihilates it.[3] Immortality is natural because death or final extinction can only be a super-natural event. By contrast to the ordinary view, Leibniz maintains that being alive does not entail being mortal; on the contrary, what has begun to live can never cease to be alive.

Leibniz's doctrine is indisputably one of the most radical forms of immortalism ever conceived, although in current scholarship its radical or even paradoxical character is often overlooked.[4] It differs from all the three standard conceptions of immortality, namely the Platonic immortality of the separated soul, Christian resurrection, and reincarnation (see Choron 1973). Of course, Leibniz's view appears to some extent closer to that of Christian resurrection, insofar as the latter includes the restitution of the body. Resurrection, however, is from death, whereas Leibniz denies precisely that death is real. Because of this radicalness, most eighteenth-century German philosophers dismissed the doctrine as a ridiculous invention contrary to both reason and common sense (e.g. Baumeister 1737). In order to explain this general dismissal, the present chapter focuses on the initial phase of the debate that Leibniz's theory of death aroused in Germany. The hostile reactions of theologians, physicians, and even philosophers

---

[2] Leibniz, *Essais de théodicée*, I, §90 (GP VI, 152; trans. Leibniz 1985, 172).
[3] On Leibniz's rejection of separated souls see Brown 1998b.
[4] Notable exceptions are Brown 1995, 1998a, 1998b; and Savile 2002.

66 THE BANISHMENT OF DEATH: LEIBNIZ'S SCANDALOUS IMMORTALISM

who, like the Wolffians, were otherwise sympathetic to Leibniz show to what extent radical immortalism could be and actually was perceived as an implausible and possibly dangerous belief.

2 History of the term

In the eighteenth century, Leibniz's doctrine became very popular under the label of *exilium mortis Leibnitianum*, 'the Leibnizian banishment of death', as though it purported to free humans not merely from the fear of death but directly from death itself. Under this label, the doctrine was variously exposed, upheld, criticized, or even denigrated.

The first to introduce the Latin phrase *exilium mortis* to designate this specific position is Elias Camerarius (1673–1734). His dissertation *De morte in exilium acta*,[5] also cited by some of his contemporaries as *Dissertatio de exilio mortis Leibnitiano*,[6] aims to provide a solid refutation of Leibniz's unusual views on death. Nevertheless, the term is later adopted by Leibniz's followers, who popularize it as the official trademark of the doctrine. The first is Bilfinger 1725, ch. 5, esp. §§366–369, followed by Hansch, Baumgarten, and Canz. For instance, Baumgarten's *Metaphysics* gives the following definition: 'The opinion [*sententia*] affirming that a human's death is nothing but the transformation of an animal is called the banishment of (absolute) death [*exsilium mortis (absolutæ)*]'.[7]

The phrase *exilium mortis* originates from Leibniz himself and can therefore be deemed authentically Leibnizian, albeit not in its Latin rendition. In 1712, Leibniz sent Pierre Coste his remarks on the three volumes of the works by Shaftesbury published the year before under the title *Characteristicks of Men, Manners, Opinions, Times*. One of Shaftesbury's collected writings in particular had gained Leibniz's enthusiastic approval. When reading the fifth treatise, *The Moralists, A Philosophical Rhapsody*, Leibniz felt as though he was 'in the *sanctuary* of the most sublime philosophy'.[8] In particular, he reports that he was favourably struck by the similarities between Shaftesbury's views and the main tenets of his own *Theodicy*:

---

[5] The work was in fact submitted as a doctoral dissertation in medicine by Ernst Christoph Caspar under the supervision of Elias Camerarius, therefore regarded as its author. The publication includes two distinct anti-Leibnizian chapters on the plague and death, respectively.

[6] See e.g. Canz 1996, §1130.

[7] Baumgarten 1739, §779. Absolute death takes place if and only if the soul's activity no longer harmonizes with the activity of *any* body; by contrast, if death only disrupts the correspondence between the soul and *a certain* body, then it is said to be relative, for the soul acquires a new body and the animal is not deceased but transformed (see §778).

[8] Leibniz, 'Remarques sur les trois volumes intitulés: *Characteristicks of Men, Manners, Opinions, Times*' (GP III, 429; trans. Leibniz 1989b, 633).

From the first I found in it almost all of my *Theodicy* before it saw the light of day. The universe all of one piece, its beauty, its universal harmony, the disappearance of real evil, especially in relation to the whole, the unity of true substances, and the great unity of the supreme substance of which all other things are merely emanations and imitations are here put in the most beautiful daylight.

(GP III, 429–430; trans. Leibniz 1989b, 633)

Leibniz politely points out, however, that Shaftesbury did not anticipate *all* the typically Leibnizian doctrines, for at least three are missing from the English treatise: 'It lacks almost nothing but my pre-established harmony, my elimination of death [*mon bannissement de la mort*], and my reduction of matter or of plurality to unities or simple substances' (ibid. 430). Here, the banishment of death is significantly listed by Leibniz among the most characteristic and fundamental tenets of his philosophy, on a par with pre-established harmony and the 'reduction' of matter to unextended monads.

Coste forwarded Leibniz's remarks to Masson, who published them in the *Histoire critique de la republique des lettres* (Leibniz 1715). In 1720, Des Maizeaux reprinted the same text under a different title in his *Recueil*,[9] thereby ensuring its widest possible circulation. The Leibnizian origin of the term is further confirmed by Camerarius himself, who at the beginning of his dissertation quotes from the *Recueil* the passage on the banishment of death and indicates it as the source of the expression *exilium mortis* and the synonymous one *proscriptio mortis* (Camerarius 1721, 21). In 1728, Hansch's *more geometrico* demonstration of Leibniz's monadology still refers to the same passage:

Theorem 119.   No living being [*nullum vivum*] ceases to exist after natural death.

Demonstration.   The natural death of no living being entails more than the involution and diminution of the present organic body of a certain dominant monad . . . .

Corollary 1.   Every living being is indestructible . . . .

Scholium 1.   This theorem is the basis of the banishment of death asserted by the Philosopher [i.e. Leibniz] in *Recueil*, II, 283.[10]

3 Early confrontations

So much for the history of the term. As for the history of the debate, Elias Camerarius was not in fact the first to attack Leibniz because of his immortalism.

---

[9] Leibniz, 'Jugement sur les oeuvres de M. le Comte de Shaftsbury,' in Des Maizeaux 1720b, II, 269–286.
[10] Hansch 1728, 170–171. On Hansch's Leibnizianism, see Pelletier 2016.

68   THE BANISHMENT OF DEATH: LEIBNIZ'S SCANDALOUS IMMORTALISM

Before him, Des Maizeaux had been very concerned about this doctrine. One year after the publication of Leibniz's remarks on Shaftesbury in the *Histoire Critique de la République des Lettres*, the 1716 issue of the same journal featured several pieces on Leibniz's *New System*. Des Maizeaux (1716a) opened the debate with his learned contribution, a revised version of which also appeared in the *Recueil* (Des Maizeaux 1720b). As the title of the first version announces, the target of Des Maizeaux's attack is Leibniz's attempt to invoke the authority of ancient philosophers in support of his strongly revisionist views on birth and death. Among such possible remote forerunners of immortalism, the *New System* mentions in the first place Democritus:

> This may be similar to something the great Democritus discussed, complete atomist that he was.... It is therefore natural that an animal, having always been alive and organized..., always remains so. And since there is no first birth or entirely new generation of an animal, it follows that there will not be any final extinction or complete death, in a strict metaphysical sense.
>
> (GP IV, 481; trans. Leibniz 1989a, 141)

What the reference to Democritus appears to suggest is that, if even such a naturalistically minded philosopher as an atomist can uphold immortalism, then this doctrine cannot be completely implausible or counterintuitive.[11] What is more, Leibniz claims that the denial of the reality of birth and death can also be ascribed to both the Hippocratic and Eleatic schools:

> With respect to ordinary animal bodies and other corporeal substances, whose complete extinction has been accepted until now, and whose changes depend on mechanical rules rather than moral laws, I noted with pleasure that the ancient author of the book *De diæta*, attributed to Hippocrates, had glimpsed something of the truth when he stated explicitly that animals are not born and do not die, and that things we believe to begin and perish merely appear and disappear. This was also the opinion of Parmenides and Melissus, according to Aristotle. For these ancients were much more solid than people believe.
>
> (GP IV, 481; trans. Leibniz 1989a, 141)[12]

If taken seriously, this passage reveals something unexpected. Lurking behind Leibniz's immortalism is the archaic intuition—shared in different ways by both

---

[11] As Leibniz makes clear elsewhere, this reference to Democritus is motivated by his position on animal resurrection: 'Il semble que Democrite luy même a vu cette ressuscitation des animaux, car Plotine luy attribute qu'il enseignoit une resurrection' (*Considérations sur la doctrine d'un esprit universel unique* [1702]; GP VI, 535).

[12] See Leibniz, *Specimen inventorum* (1688): 'Et hæc videtur fuisse expressa sententia autoris *libri de Diæta*, qui Hippocrati ascribitur, nec abhorruere Albertus Magnus et Joh. Baco, qui neque productionem neque destructionem naturalem formarum admisere' (A VI, iv, 1624).

Eleatism and Atomism—that being is eternal so that nothing ever really begins or ceases to exist. By presenting his banishment-of-death doctrine as a revival of the 'sound' ancient philosophy, Leibniz presumably aimed to make it more palatable to his early modern fellows and gain the favour of erudite scholars (see Brown 1995, 80–81). Apparently, Leibniz did not realize the danger of aligning himself with a radically eternalist position with all its anti-Christian implications; or perhaps he thought that these could be neutralized simply by positing an initial divine act of creation and ascribing to God the power of destroying His creation whenever He might want to.

Be that as it may, Des Maizeaux's reaction shows that Leibniz's move was not necessarily a false step; for this adversary puts his effort precisely into dismantling the alleged proximity between Leibniz and the ancient authors.[13] From the beginning, Des Maizeaux makes it clear that he prefers to concentrate on 'a point of criticism' rather than on 'purely metaphysical speculations, which are often both boundless and bottomless' (Des Maizeaux 1716a, 54; trans. Leibniz 1997, 227). His attack is launched on the field of classical philology and consists mainly in proving that Leibniz's reading of the Hippocratic passage from the book *On Diet* is actually misled by the incorrect translation of some key terms—first of all, the Greek term *zoon*, usually rendered as 'animal' whereas it properly means 'living being' in general. Actually, Des Maizeaux argues that in the given context the intended meaning of this term must be even broader: the ancient author used *zoon* only to comply with the popular world-view, which regards living beings as beings par excellence; but, in fact, he meant to designate 'all kinds of *beings*'.[14] In light of this reading, the ancient source invoked by Leibniz cannot count as an early statement of radical immortalism, for it merely asserts a very general and innocent principle of substance conservation that was widely received among ancient philosophers:

> So this principle of the author of the book *On Diet*—that in the world *nothing is born or dies*—comes down to precisely what all the ancient philosophers unanimously maintained, namely that nothing can be produced from nothing, and what has once existed cannot be reduced to nothing: *Nil posse creari/De Nihilo, neque quod genitum est/Ad Nil revocari*.[15]

---

[13] See Des Maizeaux 1720a, 364: 'Ce morceau roule sur la conformité que M. Leibniz a crû apercevoir entre son Hypothese touchant *l'inextinction* ou *indestructibilité* des Animaux, et le sentiment de quelques anciens Philosophes.'

[14] Des Maizeaux 1716a, 62: '...le peuple, qui ne considère les choses que par la plus forte relation qu'il a avec elles, ne compte proprement au nombre des Etres, que les Plantes et les Animaux, qui sont des *Etres vivans*'. The later version has a weaker formulation: see Des Maizeaux 1720a, 372. Contrary to Woolhouse's claim (Leibniz 1997, 244n), the body of the letter is not entirely identical to the former text. Some changes between the 1716 and the 1720 versions are the effect of Des Maizeaux's partial revision of his earlier interpretation of the Hippocratic text, as documented by Des Maizeaux 1716b.

[15] Des Maizeaux 1716a, 67; 1720a, 376; trans. Leibniz 1997, 232 (slightly modified). The final verses are from Lucretius, *De rerum natura* I.544–545.

70   THE BANISHMENT OF DEATH: LEIBNIZ'S SCANDALOUS IMMORTALISM

The other alleged forerunners of immortalism, such as Democritus and Parmenides, are discarded in roughly the same way. By means of philological arguments, Des Maizeaux concludes that Leibniz's system is entirely new and unprecedented. Rather ironically, he claims that the 'glory' of having invented 'the system of the indestructibility of animals' must be entirely ascribed to Leibniz and that no one should challenge his authorship (Des Maizeaux 1720a, 368–369).

In both the 1716 and 1720 editions, Des Maizeaux's article is followed by the letter Leibniz had written to Des Maizeaux in 1711 as a reply to an earlier draft of that article.[16] Des Maizeaux presents this letter as Leibniz's capitulation:

> But to return to M. Leibniz: it seems to me, sir, that I have shown quite clearly that the ancient philosophers whom he names had no *inkling* of anything like his theory [*hypothèse*] about the *inextinction* of *animals* when they maintained that *nothing is born, or dies* and that *the things which are thought to begin and perish, only appear and disappear*. M. Leibniz appears to agree with that himself in the letter which he did me the honour of writing to me...
> (Des Maizeaux 1716a, 70–71; 1720a, 380; trans. Leibniz 1997, 235).

In fact, this reading of Leibniz's letter sounds tendentious. Although Leibniz admits that immortalism was not the ordinary belief among the ancients,[17] he also adds that some ancients are at least likely to have shared his views. Moreover, he not only rejects Des Maizeaux's interpretation of the passage from the book *On Diet* in terms of the mere conservation of matter,[18] but also mentions again both Democritus, who may have admitted the conservation of animals, and Parmenides, depicted as a proto-Spinozist: 'Perhaps Parmenides, who (according to Plato) taught that all was *one*, had views close to those of Spinoza, and so it should not be so surprising if some [*sc.* of Parmenides' views?] should have got close to mine.'[19] This passage is far from unambiguous, but according to one of its possible readings Leibniz seems to be acknowledging that some of his views share

---

[16] Leibniz 1720b. According to Des Maizeaux's report, his 'Explication d'un passage d'Hippocrate' is a revised version of some 'Remarques' on Leibniz's *Système nouveau* that he composed in 1700 and sent to Bayle. He also wanted to send this piece to Leibniz, but as he wrote to him in 1711, the manuscript was temporarily lost, so he was only able to send a fragment. See Des Maizeaux 1716a, 52–54; and 1720a, 363–364.

[17] See Leibniz 1720b, 386: 'Pour ce qui est des Anciens, j'avoüe que leurs sentimens ordinaires n'arrivent pas à mon sentiment de l'*inextinction* des Animaux. Leur *indestructibilité* ne s'entend ordinairement que de celle de la Matière, ou tout au plus des Atomes.'

[18] See Leibniz 1720b, 387; Brown 1995, 81. In a letter to Masson of 1716, Leibniz appears less confident: see GP VI, 624.

[19] 'Peut-être que Parmenide, qui (chez Platon) enseignoit que tout étoit *Un*, avoit des sentimens aprochans de ceux de Spinosa: et qu'ainsi il ne faudroit pas tant s'étonner, si quelques-uns se seroient aproché des miens' (Leibniz 1720b, 387; trans. Leibniz 1997, 239). According to a weaker reading, 'quelques-uns' means 'some other ancient philosophers,' so that Leibniz would be simply wondering why there might not have been ancient precursors of his philosophy just as there were of Spinozism. In my view, the context favours the stronger reading.

with those of Spinoza a common Parmenidian background—which may sound indeed surprising even though, of course, it does not imply any admission of Spinozism.

On the same page, Leibniz also refutes a possible charge of anachronism. As his account of death in terms of transformation is largely inspired by scientific discoveries owed to the invention of the microscope, how could similar doctrines be ascribed to the ancients? Leibniz finds no better answer than to invoke prediction—which suggests that the core intuition of immortalism is in fact independent of empirical evidence. As Leibniz argues, the existence of 'minute animals' (*petits animaux*) might well have been predicted just as the existence of corpuscles was admitted before they were discovered, or 'just as Democritus predicted stars in the Milky Way which were undetectable before the invention of the telescope' (ibid.).

4 The immortalist club

The problem of the sources and precedents of Leibniz's immortalism is raised again in 1722, when the theologian Christoph Matthäus Pfaff publishes his schediasm *De morte naturali*, which soon becomes a mandatory reference text on death and related topics. Instead of following Des Maizeaux's strategy of isolating Leibniz from every philosophical tradition, Pfaff takes the opposite course. He casts doubt on Leibniz's originality, thereby implicitly accusing him of plagiarism. In Pfaff's writing, immortalism is discussed with respect to the question of whether death exists. The section begins with a macabre joke: 'The question of whether death exists [*an detur*] might seem redundant and useless, if among the moderns there had not been some philosophers who dared to cast doubt on the common opinion about this. One is Pierre Poiret, another one is Leibniz, and both are dead' (Pfaff 1722, §3: 9). Pfaff's grim irony clearly aims to persuade the reader from the beginning that immortalism is actually untenable, since its upholders have passed away.

More surprising is the mention of Poiret as a fellow immortalist of Leibniz's. Of course, the ground for Pfaff's juxtaposition of the two philosophers had been laid by Elias Camerarius, who had already evoked Poiret's doctrine that the soul is always united to a subtle, incorruptible body, so that what dissolves at death is only some external sheath, the gross body.[20] However, at first sight Poiret would seem to acknowledge the reality of death. In the second tome of his *Oeconomie divine*, he embraces the traditional Judeo-Christian doctrine that death is a

---

[20] See Camerarius 1721, 28: 'Dudum quoque Poiretus statuit, animæ post mortem unitum manere tenue corpus, at nec ille ejus originem potuit assignare; quî ergò eam dabunt asseclæ Viri Illustris [i.e. Leibniz's]?'

consequence of sin. He contrasts the present state of bodies, liable to corruption and decay, with their original state of perfection, adding that nature as a whole awaits to be restored to that primeval condition of glory (see 1687, II, ch. 22, §§9–18: 594–610). Since all material beings must represent their creator by their features, they must first of all represent him in terms of being and duration. Thus, the human body must have been created incorruptible and immortal, and such will be its glorious state after its second birth or resurrection (see ibid. §11: 599; §17: 607). So far, mortality appears contingent and transitory but nonetheless real.

It is in the fourth tome and precisely in the section on corporeal hell that Poiret introduces the subtle body as the foundation of natural immortality. To explain why it is impossible for the damned to destroy their own bodies so as to die once and for all and make their torment cease, Poiret draws on his account of the formation of the body by virtue of a divine force that cannot be lost or dismissed (see ibid. §20: 611). Beside recomposing the body of the damned as soon as it is torn apart, this force also guarantees the eternal indefeasibility of all human bodies:

> ...even presently, when our visible body eventually decomposes at death, it is only a rough bark [*écorse grossiére*] that we remove. Then the most essential and active [part] of the body, or its most subtle and inner portion, separates itself from it and evaporates, so to speak. It is accompanied by that divine force of conformation, which in a moment disposes it in the form of the primordial system of its creation.   (Poiret 1687, IV, ch. 2, §18: 46)

Because of the never-ending natural law that joins the soul to its body, the physical annihilation of the natural soul-body compound would constitute a 'natural absurdity and impossibility' (ibid.). Thus, the still traditional opposition drawn in the second tome between the incorruptible body before sin and the mortal body after sin has made way, in the fourth tome, for the distinction between 'our visible body' and its 'most subtle and inner portion'. In spite of the fall, the incorruptible body has not disappeared from present life but coexists with the mortal body that envelops it. This essential physical core of our body is not altered by death except insofar as death releases it from its outer shell—which in fact means that death, in the strict sense of the soul's separation from its body, is physically impossible.

As even Leibniz sometimes formulates his immortalist theory in terms of the conservation of a subtle body in spite of the loss of a gross, external integument, this may suggest some proximity between his views and Poiret's.[21] At least one

---

[21] See especially *Considérations sur la doctrine d'un esprit universel unique* (1702): 'Car pourquoy l'ame ne pourroit elle pas tousjours garder un corps subtil, organisé à sa maniere, qui pourra même reprendre un jour ce qu'il faut de son corps visible dans la resurrection, puisqu'on accorde aux bien-heureux un corps glorieux, et puisque les anciens peres ont accordé un corps subtil aux anges' (GP VI,

relevant passage was widely accessible by 1720, which stated that 'there are no created substances wholly destitute of matter. For I hold with the ancients, and according to reason, that angels or intelligences, and souls separated from the gross body, have always subtle bodies, though they themselves be incorporeal.'[22] Nevertheless, Pfaff shows no awareness of such passages and concludes that Poiret poses only a moderate threat to Leibniz's originality: 'Leibniz took another path but one not totally dissimilar from Poiret's' (Pfaff 1722, §3: 11). The real threat lies elsewhere. Closing the section, Pfaff plays his ace card and reveals the name of Leibniz's alleged source: 'Only this must be added, that Leibniz did not himself invent this opinion on death, but he learned it from a very celebrated man, Christianus Franciscus Paullini, and brought it to public light in the same year as Paullini did' (ibid. 14–15).

Christian Franz Paullini (1643–1712), a historian and friend of Hiob Ludolf and Athanasius Kircher, is mentioned by Leibniz and his biographers mostly in relation to the project of founding the *Collegium imperiale historicum*, which was indeed the main reason why Leibniz got in touch with him. Leibniz corresponded with Paullini from December 1690 to July 1695. The thirty-three letters they exchanged mainly deal with historical and antiquarian issues, but occasionally medical texts and authors are also discussed, for Paullini was a renowned physician. Pfaff sarcastically describes him as 'that very curious man, very famous far and wide among scholars for having also invented a new method for defeating almost all diseases by means of urine and excrement' (ibid. 15n). This was not Paullini's only unconventional idea. Pfaff points to a short essay, published in 1692 and reprinted in 1695, whose title can be translated as follows: 'Death (commonly considered) is a silly old fairy tale.'[23] According to Pfaff, this essay 'explains the issue with much more erudition and clarity than Leibniz does' (Pfaff 1722, §3: 15n). Despite Pfaff's explicit claim to the contrary, his accusatory intent is quite clear. His point that Leibniz's immortalism is actually drawn from Paullini's collection of oddities is tantamount to suggesting that immortalism should not be deemed a serious doctrine.

In his short text, Paullini characterizes death as the separation of soul and body, and then argues that souls *qua* forms are essential to bodies. Animated bodies never lose their souls, just as souls never lose their life. Thus, death is nowhere, while life and souls are everywhere. Everything is animated and alive, even cadavers and stones, and every being has a natural 'will and desire to eternalize

---

533). See Leibniz to Sophie Charlotte and John Toland, December 1702: 'Mais quant à la separation, elle n'est jamais entiere de tout corps; l'ame demeure tousjours unie encor eapres la mort à quelque chose d'organique quoyque fort subtil' (A I, xxi, 721); and *Principes de la nature et de la grâce*, §6 (GP VI, 601). These ideas are rooted in Leibniz's esoteric background, as is shown by his earliest speculations on immortality and resurrection: see Leibniz to Duke Johann Friedrich, 21 May 1671 (A II, i, 175). See MacDonald Ross 1982; Brown 1998a, 8–12.

[22] Leibniz's Fifth Letter to Clarke, §61, in Des Maizeaux 1720b, I, 119; trans. Leibniz 1989b, 707.

[23] 'Der Tod (insgemein beguckt) ein alt-albres Mährlein.' In Paullini 1692, I, 43–51.

74   THE BANISHMENT OF DEATH: LEIBNIZ'S SCANDALOUS IMMORTALISM

itself' (Paullini 1692, I, 47). Paullini's immortalism appears to be a consequence of his panpsychism. Assuming that there are three different levels of life and activity, he explains away the event usually called death as the mere descent to a lower level of life (ibid. 48). In support of his immortalism, Paullini cites the Hippocratic book *On Diet* and a famous saying attributed to Apollonius of Tyana: 'There is no death of anything except only in appearance, just as there is no coming-to-be of anything except in appearance only.'[24]

No less striking than the similarities between Paullini's view and Leibniz's doctrine is the temporal coincidence between the composition of his work and that of the *New System*. In 1692, Leibniz read the *synopsis* of the first volume of Paullini's forthcoming book and favourably commented on it;[25] and a later quote from the second volume suggests that Leibniz may have managed to obtain a printed copy of the entire work.[26] Nevertheless, although the actual contacts between Leibniz and Paullini attested by their correspondence could support Pfaff's hypothesis, any direct influence of Paullini on the *New System* such as that claimed by Pfaff is still purely conjectural. In fact, Leibniz's account of death as the transformation of an imperishable animal dates at least from the mid-1680s.[27]

Furthermore, Paullini's views were not entirely original either. In a later work, he refers the doctrine of the three degrees of life to the Helmontian physician Martin Kerger; but he thereby also reveals a plausible source for his elimination of death:

> But tell me, please: what is death? Death, either as the *separation of the soul from the body* or as the *cessation of* absolutely *all actions*, is in fact a pure and utter scholastic figment, provided that you well understand the three distinct degrees of life thoroughly and clearly exposed by Kerger.[28]

On the other hand, even if Pfaff's implicit accusation of plagiarism may turn out to be completely misguided, his effort to unveil Leibniz's background correctly

---

[24] Apollonius to Valerianus, in Philostratus 2006, 51. See Paullini 1692, I, 49–51. Paullini also cites a couple of scriptural passages from *Ecclesiastes* and the German scientist and physician Ambrosius Rhodius (1577–1633).

[25] See Paullini to Leibniz, 10 (20) January 1692 (A I, vii, 537); and Leibniz to Paullini, 16 (26) March 1692 (A I, vii, 626).

[26] See Leibniz to Heineccius, November 1698 (A I, xvi, 298). As soon as the first volume of the work came out, Paullini expressed his wish to send a copy to Leibniz: see Paullini to Leibniz, 20 (30) December 1692 (A I, viii, 585).

[27] See, e.g., *De natura mentis et corporis* (1683–1686; A VI, iv, 1491); *De religione magnorum virorum* (1686–1687; A VI, iv, 2464); and Leibniz to Arnauld, September 1687 (A II, ii, 235–236).

[28] Paullini 1703, 13. Actually, the whole passage echoes Kerger 1663, sect. 1, ch. 6: 'Vitæ gradus,' 46–47: 'Quid ergò? Mors nulla? Rei nullius? . . . Mors itaque talis, quæ aut sit separatio animæ à corpore, aut cessatio omnium omninò actionum, nulla est, rei nullius. Decidunt autem, quæ mori dicuntur, de statu nobiliore ad ignobiliorem, de vitæ gradu præstantiore ad gradum deteriorem.'

highlights that Leibniz was not the first to radically deny mortality. In fact, this was even truer than Pfaff himself wished: remember that his aim was to present immortalism as a specifically modern phenomenon, an innovation to censure and reject. This narrow picture was soon to be dismantled by further investigations, which revealed a long and largely submerged stream of immortalism, ranging from ancient Pythagoreanism to Renaissance naturalism, from early modern mysticism to panpsychism, from 'occult' traditions like alchemy and Kabbalah to vitalistic medicine. Gradually, a variety of sources became suspected of having preceded or accompanied and possibly inspired or confirmed Leibniz's banishment of death.[29]

As early as 1722, Creiling's commentary on the Latin version of *Monadology* suggests a connection with alchemical sources. Commenting on paragraphs 75–78, Creiling observes that in some respects their content does not differ much from the theses of a book that he came across 'by chance,' the *Pansophia enchiretica*.[30] The First Part of this pseudonymous book distinguishes four degrees of life: simple subsistence, vegetation, animality, and rationality.[31] Human death is the separation of the intellective soul, but apart from the human being nothing else dies, 'not even the human body, and therefore there is nothing mortal in the world, because everything is full of life' (Bachimius Denstonius 1682, 9). Indeed, both generation and death consist in being transferred to a higher or lower level of life respectively, in a perpetual 'circulation' from darkness to light and vice versa (ibid. 10; see Creiling 1722, 23–24). Although Creiling's commentary says nothing explicit about the alchemical character of the *Pansophia enchiretica* nor mentions that it was placed on the Index in 1688, he cannot have been unaware that he was associating the *Monadology* with a forbidden book.

In the subsequent literature, the references to pre-Leibnizian immortalist doctrines multiply. Both the upholders and detractors of the banishment of death strive to discover its ancient or recent sources. In 1728, Hansch evokes Paullini[32] and Campanella.[33] In 1737, Baumeister bets on Paullini and Giordano Bruno, and even agrees with Leibniz that ancient philosophers had already tried to banish death—but in vain, he adds (Baumeister 1737, §3).

In the wake of Pfaff, many scholars focus their attention on the subtle-body doctrine and find an impressive list of sources in Ralph Cudworth's *True*

---

[29] See Brown's distinction between 'seminal' and 'confirmatory' influences (1998a, 6–8).

[30] Creiling 1722, 22. Creiling, professor of mathematics and natural sciences, was himself a renowned alchemist: see Frick 1960; Betsch 2005.

[31] See Bachimius Denstonius 1682, 6. The author is identified with Jacobus Wenceslaus Dobrozenski 'de Nigroponte, medicus Pragensis' by the famous physician Martin Schurig (1731, sect. 5, ch. 9, §147: 640.

[32] Hansch 1728, 167. Hansch refers to Paullini 1703.

[33] Hansch 1728, 171: 'Thomas Campanella *Part. II. Metaph. Lib. VII. cap. V. art. VI. p. 145. Nullum Ens Deo mori et mundo, sed transmutari, nec dari annihilationem* variis probat rationibus, cùm mors sit propriè compositorum ex diversis.'

Intellectual System:[34] ancient Platonic philosophers, Church Fathers, modern Neoplatonists—everyone who ever admitted one or more subtle bodies or taught that the soul is never without a body appears worthy of being included in the ranks of the radical immortalists. A result of this quest for sources is that Leibniz's theory of immortality appears to be gradually downplayed as just another subtle-body doctrine.

Indeed, as early as 1699 Johann Bernoulli had already interpreted Leibniz's theory in terms of the perennial conservation of an organic corpuscle: according to this hypothesis, 'death would be nothing but the gradual destruction of the gross parts of the body'.[35] Moreover, as mentioned above, Leibniz himself did not refrain from drawing on the subtle/gross body opposition to present his views, which led many to regard that opposition as essential to the banishment-of-death doctrine.[36] So where does Leibniz's originality lie? Why does Leibniz say 'my' banishment of death?

In Leibniz's metaphysics, the traditional idea of subtle body undergoes a profound transformation, since it merges with his famous doctrine of natural machines. Traditionally, subtle and gross bodies were thought to be made of essentially different stuff: ethereal or nearly spiritual stuff the former, heavily material stuff the latter. Leibniz, by contrast, rejects any essential difference between the macroscopic and the microscopic machines and makes their only difference consist in size. For, in keeping with his mechanistic tenets, Leibniz maintains that the visible organic bodies merely replicate on a larger scale the tiniest, imperceptible mechanisms. The next section casts further light on this issue by considering Elia Camerarius' objections to Leibniz.

5 The puzzle of identity through death

Although not every physician was unsympathetic to immortalism, academic medicine did not react favourably to Leibniz's attempt to banish death. As mentioned above, after Des Maizeaux's philological criticism the first set of purely theoretical objections was raised in 1721 by Elias Camerarius, who was professor of medicine at Tübingen—the very university where Pfaff taught theology and Creiling taught mathematics. For chronological reasons, Camerarius was in a position to benefit from a larger corpus of texts than Des Maizeaux, as some of Leibniz's key works had appeared in the meantime. In addition to the *New System*

---

[34] See Cudworth 1964, ch. 5, sect. 3. For instance, conspicuous references to Cudworth are to be found in Winckler 1742, §841n: 566–570; Gerhard 1777, locus 27, ch. 2, 29n; and Müller 1779, §3 and §5.

[35] Johann Bernoulli to Leibniz, 11 (21) February 1699 (A III, viii, 54).

[36] See esp. Baumeister 1737, §2.

and the letter to Des Maizeaux, he cites *Theodicy*, *Monadology*, and the letter to Rémond of 11 February 1715.[37]

The main issue raised by Camerarius against Leibniz's doctrine concerns the precise nature and the identity over time of what is supposed to persist after death:

> There is nobody who does not see that the first and foremost difficulty arises with respect to the very indestructibility of the machine, when it is affirmed that every soul or monad remains always joined to an organic body, which is however in perpetual change, so that it does not remain the same body, although the soul remains the same, and so does the animal [*etsi anima eadem maneat, et idem animal*]. (Camerarius 1721, 27)

Four entities are mentioned: soul, animal, machine, and organic body. If one assumes, as Camerarius does, that these entities are really different from one another, it appears legitimate to ask which of them persist and which must perish, which are indestructible and which can be destroyed, which remain the same even through death and which are eventually replaced by something else. Leibniz's texts directly answer parts of these questions, as they straightforwardly affirm the persistence of the same soul and the same animal. On the other hand, his statements about the status and fate of machines and organic bodies are less clear. This issue is still far from settled nowadays, but it must have appeared all the more puzzling to eighteenth-century readers, who had limited access to Leibniz's writings.

The source of the puzzle can be pictured as follows. According to *Monadology*, §§63–64, the term 'animal' designates an entity constituted by an organic body and a soul, whereas the organic body is characterized as 'a kind of divine machine or natural automaton' (GP VI, 618; trans. Leibniz 1989a, 221). However, according to the *New System*, natural machines are indestructible and remain always the same:

> We must then know that the machines of nature have a truly infinite number of organs, and are so well supplied and so resistant to all accidents that it is not possible to destroy them. A natural machine still remains a machine in its least parts, and moreover, it always remains the same machine that it has been ....
> (GP IV, 482; trans. Leibniz 1989a, 142)

Natural machines, along with souls and animals, persist even after death. In this work, Leibniz maintains that 'there is only one reasonable view to take—namely, the conservation not only of the soul, but also of the animal itself and its organic

---

[37] This letter was made available by Des Maizeaux 1720b, II, 185–197.

machine' (ibid. 480; trans. Leibniz 1989a, 141). In conjunction with the *Monadology*'s characterization of the organic body as a natural machine, these statements should entail the indestructibility and identity through time (or even through death) of the organic body itself—which is nevertheless what Leibniz expressly denies in his 1711 reply to Des Maizeaux: 'And I hold that each soul, or monad, is always accompanied by an organic body, though one which is in perpetual change—so much so that the body is never the same, even though both the soul and the animal are' (Des Maizeaux (ed.) 1720b, II, 384–385; trans. Leibniz 1997, 238). Actually, it might seem that one can hardly affirm the contrary, as the vulnerability or plain destructibility of ordinary organic bodies may count as empirical evidence.[38] Take an insect and burn it to ashes, suggests Camerarius 1721, 28; is it not highly implausible to maintain that the body of the insect is still there? To add to the reader's confusion, a passage from the *Monadology*, §77, apparently condemns the animal's machine to the same fate of partial dissolution: 'Thus one can state that not only is the soul (mirror of an indestructible universe) indestructible, but so is the animal itself, even though its machine often perishes in part, and casts off or puts on its organic coverings' (GP VI, 620; trans. Leibniz 1989a, 223, slightly modified).

At least two questions can be raised. The first concerns the relation between body and machine. Are natural machines indestructible and persistent like souls and animals or fragile and ephemeral like organic bodies? The second question concerns the relation between body and animal. If the organic body is a constituent of the animal, how can the latter preserve its identity while the former changes and dies?

Leibniz's answer to both questions lies in his theory of infinitely manifold machines. First, Leibniz indisputably holds that the natural machine is the organic body itself. However, if the bodily machine is considered as a mere body or an aggregate of matter, then its identity is fleeting, because matter is in a perpetual flux.[39] Since variable amounts of particles are added or lost or replaced at every moment, it is entirely possible that our present body no longer contains even one single particle of the matter that composed it at birth. Thus, no organic body remains *materially* the same (i.e., the same aggregate of the same particles) through time:

> ...according to my opinion, not only are all lives, all souls, all minds and all primitive entelechies perennial, but every primitive entelechy or vital principle is equipped with some machine of nature that we call organic body, although that

---

[38] In response to the objection that 'the organic body can be destroyed', Leibniz does not deny this possibility, but insists that even in this case some *massa animata* would persist (GP VII, 330).

[39] See Leibniz to Sophie Charlotte and Toland, December 1702 (A I, xxi, 722); and Leibniz 1720a, §71 (GP VI, 619).

machine, even when it retains its overall shape, consists in a flow and is constantly repaired like the ship of Theseus.

(Leibniz to Wagner, 4 June 1710; GP VII, 530)

This is why natural machines *seem* to be destructible, for 'not only the soul but also the animal is preserved, even though its machine is a composite which seems dissoluble' (Leibniz to Sophie Charlotte and Toland, December 1702; A I, xxi, 722; trans. Leibniz 2011, 274). The point is that, however dramatic the dissolution, it never amounts to a complete and definitive destruction: 'Thus, every machine of nature has this [feature], that it is never completely destructible, because as the gross integument [*crasso tegumento*] is dissipated in whatever manner, underneath there is always a tiny machine [*machinula*] not yet destroyed, like Harlequin's clothes' (Leibniz to Wagner, 4 June 1710; GP VII, 530).

By virtue of its infinitely many folds, the natural machine 'is indestructible, and always has an entrenchment of reserve against whatever violence there might be. So much so that it subsists and remains the same throughout the developments, envelopments, and transformations, just as the silkworm and the moth *are the same animal*' (Leibniz to Sophie Charlotte and Toland, December 1702; A I, xxi, 722; trans. Leibniz 2011, 274; emphasis added). According to Leibniz, the persistence of an underlying smaller machine or subtler body is sufficient to preserve not only the identity of the machine itself but also the identity of the whole animal. For when the superficial layers of the body are lost at death, the remaining small machine preserves some deeper structure, which is common to the various shapes gradually assumed by an animal. From this structural point of view, every animal or plant remains the same animal or plant throughout its transformations: 'For although the same matter does not remain, because it is in a continual flux, there always remains the basis of the structure [*le fond de la structure*]' (ibid.; trans. Leibniz 2011, 275).

As Leibniz points out, to say that the same animal survives *qua* individual is not to say that it survives as the same kind of animal. Leibnizian persistence through death requires numerical identity, not sortal sameness—which entails that, for Leibniz, sortal sameness is not a necessary condition for numerical identity:

Hence, not only is the soul perennial, but some animal always survives [*aliquod animal semper superest*] as well, although it must not be said that a specific animal [*certum aliquod animal*] is perennial, since the animal species does not persist [*species animalis non manet*]. For instance, the caterpillar and the moth *are not the same animal*, even though the soul is the same in both.

(Leibniz to Wagner, 4 June 1710; GP VII, 530; emphasis added)

At the end of the day, the immutable identity of the soul is the deepest ground of the survival of animals as the same individuals. Of course, the relation between the deep physical structure of the machine and the unifying immaterial principle called soul would require further clarification than that provided by Leibniz's texts, as both structure and soul appear to play a fundamental role in the preservation of the animal's identity. Moreover, it is difficult to spell out what the core or 'basis' of an animal structure exactly is; all we know is that this bearer of indestructibility should be both unique to every single animal, so as to account for its individuality, and common to all its multiple machines, so as to account for its persistence. It is nonetheless clear that the theory of natural machines and the implied distinction between a material and a structural point of view are effective in making Leibniz's aforementioned problematic claims consistent with each other.

6 Death and generation

Since the reconstruction just sketched is based mainly on sources that were not publicly available to Leibniz's contemporaries, it would have been extremely hard for anyone at the time to fully grasp Leibniz's theory and reconcile its apparent inconsistencies. The objections raised by Camerarius express the general difficulty of understanding how natural machines work in preserving the animal's identity even through the most radical transformations of the body:

> ... still I cannot understand whence a new body is added to the monad or soul as this body disintegrates, or in what regard [*qua ratione*] the animal remains the same. If you say that a tiny machine [*parvulam machinulam*] remains always joined to the monad, then you will have to show whence it originates, whence it emerges, where it hides, or arises. ... the body that we observe is the same body it was in the beginning, and now it putrefies and dissolves. If you say that some tiny machine remains joined to the monad, you say nothing. For, whence does it come? Whence has it been extracted? Where was it hidden? Each and every limb of the animals dies and dissolves, hence too the entire animal machine; therefore the previous animal does not persist. In vain will you retort that the body is destroyed but the machine is not; for, is the body itself not a machine? Can it be that body and machine are two different things? How do they differ from each other? Does the monad govern two machines as long as the body lasts, that is, both the machine of the future state and the body of the present state?
>
> (Camerarius 1721, 27–28)

Basically, Camerarius rejects Leibniz's main argument for immortalism, namely the analogy or symmetry between generation and death. According to him, whereas generation can indeed be explained (as Leibniz does) in preformationist terms as the development or transformation of pre-existing seeds, death is the final extinction of an animal's life. As the animal dies, only the immaterial soul survives.

A similar strategy is adopted by Pfaff. In the wake of Camerarius, he takes a liberal or even cautiously approving attitude towards Leibniz's preformationist theory of generation, while condemning without appeal the twin theory of death:

> ... above all, what is scandalous to us in this Leibnizian system, is that he says that in death the body itself and the machine itself that is joined to the soul do not dissolve at all, but the body persists joined to the soul, while only its coverings [exuviæ] dissolve, so that it returns to the small size it had in the seed; that death makes this body only enfold [involvi], just as generation makes it unfold [evolvatur]; and even that its vital actions are merely suspended by death, but do not cease. (Pfaff 1722, §5: 21–22)

The 'scandal' consists in denying that death is real and treating it as just the reverse of generation. If preformationism is true, generation is not a real beginning of life but only a transformation of an already living being. By contrast, death is a real boundary of life, which involves the final dissolution of the bodily machine and the cessation of all vital activities. To deny this—Pfaff insists—is 'to speak against the evidence [contra solem] and wage war on common sense and experience' (ibid.). Furthermore, Pfaff attacks Leibniz's argument for the necessity of mind-body union by rejecting the claim that the soul is always united to a body as gratuitous and counterintuitive: '[D]eath itself shows that souls separate from bodies. For, the body that corrupts and dissolves is not just a covering and veil of the body, but is the very organic body that lay embedded in the seed' (ibid. 20). The doctrine that the animal survives any destruction by folding itself into some small or subtle body is dismissed as paradoxical and unintelligible:

> Who would tolerate someone saying that, when a human body is cremated, it is not the body itself that is cremated but only its covering and mantle, and that the body itself simply folds upon itself [convolvi] like a hedgehog that raises its spikes? Where in the world, I ask, does this tiny body hide? What vital actions does it perform? Whence does it originate and in what way? (Ibid. 22)

Pfaff concludes that the entire banishment-of-death doctrine has 'no semblance of truth,' for it is merely an attempt by Leibniz 'to pass off a fairy tale [fabulam] to the world that loves to be deceived and wants new and paradoxical hypotheses to be foisted on it' (ibid.). With these words, Pfaff inaugurates the longstanding critical custom of dismissing Leibniz's philosophical theories as fairy tales. (In fact, this text also contains Pfaff's early revelation that Leibniz had sent him letters in which he admitted that the whole system of theodicy and pre-established harmony was merely a philosophical amusement, a *lusus ingenii*: ibid. 17.)[40]

7 Conclusion

An ancient, vigorous strand of radical immortalism appears to have traversed early modern philosophy, theology, and medicine. Leibniz's doctrine was certainly rooted in this rich and complex tradition, but the German reaction to his banning of death nevertheless proved hostile across the board. Even Wolff, long regarded as the popularizer of Leibniz's metaphysics, kept himself aloof from the banishment of death. Not only did he never mention the issue; he developed a spiritualistic doctrine of immortality diametrically opposed to the views of his former mentor.[41] Moreover, apart from few (possible) exceptions such as Bilfinger or Hansch, those who tried to revive Leibniz's promise of an immortal body resorted to the more traditional subtle-body doctrine.[42] Did such a misinterpretation arise from mere ignorance? More plausibly, the dualistic distinction of an immortal subtle body and a mortal gross body simply appeared less problematic than Leibniz's radical immortalism; in admitting subtle bodies, one did not feel *eo ipso* committed to denying that death exists. Canz, for instance, vindicates his account of the soul's fate from the charge of being incompatible with death by arguing that since the soul loses its gross body, death *qua* separation of soul and body does actually take place (Canz 1996, §1130: 944). This suggests that the subtle-body doctrine was not taken to be equivalent in itself to the utter elimination of death. It also suggests that immortalism alarmed even its supporters as a potentially compromising position, so they took care to distance themselves from its most radical version.

As we have seen, Pfaff treated Leibniz's doctrine as being not only paradoxical but even 'scandalous'. What was the real scandal? My suggestion is that Leibniz's attempt to banish death may well have been perceived as a threat to Christian dogma, not only because of its implications concerning the soul's state after death or the resurrection of the body, but for the more fundamental reason that death is essential to Christianity. What are we to make of the Christian history of salvation once it is accepted that death is not real and every living being is naturally immortal? This conclusion invites us to revise the widespread assumption that the defence of immortality is always connected to pious concerns and apologetic aims. Indeed, the story of this philosophical engagement with death shows that immortalism can come into serious conflict with received religious beliefs.

---

[40] Scholars usually refer only to Pfaff's later revelation (1728).
[41] See Favaretti Camposampiero forthcoming.
[42] See, e.g., Canz 1996, §1125: 940–941; Winckler 1742, §§838–842: 563–571.

PART III
LEARNING TO LIVE

4

Human Life as a State of Mediocrity in John Locke

Giuliana Di Biase

1 Introduction

When, in composing his funerary epigraph, Locke described himself as a man 'who was contented with his modest lot', he was leaving a message for posterity regarding his view of human life. This message, which he repeated to his friend Antony Collins shortly before he died,[1] had ancient roots. 'Beatus esse qui mediocritate contentus vivit'—happy who lives contented with mediocrity— Horace had written,[2] and his words went on to resonate through the Christian era. The fifth-century poet Sidonius Apollinaris, for instance, lauded the 'felicissimum mediocritatis meae statum'—his extremely happy mediocre position—in one of his letters.[3] Writing a little later, Venantius Fortunatus attested to the fortunes of Horace's dictum when he described himself as 'tota mediocritate contentus'—contented with the entire mediocrity.[4] This continuity was connected to the polysemy of the term *mediocritas*. Mediocrity could denote a middling quality or average ability,[5] but also scarcity, smallness, insufficiency. When classical writers such as Cicero spoke of 'mea mediocritas', it was the latter meaning that they had in mind.[6] Along with other reverential formulas such as 'mea

---

[1] 'Siste viator, Hic juxta situs est Joannes Locke. Si qualis fuerit rogas, mediocritate sua contentum se vixisse respondet'. Near this place lies John Locke. If you are wondering what kind of man he was, he answers that he was contented with his modest lot. (Locke, *Works*, C. Baldwin, London 1824[12], vol. 1, p. xxxix). Locke to Antony Collins, 19, 9 June 1704: 'I am not envious, and therefore shall not be troubled if others find themselves instructed with so extraordinary and sublime a way of reasoning. I am content with my own mediocrity.' The 'others' to whom Locke referred was William Sherlock, who had criticized the *Essay* for the rejection of innate ideas. See Locke 1976–1989, vol. 8, p. 330.

[2] In the seventeenth-century editions of Horace edited by Theodore Marcilius (Paris, 1604), and John Bond (Paris, 1640), both of which Locke possessed, the *argumentum* prefixed to the famous ode 16 to Mecenas read 'beatum esse qui mediocritate contentus vivit', in Marcilius's edition, and 'Se mediocritate sua contentum esse', in Bond's edition. Harrison and Laslett 1971, 157. nos. 1498 and 1500.

[3] Apollinaris 461–484 CE, bk. 7, ep. 8, 1 (472 CE).

[4] Fortunatus, *Vita S. Albini Andegavensis Episcopi*, (c. 580), in Fortunatus 1862, 481.

[5] This was the meaning of mediocrity in Horace's *Ars Poetica*; mediocrity was to be appreciated in most areas of life but banned in the fine arts.

[6] See for inst. Cicero, 44–43 BC, 2, 2. See also, for inst., Statius, 89–96 CE bk. 5, *Praefatio*; Paterculus, 30 CE, bk. 2, 104, etc.

Giuliana Di Biase, *Human Life as a State of Mediocrity in John Locke* In: *Life and Death in Early Modern Philosophy*. Edited by: Susan James, Oxford University Press. © Giuliana Di Biase 2021. DOI: 10.1093/oso/9780192843616.003.0005

parvitas', admissions of mediocrity in the preface of a text answered to the rules of rhetoric, which prescribed a humble approach to the reader. Early Christian authors such as Tertullian, Cyprian, and Augustinus continued to employ this expression, in conformity to the Christian command of meekness and humility.[7] In their writings, the 'humana mediocritas'—the mediocrity of human beings— was opposed to God's infinite wisdom and omnipotence.[8]

The other meaning of mediocrity, denoting a middling quality, was encapsulated in Horace's concept of the *aurea mediocritas* or golden mean, and in Cicero's warning 'mediocritatem illam tenebit, quae est inter nimium et parum'—keep that mean which lies between excess and defect.[9] Here mediocrity was intended as the Latin equivalent of the Aristotelian $\mu\epsilon\sigma\acute{o}\tau\eta s$, the virtuous 'mean' between opposite extremes. Arguably, the consonance of the other meaning of mediocrity (smallness or insufficiency) with the Christian ideal of humility paved the way for the progressive assimilation of the golden mean to the virtue of moderation.[10] It is true that the 'mean' and moderation were not exactly synonymous: in ancient Peripatetic ethics, $\sigma\omega\phi\rho\sigma\acute{v}\nu\eta$ was the specific virtue of self-restraint, whereas the ethical mean, or middle way between excess and deficiency characterized all virtues. In some cases, abiding by the mean might be a matter of practicing moderation by restraining excesses, but vices of deficiency such as cowardice required augmentation rather than restraint. Nevertheless, as the authority of a long tradition prevailed over these exceptions, the notion of the mean was steadily assimilated to the virtue of moderation. In seventeenth-century England, the coalescence of the two was helped along by the religious climate: within early modern Protestant ethics, the possibility that the will might require augmentation rather than restraint was rarely contemplated. Instead, an emphasis on the weight

---

[7] Tertullian (a), ca. 198–204 CE ch. 10., 1; Augustinus, ca. 400 CE, bk. 6, 6; Cyprianus, III cent. CE 20,1. The expression was still of common use in seventeenth- and eighteenth-century Latin texts, as an equivalent of the personal pronoun. Cassiodorus named 'mediocritas' or 'metriasmos' the figure 'quoties rem magnam mediocre relatione proferimus'. See Cassiodorus, 'Expositio in Psalterium', 538–570 CE, in Cassiodorus, 1865, 2, 212.

[8] See for instance Tertullian 213 CE, 1, 4: 'cum propterea paraclitum miserit dominus, ut, quoniam humana mediocritas omnia semel capere non poterat, paulatim dirigeretur et ordinaretur et ad perfectum perduceretur disciplina ab illo vicario domini, Spiritu Sancto'; Tertullian (b) 198–204 CE, 3.,35; Tertullian (c), 198–204 CE, bk. 1.,18.,3. See also Arnobius, IV cent. CE, bk. 1, 38,4: 'qui, quod frugiferum primo atque humano generi salutare, Deus monstravit quid sit, quis, quantus et qualis: qui profundas eius atque inenarrabilis altitudines, quantum nostra quivit mediocritas capere et intelligere permisit et docuit'.

[9] Cicero, 44 BC, 1, 89.

[10] Origen might have played a significant role in this, because he identified humility as Aristotle's *mesotes*. Foulcher 2015, 29. Aquinas endorsed this interpretation, describing humility as a form of moderation. He conceived of temperance as the virtue appointing the mean: see [*S. Th.*], 2a2ae, q. 141, art. 6, reply to ob. 3. Temperance was 'a kind of moderation...chiefly concerned with those passions that tend towards sensible goods, viz. desire and pleasure'. See *S. Th.*, 2a2ae, q.141, art.3. In seventeenth-century England moderation and temperance were sometimes understood as synonymous. See Shagan 2012, 32, in note.

of original sin and the dangerous appetites of fallen humanity led the Reformed to conceive of all vices as excesses requiring the restraining force of moderation.

To be sure, the assimilation of mediocrity to moderation had some opponents. The golden mean was sometimes perceived as a residue of Aristotelianism, and regarded with suspicion on the grounds that heathen ethics was, as Ramus had claimed, inferior to Christian ethics. When, in his *The Marrow of Sacred Divinity*, William Ames criticized the vagueness of the rule of mediocrity, he was not simply reiterating Aristotle's warning about the difficulty of locating the mean. Like Melanchthon, Ames intended to highlight the huge gap between ancient philosophy and Christianity and underscore the irrelevance of the first to the second.[11] But attempts to dispense with the pagan notion of the mean were not always accepted, and were resisted by a number of eminent theologians such as Richard Hooker and Robert Sanderson. Drawing reassurance from the Church fathers, both these authors accepted the consonance of Aristotelian mediocrity with Christian faith, and praised the mean as a fundamental norm of ethical life.[12]

The frequent mention of mediocrity in seventeenth-century English political and literary texts suggests that there was a broad consensus in favour of the view voiced by Hooker and Sanderson. Mediocrity was equated with moderation and conceived as one of the fundamental moral virtues celebrated by the classical philosophical tradition. So much so, that the differences between Stoic, Peripatetic, and Epicurean ideals of moderation were treated as insubstantial, and reconciled within the syncretistic philosophy of Neo-Stoicism. Underlying this apparent consensus, however, a series of sharp disagreements arose about the precise meaning of mediocrity, and about how the virtue should be expressed.

One domain in which these disputes flourished was religion. Members of the national church agreed that the church's doctrine and practices exemplified the *via media*, and that popery was one of the extremes to be avoided, but disagreed about the variety of Protestantism that should constitute the other extreme. Puritans such as Samuel Ward criticized the church's *via media* as unduly lukewarm, while also maintaining the necessity of moderating turbulent zeal. In Ward's view, the mean lay in a more fervent religious practice, somewhere between the church's position and what he regarded as excessive zealousness.

The content of the mean was also a matter of dispute in political contexts, where it was used to defend different types of constitution. During the civil war, members of the Royalist and Parliamentary camps often equated the mean with mixed monarchy, but after the regicide, Marchamont Nedham associated it with a republic. Again, his contemporary Hobbes described the absolute rule of his

---

[11] See Ames 1642, 233; Melanchthon 1834, bk 2, 309. Already Lactantius 1886, 181, had insisted on a similar point in his *The Divine Institutes* (What then, I pray, 'will this mediocrity profit us?'), yet his target was stoic attitude towards passions, which recommended extirpation rather than a mediocrity.
[12] Hooker 1888, bk.1, 16, 7, 283; Sanderson 1841, 429; passim.

Leviathan as occupying the virtuous, but vulnerable mean between those who favoured a 'too great Liberty', and those who were for 'too much Authority'.[13] The habit of justifying a political position by portraying it as a middle way between extremes also remained common amongst the supporters and opponents of Charles II during the Exclusion crisis. Opposing sides in this dispute each claimed that their position had the advantage of mediocrity.[14]

There was, however, a less controversial sense in which mediocrity was invoked as a norm in the seventeenth century. Apollinaris had spoken of a 'status mediocritatis', by which he meant an undistinguished social position, and in a 1625 sermon, John Donne praised the 'middle state' or 'mediocrity' between richness and poverty, which preserved human beings from the excesses of pride and desperation. This idea was widely accepted, as was the cognate conception of the middle state as a condition of partial ignorance and imperfection, a legacy of original sin.[15] The philosopher John Locke developed this idea in an original way, in an account of the state of mediocrity that formed the core of his reflections on human life. Men's ontological condition corresponded to this state, the universality of which contrasted with the variability of individual talents—a sphere governed by the Aristotelian mean. Life was a time of mediocrity; death opened the way to the excesses of extreme misery and eternal happiness, according to individual merits and faults. My purpose is to reconstruct the distinctive traits of this idea in Locke's thought, its genesis and evolution. Initially, he seems to have conceived of the middle state essentially as one of intellectual mediocrity, as is suggested by a 1677 entry in his journal. The lengthy debate about scepticism, dating back to the early Church fathers, seems have been his main source of inspiration in this first stage. Subsequently, he developed this idea in a more original way, insisting on the natural suitability of human beings to their mediocre state. The reading of Pierre Nicole and Pascal, who both heavily emphasized the catastrophic consequences of original sin on human nature, may have prompted Locke to redefine the state of mediocrity in more optimistic terms. Finally, the uneasiness that characterizes this state in the *Essay* somehow reduces Locke's optimism; the human condition on earth appears to be an imperfect state of insatiable desire, aimed at directing attention towards eternal life. However, the perfect knowledge of morality attainable in this world redeems our mediocre state.

---

[13] Hobbes 1994, 1 (Dedicatory Letter).   [14] See Scodel 2002, 4–8.

[15] In a very few cases, the middle state was intended negatively, for instance when it was associated with the idea of a compromise between mundane and eternal interests: in this sense, the Puritan clergyman Thomas Manton refused to equate Christian life with the 'middle state' between total subjugation to the flesh's desires and obedience to God's commandments. See Manton 1873, II, sermon 5, 233. The 'middle state' and the 'tolerable mediocrity' against which the Presbyterian William Bates preached in one of his sermons was Purgatory, a belief of the Roman Church. See Bates 1700, 537.

2 Locke's 'state of mediocrity' in 'Study'.
Intellectual mediocrity

The expression 'state of mediocrity' appears for the first time in Locke's manuscripts in a journal note he began to write when he was in France between 16 and 26 March 1677, and finished in April or May. The note, entitled 'Study',[16] may have been written to comply with the request of one of his friends, the doctor of Divinity Denis Grenville. Around the middle of March, Locke had received a letter from Grenville, whom he had befriended in Montpellier,[17] asking him to pen his thoughts about how much time and energy a scholar should devote to each of his occupations, namely recreation, business, conversation, study, and devotion. Grenville was afraid of being unable to avoid excesses in allocating his time, and placed great trust in the judicious advice of his friend. As he explained, 'I would faigne hit the Meane if I could tell how.'[18] Locke's initial reply took the form of a letter to Grenville, dealing with the first occupation he had mentioned, namely recreation.[19] Here Locke denied the possibility of establishing a definite, universal measure of the time and energies to be devoted to this activity. It was doubtful, he maintained, 'whether there be any such exact proportion of recreation to our present state of body and mind, that soe much is exactly enough and what soever is under is too litle what soever is over is too much'.[20] Following Aristotle, Locke insisted on the variability of the parameters that constitute the extremes on either side of a mean.

This objection reappears in 'Study', where Locke turns to enquire into the 'just measure' of time and energies that scholars like Grenville should devote to learning. The discourse enlarges on the limits of knowledge, its purpose, and its relevance to human life. The arguments Locke offers here were subsequently developed in *An Essay concerning Human Understanding* and *Some Thoughts concerning Education*, but they made their first appearance in this 1677 journal note. 'The end of study', he begins, 'is knowledge, and the end of knowledge practice or communication.'[21] To achieve knowledge that we can communicate and put into practice, we ought to consider the disproportion between the vast extent of what is knowable and our limited human capacities, and take account of the shortness of human life. 'The whole time of our . . life [. . .] is. not enough to acquaint us with all those things, I will not say which we are capable of knowing,

---

[16] Locke, 'Study', in King 1830, 1, 171–203.

[17] Denis Grenville to Locke, 6/16–8/18 March 1677, in Locke 1976–1989, 1, 470–472.

[18] Ibid., 472.

[19] Locke to Denis Grenville, c. 9/19–11/21 March 1677, ibid., 472–474. The covering letter is lost. Locke obtained a copy of the surviving part from Grenville in November 1678 and copied it in his journal heading it 'An Essay concerning Recreation in answer to D G's desire Mar 77'. See Bodleian. MS Locke f.3, 351–357.

[20] Locke to Denis Grenville, c. 9/19–11/21 March 1677, in Locke 1979–89, 1, 474.

[21] Locke, 'Study', in King 1830, 171.

but which it would not be only convenient but very advantageous to know.'[22] Of all the things we might come to know, the most advantageous concern God, the way to heaven and prudence, because our happiness in this and the next life depends on them. Any man has therefore a duty to cultivate knowledge of these kinds. Study, however, is the 'particular calling' of scholars, and the means by which they fulfil the divine commandment to work.[23] To fully comply with this obligation, however, they should not waste their time on disputes about subtle verbal distinctions, which can hardly advance their knowledge. Although the different opinions expressed by the learned can alert us to the 'vanity and ignorance of mankind',[24] these issues should not be a scholar's main concern. Nor should scholars occupy themselves with sterile pursuits such as honing the purity of their language, studying classical idioms, or immersing themselves in erudite historical investigations.

Having set out these negative rules, Locke moves on to make some more positive recommendations about how to pursue knowledge in accordance with the 'just measure of our strength'. Scholars should content themselves with a 'moderate knowledge' so as not to impair their health. They should keep in mind the fact that the end of knowledge—'the benefit of ourselves and others in this world'[25]—will be impossible to attain if our bodies and minds are too heavily loaded with learning. Yet these precepts, important as they may be, are not sufficient to determine the middle way for which scholars should strive. Something else must be taken in consideration.

> The great secret is to find out the proportion; the difficulty whereof lies in this, that it must not only be varied according to the constitution and strength of every individual man, but it must also change with the temper, vigour, and circumstances, and health of every particular man, in the different varieties of health, or indisposition of body, which every thing our bodies have any commerce with is able to alter: so that it is as hard to say how many hours a day a man shall study constantly, as to say how much meat he shall eat every day, wherein his own prudence, governed by the present circumstances, can only judge.[26]

On subsequent pages, Locke continues to underline the individual character of the parameters necessary to determine the mean; the objects of study, and the time and energy to be employed in this and alternative occupations such as relaxation, meditation and conversation, should vary 'according as every one finds most successful in himself to the best husbandry of his time and thought'.[27]

A first requirement on scholars is therefore that they should identify and follow their own personal mean. But this is by no means their only task. To comply with

---

[22] Ibid., 172.   [23] Ibid., 181.   [24] Ibid., 176.   [25] Ibid., 182.   [26] Ibid., 183.
[27] Ibid., 185.

their scholarly duty, they must also focus their efforts on grasping the truth, the proper object of the mind, and the essence of God, 'who is truth itself'.[28] A second universal rule is therefore that study should aim at truth; but here a third limit comes into view. Alongside the shortness of our lives and our meagre mental and physical capacities, our scholarly efforts to pursue knowledge are liable to be derailed by a despairing lack of confidence in our judgement, or an overwhelming pride in our understanding. To steer between these extremes, scholars must accept their mediocrity. As Locke explains:

> he that thinks his understanding capable of all things, mounts upon wings of his own fancy, though indeed Nature never meant him any, and so venturing into the vast expanse of incomprehensible verities, only makes good the fable of Icarus, and loses himself in the abyss. We are here in the state of mediocrity; finite creatures, furnished with powers and faculties very well fitted to some purposes, but very disproportionate to the vast and unlimited extent of things.[29]

The image of Icarus to which Locke appeals had been used by Bacon in *De Sapientia Veterum*, where he too had praised the middle way. Icarus transgressed against his mediocrity by disregarding his father's advice not to fly too high or too low.[30] Bacon notes that this image is usually associated with moral rather than intellectual mediocrity, and epitomizes a view of virtue as the *via media* between excess and defect. By contrast, discussions of scientific method usually appeal to the passage between Scylla and Charybdis, understood as the 'rocks' of distinctions and the 'abysses' of universals. In the Preface to *Novum Organon*, Bacon also proposes a less mythological image of intellectual mediocrity, inspired by Sextus Empiricus' distinction between the various schools of philosophy. His own form of sceptical scientific inquiry, he claims, is the middle way between dogmatic and Academic extremes, between the 'presumption of pronouncing on everything and the despair of comprehending anything'.[31]

Following out Bacon's line of thought, Locke claims in 'Study' that 'It is of great use in the pursuit of knowledge not to be too confident, nor too distrustful of our own judgement, nor to believe we can comprehend all things nor nothing.'[32] Like Bacon, he praises the *via media* between the extremes of dogmatism and scepticism, though he chooses the image of Icarus to highlight the importance of intellectual mediocrity. His purpose in doing so is to emphasize the need for a careful enquiry into the extent of our faculties. If we are to avoid a fate like that of Icarus, we must be mindful of the intellectual limits imposed by our mediocre state.

---

[28] Ibid., 187.   [29] Ibid., 197.   [30] Bacon 1900, 13, 53.   [31] Ibid., 8, 59.
[32] Locke, 'Study', in King 1830, 196.

92 HUMAN LIFE AS A STATE OF MEDIOCRITY IN JOHN LOCKE

In the rest of his journal entry, Locke pursues this objective. Some topics of enquiry, he claims, are unsuited to the power of our intellect; these include 'things infinite', the 'essences of substantial beings' and the 'manner also how Nature, in this great machine of the world, produces the several phenomena, and continues the species of things in a successive generation'.[33] By contrast, 'the improvement of natural experiments for the conveniences of this life, and the way of ordering himself so as to attain happiness in the other'[34] lie within the reach of our natural faculties. By using these faculties properly, we can come to understand not only the moral requirements to which we are subject, but 'religion too, or a man's whole duty'.[35] Our intellectual mediocrity therefore does not impede us from fulfilling the duties specified by the fundamental norms of the law of nature (to honour God, to preserve ourselves through work, and to be useful to others).[36] The 'dim twilight'[37] in which we live provides human beings with sufficient illumination, given their 'instinctive knowledge of the truth'.[38]

In defending this view, Locke is implicitly taking sides in a long debate stretching back to the fathers of the church. Although he does not mention these predecessors, there is every reason to think that he knew about them, because he owned some of the principal works in which their positions in this debate emerged. One of these works is the *Octavius* by the third-century Roman apologist Minucius Felix, which was extremely popular in the seventeenth century and went through many editions.[39] Locke's library contained two of them—a 1612 Latin edition by Geverhartus Elmenhorst and a 1664 French edition by D'Ablancourt.[40] Another important text is Lactantius' *Divinarum Institutionum*, of which Locke owned two copies.[41]

One of the issues which Minucius and Lactantius debate is the question of how insufficient our human knowledge is. Does our intellectual mediocrity consign us to complete ignorance of God and the things we need to know in order to live well? Or does it enable us to acquire enough knowledge to fulfil our fundamental

---

[33] Ibid., 198.   [34] Ibid.   [35] Ibid.

[36] The list of subjects in 'Study' is reminiscent of Aquinas' teaching, according to which the three fundamental laws of nature were the study of God, the preservation of oneself, and living in society; in the *Essays on the Law of Nature*, Locke declared these three laws 'embrace all that men owe to God, their neighbour, and themselves', and in 'Study' he restated this conviction. Cfr. Locke 1954, 156–159. See also Locke, 'Knowledge', in Locke 1936, 86–89.

[37] Locke, 'Study', King 1830, 182.   [38] Ibid., 194.

[39] Several editions appeared since the first years of the seventeenth century: that of Gevehartus Elmenhorst, published in 1603, was reprinted many times in the subsequent years. *Octavius* was printed at Oxford in 1631 and 1636, in London in 1695; another important edition was that of Revees 1709. Minucius was the only Christian apologist not to enter into Christological problems: he confined himself to the items of monotheism, divine providence, the purity of Christian life and the immortality of the soul. This might explain his fortune in a century of religious controversies. Regarding the debate of the reliability of early Church fathers in seventeenth-century England, see Quantin 2009.

[40] See Harrison and Laslett 1971, 190, nos. 1101 and 1999a.

[41] Ibid., 167, nos. 1651 and 1651a. The first is a 1570 edition, the second a 1539 edition edited by Erasmus.

duties, as Locke has so far claimed? In his *Octavius*, Minucius describes the human condition as a state of ignorance, equally far from the extremes of knowledge of natural and of supernatural things:

> the mediocrity of human intelligence is so far from (the capacity of) divine investigation, that neither is it given us to know, nor is it permitted to search, nor is it religious to ravish, the things that are supported in suspense in the heaven above us, nor the things which are deeply submerged below the earth.[42]

The context of this quotation is important. The *Octavius* is written in the form of a dialogue between the pagan Caecilius and the Christian Octavius. The words just quoted are spoken by Caecilius, who has been rebuked by Octavius for his superstitious beliefs, and sets out to defend himself. Caecilius begins by reminding Octavius that all things in human affairs are doubtful and uncertain, and laments the fact that Christians, who are for the most part illiterate, dare to speak with confidence about the nature and power of God. Their intellectual presumption, he claims, is inconsistent with human mediocrity. In this context, the expression *humana mediocritas* seems to possess a double meaning, both evaluative and descriptive. On the one hand, it refers to a condition of intellectual insufficiency; on the other hand, to an intermediate position between the natural and the divine. This *medium per distantiam* is also a *medium per abnegationem*, a state of total ignorance of the extremes.

Against this pagan argument for *mediocritas* as a form of incurable ignorance, Minucius argues in the voice of Octavius that a degree of wisdom is implanted by nature in every human being, literate and illiterate, rich and poor. Everyone is thus entitled to enquire into divine things, and express his thoughts on the subject.

Minucius's ideal of an intellectual mediocrity free from its sceptical implications is in turn developed by Lactantius in his *Divinarum institutionum*. While divine *sapientia* represents the absolute limit of knowledge and is opposed to total ignorance, humans can attain a moderate level of understanding in between the two.

Some thought that all things could be known: these were manifestly not wise. Others thought that nothing could be known; nor indeed were these wise: the former, because they attributed too much to man; the latter, because they attributed too little. A limit was wanting to each on either side. Where, then, is wisdom? It consists in thinking neither that you know all things, which is the property of God; nor that you are ignorant of all things, which is the part of a beast. For it is something of a middle character which belongs to man, that is, knowledge united and combined with ignorance.[43]

---

[42] Minucius Felix 1885, 175.   [43] See Lactantius 1886, 73.

According to Lactantius, the measure of *sapientia* assigned to human beings places them between God and the beasts. These are the extremes on either side of human intellectual mediocrity, one of excess and the other of deficiency. Moreover, since human beings have been endowed with a 'middle character', and can become wise only by believing in the one God, pagan philosophy cannot help them.

The Academics argued from obscure subjects, against the natural philosophers, that there was no knowledge; and satisfied with the examples of a few incomprehensible subjects, they embraced ignorance as though they had taken away the whole of knowledge, because they had taken it away in part. But natural philosophers, on the other hand, derived their argument from those things which are open, *and inferred* that all things could be known, and, satisfied with things which were manifest, retained knowledge; as if they had defended it altogether, because they had defended it in part. And thus neither the one saw what was clear, nor the others what was obscure; but each party, while they contended with the greatest ardour either to retain or to take away knowledge only, did not see that there would be placed in the middle that which might guide them to wisdom.[44]

By adapting Sextus Empiricus' distinction between the three schools of philosophy—the dogmatists, Academic Sceptics, and Pyrrhonists—to the Aristotelian scheme of a mean between two extremes, Lactantius constructs an argument that would be employed by Montaigne,[45] and later on, by Bacon. Locke not only owned Lactantius's book, but it is also likely that he was familiar with the variation of Lactantius's conception of *mediocritas* developed by Augustine, for whom human wisdom is the mean between 'the folly of man, and the pure Truth of God.[46] According to Augustine, men can only become wise by uniting closely with their Creator, yet are endowed with an intellectual mediocrity that can preserve them both from the rationalistic excess of Pelagius, and from the sceptical excesses of heretics.[47] The *docta ignorantia* reconciles the two extremes of knowledge and ignorance, thereby attesting to God's benevolence towards humanity.[48]

Intellectual mediocrity continued to be lauded in religious writings across the centuries. In seventeenth-century England, John Donne, for example, warned against overestimating knowledge and recommended the 'middle-state'. 'Every

---

[44] Ibid.   [45] See Montaigne 1652, 364, 770, etc.

[46] Augustinus, 391 CE, 15, 33: 'sapiens sit Deo ita mente coniunctus, ut nihil interponatur quod separet; Deus enim est veritas; nec ullo pacto sapiens quisquam est, si non veritatem mente contingat: negare non possumus inter stultitiam hominis et sincerissimam Dei veritatem medium quiddam interpositam esse hominis sapientiam'.

[47] Augustinus, 418 CE.

[48] Augustinus, ca . 411 CE, 15, 28: 'Est ergo in nobis quaedam, ut dicam, docta ignorantia, sed docta spiritu dei, qui adiuvat infirmitatem nostram.' Bonaventure of Bagnoregio would describe the learned ignorance as an *excessus mentis* (an extreme at the top of the mystical ascent, inaccessible to human intellect: see Bonaventure 1259, ch. 4, 6), whereas Nicholas of Cusa would ground it in the neo-platonic coincidence of opposites. The extremes of knowledge and ignorance were reconciled in the mean, intended as a *medium per partecipationem*.

man becomes a fool by knowledge,'[49] he admonished, quoting Scripture to this effect. The Puritan John Howe claimed that God had left man 'in medio' or 'undetermined' in this world, revealing only what was necessary to 'the being or well-being of religion,' and the Anglican Isaac Barrow praised the providential design that had assigned to man only a 'suitable mediocrity' of knowledge, wealth, health, and power. Backing this broad consensus over intellectual mediocrity was the Pauline admonition 'sapere ad sobrietatem'—think with sober judgement.

In Locke's 'Study', the image of Icarus recalls classical rather than Christian sources, and the Christian universal meaning of the state of mediocrity remains in the background. This state is essentially presented as a condition of limited intellectual ability, whose acceptance preserves scholars from the extreme of scepticism. Locke admonishes them not to be overconfident in their judgement if they wish to avoid the painful situation of 'incurable doubt and perplexity of mind'.[50] However, in a subsequent response to Grenville, Locke will clarify his view of the state of mediocrity as a universal condition.

3 'Scrupulosity'

Locke did not send his 'Study' to Grenville. However, a year after his initial request, in March 1678, Grenville again asked Locke's advice on how 'to keep the meane' in business, study and conversation,[51] and received an answer from his friend within a few days.[52] There is a draft of Locke's letter to Grenville in his journal, with the marginal caption 'Scrupulosity'.[53] Two other copies exist, suggesting that the contents of the letter had a wider circulation among Locke's acquaintances.

In 'Scrupulosity', Locke does not deal separately with the topics Grenville had listed; rather, he writes a sort of introduction to their treatment. He begins by focusing on what he considers to be the true reason for Grenville's request, his idea that 'a man is obleiged strictly and precisely at all times to doe that which in it self is absolutely best, and that there is always some action soe incumbent upon a man, soe necessary to be donne preferable to all others, that if that be omitted, a man certainly failes in his duty'.[54] Locke opposes three arguments to Grenville's view. First, such an obligation could not be reconciled with the practical realities of human life, where our duties are rarely so evident as to leave no doubt about the

---

[49] See John Donne, 'Sermon 65', in Donne 1839, 3, 151. The sentence is a quotation from Jer 10, 14.
[50] Locke, 'Study', in King 1830, 198.
[51] Denis Grenville to Locke, 2/12 March 1678, Locke 1976–1989, 1, 550.
[52] Locke to Denis Grenville, 13/23 March 1678, ibid., 555–560.
[53] See Bodleian Library, MS Locke f. 3, 69–79. Hereafter, I shall name as "Scrupulosity" the content of Locke's letter to Grenville of 13/23 March 1678.
[54] Locke to Denis Grenville, 13/23 March 1678, Locke 1976–1989, 1, 556.

rightness of an action. Second, such an obligation is starkly at odds with the infinite goodness of God, who, 'considering our ignorance and frailty, hath left us a great liberty' in matters not contrary to his fundamental laws. To always do our best, we should have to scrupulously consider all possible actions, 'even the minutest of them', and in doing so would waste time, to the detriment of other occupations. In addition, the need to reflect so carefully on what we ought to do would prevent us from being useful to others. In the end, 'we should never come to action'.[55]

Locke's third argument touches on our state of mediocrity.

> I have often thought that our state here in this world is a *State of Mediocrity* which is not capable of extreams though on one side or other of this mediocrity there might lie great excellency and perfection. Thus we are not capeable of continuall rest nor continuall exercise, though the later has certainly much more of excellency in it. We are not able to labour always with the body nor always with the mind. And to come to our present purpose, we are not capeable of liveing altogeather exactly by a strict rule, nor altogeather without one. not always retird nor always in company.[56]

Here Locke's idea of a state of mediocrity assumes a more definite shape. Intellectual mediocrity emerges as just one facet of a broader condition encompassing physical, moral, social, and political mediocrities. For example, the 'very moderate sovereignty' lauded in the *Two Treatises on Government* as the middle way between the excesses of anarchy and tyranny[57] gains its justification as an aspect of human mediocrity, as does the moderate sociability of human beings.[58] Mediocrity, we can now begin to see, is not only a state but also the foundation of a sort of super-ordinate moral norm, that guides and disciplines human efforts to live a good life. Over high aspirations for moral perfection are an excess to be avoided as is their opposite, a hopeless surrender to our ignorance of the good.

---

[55] Ibid., 559.   [56] Ibid.

[57] See Locke, "The Second Treatise", in Locke 1960. § 108, 358. Richard Ashcraft argued that mediocrity was the characteristic trait of Locke's description of the state of nature as a state of uncertainty and uneasiness: see R. Ashcraft 2010, 237. However, also the civil state represented for Locke a 'state of mediocrity', being not the opposite extreme. The law of nature continued to be the supreme rule in it; the defects of the state of nature were somehow amended in the civil state, but perfection was not attainable in this life.

[58] See Locke, "The Second Treatise", in Locke 1960. § 77, 318, where Locke affirmed that God 'made Man such a Creature' as to be under 'strong Obligations of Necessity, Convenience, and Inclination to drive him into Society, as well as fitted him with Understanding and Language to continue and enjoy it'. The mingling of terms like 'necessity' and 'convenience' with 'inclination', 'understanding', and 'language' suggest the idea of a moderate instinct of sociability. Solitude for Locke was not an unnatural condition for human beings: see Locke 1975, II. xxviii. 12, 357: 'Solitude many Men have sought, and been reconciled to.'

Both in 'Study' and 'Scrupulosity', the state of mediocrity only comes to the fore after Locke has highlighted the variable nature of the mean, in a manner reminiscent of Aristotle's teaching. 'Matters concerned with conduct and questions of what is good for us,' Aristotle had said, 'have no fixity'. These questions do 'not fall under any art or precept but the agents themselves must in each case consider what is appropriate to the occasion'.[59] As Aristotle presents it here, the mean not only differs from person to person, but also from situation to situation, and the second type of variation is also emphasized in 'Scrupulosity'. However, as in his earlier 'Study', Locke's attention shifts from the difficulty of determining the mean in any given case, to a different and more stable conception of mediocrity. As he now presents it, mediocrity is an ontological condition. As human beings, our capacities lie somewhere in the middle between perfection and imperfection, and this fact is a basic principle to which we need to adhere in every aspect of our lives. Viewed like this, the state of mediocrity provides a universal foundation for assessing our aims and actions that goes beyond our individual differences.

Locke presents the view he expresses in 'Scrupulosity' as somewhat original. Writing to Grenville, he describes it as an 'odd notion of mine', a 'phansy' which should not be viewed as 'a great argument in the case', being an idea of his own.[60] In fact, however, the idea that our state of mediocrity bears on many areas of life was widely present in seventeenth century debate. First of all, as a physician Locke would have been familiar with the ancient expression *in statu mediocritatis*, which was still employed in the medical literature of his time to identify either the state between illness and health, or the state of health.[61] But mediocrity also played a central part in the Christian analysis of social virtues, where it was almost unanimously associated with a condition between poverty and wealth. Following scriptural sources,[62] both Puritans and Anglicans lauded the 'financial' middle state as a condition preserving human beings from the excesses of pride and despair. The writings of Sir Matthew Hale epitomized this conviction: in *Jacob's vow*, he strongly recommended the 'state of mediocrity' between poverty and wealth as the 'quietest condition' in human life, a 'state of tranquility' free from the 'perturbations and temptations' afflicting the extremes.[63]

---

[59] Aristotle 2009, II. 2, 24.

[60] Locke to Denis Grenville, 13/23 March 1678, Locke 1976–1989 1, 559.

[61] See Lugt 2011, 13–46. See for instance, Lusitanus 1635, 101: 'Verumtamen nihil prohibit aliter supponere, & comparationem ducere non a redundantia sanguinis praeter naturam, sed ab statu mediocritatis, a quo si minuatur sanguinis, debilior aeger evadet'; Piquer 1762, 17: 'facile patet, naturam humanam Medicinae subjectum debere esse eam, qua posita, homo sanus existat, & qua deficiente, fiat aegrotans, eaque necessario consistere debet, in organica corporis structura, certis dispositionibus praedita, & determinatibus legibus subjecta, quae necessariae sint ad eius conservationem, in statu mediocritatis sustinendam'.

[62] In particular, Proverbs 30.8 (the Augur's prayer).

[63] See Hale 1805, 2, 173–177. Another example may be found in Brownrig 1661, 455: 'This *holy* man [the psalmist] makes *this prayer* against *too little*, or *too much*, 'tis *approbation Mediocritatis*, out of the *true estimate* of a state of *Mediocrity*'; 466: 'Riches, O, they are full of *snares*; Poverty, that hath its *temptations*; the state of *mediocrity*, and *competencie*, that's the *safest*.' Not all authors introduced the

98 HUMAN LIFE AS A STATE OF MEDIOCRITY IN JOHN LOCKE

Some years before, in a 1625 sermon, John Donne had also focused his attention on the financial middle state. He too had argued that the 'middle state' appeared to be the 'safest condition' in human life, provided that it was 'not so low as to be made the subject of oppression, nor so high as to be made the object of ambition'. But how should this state be described? This was the hard task, for Donne. Mediocrity might be said to correspond to a certain 'competency' urging man to better himself, but it was crucial that this ambition should not be poisoned by excessive self-confidence. As Donne explains the problem, 'God produced plants in Paradise therefore, that they may grow; God hath planted us in this world, that we might grow; and he that does not endeavour that by all lawful means, is inexcusable.' Yet it is pure vanity 'to imagine such a mediocrity, such a competency, such a sufficiency in myself, as that I may rest in that, that I think I may ride out all storms, all disfavours, that I have enough of mine own, wealth, health, or moral constancy, if any of these decay'.[64] Donne's idea of a 'middle state' not only emphasizes the importance of humility in Christian life, but also highlights the 'capacity' with which God has entrusted human beings, and which it is their duty to develop.

When Locke writes about the 'state of mediocrity' in 'Scrupulosity', he echoes Donne's emphasis on its implications for action, but develops them in an original way. God has given us a capacity for action, which is increased by our mediocrity: the middle state is a state of industry because of its being mediocre. Given their moderate sociability, moderate attitude towards restrictions, and moderate physical and mental strengths, humans are well suited to a middling way of life. Indeed, their mediocrity attests to God's benevolence: how could a compassionate God have wanted humans to be incessantly afflicted by scruples? Knowing their 'ignorance and frailty',[65] the Creator has given them 'great freedom' in all things indifferent, thus protecting them from the burden of continuous and unavoidable sin.

This positive view of the state of mediocrity is in sharp contrast with that found in the works of Pierre Nicole and Blaise Pascal, who exerted an enormous influence on Locke. During his residence in France, Locke studied these authors with the utmost attention, and their emphasis on human weakness is reflected for the first time in the journal notes he wrote during those years. Locke read several of Nicole's *Essais de morale* and translated three of them into English.[66] Included

---

idea of a state: in his *Sermons Preached upon Several Occasions*, 297, John Wilkins praised a 'virtuous mediocrity in the right use of our wealth, directing a man to a due measure, both in the acquiring and keeping of his estate, but chiefly in giving and disposing of it upon fitting occasions'. Wilkins 1682, 297.

[64] John Donne, 'Sermon 65', in Donne 1839, III, 151–152. Locke owned Donne's *Poems*: see Harrison and Laslett 1971, 126, no. 990.

[65] Locke to Denis Grenville, 13/23 March 1678, in Locke 1976–1989, 1 in 556.

[66] Locke owned various editions of the first four volumes of Nicole's *Essais*: volume 1 in both the first edition of 1671 and the fifth edition of 1679; volume 2 in the third edition of 1678; volumes 3 and 4 in their first edition respectively of 1675 and 1679. See Harrison and Laslett 1971, 192, nos. 2040, 2040a

in this trio was 'De la faiblesse de l'homme' (*The Weakness of Man*), where Nicole focuses on a series of characteristic Jansenist themes: the feebleness of man's faculties, the corrupted nature of human beings, and the brevity of human life. Nicole enlarges on our pride and vanity, our tendency to overestimate our intellectual and physical abilities, our frailty and ignorance, and our utter dependence on God who alone can raise us from a condition akin to that of beasts. 'Moins l'homme agit en homme, plus il est content. Les actions, où la raison a beaucoup de part, le lassent & l'incommodent, & sa pente est de se réduire autant qu'il peut à la condition des bêtes.'[67] Even the most perfect of men, blessed with divine grace, are in danger of losing themselves in their sins.

In 'Study' Locke echoes some of Nicole's opinions. Like Nicole, he claims that knowledge can be distinguished into three kinds (of words, history, and things), that human knowledge is limited and, most importantly, that humans have an 'instinctive knowledge' of the truth.[68] This conviction had already been expressed in the *Essays on the law of nature*, where Locke affirmed that natural law is in conformity with men's rational nature.[69] Despite his rejection of innate ideas, he maintained that reason naturally tends towards those truths that one must know in order to lead a good life, which constitute the substance of the law of nature. This tendency of human reason corresponded to the *naturalis inclinatio* towards the good and the truth which Aquinas had assigned to human beings,[70] and represented a substantial point of agreement between Nicole and Locke in 'Study'.

However, Locke's views about human weakness stand in sharp contrast to those of Nicole.[71] According to Nicole, our material needs, which we share with animals, and the small portion of truth that God has allowed us, serve to humiliate us and reduce us to a bestial level.[72] Moreover, it is only through this humiliation that our tendency to vainglorious presumption can be cured. Locke does not agree. His

---

and 2040b. Locke intended to publish his translation, but was forestalled by the appearance of a complete edition of Nicole's *Essais* in English in 1677–1680. See Lough 1953, 111 and 202 , Cranston 1957, 175–177, Woolhouse 2007, 128, 142, and especially Marshall 1997, 89–90, 131–137, 151–152, 157, 168, 178–186, 188–197, etc., who pays close attention to the first and the third of the three essays of Nicole that Locke translated. A mention of Nicole's *Essais* is in a journal note Locke wrote on July 29, 1676 (Locke 1936, 81–82).

[67] I quote from Yolton (ed.) 2000, 106; Yolton's book includes the 1677 edition of Nicole's *Essais*, the one Locke possessed. Locke's translation of this passage reads: 'Men are the more satisfied, the lesse they doe like men. These actions, where in reason beares a part, are irkesome to them. The inclination of man carrys him downwards, to bring him self, as neare as he can, to the condition of a beast.' See ibid., 107. Nicole had not mentioned man's inclination; he had affirmed that humans' *only concern* is to bring themselves as near as they can to the condition of animals.

[68] See Locke, 'Study', King, 1830, 194; Yolton (ed.) 2000, 78.   [69] Locke 1954, 111, 199f.

[70] Aquinas, *S. Th.*, q.94, art. 2. 1a2ae, q. 94, art. 2.

[71] Sometimes Locke modified Nicole's text so as to lessen its polemical verve: for example, Nicole affirmed 'Les discours ordinaires des hommes sont tous pleins des Eloges qu'ils se donnent les uns aux autres pour ces qualités d'esprit,' a sentence which Locke translated as 'The philosophie of the heathens is stuffd with elogies, of the nature of man, and the endowments of his minde.' See Yolton (ed.) 2000, 68–69.

[72] Ibid., 50: 'Tout ce que la vérité peut faire, est de nous humilier'; 66–67.

100 HUMAN LIFE AS A STATE OF MEDIOCRITY IN JOHN LOCKE

conception of mediocrity seems to emerge from a critical engagement with Nicole, which may in turn have been stimulated by his reading of Pascal, and particularly by Pascal's idea of a *milieu*.

Locke had a tremendous admiration for Pascal, as the *Essay concerning Human Understanding* reveals. Pascal, he writes, was one of 'those glorious Spirits' to whom God had been pleased to attribute some of his perfections, 'as far as created finite Beings can be capable'.[73] Locke's journal for 1677 confirms that he was reading Pascal's *Pensées*; and as one of his notes records, he was struck by Pascal's discussion of two extremes, the infinitely small and the infinitely great.[74] Pascal described the human condition as a *milieu*, a middle state between the two. Man, he says, is 'Un neant à l'égard de l'infiny; un tout à l'égard du neant, un milieu entre rien et tout.'—nothing in relation to the infinite, everything in relation to nothing, a mean between nothing and everything.[75] Here *milieu* has a pejorative sense; man's middle position precludes him from piercing the essences of phenomena, since he cannot hope to see into the workings of infinite greatness or of infinite smallness, and must therefore be satisfied with incomplete knowledge. However, in another fragment entitled 'Pyrronism', Pascal praises intellectual mediocrity as a worthy condition for human beings.

> L'extrême esprit est accusé de folie, comme l'extrême déffaut. Rien ne passe pour bon que la mediocrité. C'est la pluralité qui a establi cela, & qui mord quiconque s'en eschappe par quelque bout que ce soit. Je ne m'y obstineray pas; je consens qu'on m'y mette: & si je refuse d'estre au bas bout, ce n'est pas parce qu'il est bas, mais parce qu'il est bout; car je refuserois de mesme qu'on me mist au haut. C'est sortir de l'humanité, que de sortir du milieu: la grandeur de l'ame humaine consiste à sçavoir s'y tenir: & tant s'en faut que sa grandeur soit d'en sortir, qu'elle est à n'en point sortir.[76]

Excess, like defect of intellect, is accused of madness. Nothing is considered as good but mediocrity. The majority has settled that, and finds fault with him who escapes it at whichever end. I will not oppose it. I quite consent to put myself there, and refuse to be at the lower end, not because it is low, but because it is an end; for I would likewise refuse to be placed at the top. To leave the mean is to abandon

---

[73] See Locke 1975. II, x, 9, 154.

[74] See the note Locke wrote on February 8, 1677, 'Knowledg its extent & measure', in Locke 1936, 84–90.

[75] Pascal 1675, 176. This edition was in Locke's library (Harrison and Laslett 1971, 204, no. 2222a), along with the 1678 edition by G. Desprez (204, no. 2222). Locke also owned Filleau de la Chaise' *Discours sur les pensées de M. Pascal*, 1672 (204, no. 2223).

[76] This passage is to be found on page 276 of the 1678 edition by G. Desprez of Pascal's *Pensées*, which Locke owned (Harrison and Laslett 1971, 204, no. 2222), but not in the previous editions. The 1678 edition appeared too late to influence Locke's early conceptualization of mediocrity in 'Study'.

humanity. The greatness of the human soul consists in knowing how to preserve the mean. So far from greatness consisting in leaving it, it consists in not leaving it.

This eulogy to mediocrity is potentially deceptive. The intellectual mediocrity lauded by Pascal is not Montaigne's *juste milieu*, characterized by self-satisfaction, but rather the dramatic consequence of original sin. Through sin, humans are condemned to experience both the desire for knowledge that elevates them above animals, and the inability to bring this desire to fruition. Their middling condition is not a place where extremes can be reconciled, but a paradoxical expression of their irreconcilability. Locke's notion of mediocrity seems to release this tension. Humans are naturally suited to their mediocre state and can therefore be contented with it. Their imperfect knowledge does not condemn them to experience frustration, nor need it be a source of humiliation, but rather represents an opportunity for action that elevates them above animals.

At this stage of his intellectual development, Locke therefore stands by a conception of mediocrity that is strongly opposed to the pessimistic attitudes of Nicole and Pascal. Instead, he aligns himself with a more positive Christian conception of mediocrity, which is also strongly present in seventeenth-century debate. Mediocrity is indeed our lot; but within it we can cautiously extend our knowledge and learn to live more virtuously.

By the time he writes the *Essay*, however, Locke's view is changing. Our mediocrity, he comes to feel, is afflicted and unsettled by uneasiness, an idea that recalls Pascal's conception of the *milieu*. However, since the perfection that our moral knowledge can attain in this life redeems our state, our condition, as Locke continues to see it, is still not one of total degradation. This idea seems to begin to emerge in Locke's writings at the beginning of the eighties, in a letter to Damaris Cudworth.

4 Locke versus John Smith. Mediocrity and moral excellence

Locke seems to have discussed the view of mediocrity that he defends in 'Scrupulosity' with his friend Damaris Cudworth. This is suggested by the conclusion of her *Discourse concerning the Love of God*, where she writes,

> In short, our Natures are so suited to a mediocrity in all things, that we can scarce exceed in any kind with Safety, To be always busy in the Affairs of the World, or always shut up from them, cannot be born: Always Company, or always Solitude, are Dangerous: And so are any other Extreams.[77]

---

[77] Masham 2004), 126.

102 HUMAN LIFE AS A STATE OF MEDIOCRITY IN JOHN LOCKE

But the issue also comes up in a letter Locke wrote to her in 1682, replying to her request for his opinion of John Smith's *Select Discourses*. In his answer, Locke raises some objections to Smith's claim that there are four kinds of knowledge, corresponding to four types of men.[78] In Smith's view, individuals of a first type are unable to distinguish the voice of reason from that of the senses, and are consequently ruled by opinion and imagination. Those of a second type believe that the soul has a supremacy over the body and strive to follow the dictates of reason; but they easily fall prey to bodily passions. Individuals of a third kind are completely detached from sensuous appetites and aspire to a true knowledge of God, but are nevertheless easily diverted from virtue. Finally, a fourth kind are so devoted to contemplation that their souls are united with the divine essence. Locke objected that Smith's distinctions correspond to different 'degrees of the love of god and practice of virtue', rather than to different types of knowledge; it would be wrong, he declared, to claim knowledge of objects lying above man's reason. Instead, he proposed a threefold partition of mankind:

> I cannot quit my former division of men who either thinke as if they were only body and minde not soule or spirit at all, or those who in some cases at least thinke of themselves as all soule seperate from the commerce of the body and in those instances have only visions or more properly imaginations, and a third sort who considering themselves as made up of body and soule here and in a state of mediocrity make use and follow their reason.[79]

Members of the third of these groups who accept the mediocrity of the human state, represent the mean between the religious extremes of atheism and enthusiasm. In a note of the same period, Locke remarks that enthusiasm is an excess. Following out a suggestion made by Plutarch about the 'mediocre' nature of true religion, he explains that 'Enthusiasme is a fault in the minde opposite to bruitish sensuality as far in the other extreme exceeding the just measures of reason as thoughts groveling only in matter and things of sense come short of it.'[80] A right use of reason is therefore necessary if one is to hold to the mean between two forms of irreligion.[81]

---

[78] See Smith 1660, 17–20.

[79] Locke to Damaris Cudworth, c. 21 February 1682, Locke 1976–1989, 2, no. 687, 488; this is a partial copy of the letter. The full text is in Locke 1936, 123–125. The 'former division' might be that in a journal note for 20 February 1682, which focused on the different beliefs regarding the immortality of the soul (a topic which Smith treated in the fourth of his *Discourses*). See ibid., 121–123.

[80] The note was written on 19 February 1682; see Locke 1936, 121.

[81] In *On Superstition*, Plutarch had affirmed that the true religion lies between the extremes of superstition and atheism, for 'atheism is falsified reason, and superstition is an emotion engendered from false reason'. See Plutarch, 1928, 2, 458. Plutarch associated the Aristotelian notion of the mean with values originally quite foreign to it.

In the same letter, Locke also discusses two further aspects of mediocrity, the first of which concerns our dual nature. Smith had claimed that men belonging to his third kind are 'continually flying off from the Body', trying to escape a union of body and soul that impedes the growth of their knowledge. Commenting on this view, Locke condemns it as an example of enthusiasm. The union of body and soul, he argues, is essential to the proper working of reason. Diverting our thoughts from the sensible world and concentrating 'more on heavenly objects' cannot lead to knowledge, and will only produce opinions and persuasions without any rational foundation.[82] To appreciate our state of mediocrity is therefore to recognize that we are embodied creatures, whose reasoning should focus on the sensible world.

Turning to a further aspect of mediocrity, Locke considers Smith's first category of humans, who cannot distinguish reason from the senses. These 'Complex and Multifarious' men are 'made up of Soul and Body' and have 'Knowledge wherein Sense and Reason are so twisted up together, that it cannot easily be unravel'd'.[83] But where Smith regards such human beings as deficient, Locke argues that, once we take account of our mediocrity, we can save ourselves from at least some of the errors that arise from our senses and imagination, and also from the opposite mistake of aspiring to a form of perfection that is beyond us. At least where speculative knowledge is concerned, humans of Smith's fourth kind are, so Locke contends, an enthusiastic fantasy, typical of 'Visionarys'.[84] In practical matters, however, the conclusion is different. As Locke admits, men endowed with 'Seraphyke love and Heroick virtue', whose lives attest to 'great degrees of Excellency and perfection', do exist.[85] In a journal entry for 1676 he had already noted this in reference to humans' ability to love: there are some men of an 'excellent make' who are delighted with 'the existence and happiness of all good men', and even with that of all humanity.[86] They exceed the average human capacity for love.

As Locke has so far presented it, our state of mediocrity prevents us from achieving moral excellence. Here, however, he begins to make space for this capacity. This important shift prefigures a series of changes in Locke's position that emerge more fully in the *Essay concerning Human Understanding*. Despite the deep pessimism about human nature, which is deprived it of its instinctive knowledge of the truth and placed in a state of constant uneasiness, the *Essay* endows humans with the ability to acquire perfect moral knowledge.

---

[82] Locke 1936, 124.   [83] Smith 1660, 17.   [84] Locke 1936, 125.   [85] Ibid.

[86] John Locke, 'Pleasure and Pain. The Passions', in Locke 1954, 266. Here Locke distinguishes between four sorts of people, according to their way of loving others: this fourfold distinction might have been inspired by Smith.

5 The state of mediocrity in the *Essay*

The state of mediocrity is mentioned twice in the fourth book of the *Essay*, towards the very end of the work. This position appears to be strategic, since Locke has by then already dwelt on the limits of human understanding, both of natural and divine things. The mechanism of sensation, the cohesion and divisibility of matter, and the communication of motion baffle our capacities, and the real essences of things are inaccessible to our human faculties. God's attributes, substance and infinity are 'incomprehensible', as is the nature of finite spiritual substances.[87] Moreover, the secrets of the things beyond and above us appear to be impenetrable, as Caecilius had claimed in the *Octavius*. Knowledge of the physical world can only be enhanced 'by Experience and History'; this is 'all that the weakness of our Faculties in this State of *Mediocrity*, which we are in this World, can attain to'.[88]

Our intellectual mediocrity therefore has a catastrophic impact on natural philosophy, which can never become a science. Although experiment and observation may improve the 'conveniences of life', they cannot disclose the essence of things. But we are better placed to attain moral knowledge. In *Essay* IV, xii, Locke opposes our stagnant comprehension of substances to the certainty we can attain in the moral domain. In this domain, our knowledge can achieve the same level of certainty as mathematics, so that learning about morality represents '*the proper Science, and Business of Mankind in general*'.[89] Here, too, our mediocrity is not a disadvantage. Rather than adversely affecting our capacity for moral knowledge, it is instrumental in highlighting how much human beings are suited to this kind of enquiry, being 'both concerned, and fitted to search out their *Summum Bonum*'. Although Locke no longer sees them as endowed with an instinctive knowledge of the truth—a talent which is banned from the *Essay*, where human's only natural inclination is towards happiness—they may still achieve full scientific knowledge of their duties.

In a subsequent, very short chapter of the *Essay* devoted to judgement, Locke returns to this idea. God has given human beings only a 'Taste of what intellectual Creatures are capable of, to excite in us a Desire and Endeavour after a better State'. He has

> afforded us only the twilight, as I may so say, of *Probability*, suitable, I presume, to that State of Mediocrity and Probationership, he has been pleased to place us in here; wherein to check our over-confidence and presumption, we might by every day's Experience be made sensible of our short-sightedness and liableness

---

[87] Locke repeats this several times: see Locke 1975, I, iv, 15, p. 93; I, iv, 17, p. 95; II, i, 15, 113; II, xiii, 18, 174; II, xv, 8, p. 200; II, xvii, 2, p. 210; II, xxiii, 33, p. 314; etc.
[88] Ibid., IV, xii, 10.   [89] Ibid., IV, xii, 11, 646.

to Error; the Sense whereof might be a constant Admonition to us, to spend the days of this our Pilgrimage with Industry and Care, in the search, and following of that way, which might lead us to a State of greater Perfection.[90]

For the first time, the state of mediocrity is associated with desire or uneasiness, the painful sensation caused by 'the absence of any thing, whose present enjoyment carries the *Idea* of Delight with it'.[91] Happiness consists in a complete removal of uneasiness, which, however, is impossible in this 'imperfect State', as Locke explains, because of the 'multitude of wants, and desires, we are beset with'.[92] By placing us in a mediocre state, God intended to arouse the desire for a better condition in us. (This idea is reminiscent of the Pauline Epistles,[93] of Augustine and Pascal.) Uneasiness should prompt us to act morally, in order to obtain the greatest good which is our true happiness. The 'pursuit of true and solid happiness' is 'the highest perfection of intellectual nature', Locke claims.[94] The state of mediocrity provides further assistance in this, being a state of apprenticeship.

Clearly, Locke thinks that the middle state is a condition with which to be contented, despite being characterized by uneasiness, weakness, and error. The paradoxical nature of Pascal's *milieu* is extraneous to it. Locke's disagreement with traditional views of original sin in *The Reasonableness of Christianity* finds another expression in his description of the state of mediocrity; the goodness and justice of God cannot be reconciled either with the idea that all people are subject to eternal punishment because of Adam, or with a view of human life as a miserable, humiliating condition. The middle state is the ingenious work of the divine architect, who has harmoniously disposed the various species of creatures in the chain of being and assigned an intermediate position to man.[95] Each step in the chain has its own degree of perfection, and morality is the perfection proper to the state of mediocrity. Human beings are naturally suited to this state, Locke insists in the *Essay*. If they have not been endowed with 'Microscopical eyes' or more acute senses by their Creator,[96] it is because these might have hindered their capacity to strive for moral perfection.

---

[90] Ibid., IV, xiv, 2, 652.   [91] Ibid., II, xx, 6, 230.

[92] See ibid., II, xxi, 46, 263. Happiness could only be mediocre on earth: the 'extreme' happiness which Locke described as the supreme end of human life would be enjoyed after death, since it was the 'immoderate' state the apostle Paul spoke of, 'what Eye hath not seen, Ear hath not heard, nor hath it entered into the Heart of Man to conceive'.

[93] Cfr. 2 Cor. 5, 2: ' For in this [condition] we groan, earnestly desiring to be clothed with our habitation which is from heaven.' Locke would comment on this passage in his *A Paraphrase and notes on the Epistles of St Paul*. See Locke 1987, 1, 284, note 4.

[94] Locke 1975, II, xxi, 51, 266.   [95] Ibid., III, vi, 12, 447.   [96] Ibid., II, xxiii, 12, 303.

5

Learning to Live a Human Life

Lisa Shapiro

There is a stark contrast between life and death: things come into existence and persist—they live—as the things they are, and then they die, or go out of existence. In this paper, my aim is not to explore this metaphysical distinction, but rather to focus on the *living* of a human life. For once we are alive, our existence is not static. Human beings, like other living things, develop, and this fact that we change over time is part of our essence. This development can be physiological, as we grow and mature and age, it can be moral, as we cultivate good habits of action and interaction, or virtues, but it can also be the development of understanding, of the world and of just what kind of thing we are.

A central part of our development involves learning. We *learn* how to move ourselves and manoeuvre our bodies, we *learn* how to live well, and we *learn* how to think. The discussions around learning in the early modern period promise to be particularly interesting if only because of efforts at educational reform of the period. The Jesuits overhauled the French education system in the early seventeenth century, beginning with their flagship *collège* at La Fleche, and writings on the proper form of education proliferate in England and France in the second half of that century. John Milton's 1644 letter to Samuel Hartlib on education, which was published, is responsive to a movement to reform education of children in England,[1] Hartlib himself in 1646 publishes a guide for presbyters, elders, and deacons to educate poor children, and there are many dozens of published sermons with similar themes. The philosophical thinking about what it is to learn no doubt informed and were responsive to these discussions, as Locke's *Some Thoughts Concerning Education*, originally published in 1693 (Locke 1989), surely is. Philosophical thought about learning is also of interest because of its focus on women's education, in particular by so many women thinkers of the period. That discussion can be traced from a short argument in Marie de

---

[1] Milton's suggested reforms are designed to bring children closer to God by starting from a foundation of basics—instruction in languages, and grammar—before moving to classical literature and poetry, and then gradually moving to more abstract subjects, like Geometry and Historical Physiology, then the application of those sciences to practical matters, and ultimately to morals, law and politics. He concludes his letter by focusing on the importance of physical activity, in particular sport like fencing and wrestling, as well as travel and diet, for insuring that the children grown into healthy and well-rounded adults.

Lisa Shapiro, *Learning to Live a Human Life* In: *Life and Death in Early Modern Philosophy*. Edited by: Susan James, Oxford University Press. © Lisa Shapiro 2021. DOI: 10.1093/oso/9780192843616.003.0006

Gournay's *De l'égalité des hommes et des femmes*, originally published in 1622 (Gournay 2002a), to Anna Maria van Schurman's *Dissertatio De Ingenii Muliebris ad Doctrinam et meliores Litteras aptitudine*, published in 1641 (Schurman 1641), to Bathsua Makin's appropriation of that work in her *Essay to Revive the Antient Education of Gentlewomen* (Makin 1673), to François Poulain de la Barre's *Discours physique et moral de l'égalité des deux sexes*, originally published in 1673 (Poulain 2011), and followed by *De l'éducation des dames pour la conduite de l'esprit dans les sciences et dans les moeurs*, originally published in 1674) (Poulain 2011)[2] to Mary Astell's *A Serious Proposal to the Ladies*, the first part of which was published in 1694, with the second part following in 1697. (Astell 2002), just to note some highlights.[3] It seems clear that philosophical thought about learning had real practical impact, an impact comparable to that of philo-sophical thought about matter on natural philosophy. In this paper, I explore how philosophers of the period conceive of learning, how that conception intertwines with models of education, and how it ties into what can only be characterized as a movement to educate women in particular.

I focus on discussions that take the overarching aim of the education of human beings to teach us both that we are free and how to use that freedom well. At the same time that central lesson occurs against a background of the institution of education itself, inculcating customs and habits in students. A central question thus arises about how custom and habit, which are in many ways are not only apparently antithetical to our freedom but also interfere with our understanding that we are free, are integral to our learning how to live a fully human—free—life, and to leading it well.

I begin with Descartes. For Descartes, it is clear, the will is essential to what it is to be human, and we human beings need to learn both that we are freely willing and to use that will well. But how we learn these things is less clear. While the *Meditations* paint a picture of us as independent learners or autodidacts, Descartes's own pseudo-biographical remarks in the *Discourse on the Method for Rightly Conducting Reason* suggests a more complicated picture, one in which custom and habit play might ineliminable roles in our recognition of our own freedom. Locke's account in his *Some Thoughts concerning Education* can help to flesh out just what these roles might be. For Descartes and for Locke, however, finding freedom within the context of habituation seems a relatively straightfor-ward matter. The Cartesian François Poulain de la Barre problematizes that idea. While he agrees with Descartes that the exercise of free will comes against a background of custom and habit, he does not find overcoming the force of custom

---

[2] Followed in 1675 by the peculiar *De l'excellence des hommes contre l'égalité des sexes* (Poulain 2011).

[3] Desmond Clarke's excellent edition of Gournay, van Schurman, and Poulain's essay on the equality of sexes in *The Equality of the Sexes: Three Feminist Texts of the Seventeenth Century* (Clarke 2013) lays bare a part of the story of the lines of influence.

108 LEARNING TO LIVE A HUMAN LIFE

quite so straightforward. Nonetheless, for him, as for Descartes, it does not seem as if willing is something that can be taught to us by others. Mary Astell recognizes that the ways in which custom can interfere systematically with our leading a fully human life, and is faced with the daunting task not only of reforming the education through which we learn to direct our own power but also in convincing women that their education has been sorely lacking, and indeed interferes with their ability to be recognize and exercise their will.

1 Descartes on the nature of a human being: the centrality of the will

For Descartes, that human beings have a free will is constitutive of our nature along three dimensions. The will is the fulcrum on which our capacity for knowledge turns; it is the source of our authority or ownership of our actions, including our thoughts; and it is the proper source of our self-esteem. That having knowledge depends on our will is clear from the diagnosis of our errors in both the Fourth Meditation and the *Principles of Philosophy*. It is the nature of the will to be inclined towards the true (and the good), and so if our ideas are 'sufficiently clear' we will experience 'a great inclination in the will' (AT 7:59; CSM 2:41)[4] to believe what we perceive. We can succeed in arriving at the truth if we use the will well, affirming those ideas perceived clearly and distinctly perceived. If, however, we are not so compelled, but are rather indifferent—pulled in one direction by some reasons, pushed in the opposite direction by other ones—we misuse the will if we do anything but withhold judgement. In the *Principles* Descartes notes that 'the supreme perfection of man' is that 'he acts voluntarily, that is, freely, and that this makes him in a special way the author of his actions and deserving of praise for what he does.' (Pr.1.37; AT 8A:18; CSM 1:205). This idea that our actions are owned by us is expressed in the conclusion to the Fourth Meditations, an affirmation of the newly discovered method for avoiding error: 'if, whenever I have to make a judgement, I restrain my will so that extends to what the intellect clearly and distinctly reveals, and no further, then it is quite impossible for me to go wrong' (AT 7:62; CSM 2:43). That this resolution involves an exercise of will upon itself—a willing to use one's will well—signals that the adoption of the

---

[4] Descartes's works are cited internally to refer to Descartes' *Oeuvres Completes* (Descartes 1997), edited by Paul Adam and Charles Tannery and the standard translation of his philosophical works (Descartes 1984-1991), edited and translated by John Cottingham, Robert Stoothof, and Dugald Murdoch (with Anthony Kenny who also edited the third volume). The internal parenthetical notations are as follows: AT [Volume of Descartes 1997]: page; CSM [Volume of Descartes 1984–1991]: page). When there is no reference to Descartes 1984–1991, the translation is my own. I use the following abbreviations to refer to specific works of Descartes contained in those volumes: Pr: *Principles of Philosophy* (followed by part and article number, for instance, Pr.1.37). PA: *Passions of the Soul* (followed by article number, for instance, PA a.153).

method is taken with self-awareness and so is an action that is properly one's own. That our exercise of will is distinctively our own makes it the proper source of self-esteem, as is clear from the definition of generosity in the *Passions of the Soul*. There, Descartes writes:

> . . . true generosity, which makes a man esteem himself as much as he legitimately can, consists only in part that he knows that there is nothing that truly belongs to him but this free disposition of his will, and that the only reason that he ought to be praised or blamed is that he uses it well or badly, and in part in that he feels in himself a firm and constant resolution to use it well, which is to say, never to lack the will to undertake and execute all those things which he judges to be the best.
> (PA a. 153, AT 11:445–446; CSM: II.384)

We can, however, describe features of the will without fully understanding that we ourselves have a free will. Descartes's exchange with Pierre Gassendi in the Fifth Objections and Replies (published with Descartes's *Meditations*) brings this issue to the fore. In his Objections, Gassendi is concerned about Descartes's account of the will and in particular about his conception of the will's indifference as being pushed and pulled in opposite directions by competing reasons. Descartes replies by simply asserting:

> I am not prepared to set about proving [these propositions] here. These are the sorts of things that each of us ought to know by experience in his own case, rather than by having to be convinced of them by rational argument; and you, O Flesh, do not seem to attend to the actions the mind performs within itself. You may be unfree, if you wish; but I am certainly very pleased with my freedom since I experience it within myself.   (AT 7:377; CSM 1:259)

From Gassendi's perspective, this response would not seem to be on point. Part of Descartes's point, however, is that no definition of the will by a set of propositions will be sufficient. Rather, it seems, our understanding of the will must derive from knowledge of our own freedom, that which truly belongs to us, and on the basis of which we can be morally evaluated, and that knowledge is grounded in our own experience of exercising our will. Descartes goes on to remark to Gassendi that he does think Gassendi is free, but is simply failing to notice his own demonstration of that freedom—denial of Descartes's views. If he were simply to notice just what he was doing, Descartes implies, Gassendi would learn the nature of his own freedom. These remarks reflect Descartes's reasons for his self-conscious adoption of the method of analysis in the *Meditations*, as described in the Second Replies:

> the true way by means of which the thing was discovered methodically and as it were *a priori*, so that if the reader is willing to follow it and give sufficient

110   LEARNING TO LIVE A HUMAN LIFE

attention to all points, *he will make the thing his own and understand it just as perfectly as if he had discovered it for himself.*

(AT 7:155, CSM 2:110, emphasis added)

Descartes is thus pointing Gassendi to do just what the meditator himself has done: to recognize that in denying he has acted voluntarily, and then to use that exercise of will to discover the nature of his own freedom and what it is to use that will well.

The meditator, however, seems to discover the will as if by accident. In the First Meditation, the meditator moves 'to turn my will in completely the opposite direction and deceive myself, by pretending for a time that these former opinions are utterly false and imaginary' (AT 7:22; CSM 1:15), resisting his habitual former beliefs by denying rather than affirming them.[5] He then, simply through self-examination, learns just what the nature of the will is and so how to use his will well. In some sense, despite Descartes's efforts to direct his attention, Gassendi still has to learn for himself that he is free and so the nature of the will.

The meditator is presented as an autodidact. He turns away from his previous beliefs, the habits of thought that have been inculcated in him, and is left with simple reflection—his own nature as a thinking thing. The suggestion is that simply through this reflection he can learn, essentially teaching himself, everything he needs to know, his own nature as a thinking thing, and both what that nature depends upon (namely, God) and what it implies. Someone else can perhaps point out what ought to be attended to, as Descartes does with Gassendi, but he would be hard pressed to teach what needs to be learned. Just as Gassendi needs to learn for himself, so too do each of us. The real way to learn, it appears, is to be self-taught.[6]

There is, however, in the background the suggestion that things may not be so simple. Descartes's reply to Gassendi takes Gassendi's denial of Descartes's account of the will as evidence of his freedom, and in the body of the *Meditations*, the meditator recognizes that he has a will in denying his habitual beliefs. One does not learn that one is free *ex nihilo*, but rather somehow by rejecting something that is given.

---

[5] In the *Principles* I.6, the paradigmatic act of will is that of withholding assent rather than denial: 'We have free will, enabling us to withhold our assent in doubtful matters and hence avoid error' (AT 8A:6, CSM 1:194).

[6] Anna Maria van Schurman's *Dissertatio* (Schurman 1641 and in translation in Clarke 2013) can be seen as written in this vein. As a series of syllogisms demonstrating that it is fitting for a Christian woman to be educated, it enacts what it aims to prove, and so provides evidence of a woman's natural ability to reason (though this is not quite the same as willing for her). Insofar as the work presupposes that women are uneducated, the author presents herself as self-taught, an autodidact.

2 The *Discourse*: a more complicated picture

The autobiographical remarks in Parts I and II of Descartes's *Discourse on Method* appear to provide an early version of the autodidact narrative. Through his travels and reflection on his experience, Descartes, as he characterizes it, 'gradually freed myself from many errors which may obscure our natural light and make us less capable of heeding reason' (AT 6:10, CSM 1:116). He holes himself up 'alone in a stove-heated room' so as to be 'completely free to converse with myself about my own thoughts' (AT 6:11; CSM 1:116) and becomes resolved 'get rid of' 'the opinions to which I had hitherto given credence' 'all at one go' (AT 6:13; CSM 1:117). From there, he goes on to develop the method for rightly conducting his own reason that, through the work, he shares with others. Moreover, he insists that he is putting forward his method not so much to teach what he has learned, but as a model from which his readers can learn something they might want to teach themselves:

> I am presenting this work only as a history, or if you prefer, a fable, in which among certain examples worthy of imitation, you will perhaps also find many others that it would be right not to follow.   (AT 6:4; CSM 1:112)[7]

However, in the telling of the story, Descartes begins with his own education, one centred on letters, and it is quite striking just how long Descartes goes on about it, what he was taught in school and the customs in which he was inculcated. As Descartes tells it here, he 'did not, however, cease to value the exercises done in the Schools' (AT 6:5; CSM 1:113). Languages, fables, history, reading good books, oratory, poetry, mathematics, morals, philosophy, jurisprudence, medicine and the other sciences all have some value—languages are required to read works of the ancients, fables awaken the mind, histories help shape judgement, oratory and poetry provide aesthetic pleasures, mathematics serves the arts, morals exhort us to seek virtue, philosophy, jurisprudence, medicine and the other science benefit our reputation and status in society—even if they are 'full of superstition and falsehood' (AT 6:6; CSM 1:113). If his education did leave him full of doubt, cognizant of his ignorance, with the thought that 'as soon as I was old enough to emerge from the control of my teachers, I entirely abandoned the study of letters' (AT 6:9; CSM 1:115) and having 'learned not to believe too firmly anything of which I had been persuaded only by example and custom,' (AT 6:10; CSM 1:116),

---

[7] Indeed, Descartes is at pains to insist that he has never had plans to teach anyone: 'my plan has never gone beyond trying to reform my own thoughts and construct them upon a foundation which is all my own'. (AT 6:15; CSM 1:118). His insistence that the foundation of his thoughts is his own suggests that we can only be the author of our own thoughts if we to teach ourselves.

112 LEARNING TO LIVE A HUMAN LIFE

one wonders why we are presented with such a longwinded summary of his schooling.

There is a suggestion that there is a real sense in which he never would have discovered his method without that education, that is, without his having been suitably acculturated, having read a set of texts taken to have played an important role in forming the community of which he is a part, being given the tools to help address the problems his community faces, and learning the rules that govern that community. This suggestion is borne out in other remarks in the *Discourse*. Descartes remains quite careful in circumscribing just what he aims to unseat. He pointedly denies advocating for radical political upheaval (AT 6:13), or even reform (AT 6:14–15), and disavows recommending to 'reform the body of the sciences or the established order of teaching them in the schools' (AT 6:13; AT 1:117). Equally, the first of the maxims in the *morale provisoire* set out in Part Three of the *Discourse*, also assigns a positive value to custom, asserting that one ought

> to obey the laws and customs of my country, holding constantly to the religion in which by God's grace I had been instructed from my childhood, and governing myself in all other matters according the most moderate and least extreme opinions.   (AT 6:23; CSM 1:122)

The second and third maxims of the *morale* put the use of will front and centre, the second resolving to be firm and decisive in acting in the way judged to be the best and the third to master oneself—that is, one's thoughts and one's will—rather than the order of the world.[8] These latter maxims can perhaps be read as dependent on the first.

However, the question remains of how his ability to learn for himself, to own his thoughts, depends on the prior customs and habits taught to him by others. Certainly, acculturation and education gives us the language through which to express our thoughts, and through our discursive capacity we come to be able to reflect on those thoughts, to consider the possibility that they might be false, and to decide to disbelieve what one has formerly believed. This point is consistent with Descartes's position that language is central to distinguishing human beings from other animals. Education also exposes us to an array of different events and experiences, attitudes towards the commonplace and the extraordinary, problems that one has never imagined or encountered and means of addressing them. This expansion of one's experience from the local context might well afford the opportunity to notice differences between the ways in which one lives and those

---

[8] Descartes defines virtue as being resolved to do what one judges to be the best. See for instance his letters to Elisabeth of 4 August 1645 (AT 4:265) and 1 September 1645 (AT 4:284). See also *Passions of the Soul* a. 148 (AT 11:142).

described in what one has been studying. Remarking these differences in turn can engender the imagination that things might well be otherwise, and that one might do otherwise. The study of logic and mathematics help in identifying and resolving problems, and through these studies one learns the norms of rationality, with the ability to identify faulty syllogisms and miscalculations. These skills help us in formulating choices clearly, and so to recognize that we have choices. We thus do depend on our education for all the tools that we use, the background we need, in order to exercise our will.[9]

These explanations, however, are not entirely satisfactory. All we need to demonstrate our freedom is the opportunity to deny something. That object of denial need not have been institutionalized in an educational context. We could still conceivably, on this line, be raised by wolves and manage to discover for ourselves that we are free (at some point, after all, it would occur to us that we are not wolves).

3 John Locke and the role of habit

As I noted at the outset, writings detailing the standard education in England are easy to come by. Invariably, readers are presented with a set of prescriptions of what to study, what order to study it in, the course of exercise and diet, and so on, but with little explanation of why this course rather than any other. John Locke's *Some Thoughts Concerning Education*,[10] however, does provide a justification for the course of education and through it we can see that there is a more intimate connection between custom and habit and our recognition of our being freely willing. According to Locke, education should instil the habits that promote virtue:

> [t]he great thing to be minded in education is what *habits* you settle: and therefore in this, as all other things, do not begin to make anything *customary* practice whereof you would not continue and increase.   (STCE §18)

His account provides insight into just how far-reaching educational efforts at inculcating habits are. He begins by considering matters of the body and health—

---

[9] Marie de Gournay offers an argument in her essay 'On the Equality of Men and Women' (Gournay 2002a and in translation in Clarke 2013 and Gournay 2002b) about the important role differences in education play in explaining the differences between Italian women (cloistered and inexperienced) and English and French women (active in the world) and similarly their male counterparts (Italian men are well educated, while French and English men are not) showing that differences in apparent rationality are not natural but the result of education

[10] I cite *Some Thoughts Concerning Education* (Locke 1989) internally as STCE followed by paragraph number.

114 LEARNING TO LIVE A HUMAN LIFE

what exposure children should have to fresh air, how much exercise, sleep, what to eat and drink, what clothes to wear—before he turns to matters of the mind. Physical activity, clothing, food cultivate a set of bodily habits that will 'endure hardships' and serve a child well as he grows into an adult, travels to different regions and even countries, and, most significantly, develops his understanding. The development of the habits of mind serve a similar purpose, but here the hardships that the mind must learn to endure in cultivating virtue are those of his own desires:

> And the great principle and foundation of all virtue and worth is placed in this, that a man is able to *deny himself* his own desires, cross his own inclinations, and purely follow what reason direct as best though the appetite lean the other way.
> (STCE §33)

As Locke sees things, human beings are driven by our uneasiness in feeling the absence of those things which give us pleasure: we desire to remove that uneasiness, and so regain our feelings of satisfaction and joy (ECHU 2.20.6).[11] But these desires need not themselves conform to reason, and we need to learn early to deny ourselves the satisfaction of our errant desires. The role of education is to inculcate in us early the habits of this denial:

> It seems plain to me that the principle of all virtue and excellency lies in a power of denying ourselves the satisfaction of our own desires where reason does not authorize them. *This power is to be got and improved by custom, made easy and familiar by an early practice.*   (STCE §38; emphasis added)[12]

It is important, for Locke, that children not be told what they ought to do, provided with rules that they are to commit to memory and be obliged to follow, but rather that they be trained to do what they ought to by practising the routine:

> This method of teaching children by a repeated practice, and the same action done over and over again under the eye and direction of the tutor till they have got the habit of doing it well, and not by relying on *rules* trusted to their memories, has so many advantages whichever way we consider it that I cannot but wonder (if ill customs could be wondered at in anything) how it could possibly be so much neglected   (SCTE §66)

---

[11] Locke's *Essay Concerning Human Understanding* (Locke 1975) is cited internally as ECHU Book. Chapter.Paragraph.

[12] See also: The habit of resisting 'the importunity of *present pleasure or pain* for the sake of what reason tells him is fit to be done … is the true foundation of future ability and happiness'. (STCE §45)

It's not that explanations and the setting of rules have no place. Children are, Locke recommends, to be 'treated as rational creatures' and offered motivations to act in a way that accords with their age and understanding (SCTE §81). But the best means of instruction, he notes, is simply to 'set before their eyes the *examples* of those things you would have them do or avoid' (STCE §82), both by providing models of the actions expected by the child, but also by securing a tutor who, in his every action, sets a good example. Once good habits and customs are instilled, children are then open to learning (STCE §147), and Locke outlines a programme that includes: reading, writing, drawing, French, Latin, geography, arithmetic, chronology, history, geometry, astronomy, ethics, law, rhetoric, logic, natural philosophy, dancing, music, fencing, trade, painting, gardening, and joinery.

On the face of it, it seems that Locke's view that education consists in the instilling proper habits runs counter to the role I have been suggesting it plays in Descartes's *Discourse*. There is little room, for the development of freely willing human beings insofar as we are all to be schooled in how we ought to conduct ourselves, fully inculcated into the manners, customs and habits that are fitting to our positions. Yet as with Descartes, for Locke the exercise of will involves denying something that is given to us. In the *Essay Concerning Human Understanding* he writes:

> Volition, it is plain is an act of the mind knowingly exerting that dominion it takes itself to have over any part of the man, by employing it in, or withholding it from, any particular action. (ECHU 2.21.15)

And that we have this volition is central to his account of human nature. It seems then that the two must be reconciled.

We can see education, on his account, as providing precursors to the exercise of volition. As we have seen, Locke explicitly conceives of a good education as teaching us to deny our desires, the motivations that our nature has given us. This denial, however, is not achieved explicitly. Telling a child to sit still and pay attention will do little good. Instead, the child has to learn the habit of rechanneling his energy to focus on a single activity. The acquisition of this habit is hardly voluntary, but that is because the child is not *knowingly* redirecting his desires. But the instilling of the habit, nonetheless, gives him practice in denying his desires, so that, when he does actively will to do one thing rather than another, he can exercise his will without difficulty. Education, as Locke details it not only provides the tools we need to exercise our will, it also provides us with a kind of practice in denying what has been given to us. Insofar as we have come into the habits of refusing the satisfaction of our desires and redirecting them, we are preparing to knowingly choose to do or not to do something, whether that be believing or some other action.

116 LEARNING TO LIVE A HUMAN LIFE

This account of the role our education plays in facilitating our exercising our will, and so in realizing our nature as human beings, also helps to hone the question of how we learn that we have a will in the first place. Descartes's suggestion that we can only learn of our will on our own leaves that discovery as somewhat of a mystery. We either figure it out, or, like Gassendi, we do not. The role of habituation I am suggesting Locke's account of education plays in preparing us to will pinpoints where the mystery lies. How do we move from being habituated to denying our desires to *knowingly* making a choice, typically, in the first instance, denying something we have taken for granted? That is, how do we move to knowingly reject the habits to which we have been accustomed? Locke himself says little in this regard. Indeed, Descartes makes it seems relatively easy to recognize that one has a free will. One inevitably becomes disenchanted with the way one was brought up, and it just happens that one decides to do otherwise. Maybe this exercise of will is relatively conservative—as noted, Descartes pointedly refrains from questioning the political system in any way, and equally from challenging the educational system and the body of knowledge it teaches, only challenging his own beliefs. And maybe since the role of the philosopher inevitably involves raising objections, for us who are so habituated to thinking otherwise, it can seem easy. But it is important to recognize that it is often not easy to call into question one's habits, especially if they are deeply entrenched and serve to structure our everyday lives.

4 Poulain de la Barre: the force of prejudice

The Cartesian François Poulain de la Barre recognizes this point. In the preface to his *A Physical and Moral Discourse concerning the Equality of Both Sexes*, published in 1673 Poulain notes the points worthy of imitation in the fable Descartes presented his readers, calling into question traditional education, the pursuit of truth as individuals, examining one's own beliefs, noting and correcting one's prejudices.[13] For Poulain, a prejudice is not simply a false belief, though it is also that. 'Prejudice' is a technical term, referring to judgements we make unreflectively, that is, without examination that are 'entrenched' or solidified, inculcated through habit and custom, and so serve to structure our understanding of the world around us. These prejudices are not simply the inevitable consequence of

---

[13] 'The best idea that may occur to those who try to acquire genuine knowledge, if they were educated according to traditional methods, is to doubt if they were taught well and to wish to discover the truth themselves. As they make progress in this search for truth, they cannot avoid noticing that we are full of prejudices, and that it is necessary to get rid of them completely in order to acquire clear and distinct knowledge.' (TFT, 119) I use the translations in Clarke 2013, cited internally as TFT followed by page number.

our imperfect knowledge, but rather are akin to, in contemporary terms, implicit biases.[14] This becomes clear through his illustration.

Poulain takes the Cartesian method to be invaluable for eradicating these prejudices (something, as noted, that Descartes himself refuses to apply it to). To illustrate its value in this regard, he aims to select one particular opinion that seems to be held universally and so must be true, is in fact a prejudice, and ill-founded. The opinion on which he focuses is the inequality of the sexes:

> Among all the prejudices, no one has found a more appropriate one with which to illustrate my thesis than that which commonly accepts about the inequality of the sexes.   (TFT, 120)

The only basis for this belief, Poulain aims to show, is 'custom and superficial experiences,' and that it is because of way that 'women have been dominated and excluded from the sciences and from public life' that they appear to be unequal to men. That is, any 'alleged deficiencies are imagined or insignificant . . . [and] result exclusively from the education they receive' (TFT, 120). Poulain's choice of this particular belief for examination exposes how our beliefs, insofar as they are based simply on custom and habit, are enmeshed in a social and political order in which some things are taken to be more valuable than others and the ways in which people are educated serve to affirm these measures of relative value. And because of the extent to which this belief is intertwined through so many of our other beliefs, dislodging, or even leaving it open for revision, proves to be challenging.

For Poulain, the best reasons people have for believing that women are inferior amount to little more than an appeal to custom. They are convinced that 'if some practice is well established, then we think that it must be right' (TFT, 125), committing a classic naturalistic fallacy by arguing that if things have always been such they currently are, it is because they ought to be so. So, because women do not currently study the sciences and hold office, and indeed there is no current record of their having done so, this is because women are not capable of studying the sciences and holding office. And because women are observed both within Europe and elsewhere to be by and large subject to the will of men, playing uniquely household-related roles that must be because this is women's natural place. But pointing out that 'is' does not imply 'ought' is of little use. This conviction that our practices capture the nature of things entails that they are hardly open to revision. Indeed, the beliefs are so entrenched, Poulain, notes, that it seems as if women themselves 'tolerate their condition.' (TFT, 126)

The strategy Poulain uses to call into question the belief in the natural inequality between the sexes is interesting. He offers a causal history of how the social

---

[14] Amy Schmitter makes this point in her 'Cartesian Prejudice: Gender, Education, and Authority in Poulain de la Barre' (Schmitter 2018).

118 LEARNING TO LIVE A HUMAN LIFE

order ended up as it is.[15] Social relationships, he claims, arise from a series of moral accidents that begin from efforts to usurp power arising from the inevitable attempts of one community to secure advantages from another by invasion, through which 'the condition of women became even more intolerable than before,' (TFT, 128) to the systematic exclusion of women from political power, as governing increasingly involved rule by physical domination, and then as a result to their exclusion from the sciences simply because their work in maintaining households did not afford them the leisure time to pursue studies. In short, what starts as a series of accidents becomes a customary practice that becomes more and more entrenched as those practices serve the interests of some over others.

With this alternative explanation of observed differences between men and women made plausible, and so the idea that inequalities between men and women might well be a matter of luck rather than 'insurmountable necessity' (TFT, 132), Poulain moves to argue that there is as much potential for authority, both epistemic and political, in women as in men:

> I do not claim that they [women] are all suited to the sciences and public office, or that each woman is capable of doing everything. No one claims that about men either. I ask only that, considering the two sexes in general, we recognize that there is as much aptitude in the one as in the other. (TFT 132)

The arguments Poulain offers turn on remarking the strengths that women demonstrate—their discernment and precision, their articulateness, their sense of peace and justice—in what they have been acculturated to do and maintaining that those same strengths are precisely those that serve the pursuit of knowledge and holding public office. Poulain's argumentative strategy is thus to first show that what we observe—the social roles that situate men and women as unequal—is not a reflection of nature but rather a matter of entrenched custom. He then moves to argue that the particular claims about women's abilities, claims that take the social roles they play and do not play as evidence, are ill-founded, and to point to other evidence that women and men have comparable abilities across the range of human activity and social roles. To dislodge the prejudice of the inequality of the sexes Poulain recognizes it is insufficient to simply raise an objection to the logic of the position. Rather, he has to construct a whole new narrative that can move us to see the world in a different way and thereby to revisit our evaluations of particular traits. This is no longer a simply act of denial but rather a wholesale revision.

---

[15] The story may seem familiar. Rousseau's narrative in his *Discourse Concerning the Origins of Inequality* has a very similar form, though it was written seventy-five years later (Rousseau 2009).

Poulain in his second work on the same theme, *On the Education of Women in Guiding the Mind in the Sciences and in Morals* published in 1674, makes explicit his view that most of our beliefs are instilled in us by others.[16] In the second of the five conversations, that comprise the work, he draws attention to the problem we all face in so far as we depend on others for our most basic needs from birth and so simply accept their authority with respect to what there is, and the value of those things.

> Timander offered a summary. 'So then, the relationships that we establish when we open our eyes, which on the one hand are so essential to us, become, on the other hand, more pernicious as they make us rasher in our judgements and more incarnate, as it were, in our thinking.
>
> Stasimachus went on: 'Our condition isn't improved when we make new associations as our hearing is sensitized and we start to understand meaning with our ears. Since people are not merely showing us new things when they speak to us but are also indicating whether those things are good or bad, the impression of the things we see is fortified by that which we receive through our ears, and the weight and speed of our imagination become so frantic that we are hardly able to resist that impression.
>
> ... what we should be considering further is that our need of those who are raising us gives them absolute authority over our minds and that authority is subsequently increased by various specific incidents.
>
> ... We must acknowledge therefore that the first principle of everything you know and believe and do is the trust you placed in your parents and your masters; and the second principle, which follows from the first, is the blind trust you place in the customs and example of your peers. Those are the sources of all our ideas of truth, knowledge, virtue, justice and civility.' (*Education of Ladies*, 161–163)[17]

From the time we are born, our physical dependencies make our minds susceptible to the influence of others, first our parents and families, and then those around us with whom we become properly socialized. Our task is to recognize the contingency of our social practices and moral evaluations, and to look inward to discover our own faculty of judgement and to use it well to determine for ourselves what we ought to believe.

Poulain recognizes that it is hard to maintain confidence in one's own judgement. After all, the move to assert our own authority is premised on the

---

[16] The work is structured as a series of five conversations between Sophia, the epitome of wisdom, Eulalia, an uneducated yet well-spoken and honest young woman, Timander, a gentleman persuadable by reason and good sense, and Stasimachus, the alter-ego of Poulain, and the peacemaker who offers, with Sophia, reasons.

[17] Citations are to the translation of Poulain 2002, followed by the page number.

recognition that we fall into 'error and prejudices.' It can be, as Timander highlights, tempting to simply defer to 'the public voice; we should take as most surely certain what is decreed by general consensus' for a 'large number of people, particularly, smart, bright people who know what they are doing and wouldn't have made their opinions public if they hadn't been the best' are unlikely all to be wrong (*Education of Ladies*, 165). To avoid this temptation requires recognizing that a principle of equality mandates that between two people, each is as likely to be mistaken as the other, and so 'it would be imprudent to give our consent to what one man says to us simply because he says it. In that state of equality, we might as well believe ourselves as other people' (*Education of Ladies*, 165–166). Challenging our habitual beliefs, Poulain recognizes, involves a special kind of confidence, one that our ability to justify our beliefs is on level footing with that of others. That is, in order to ensure that we do not succumb to prejudice we need to recognize our own authority in settling on our thoughts. With this authority comes a responsibility for ensuring that our thoughts are well-founded, based on good reasons, and not simply on common practice. This does not mean that we are to arrive at our beliefs independently, but rather we ought to defer to others' judgement only when another person has demonstrated expertise through their ability to convey to us clearly their own understanding. That is, we ought to rely on the testimony of others only when they have taught us what they know in such a way that we too can understand it.

It does not seem that Poulain thinks it is particularly difficult to find the confidence in our own authority. It may require being placed in the right circumstances—a series of conversations with those who have already confidence in their own judgement, for instance, and recognize the same authority in others—but insofar as these conversations are relatively easy to come by, it seems, he thinks it a rather straightforward matter to cultivate our minds. Is this in fact the case? Can the forces of custom and acculturation be so strong as to impede our ever discovering our own natural capacity for judgement, or at least to the degree that we have confidence in our own epistemic and moral authority? The particular context of Poulain's discussion adds force to the question. This is, after all, the peculiar problem women face in challenging their own lack of epistemic and political authority, and why they 'tolerate' their condition. Why, given this condition should women ever think that they can listen to their own reason rather than defer to popular opinion?

5 Mary Astell: freeing oneself from bad habits

As Locke himself acknowledges, his thoughts on education are for the education of a young gentleman, and this course 'will not so perfectly suit the education of *daughters*; though where the difference of sex requires different treatment, it will be no hard matter to distinguish' (STCE §6). Mary Astell in her *Serious Proposal to the Ladies* [hereafter SP] aims to unseat this idea, and indeed she identifies the kind of education that women have received, the habits that have been inculcated in them and the customs to which they have been acculturated, as undermining their ability to properly understand just what they are, and so to value themselves properly. Her *Serious Proposal* aims to rectify this situation, and the difficulty she found getting uptake of the proposal indicates just how challenging it is to teach someone that she is free and equally for her to learn that for herself.

As Astell presents it, women focus their attentions on the minute details of their physical appearance—be it their dress, their carriage, their movements in dancing, their conversation, so as to charm—ultimately in the service of securing a husband. In doing so, Astell is clear, they value themselves incorrectly in two distinct ways:

> entertain[ing] such a degrading thought of our own *worth*, as to imagine that our Souls were given us only for the service of our Bodies, and that the best improvement we can make of these, is to attract the eyes of men. We value *them* too much, and our *selves* too little, if we place any part of our worth in their Opinion; and do not think our selves capable of Nobler Things than the pitiful Conquest of some worthless heart. She who has opportunities of making an interest in Heaven, of obtaining the love and admiration of GOD and Angels, is too prodigal of her Time, and injurious to her Charms, to throw them away on vain insignificant men. She need not make her self so cheap, as to descend to Court their Applauses; for at the greater distance she keeps, and the more she is above them, the more effectually she secures their esteem and wonder
>
> (SP, 55–56).

First, women take their bodies to be the locus of their value, and so their minds are put to work on how best to perfect their bodies, and second, they value the opinion of the men whose approval they seek. In doing so, they fail to see their minds as the source of their value, but also they cede the standards by which they will be valued to the men they are aiming to attract.[18] The problem Astell diagnoses is in

---

[18] See also:

And were Womens haughtiness express'd in disdaining to do a mean and evil thing; wou'd they pride themselves in somewhat truly perfective of a Rational nature, there were no hurt in it. But then they ought not to be denied the means of examining and judging what is so; they should not be impos'd on with tinsel ware. If by reason of a false Light, or undue Medium, they chuse amiss; theirs is the loss, but the Crime is the Deceivers. She who rightly understands wherein the perfection of her Nature consists, will lay out her Thoughts and Industry in the acquisition of such Perfections. But she who is kept ignorant of the matter, will take up with such Objects as first offer themselves, and bear any plausible resemblance to what she desires; a shew of advantage being sufficient to render them agreeable baits to her who wants Judgment and Skill to discern between reality and pretence. From whence it easily follows, that she who has nothing else to value her self upon, will be proud of her

122 LEARNING TO LIVE A HUMAN LIFE

keeping with what Descartes and Poulain identify as essential to human being. It is not simply that women do not value their capacity for thought, it is that they do not acknowledge their own epistemic and moral authority. Insofar as they lack that authority, they simply, unwittingly, follow custom and habit, with no disinclination to go against it. And insofar as they fail to deny that has been given to them, what is expected of them, they fail to exercise their will, or even recognize that they have the option to do so.

That women are misguided in these ways is not something intrinsic to the female condition but rather is the result of their education, 'which like an Error in the first Concoction, spreads its ill Influence through all our Lives . . . . Women are from their very Infancy debar'd those Advantages, with the want of which, they are afterwards reproached, and nursed up in those Vices which will hereafter be upbraided to them' (SP, 59–60). And Astell continues:

> Women were they rightly Educated, had they obtain'd a well inform'd and discerning Mind, they would be proof against all those Batteries, see through and scorn those little silly Artifices which are us'd to ensnare and deceive them. Such an one would value her self only on her Vertue, and consequently be most chary of what she esteems so much. She would know, that not what others say, but what she her self does, is the true Commendation and the only thing that exalts her.   (SP, 64)

A proper education would afford women the confidence in their own judgement, and so the ability to resist the force of those 'silly Artifices' and other customs and habits that are foisted upon us.

Astell's challenge, however, is to convince those that have been poorly educated to undertake a process of reeducation. How is she to do this? Because of the way in which the habits and customs governing female behaviour have become entrenched through their education, that is, because of the force of prejudice, it is not an option for them to discover their own free will by accident, as did the meditator, or as is open to Gassendi. Nor does it seem that the remedy of engaging these women in rational conversation, as Poulain envisages, will have much effect. For not only has their education left women with little experience in reasoning from premises to conclusions, one might imagine that the pull of the social forces—what we might call peer pressure—would be so strong as to draw any

Beauty, or Money, and what that can purchase; and think her self mightily oblig'd to him, who tells her she has those Perfections which she naturally longs for. Her inbred self-esteem and desire of good, which are degenerated into Pride and mistaken Self-love,1 will easily open her Ears to whatever goes about to nourish and delight them; and when a cunning designing Enemy from without, has drawn over to his

Party these Traytors within, he has the Poor unhappy Person at his Mercy, who now very glibly swallows down his Poyson, because 'tis presented in a Golden Cup; and credulously hearkens to the most disadvantagious Proposals, because they come attended with a seeming esteem (SP, 62–63).

individual woman she is trying to persuade back to her old habits. It is not clear that even an alternative natural history of the sort Poulain provides would hold much sway—even Poulain acknowledges that the force of custom is so strong that his account would be subject to ridicule. Astell resorts to a polemic of a sort, a kind of sermonizing. She works on the emotions of her intended audience, playing on their fear of falling out of fashion, either through the natural ageing process or simply not being current about what to wear, of loss of social status, of failing to realize cultural expectations, and presents the love of God (which she simply asserts without argument as the true source of value) as an antidote to all these concerns.[19] Nonetheless, the pleasures of following customary ways are well-entrenched, even if they might be fleeting. Why would someone forsake those known pleasures for the promise of an alternative life that seems ascetic by comparison. If one does not start out loving God, and feeling that particular and enduring pleasure, why would one take the risk to follow this path? What is the incentive, after all?

The second part of the work, published three years later, tries a different tack. She drops her polemical tone, and presents the programme of her educational system in a straightforward manner. And the programme bears a striking resemblance to Descartes's method, as it is articulated in the *Discourse:* properly circumscribe the question, reason only with clear ideas, in order, from the simplest to the more complex, through a full enumeration of its various aspects, remaining focused and withholding judgement from that which we do not understand. She proposes quite simply to give the women she aims to reach practice in reasoning, hoping that these habits of thought can be applied to other things, to critically evaluate the manners and customs in which they have been raised. She also recognizes that it is hardly enough to simply assert the love of God as the source of value. For even if this idea is grasped, the idea alone will not be sufficient to motivate a change of behaviour. Rather, there is a need to cultivate the sentiments that attach to that understanding of value

> But considering how weak our Reason is, how unable to maintain its Authority and oppose the incursions of sense, without the assistance of an inward and Spiritual Sensation to strengthen it, 'tis highly necessary that we use due endeavours to procure a lively relish of our true Good, a Sentiment that will not only Ballance, but if attended to and improv'd, very much outweigh the Pleasures of our Animal Nature.   (SP 143–144)

How are we to arrive at this sensation? Through just the kind of reflexive act of will that Descartes takes as committing us to pursuing the good:

---

[19] Her proposal for a convent, in which women can separate themselves from society to cultivate their minds, fell flat.

124 LEARNING TO LIVE A HUMAN LIFE

> Now this is no otherwise to be obtain'd than by directing the Will in an elicit Act
> to GOD as its only Good, so that the sole End of all its movements may be to
> draw near, to acquiesce in and be united to him. For as all Natural Motions are
> easie and pleasant, so this being the only Natural Motion of the Will must needs
> be unspeakably delightful to it (SP 143–144).

For Astell, we recognize that we have a will, just as does Descartes' generous person, by directing it through its 'natural motion'. That natural motion, by its very nature, is towards the good—God. In virtue of affirming our will to pursue that good, we feel a distinct pleasure, a love, or a spiritual sensation. And insofar as it is the distinctive pleasure it is, it provides the seeds through which the pleasures of conformity to custom can be resisted.

7 Conclusion

If you think that being freely willing is essential to human nature, living well, that is, acting well, involves using one's will well or realizing one's freedom. However, simply being freely willing is not sufficient to realizing one's freedom. The realization of one's freedom is something that occurs as a part of human development. Realizing one's freedom involves a special sort of knowledge, one that one has to learn for oneself by actually refusing what has come to be expected, by intentionally denying what one has been taught or flouting custom and habit. However, just because we have to learn it for ourselves does not mean that it cannot be taught.

Education not only provides us with the background against which we exercise our will and so demonstrate it, but education also needs to cultivate within us the habits that will allow the critical exercise of our freedom to emerge and be expressed—habits which give us practice in denying the satisfaction of immediate desires, and which at the same time allow for us to recognize our own authority to pursue a line of thinking or an action, and so to make a mistake. Education thus enables the development of freely willing humans.

However, our education can go wrong and impede development. It can cultivate bad habits, habits which occlude our freedom from view, entrenching customs so that they become prejudices that are difficult to dislodge. It is difficult but not impossible to overcome this bad education. There are a range of strategies to be deploying: imagining things to be otherwise, engaging in intimate conversations which build confidence and provide models of reasoning, inciting the sorts of emotions that can counterbalance the pull of custom. However, ultimately, it seems, we are each left to work on our own minds, practicing thinking things through, simply and systematically, so that we can live our best lives as human beings.

6

Spinozan Meditations on Life and Death

Julie R. Klein

In a well-known proposition in *Ethics* 4, Spinoza argues that 'A free man thinks of nothing less than of death, and his wisdom is a meditation on life, not on death' (E4p67).[1] Spinoza's argument for this claim depends on his view of imagination, reason, and *scientia intuitiva* and on his notion of *conatus*. We can reconstruct his position as follows. All things strive to persevere in existing (E3p6). As a matter of course any mind thus strives to imagine things that enhance its body's power to persevere in existing and to repel the idea of anything destructive (E3p12–13). To the extent that our efforts at self-preservation are predominantly imaginative, they are insufficiently powerful to moderate our reactions to forces that affect us or to enable us to forge stable bonds with others who may help us. Just this limited power explains what Spinoza calls our servitude. Imaginative thinking, which produces our only (and in fact inadequate) idea of the 'duration of our Body' (E2p30), moreover models nature temporally, giving us a sense of things as present (E2p17s) and a picture of nature as a series of past and future contingencies (E2p44s, 4p62s).[2] Unpleasant as it may be, minds in the grip of imagination are vulnerable to being pushed to fearful images of their demise. Hence, they think of and meditate on death.[3] So much in the common order of nature can provide *memento mori*.

The free person of E4p67 is in contrast a rational person, and to be rational means to be active rather than passive and oriented by necessity rather than contingency. Spinozan reason by its very nature operates with 'common notions and adequate ideas of the properties of things' (E2p40s2) and comprehends things

---

[1] In Spinoza citations, E = *Ethics* (d = definition; ax = axiom; p = proposition; dem = demonstration; c = corollary; s = scholium; pref = preface; app = appendix); CM = *Metaphysical Thoughts*; TTP = *Theological-Political Treatise*; TP = *Political Treatise*; L= Letter; G = Gebhardt's *Spinoza Opera* (4 vol.). English translations are Edwin Curley's from Spinoza 1985 and 2016. For the TTP, I follow Curley's adoption of Bruder's paragraph numbering and give Gebhardt's pagination. Although Gebhardt's presentation of the TTP and *Ethics* are superseded by volumes III–IV of Spinoza 2009-, under the general direction of Pierre-François Moreau, his edition remains a reference point.

[2] Letter XII calls measure, time, and number as 'nothing but modes of thinking, or, better [*sed potius*] imagining' (Giv 57).

[3] Cf. TTP V.22 (Giii 74) and TP V.6.

Julie R. Klein, *Spinozan Meditations on Life and Death* In: *Life and Death in Early Modern Philosophy*. Edited by: Susan James, Oxford University Press. © Julie R. Klein 2021. DOI: 10.1093/oso/9780192843616.003.0007

'without any relation to time, but [rather] *sub specie aeternatitis*' (E2p44c2).[4] E5p29 crisply articulates the difference between the temporality of imagination and the eternal viewpoint of reason and intellect: 'Whatever the Mind understands *sub specie aeternitatis*, it understands not from the fact that it conceives the Body's present actual existence, but from the fact that it conceives the Body's essence *sub specie aeternitatis*.' E5p38 shows the implications for destructive affects and the fear of death: 'the more the Mind understands things by the second and third kind of knowledge, the less it is acted on by affects that are evil, and the less it fears death'.[5] Simply put, free people do not meditate on death because they cannot: their minds are otherwise occupied.[6] If we are not thinking of death, it can have, as an author well known to Spinoza said, no sting.[7] To the extent, then, that we are rational and free, death is a non-issue. Indeed, to the extent that we are able to meditate on life *sub specie aeternitatis*, we actually experience joy, love (E5p20s, p32c), eternity (5p23s), and 'the greatest satisfaction of the Mind' (E5p27).

Reading these arguments, no doubt more than a few readers have sighed, 'If only...' Spinoza's vision is inspiring; would that we could achieve it. Spinoza's insistence that reason and intuition develop through cultivation and in conducive environments is a sobering reality.[8] His analysis of human individuals and communities as exceedingly small forces in nature can further dampen our aspirations. We are 'infinitely surpassed by the power of external causes' (E4p3), such that no human being can 'undergo no changes except those which can be understood through his own nature alone, and of which he is the adequate cause' (E4p4). We may to some extent become rational and even intuitive, but our limited power suggests that returning to imagination (E2p17s, 29s) and sad passions (E3p11, 4p4c) is inevitable. Becoming rational and free is an ongoing project, with advances and regresses, successes and failures. If, *per impossibile*, there were individuals or communities unaffected by more powerful forces in their environments, they would be free of inadequate ideas and passive affects. They

---

[4] E.g. E3p3, p3c; E4p62dem: 'Whatever the Mind conceives under the guidance of reason, it conceives under the same aspect of eternity or necessity [*aeternitas, seu necessitate species*] (by 2p44c2) and is affected with the same certainty (by 2p43 and p43s).'

[5] Cf. E3p18s2, E4p47s, and TTP XVI.32 'The only free person is the one who lives wholeheartedly according to the guidance of reason alone' (Giii 194). TP II.11 further clarifies the idea of degrees of rational guidance and freedom.

[6] *Scientia intuitiva*, the third kind of knowing, involves 'adequate ideas of the essences of things' (E2p40s2) and takes place 'without relation to the Body', i.e. without relation to time and duration (E5p40s).

[7] I Corinthians 15:55. Garber 2005 reads Spinoza's discussions of death and the eternity of the mind as efforts to free us from fear.

[8] Spinoza denies that that anyone is born rational or intuitive. We are 'born ignorant of the causes of things' (E1app Gii 78). TTP XVI.7 is stronger: 'Everyone is born ignorant of everything' (Giii 190). E4p68 and p68s, which presume the identification of freedom and reason, repeat the point. The proposition runs, 'If men were born free, they would form no concept of good and evil so long as they remained free.' The scholium immediately rejects the proposition: 'It is evident...that the hypothesis of this proposition is false.'

would experience only and always 'absolute affirmation of existence' (E1p7s) and 'infinite intellectual love' (E5p35). Actual human individuals and communities, however, are constituted by ratios of adequate and inadequate ideas (E3p3, p9dem), that is, by meditations on life and imaginative ideas of death.

Other readers have found Spinoza's account of life and death distinctly wanting. Matson, for example, laments that 'In the end, the difference between life and death reduces to this, that in life one is continually vexed by inadequate ideas, all of which cease at death. We must keep on looking, if our search is for a philosopher who will join us with all his heart in the toast *L'chaim*.'[9] Despite Spinoza's condemnation of asceticism as a 'sad and savage superstition' and his praise of pleasure and beauty (E4p45s), Matson finds only the offer of a Stoic waiting room for death. Other commentators have found some of the core ideas relevant to Spinoza's account of reason, freedom, and therefore life, such as adequate knowledge and adequate causation, highly problematic in view of the relative or absolute difficulty of achieving them.[10] Freedom, in particular, as the most excellent form of life, has come in for substantial critique as unachievable.[11] For yet other readers, Spinoza's claim that destruction can come only from external causes makes his account of death, particularly death by suicide, incoherent, and in any case the literature offers multiple, incompatible readings.[12]

But what precisely are the life and death to which Spinoza refers? The aims of the present paper are to clarify these terms in the *Ethics* and to assess the cogency of Spinoza's position. Since the *Ethics* is related in complex ways to Spinoza's other works, I shall refer to them along the way. Letter 32 in particular will play a crucial role in clarifying Spinoza's account of how extended things cohere and his analysis of how we differentiate individuals. Along the way of clarifying Spinoza's views, I shall attempt to answer his critics, showing first that Spinoza envisions the prospect of an increasingly rational and joyful life, and emphasizing second that he envisions adequate knowledge and freedom in relative rather than absolute terms. The most serious and interesting problem for Spinoza, in my view, is his claim that death comes from outside (E3p4), which appears to conflict with his metaphysical and physical views.

My analysis unfolds in five parts. Section 1, 'Life as *potentia*', traces Spinoza's view of life, from God's life in the early *Cogitata Metaphysica* II.6 to the *Ethics*,

---

[9] Matson 1977, 415.

[10] Garber memorably calls Spinoza's doctrine of adequate ideas 'extremely intricate, rather technical, and perhaps not altogether coherent' (Garber 2005, 107). Della Rocca 1995 questions whether human knowers have adequate ideas (183, n.29); subsequently he accepts a scalar construal of adequacy (Della Rocca 2008). Marshall admits adequate ideas of God and infinite modes but not adequate ideas of finite modes (2008). Kisner endorses modified adequacy for human knowers (2010, 41–45).

[11] Garber characterizes Spinozan freedom as unrealistic (2005, 203–204). Youpa regards it as unattainable (Youpa 2010, 66). Kisner (2010, 101) considers Spinozan freedom à la E4p67 confused. Marshall identifies freedom with adequate causation (2013). My view accords with Nadler 2015, which depicts Spinozan liberation as difficult but achievable to some degree.

[12] E.g. Bennett 1984; Gabhardt 1999; Miller 2005; Nadler 2016; Grey 2017.

where *potentia* emerges as the primary term and *vita* is reserved for singular things. Section 1 concludes with a consideration of Spinozan singular things as determinate expressions of *potentia* and Spinozan life as their striving to persevere in existing.

Section 2, 'Living bodies', considers the lives of natural and social bodies.[13] Spinoza characterizes extended individuals in terms of *rationes* of motion and rest communicated among parts. Spinozan *rationes* are stable but somewhat flexible organizational patterns through which bodies hang together and perpetuate themselves. Minimally speaking, embodied life is self-perpetuation with just enough power to endure affections, regenerate one's *ratio*, and affect other bodies. More robustly, embodied life involves increasing one's power to express one's *ratio*.[14] Spinoza's Adam represents the former; successful human development, represented by the sage, shows us the latter.

Section 3, 'Death *sub attributo extensionis*', explores Spinoza's argument that destruction comes from external causes (E3p4) and his specific definition of the death of the body as the destruction of an individual's ratio and rearrangement of its parts into an incompatible *ratio* (E4p39s). E4p39s also introduces the idea of corpse-less death, which provides the occasion to consider the flexibility and complexity of an individual's *ratio* or nature. Spinoza's insistence that conversion is the rule in nature raises the question of how to determine the point at which elasticity turns to destruction.

Section 4 examines life and death *sub attributo cogitationis*. What we would call 'the life of the mind', Spinoza calls the mind's power of understanding. As Spinoza argues in E4p24, 'Acting, living, and preserving our being' 'signify the same thing' and all depend on understanding (E4p24). Death requires more explanation. In one sense, since the mind is the idea of an actually existing human body, decomposition of the body is decomposition of the mind. In another sense, the essence of the mind is, qua essence, eternal—the same is true of the essence of the body—and, to the extent that the mind knows its essence formally, the mind is eternal. Spinoza uses idioms related to death with respect to imagination and affects. I argue that these deaths are best understood as shifts in cognition and the quality of experience.

To conclude, Section 5 returns to destruction by external causes. To the extent that talk of internality and externality presumes or implies really separate and discrete finite things, it is incompatible with Spinoza's understanding of nature as expressed in, among other places, E1p28, E2lemm3, and the critique of free will. As Deleuze remarks, 'An animal, a thing, is never separable from its relations with

---

[13] With a few exceptions, such as Jonas 1965, Spinoza's biology has not received much attention in Anglophone scholarship. In French, Andrault 2014 is a rich study of bodily vitality in Spinoza, Leibniz, and surrounding figures. Andrault 2019 specifically reconstructs Spinoza's medical knowledge and so sheds considerable light on the elements of physiology visible in such familiar texts as Letter XXXII.

[14] I consider this same issue from a different perspective in Klein 2020.

the world. The interior is only a selected interior and the exterior, a projected exterior.'[15] Letter XXXII enables us to see selection and projection as imaginative operations and so returns us to the death or cessation of an individual—myself or another—as an imaginative idea. It thus returns us to Spinoza's insistence on the difference between imagining and understanding and to his suggestion of a path from one to the other.

1 Life as *potentia*

Ethics 1 presents Spinoza's central ways of thinking about substance or God or, as E4pref has it, Nature. Many characteristics of Spinoza's God echo traditional metaphysical-theological notions, which Spinoza transposes, often with significant modifications, into his own distinctive philosophical framework. By the time Spinoza is finished with terms like cause or freedom, no more conventional thinker could possibly be satisfied. Indeed, his contemporaries were not satisfied at all, and denounced his revision and (ab)use of the philosophical lexicon.[16] In the *Ethics*, one traditional attribute of God noticeably escapes Spinoza's strategy of re-interpretation and re-appropriation: life. Spinoza's exclusion of this perhaps especially anthropomorphic item is of a piece with his continuous and scathing critique of all anthropomorphic depictions of God. Nor can the association of life with religiously inspired discussions of eternal life been much of an enticement to reclaim the idea.[17] That said, Spinoza was not averse to the idea of divine life in his earliest published work, the *Cogitata Metaphysica*, which appeared as an appendix to his presentation of Descartes' *Principia philosophiae*. While the *Cogitata Metaphysica* is mostly a critical examination of Scholastic and Cartesian views, Spinoza does at times offer his own view directly. Divine life is such a case, and both historical review and philosophical refashioning figure in the discussion.

A note at the beginning of Balling's Dutch version of *Cogitata Metaphysica* II announces Spinoza's intention to establish how 'God's existence differs entirely from the existence of created things' (Gi 249/Ci 315). Chapter II.6, 'Of God's Life', is a pivotal part of the plan. Spinoza first reviews 'the opinion of the Peripatetics', which he characterizes as confused but declines to refute in detail, noting that he prefers to take it upon himself to explain 'what is denoted philosophically' by 'life'. Speaking in his own name, Spinoza defines life as the force of persevering in existence:

---

[15] Deleuze 1988, 125.   [16] Laerke 2014.

[17] E5p34s dismisses 'the common opinion of men' who confuse the eternity of the mind with post-mortem duration and suppose that imagination and memory remain after death. E5p41s calls the idea of an afterlife and the attendant ideas of reward and punishment to come 'absurd' and 'hardly worth mentioning'.

We understand by *life* the *force through which things persevere in their being* [*nos per vitam intelligimus vim, per quam res in suo esse perseverant*]. And because that force is different from the things themselves, we say properly that things themselves have life [*habere vitam*]. But the power by which God perseveres in his being is nothing but his essence, so they speak best of all who call God life [*Vis autem, qua Deus in suo esse perseverat, nihil praeter ejus essentiam, unde optime loquuntur, qui Deum vitam vocant*]. Some Theologians think it was for this reason, i.e. that God is life [*Deus sit vita*], and is not distinguished from life, that the Jews, when they swore, said *chay yëhovah*, living Jehovah [*vivus Jehovah*], as Joseph, when he swore by the life of the Pharaoh, said *chey phar'oh* [*vita Pharaonis*].

Spinoza's dismissal of unnamed 'Peripatetics' aside, the discussion of life is borrowed nearly verbatim from Maimonides. Like his medieval predecessor, Spinoza argues that pharaoh and pharaoh's life are differentiable, but God and God's living are one and the same.[18] Where we can distinguish the essence and the existence of the pharaoh, such that the pharaoh *has* life from a source that 'is different', God's essence and existence are indistinguishable, such that God *is living*, and there is no otherness, exteriority, or composition. In the idiom of the *Ethics*, God's essence, like God's life, is to exist (E1d1, 1p7, 1p11, 1p20), but the pharaoh exists through a cause outside human nature itself (E1p8s2, p24, p33s1). As becomes clear later, Spinoza cannot unambiguously speak in a Maimonidean voice. In the *Ethics*, Spinoza's embrace of the decidedly heterodox (to Aristotelians) phrase *causa sui* (E1d1), not to mention his rejection of creation (E1p8s2) and affirmation of a single order of causation (E1p25s), mark distance from Maimonides, but the idea of a force of persevering in existence and the idea of things whose existence is not necessary *per se* but only *in alio* remain.[19] Spinoza's relation to Maimonides in the TTP is, moreover, formidably complex.

In the *Ethics*, God's power (*potentia*) replaces God's life. Spinoza presents God as having 'an absolutely infinite power of existing' (E1p11s), and he subsequently identifies God's power with God's essence: 'God's power is his essence itself' (E1p34).[20] Everything that exists, exists in God (E1p15), and God's infinite power is, moreover, infinitely productive, such that infinitely many things follow in infinitely many ways (E1p16). God is thus the efficient cause of both the essence and the existence of things (E1p25), or, in other words, 'particular things are nothing but the affections of God's attributes, or modes by which God's attributes

---

[18] Maimonides, *Book of Knowledge*, Foundations of the Law II:10, *Eight Chapters* VIII, and *Guide of the Perplexed* I.68.

[19] For different approach to the Maimonides-Spinoza relationship, see Fraenkel 2006.

[20] See also E1p17s, which refers to 'God's supreme power, or infinite nature' (Gii 62) and E2p3s, which explicitly recalls 1p34 to identify 'God's power' and 'God's active essence'. See also TTP XVI.3 (Giii 189).

JULIE R. KLEIN 131

are expressed in certain and determinate ways' (1p25c). Speaking of what follows from God, Spinoza argues that 'whatever exists expresses the nature, or essence of God in a certain and determinate way [*certo ac determinato modo*] (by p25c), i.e. (by p34), whatever exists expresses in a certain and determinate way the power of God, which is the cause of all things' (E1p36dem). In short, a human being's power 'is part of God or Nature's infinite power' (E4p4dem).[21]

Subsequent parts of the *Ethics* expand our understanding of *potentia* by introducing closely related terms for orderly analysis in different realms of inquiry.[22] In *Ethics* 2, Spinoza uses force (*vis*) as a synonym for *potentia* in connection with singular things, noting in E2p45s that 'the force by which each [singular thing] perseveres in existing follows from the eternal necessity of God's nature'.[23] *Ethics* 3 introduces *conatus*, the striving of any singular thing to persevere in existing, which he explicates as the singular thing's power and essence via propositions from *Ethics* 1 (E3p6–7). *Ethics* 4 links power and essence to human virtue, which Spinoza understands as 'power of bringing about certain things' that can be understood though the laws of human nature (E4d8). Spinoza identifies this active power with reason and adequate ideas (E3p1, p3, 4p24). In the concise formula of E4p52dem, 'man's true power of acting, *or* virtue, is reason itself (by 3p3)'. Completing the series of expansions of the idea of *potentia*, *Ethics* 5, 'On the Power of the Intellect, or on Human Freedom', rearticulates these links with respect to the third kind of knowing. Spinoza describes *scientia intuitiva* as the most powerful form of knowing (E5p36s). E5p36s also links *scientia intuitiva* with *beatitudo*, and E5p42 identifies *beatitudo* and *virtus*. Thus the concluding pages of the *Ethics* return us via multiple paths to the central idea of power and its expression in and as determinate things.

Potentia does not entirely replace *vita* in the *Ethics*. Where power, force, and essence pertain to all things, and where Spinoza's enigmatic claim in E2p13s that all individuals are to some degree 'animate' is also universal, life refers mainly to human beings and their affairs. The word first appears in E2p49s, in the midst of Spinoza's argument that fantasies of the will and its freedom devastate our capacity for knowledge and action. Spinoza warns the reader to distinguish carefully among 'ideas, images, and words', 'for the sake of speculation, and in order to arrange one's life wisely [*ad vitam sapienter instituendam*]' (Gii 132). In this instance, *vita* points to a 'way of life', not merely to being alive. Spinoza does ultimately relate his account of the best way of living to his account of what human beings are and how they persevere in existing. The first sentence of E3pref directs us to the *hominum vivendi ratio*, which can be understood as both 'the

---

[21] Cf. TTP IV.3 (Giii 58).

[22] As Renz observes, the *Ethics* 'seeks to map out how specific problems are related to each and thus to determine what kind of knowledge can legitimately be consulted to answer different kinds of questions' (Renz 2018, 21).

[23] E4p60dem and E5pref (Gii 280) use *vis seu potentia*.

132 SPINOZAN MEDITATIONS ON LIFE AND DEATH

human way of living' and 'the *ratio* [or structure] of the living human'. E3p57s plays on *vita* in a similarly double way, speaking of the life with which an individual is content and of life as 'the idea, or soul, of the individual'. In the first sense, E5p10s emphasizes the need for a correct *ratio vivendi*.[24] The second sense, which points to the human body as an organized composite, will prove to be especially important in distinguishing life and death. I turn to it in Sections 2 and 3 below. Minds, too, have *rationes*. E3p9, for example, develops the idea of the human mind's *conatus* as the activity or striving of a set of ideas, some adequate and others inadequate. I consider mental *rationes* in Section 4.

Spinoza conceives modes, and therefore singular things, as determinate expressions of the power of God (E1p25c, 2p45s, 4p4dem). As we saw above, E1p11 and p34 identify God's power and essence. In the case of singular things, Spinoza sometimes distinguishes their essences and existence in thought, and he sometimes identifies their essences and existence. These two ways of considering essences depend on grasping the difference between conceiving an essence as formal, in which case we refer only to structure and not to persevering in existence, and conceiving an essence as actual, in which case we refer precisely to persevering in existence.[25] Spinoza's familiar claim that the essence of a finite thing does not entail existence but requires a cause for existing exemplifies the formal case, depending as it does upon our ability to distinguish essence and existence in thought. E3p7dem, which concludes with the statement that 'the power, *or* striving' by which each things 'strives to persevere in its being is nothing but the given, or actual, essence of the thing itself', exemplifies his treatment of the identity of the actual essence with existence. In my view, Spinoza's anti-Platonism requires that the formal essence and the actual essence are the same essence conceived in two ways.[26] Thinking about singular things this way enables us to see that to exist as a singular thing is to have sufficient power to persevere in a certain structure or characteristic nature. Any given singular thing exists as a this or a that, and its striving to persevere in existing is evident in a pattern or organization.

Living, the human way of existing, is thus not formless existence or some kind of brute and general power of existence, but instead always the power of existing

---

[24] Cf. the opening of TTP IV, which defines law as a *ratio vivendi* and the title of TTP XIII. *Vera vita*, the characteristic TTP phrase for a life guided by reason, does not figure in the *Ethics*.

[25] Spinoza's technical term 'involvement' captures the connection. The essences of existing singular things are comprehended in one of God's attributes and 'involve the existence through which they are said to have duration' (E2p8c).

[26] Spinoza's rejection of the post-fourteenth-century metaphysics of real possibility leads him to hold that there are no essences without things, and no things without essences (E2d2, p10s). Nevertheless Spinoza's readers often emphasize either power or essence and intelligibility. For the former, Matheron 1991a and 1991b are exemplary; Laerke 2017 emphasizes the anti-Platonic motivation of this group. See also Nadler 2012. For the latter, Della Rocca 2008 is a classic case for the priority of intelligibility, and Garrett 2018 exemplary. Viljanen's 'dynamic essentialism' (Viljanen 2011, 5) attempts a third way.

indexed to a nature. As will become clear below, Spinoza conceives human beings as variable in two respects, power and structure. *Ethics* 3 conceives our variations in power and the mechanisms that cause them under the heading of affect. Affect proves an especially useful concept because it pertains to human bodies and minds simultaneously. One of Spinoza's signature claims is that both are active and passive (E3d3, p2s, p11s). As we saw in the Introduction, the more imagination organizes our experience of the world, the more passive we are, and the more reason predominates, the more active. The affect of passivity is sadness, that of activity, joy. Elsewhere in the *Ethics*, the idea of perfection does similar work. E1app, for example, instructs us to judge the perfection of things 'solely from their nature and power' (Gii 83), and E4pref indexes assessments of power to a thing's nature:

> [W]hen I say that someone passes from a lesser to a greater perfection, and the opposite, I do not understand that he is changed from one essence, or form, to another. For example, a horse is destroyed as much if it is changed into a man as if it is changed into an insect. Rather, we conceive that his power of acting, insofar as it is understood through his nature, is increased or diminished
> (Gii 208–209).[27]

While all finite things act and are affected, to be more perfect is to have more *potentia agendi*, that is, to be able to express one's power as activity and less subject to determination by others. For the human being, perfection depends on reason and intellect: 'Man's true power of activity, or his virtue, is reason itself' (E4p52), and the third kind of knowing is the most immediate experience of our power as an immanent expression of the power of God or Nature (Ep36s). Let us turn now to variation conceived in terms of structure.

2 Living bodies

While it may at first seem odd to begin with the life of bodies, Spinoza's demonstration that the human mind is the idea of an actually existing body (E2p11,13) and the prominent place accorded to physics in *Ethics* 2 underscore the importance of examining his view of bodies and their liveliness. Moreover,

---

[27] Cf. Letter XXXVI: 'I should like you to note what I said just now about the term imperfection, namely, that it signifies that something is lacking to a thing which pertains to its nature. For example, Extension can be called imperfect only in relation to duration, position, or quantity, because it does not last longer, or does not keep its position, or is not larger. But it will never be called imperfect because it does not think, since its nature, which consists only in extension, that is, in a definite kind of being, requires nothing of that sort' (Giv 185/Cii 30).

134 SPINOZAN MEDITATIONS ON LIFE AND DEATH

Spinoza often proportions mental power to bodily power, as in this passage from E2p13s, just before the so-called 'physical interlude':

> in proportion as a Body is more capable than others of doing many things at once, or being acted on in many ways at once, so its mind is more capable than others of perceiving many things at once. And in proportion as the actions of a body depend more on itself alone, and as other bodies concur with it less in acting, so its mind is more capable of understanding distinctly (Gii 97).

What Spinoza suggests here, and follows with a sketch of the elements of a general physics and rudimentary human physiology, he subsequently demonstrates. On the basic of the physics, E2p14 formally argues that 'The human Mind is capable of perceiving a great many things, and is the more capable [apta], the more its body can be disposed [disponi potest] in a great many ways.' Later Parts of the Ethics repeat the argument. E3p11, for example, uses the same strategy to explain how the mind's power of thinking varies: 'The idea of any thing that increases or diminishes, aids or restrains, our Body's power of acting, increases or diminishes, aids or restrains, our Mind's power of thinking.'[28] As we shall see shortly, Spinoza reiterates the proportional relation of mind and body in a crucial discussion of life and death at the conclusion of Ethics 5.

Spinoza defines body in E2d1: 'By body I understand a mode that in a certain and determinate way expresses God's essence insofar as he is considered as an extended thing (see 1p25c).' To be a body is just to be a determined and determining mode under the attribute of extension. Turning to human experience, Spinoza regards it as axiomatic that 'we feel a certain body is affected in many ways' (E2ax4) and that 'We neither feel nor perceive any singular things [NS: or anything of natura naturata] except bodies and modes of thinking.' The singular things at issues are defined in E2d7, whose reference to causal power and structure will orient our discussion. It reads:

> By singular things I understand things that are finite and have a determinate existence. And if a number of Individuals so concur in one action together that they are all the cause of one effect, I consider them all, to that extent, as one singular thing (E2d7).

Like E2d1, the first sentence of E2d7 recalls E1p25c, emphasizing that singular things exist amidst and in relation to singular things. The second sentence then

---

[28] See also E4p38, E4 App xxvii, and E5p39 and its scholium, which I discuss in detail below. The idea of sameness in E2p7 and p7s underwrites proportionality without violating the E3p2 prohibition on cross-attribute causation.

directs our attention to causal efficacy and internal multiplicity. Far from being atoms, singular things are concurring assemblages of individuals that produce effects. Spinoza's formulation of E2d7 plays on common usage, which treats *res singularis* and *individuum* as synonyms,[29] but his distinctive usage emerges in the physics, which introduces *individuum* as a technical term for analysing the *ratio* or organization of composite extended things. Where understanding something as a *res singularis* treats it as the unified cause of an action and makes mention of internal structure, calling it an *individuum* points to its internal structure. Finally, the second sentence also indicates that singularity can be predicated in relative terms and at different scales. If things are one insofar as (*quod si*) they concur, defining the extent and/or the axis of concurrence will demarcate the boundaries of singular thing. In Section 5 below, I consider the problem of demarcating boundaries in Spinoza's physics and metaphysics. Here, I focus on structure and organization as features of bodily life.

Considered from the standpoint of physics, human bodies are complex wholes made up of heterogeneous parts, each of which in turn has its own constituent parts. In Spinoza's idiom, human bodies are composites of composites, and composition has no end: 'The human Body is composed of a great many individuals of different natures, each of which is highly composite' (E2post1). From Spinoza's standpoint, the important issue is that the bodies that constitute an *individuum* such as the human body exhibit structure. They communicate their motions 'in a certain fixed *ratio* of motion and rest':

> When a number of bodies, whether of the same or of different size, are so constrained by other bodies that they lie upon one another, or if they so move, whether with the same degree or different degrees of speed, that they communicate their motions to each other in a certain fixed *ratio*, we shall say that those bodies are united with one another and that they all together compose one body or Individual, which is distinguished from the others by this union of bodies
> (Gii 99–100/Ci 460).

Spinoza's definition is notably comprehensive, lending itself to aggregates of bodies produced by contiguity and constraint—we can think here of a clump that seems to hang together, a heap or pile-up, or, in politics, a multitude—or to the component parts of a complex whole—as in the finely balanced, delicately interlocking parts of a human body, an ecosystem, or a well-organized *res publica*. Given sufficient agreement or similarity to sustain communication, we can speak of an individual. In all of these cases, the *ratio* dynamically specifies how the

---

[29] Renz 2018 chapter 3 provides an illuminating discussion that contextualizes Spinoza.

136 SPINOZAN MEDITATIONS ON LIFE AND DEATH

elements interact and so defines the individual's unity. Spinoza also calls the individual's *ratio motus et quietus* its *natura* and its *forma* (E2Lemm4–7).[30]

Beyond the *Ethics*, both the TTP and Letter XXXII add 'law' as synonym for *ratio*.[31] Letter 32 is particularly helpful insofar as it provides some detail about how communication works. Spinoza describes it as a process of mutual adaptation (*accommodatio*) among the parts of a whole, be it the blood or nature itself. This process of mutual affordance generates coherence (*cohaerentia*) and agreement (*convenientia*):

> Now all bodies in nature . . . are surrounded by others, and are determined by one another to existing and producing an effect in a fixed and determinate way, the same *ratio* of motion to rest always being preserved in all of them at once, [that is, in the whole universe]. From this it follows that every body, insofar as it exists modified in a definite way, must be considered as a part of the whole universe, must agree with its whole and must cohere with the remaining bodies [*cum suo toto convenire & cum reliquis cohaerere*] (Giv 172–173a/Cii 19–20).

Spinoza's list of individuals in E3p57s includes human beings, horses, fish, and birds. E4p18s introduces human pairs and communities as individuals.[32] Thus further examples for thinking about accommodation as a mutual and dynamic process might include the subtle adjustments that occur when lovers embrace or a parent picks up a child, the adaptations carried out in the human biome, or the cooperative functioning of musicians and listeners, whether on the model of the Belcea Quartet, John Zorn's ensembles, or John Cage's 4′33″. In each case, bodies are affected and affect others as they persevere in existing.

Defined minimally, the living body is composed of accommodating extended parts that cohere according to a stable *ratio*, and it possesses a sufficient degree of power to persevere in existing. That is, the living body is composed of or by, exists among, and encounters other bodies, and it continues its characteristic pattern of motion and rest. Because Spinozan nature does not stand still, the life of the human body is regenerative motion: 'The human body, to be preserved, requires a great many other bodies, by which it is, so to speak, regenerated' (E2post4). Bodily life is measured by the persistence of the *ratio*, which requires the replenishment of parts. Like the power of being mutually accommodating, the need for replenishment also suggests that individuals are to some degree flexible. They admit of

---

[30] Thus Lin 2005 refers to thing's *ratio* as its 'blueprint' or 'architecture', which he defines as a 'coherent, stable, and well-defined relationship, couched in terms of motion and rest, and obtaining between a complex individual's parts' (250–251). Youpa 2003 is also helpful.

[31] E.g. TTP IV.1–2 on law as the *ratio vivendi* of an individual or group that acts in a fixed and determinate way (Giii 57–58). For a political community, law is determined by human decision.

[32] On the contested issue of treating a political bodies as individuals, see Santos Campos 2010 and Sharp 2017. Classic discussions are found in Matheron 1988/1969), especially 346–347, and Moreau 1994, 441–459.

some elasticity and variability below the threshold of destruction, and they must have some reparative capacities. Hunger, sleep, and mild to moderate sicknesses from which an individual recovers seem obvious examples in this regard.[33] Without some tolerable degree of variation and repair, individuals would have no continuity but rather be in constant re-configuration.

But how does preservation work? Most obviously, bodies require other bodies as objects of consumption, as in the case of the foods we integrate into ourselves, or as resources for our use, such as tools and other materials necessary to sustain ourselves. Recalling E2post4, E4p18s emphasizes that 'we can never bring it about that we require nothing outside ourselves to preserve our being, nor live without having dealings with things outside us'. Spinoza thinks that the satisfaction of the requirements for self-preservation can take a predominantly passive or predominantly active cast: we can happen upon sustenance, find that it is offered to us, or arrange to provide it. In broad terms, the first two possibilities are imaginative and unpredictable, resulting in instability; the third possibility depends on our rational efforts, which lend stability. While passive satisfaction does enable us to survive and can increase our power, we are in such circumstances only partial causes and our ideas are inadequate (E3d3, p1). In practical terms, congenial affections are to some degree beneficial, but because we are unable to understand how they bring us joy and how we are part of an order of nature that exceeds us, we are unable either to reliably repeat the beneficial pattern or cope constructively with its absence. Imaginative satisfaction, in other words, can easily turn to dissatisfaction, and imagination by itself provides few tools for managing shifting fortunes and affects. In the worst cases, inadequate ideas can lead to terrible, even mortal, errors and profound misery. Letter XVIII explains how Adam, living only on the basis of imagination, confused poison for food and thereby shortened his life; someone more rational would have understood what to eat to further self-preservation and what to avoid.[34] E4p68s similarly emphasizes the baleful consequences of Adam's ignorance. Eating the fruit of the prohibited tree of knowledge of good and evil made him fear death rather than desire to live. The same meal, further, made it impossible for him to realize that Eve 'agreed completely with his nature'. Adam imagined satisfaction but experienced despair.[35]

If Adam exemplifies the precarious life of the ignorant, E4p45s sketches the flourishing life of the wise, for whom reason enables constructive action on exigencies of living and for whom human limitations prove more bearable.

---

[33] E3p59s introduces the idea of a change in bodily constitution or structure (*fabrica*) to explain hunger. E3p2 refers to sleep. Given the complexity of human beings, there may also be cases in which changes to a part do not change the ratio of the whole; cf. Matheron 1988/1969, 38–43 and Garrett's critique (Garrett 2018, 305–306).

[34] See the parallel discussion at TTP IV.26–27 (Giii 63) and the commentary in Deleuze 1988, 30–43.

[35] On Adam's becoming animal, p. 585.

E4p59dem instructs us that 'to act from reason is nothing else but to do what follows from the necessity of our own nature'. E4p25s notes that appropriate sustenance enables the whole body to be 'equally capable of all the things that follow from its nature' and, with it, the mind to be 'equally capable of understanding many things'. E4p45s explains that rational knowledge enables the wise person 'to refresh and restore himself in moderation with pleasant food and drink' and to enjoy beauty of all kinds, whether natural or artistic. Unlike Adam, the sage refrains from eating poison and actively pursues what is known to be sustaining and enhancing. E4p45s also indicates that the wise experience some variations in power without being destroyed. The wise need refreshment and restoration, i.e., replenishment. Reason and wisdom thus do not eliminate what we require—our need—but rather enable us to act with regard to it.[36] The wise individual neither overindulges, nor falls victim to the 'savage and sad superstition' that prescribes self-denial and suffering. In situations where we experience 'things contrary to what the principle of our advantage demands', the wise person is satisfied by knowing herself to be a 'part of the whole of nature, whose order we follow', that is, by agreement with nature (E4app xxxii). Where Adam's life quickly turned from enjoyment to fear, the wise experience the joy of rationally informed self-preservation. Conceived less minimally, then, human living is the active and actively increasing pursuit of self-preservation under the guidance of reason.

Spinoza's analysis of human development in E5p39s, particularly his account of the difference between life and death, brings the issues considered so far into sharp focus. The scholium draws nature or form together with power, underscores the relationship between mental and bodily capacity, and differentiates between passive and active regeneration. The infant, Spinoza informs us, 'has a Body capable of very few things, and very heavily dependent on external causes', and 'a Mind which considered solely in itself is conscious of almost nothing of itself, or of God, or of things' (E5p39s). Although Spinoza does not cite E2p13s or E2p14 here, his reference to the correlation between the body's capacity to be disposed in many ways with the mind's capacity to perceive many things recalls these antecedents. Where E2p13s stressed that understanding requires a body whose actions 'depend on itself alone', E5p39s considers the infant, whose life depends on 'external causes'. In this respect, E5p39s also picks up a discussion of the child's weak body and mind found in E3p32s. There, Spinoza observes that, far from reasoning for herself and acting on her own nature, the very young child immediately and without resistance receives and imitates the desires and feelings of others. The young child's body, in other words, has sufficient power to absorb impressions without being destroyed, but it lacks the power to reconfigure

---

[36] E5p4s sums up the difference, noting that one and the same necessity can be experienced as a passion or an action: 'all the appetites, or Desires, are passions only insofar as they arise from inadequate ideas, and are counted as virtues when they are aroused or generated by adequate ideas'.

affections in active terms and to direct itself. Consequently, the child's relation to others is dependent, mimetic, and imaginative. E5p6s confirms this picture, describing infants as unable to speak, walk, and reason. Children, according to Spinoza, 'live so many years, as it were, unconscious of themselves'. Their existence is, in Spinozan terms, more minimal than robust.

E5p39s contrasts the child who is overwhelmed by external affections, and consequently dies, with the child who lives in a constructive environment. Since we shall consider death in detail below, let us focus here on the living child. The living child, Spinoza explains, can 'change for the better', becoming happy (*felix*) by acquiring a body 'capable of a great many things' and a proportionately capable mind, one 'very much conscious of itself, and of God, and of things' (5p39s). Thus, the child begins in a state of weakness and ignorance, knowing 'neither himself, nor God, nor things' and, should affections cease, so would he. The same child can 'become conscious of himself, and of God, and of things' and so become active (E5p42s). Spinoza indexes this change in capacity to the child's nature: 'we strive especially that the infant's Body may be changed, as much as its nature allows and is conducive to it, into another capable of a great many things [*conamur ut Corpus infantiae in aliud, quantum ejus natura patitur, eique conducit, mutetur, quod ad prima aptum sit*] and related to a Mind very much conscious of itself, of God, and of things' (E5p39s). As the sequence of verbs suggests, in trying to make the infant's body more able, we must attend to what its nature can sustainably undergo and be advantaged by, lest our efforts produce a corpse instead of an adult.[37] Edwin Curley's transition of *patitur* as 'allows' and *conduco* with the dative pronoun as 'conducive' captures the sense in this passage that human nature admits some affections as useful but resists others as destructive. Dramatic as the change from infancy to maturity may be, Spinoza conceives it a change in power permitted by and facilitated by, the individual's nature, not a change of nature.

So far, we have been considering natural bodies. Social bodies illustrate what Adam's agreement in nature with Eve and the child's need for supportive adults suggest: our self-preservation requires other bodies not merely instrumentally, in the sense of subordinating them for our use, but also as complementary parts in mutually enhancing wholes. Human beings are too weak to survive alone, and connecting with others increases our power: If 'two individuals of the same nature are joined to one another, they compose an individual twice as powerful as each one'. The benefits of human connection are in principle unlimited:

---

[37] Another, more associative, way to think about *patitur* and *conduco* in this passage would be to stress that, in order to for undergoing to eventuate in the child's activity, we must affect the body in ways that it can bring together or connect.

140 SPINOZAN MEDITATIONS ON LIFE AND DEATH

> Man, I say, can wish for nothing more helpful to the preservation of his being than that all should so agree [*conveniant*] in all things that the Minds and Bodies of all would compose, as it were, one Mind and one Body; that all should strive together, as far as they can, to preserve their being; and that all, together, should seek for themselves the common advantage of all   (E4p18s).

Compared to the solitary person, the social body is better able to provide for its needs and withstand or repel threats. A Spinozan human being 'can hardly live a solitary life', and we 'derive, from the society of our fellow men, many more advantages than disadvantages'; 'by helping one another' human beings 'can provide themselves much more easily with what they require', and for 'only by joining forces can [human beings] avoid the dangers that threaten on all sides' (E4p35s). Hence 'The rational principle of seeking our own advantage teaches us the necessity of joining with men' (E4p37s1). The TTP in particular elaborates on the benefits of a social body for matters of security, sustenance, and the pursuit of human perfection. From agriculture and cooking to industry, art, and science, a life 'without an organized community' and 'mutual assistance' is 'wretched and almost brutal' (TTP V.18–20/GIII:73). TP II.15 makes the same point: 'Men can hardly sustain their lives and cultivate their minds without mutual aid.'

Like all bodies and so like human individuals themselves, social individuals are constituted by agreement (*convenientia*) (E4p18s). Spinoza argues that 'the more a thing agrees [*convenit*] with our nature, the more useful or better it is for us' (E4p31c). Given Spinoza's nominalism, perfect agreement is impossible; singulars things may be similar in virtue of commonalities (E4p29), but no two are identical (E3p57). For human beings, durable agreement depends on reason. Indeed, there is 'no singular thing in Nature that is more useful to a man than a man who lives according to the guidance of reason' (E4p35c1). As we saw above, reason enables us to act on the necessities of our nature; we keep ourselves together, and increase our power, by knowing what we need. In the case of social bodies, these necessities include social bonds, which reason generates and enhances insofar as it originates in and cultivates what is common, i.e. shareable and joinable (E2p40s1, E4p36). Rational people want for others what they want for themselves (E4p37). Like agreement, reason comes in degrees. Human beings may have relatively more or less (though not, per E4p29, nothing) in common, and their commonalities may be enhanced or diminished. To the extent that individuals are guided by reason— whether they are themselves genuinely rational or are induced to act as if they are rational by laws, practices, institutions, and social imaginaries—they are able to join together in a shared nature and strengthen their bonds. When, in contrast, human beings live by the guidance of imagination, they 'can disagree in nature insofar as they are torn by affects which are passions' (E3p33). Hence, they are 'often drawn in different directions (by E4p33) and are contrary to one another (by E4p34)', even 'while they require one another's aid' (E4p37s2). TTP XVI.14

concurs: 'By the laws of appetite, everyone is drawn in different directions' (Giii 191).

Without some degree of moderation by reason or, in more dire cases, by threats and force (E4p37s, TTP V.20 Giii 73), imaginative life yields commonalities too weak or abstract for durable and beneficial cohesion. Imaginative life does not, in other words, reliably sustain the processes of accommodation that characterize the agreement obtaining among the parts of a whole that we saw described in Letter XXXII.[38] Even the powerful dynamics of affective imitation (E3p27s) occur amidst the ambivalence and vacillations of mind that arise from the complex constitution of the body (E3p17s), the over-determination of images and affects (E2p18s, E3p27–57), and the sheer diversity of human beings and their desires (E3p57). If, moreover, we bear in mind Spinoza's insistence that that no one can completely alienate her natural right (TTP XVII.2 Giii 201), the challenge of establishing a harmonious and stable political *ratio* and thus the corresponding fragility of social bodies come clearly into view.[39] Spinoza's analyses in the TTP of the rise and fall of the Hebrew Commonwealth and other states, together with related discussions in the TP, are case studies in the integration and disintegration of social bodies.

3 Death *sub attributo extensionis*

Spinoza argues that destruction comes from exogenous forces: 'No thing can be destroyed except though an external cause' (E3p4). The demonstration presents the proposition as self-evident in view of the fact that a thing's definition 'affirms, and does not deny, the thing's essence, *or* it posits the thing's essence, and does not take it away'. By way of further explanation, Spinoza suggests that the thing's essence is an internal principle of identification, such that, if we attend to 'only to the thing itself, and not to external causes, we shall not be able to find anything in it which can destroy it' (E3p4dem).[40] In short, things do not self-destruct, for selfhood by its very nature involves preservation. For the same reason, 'Things are of a contrary nature, i.e. cannot be in the same subject, insofar as one can destroy the other' (E3p5). These propositions develop a point suggested in E1d2, namely, that finite things owe their finitude not to themselves, but to others: 'That thing is said to be finite in its own kind that can be limited by another of the same nature.'[41] Destruction is nothing if not evidence of finitude. E4p20s, which considers apparent suicides, reasserts the impossibility of self-destruction and

---

[38] E4appvii discusses political accommodation, and E4p70s advises the wise living amongst the ignorant.

[39] Cf. E4pp xii-xii on *ars et vigilantia* and TP VI.3, which defines the political *ars* as the production of *concordia*.

[40] E4p17s also presents E3p4 as self-evident.   [41] See Section 5.

142 SPINOZAN MEDITATIONS ON LIFE AND DEATH

offers a threefold classification of how external causes might operate. Since 'no one avoids food or kills himself from the necessity of his own nature', apparent acts of self-destruction are to be explained as externally coerced action, efforts to respond to coercive force by submitting to a lesser evil to avoid a greater evil, or instances of being overcome by hidden but effective causes.[42]

Spinoza treats human death in *Ethics* 4, whose sole axiom acknowledges the inevitable destruction of singular things: 'There is no singular thing in nature than which there is not another more powerful and stronger. Whatever one is given, there is another more powerful by which the first can be destroyed' (E4ax). As we saw in the Introduction, human beings are weak singular things, 'infinitely surpassed by the power of external causes' (E4p3), and consequently vulnerable to destruction, not masters of our fates (E4p4). As much as a Spinozan human being 'follows and obeys the common order of nature, and accommodates himself to it as much as the nature of things requires', accommodation is sometimes only partial, resulting in passions (4p4c) and sometimes in alterations of one's nature. Of course, accommodation sometimes proves impossible. Although we strive to avail ourselves of things that dispose the human body 'so that it can be affected in a great many ways' and become capable of affecting external bodies in a great many ways' (E4p38), other entities exceed our power to the point of threatening and eventually overcoming our capacity for self-preservation. E4appxxxiii emphasizes that much happens to us 'contrary to what the principle of our advantage demands' because we are an exceedingly finite 'part of the whole of nature, whose order we follow'.

If life is the minimal degree of organized power to be affected in many ways and persevere in existing through regeneration, death is the opposite extreme, a loss of organization and an incapacity to undergo affections. Where life involves hanging together, death is the process of being taken apart and reassembled into something else. In E4p39s, Spinoza defines the death of the body as encounter with

> things which bring it about that the human Body's parts acquire a different proportion of motion and rest to one another bring it about (by the same Definition) that the human Body takes on another form, i.e. (as is known through itself, and as I pointed out at the end of the preface of this Part), that the human Body is destroyed, and hence rendered completely incapable of being affected in many ways.

The definition at issue is the *individuum* in physics. Strictly speaking, death is de- and re-configuration, not absolute annihilation: 'I understand the [human] Body

---

[42] TTP 17.104 (Giii 219) gives the example of people so 'worn out by a great calamity or plague' that 'they all preferred death to life'.

to die when its parts are so disposed that they acquire a different proportion of motion and rest to one another' (E4p39s).[43] 'My' death is the regenerative process of some 'other' body that acquires parts of my body or even my body as a whole for its own preservation. To say that I die amounts to saying that the other body makes it impossible for me to exist at present and my parts are re-distributed to another or other bodies (E3p11s). Death is the expropriation of my parts for an incompatible *conatus*. Where I was, something else is.[44]

If the E4p39s definition of bodily death is fairly straightforward, the remainder of the scholium is decidedly more obscure. In a cryptic, elliptical passage, Spinoza remarks that death need not involve a corpse:

> Even though the circulation of the blood is maintained, as well as other [signs] on account of which the Body is thought to be alive—the human Body can nevertheless be changed into another nature entirely different from its own. For no reason compels me to maintain that the Body does not die unless it is changed into a corpse.

If some degree of alteration is consistent with persevering in one's ratio, Spinoza raises the question, 'How much?' and, further, 'In what regard?' As an example of corpse-less death, he gives us the unnamed Spanish Poet, who fell ill and upon recovering could not recognize his own works, appears to have died and become someone else: 'Sometimes a man undergoes such changes that I should hardly have said he was the same man.'[45] Much depends on the meaning of 'same', and it is difficult to determine the degree of alteration that marks the transformation of one ratio into another, such that the man formerly known as the Spanish Poet is no longer knowable under that description. If illness and recovery represent the elasticity and homeostatic resilience of an individual, an illness severe or systemic enough to alter the individual's defining capacities would seem to bring about a kind of transformation. Here we seem to have the alteration in one's nature to which Spinoza alludes in E4pc. But Spinoza gives us little guidance for determining the boundary between alteration compatible with one's nature and transformation into a different nature. Although the transformations of illness have made the Spanish Poet's history as poet inaccessible—in technical terms, the traces of those events in his body cannot be recalled and reactivated (E2p17–18)—he nevertheless remains alive and remains human. Even had he 'forgotten his native

---

[43] Cf. Letter XXXVI: 'To destroy a thing is to separate it into parts of the same kind so that none of them express the nature of the whole [*rem destruere est illam in ejusmodi partes resolvere, ut nulla earum omnium naturam totius exprimat*]' (Cii 29/Giv 184). E4p37s1 treats animal death.

[44] Rorty 1987 suggests that my investment in some notion of myself is 'temporary and temporizing' (Rorty 1987, 299), i.e. as I shall argue, anchored in imagination.

[45] For a different reading of the Spanish Poet, see Monaco 2018.

language' and so become 'a grown-up infant', he would similarly remain alive and remain human. And yet his life would not be fully continuous with his previous life; once a practicing Spanish Poet, the man has assumed a different form of life. Spinoza's idea of corpse-less death seems to acknowledge this situation of shifting identity and to indicate that we can speak of identity at different scales or degrees and in different respects. One can remain a man, but cease to be a poet.

A second enigmatic addition to the scholium introduces human growth and development as a comparison case. If the poet's corpse-less death seems 'incredible', Spinoza invites us to consider the example of the elderly person who cannot believe he was ever an infant. Spinozan elders grasp the continuity of their own history only because they see others develop; lacking introspective awareness, they must observe others and make inferences about themselves, however odd or implausible the inference may seem. Unfortunately for us, the scholium ends abruptly, without a clear conclusion. Citing the need to avoid arousing superstitious speculation, Spinoza offers only an abrupt promise to provide a more systematic explanation of continuity and change in human development later.[46] E5p39s, which we examined above in Section 2, resumes and resolves the discussion, explaining human development in terms of changes sustainable by the infant's nature, which it contrasts precisely to the production of a corpse and the losses of the Spanish Poet.

Let us consider one more case of corpse-less death, the biblical Adam in E4p68s. Compared to the Spanish Poet, Adam represents an alteration in some ways more extreme. As we saw above, Adam's fateful meal caused him to reject his wife 'who agreed completely with his nature'. Through this same process, Adam became more animal than human. Because 'he believed the lower animals to be like himself', Adam 'began to imitate their affects (see 3p27) and to lose his freedom'. E3p57s and E4p37s1 argue that animals are normally too different from our ratio for us to join with them, but Adam's misperception of likeness altered his ratio, generating non-human affects and undermining his own capacity for activity. Adam's becoming bestial is thus not the production of a corpse, but it is process of becoming other than human. He relinquished what Spinoza elsewhere describes as the capacity to live a human as opposed to an animal life: 'When we say, then, that the best state is one where men pass their lives harmoniously, I mean that they pass a human life, one defined not merely by the circulation of the blood, and other things common to all animals, but mostly by reason, the true virtue and life of the Mind' (TP V.5). The political equivalent of this corpse-less death would be the de- and re-configurations of civil strife and regime change.

---

[46] Curley thinks Spinoza was trying to avoid discussing immaterial souls and transmigration. Curley 1985. 569, n.22).

4 Life and death *sub attributo cogitationis*

So much for the life and death of bodies. What about minds? Spinoza uses the expression 'the life of the mind' only once in the *Ethics*: 'No life, then, is rational without understanding, and things are good only insofar as they aid man to enjoy the life of the Mind, which is defined by understanding' (E4app5). As we just saw, the phrase also appears in TP V.5, which contrasts mere animal life with 'the true virtue and life of the Mind'. As we have seen, Spinoza prefers *potentia* to *vita*. Thus, E5pref uses the expression *mentis, seu rationis potentia* (Gii 277) and insists that 'the power of the Mind is defined only by understanding' (*mentis potentia sola intelligentia definitur*) (Gii 280). These early expressions in *Ethics* 5 recall earlier propositions about virtue and draw together central terms in Spinoza's lexicon. In E4p20dem, Spinoza identifies virtue with 'human power itself [*ipsa humana potentia*]'. Almost immediately thereafter, he calls the striving to persevere in existing as the 'first and only foundation of virtue' (p22c) and identifies *conatus intelligendi* as the 'first and only foundation of virtue' (p26dem). Spinoza sums up these results in E4appiv, noting that the best life is the one devoted to perfecting the intellect, i.e. to acquiring intuitive knowledge of God, oneself, and things one can understand. What E4appiv sketches, Part 5 elaborates. There, Spinoza also replaces the idea of the 'life of the mind' with the idea of the intellect as the eternal part of the mind (E5p23, 29, p40c). We 'feel and know that we are eternal' (E5p23s), or, as Spinoza tells us in E5p36s, the third kind of knowing is 'more powerful' than the second kind because the intuiting mind experiences the immanent causal power of God or Nature. Here we very clearly see the connection of power, necessity, and eternity in Spinoza's philosophy.

Thus far, we have examined how Spinoza relates the increasing power, or life, of the mind to the increasing power, or life, of the body. In a curious and somewhat puzzling way, Spinoza's account of increasing one's power of understanding also alludes to death *sub attributo cogitationis*. As in the case of bodies, death in minds is de- and re-configuration. In one sense, since a human mind is nothing but the idea of its actually existing body (E2p11,13), a reshaped body comes with a reshaped mind.[47] E5p23s is clear: 'Our mind...can be said to endure...only insofar as it involves the actual existence of the body.' There is in addition a second, more subtle, and arguably more important sense of death *sub attributo cogitationis*. As we saw above in the Introduction, Spinoza holds that 'the essence of the Mind is constituted by adequate and by inadequate ideas (as we have shown in p3)' (E3p9dem).[48] Since the mind is its ideas (E2p48s), E3p9 means that

---

[47] Cf. Lin 2005, 255–258.
[48] E2p7s suggests *ratio mentis* on the model of the form of a body. E2p21 argues that the form of the mind is the idea of the mind, but the discussion at E3p9 seems much clearer.

changes in the relative proportions of the constitutive ideas are changes in the essence of the mind. The more a mind is constituted by, or, as Spinoza sometimes says synonymously, is occupied by,[49] imaginative ideas, the more passive the knower is. The more a mind is constituted by knowledge of the second and third kind, the more active she is (E3d2, p1). In other words, an increasingly active individual is more able to persevere in existing (E4p24), experience her power as part of the power of nature, and feel joy and intellectual love (E5p36s). In *Ethics* 5, Spinoza describes this increase in power in terms of the cessation of passions and the perishing of imagination. Thus corpse-less death figures in cognitive development.

E5p3 presents affective re-configuration as cessation. As we reinterpret images in terms of their constituent causal networks, the active joy of understanding supplants the passions characteristic of imaginative experience: 'An affect which is a passion ceases to be a passion as soon as we form a clear and distinct idea of it' (E5p3). Passions 'cease'—die—when confused and mutilated ideas are rethought as ordered and connected. To be sure, E5p4s emphasizes that our capacity to form clear and distinct ideas of our affects is limited, and E5p20s explains that increasing our power of understanding does not 'absolutely remove' the affects, but rather 'brings it about that they constitute the smallest part of the Mind' (E5p20s). Spinoza is also quite explicit that the acquisition of knowledge of the second and third kind neither eradicates nor abolishes the bodily affections that imagination presents. Imaginative ideas really do 'indicate the natural constitution of the Body, or that its power of acting is increased or diminished' (E4p1).[50] The cessation of imaginative affects—passions—occurs instead in thought, as a shift in the way of thinking about events that actually happen in the body. To some extent, rational individuals experience more joy because they more usefully navigate their environments. Given, however, the weak force of human beings (even as collectives) in nature, not all shifts in thinking will be manifest as more prolonged or more vigorous bodily life.[51] Spinoza thus points beyond our power to optimize durational affairs and toward changes in how we experience what happens to us and what we do.[52] As the concluding paragraph of E4app suggests, coming to understand events in causal terms that include but extend beyond us attunes us to the order of necessity, true knowledge of which alleviates suffering and provides satisfaction. To the extent that the mind is able to connect the body's affections to

---

[49] E.g. E5p39dem.

[50] See also E5p21, which uses E2p8c and p26 to show that imagining exhibits the actual existence of the body.

[51] Thus, Seneca's adherence to his principles lead to death (4p20s). E4pref also indicates that expressing one's nature and power—what he calls activity—is not equivalent to longevity: 'No singular things can be called more perfect [sc. more real] for having persevered in existing for a longer time. The duration of things cannot be determined from their essence, since the essence of things involves no certain and determinate time of existing' (Gii 209). Youpa 2003 treats this issue at length.

[52] In Klein 2014 and 2020, I analyse the change as a perspectival shift.

the idea of God, that is, understand them adequately, it rejoices and experiences an uncorruptible love (E5p18, p20s). Where imagination presents bodily events as affections, reason expresses our power of actively engaging the same events.

E5p38s refers to 'the part of the Mind which we have shown perishes with the body', i.e. the imagination, as being 'of no moment in relation to what remains'. Here, too, we encounter the idea of a re-organization in ideas and a different way of thinking about what we experience. In the second and third kinds of knowing, imagination 'perishes' in the sense of being left aside or receding from view as the common notions organize the mind (e.g. E2p29s, 2p38–40s1). As the mind is more extensively occupied by adequate ideas, inadequate ideas are displaced and their power shrinks. Thus 'being of no moment' means being of no relevance. A few key propositions make the differences between imagining and understanding apparent. With respect to imagining, E2p30 argues that 'we can have only an entirely inadequate knowledge [*cognitio*] of the duration of our body'. The reason is that we know our body through its affections, ideas of which are confused insofar as they are isolated in relation to our body alone (E2p28) rather than considered in wider causal networks.[53] As we saw in the Introduction, this same imaginative process leads to the idea that things are contingent and corruptible, i.e. natal and mortal (E2p31c). By contrast, reason 'perceives things under a certain species of eternity [*sub quadam aeternitatis specie*]' (E2p44c). Beyond reason, intuition, which apprehends singular things in relation to God, involves understanding 'the very nature of existence', not 'duration, i.e. existence insofar as it is conceived abstractly' (E2p45s). On this issue, E4p62dem, which equates conceiving things *sub specie aeternitatis* with conceiving them *sub specie necessitatis*, provides a crucial clarification.

Considering death *sub attributo cogitationis* also brings us to Spinoza's claims about the eternity of the mind and the sense in which neither life nor death is relevant to eternity. Spinoza introduces the discussion of *scientia intuitiva* by noting in E5p20s that 'it is time to pass to those things which pertain to the Mind's duration without relation to the body'. The deep and perhaps instructive irony of announcing a time to pass beyond time notwithstanding, the remaining propositions concern the eternity of the mind we feel in *scientia intuitiva*. E5p23 argues that, even if the human body is destroyed, there is a sense in which the Mind remains: 'The human Mind cannot be absolutely destroyed with the Body, but something of it remains which is eternal.' This 'something that pertains to the essence of the Mind' (E5p23dem), precisely as eternal—Spinoza is here drawing on, but does not cite, E1d8—is 'neither defined by time nor [has] any relation to time' (5p23s). This 'something' 'expresses the essence of the body *sub specie aeternitatis*', i.e., is a mode of thinking which is eternal and necessary. It is, in

---

[53] Cf. E4p18s: 'If we consider our Mind, our intellect would of course be more imperfect if the Mind were alone and did not understand anything except itself.'

148 SPINOZAN MEDITATIONS ON LIFE AND DEATH

other words, the formal reality of the mind as a mode in the attribute of thought.[54] Spinoza's provocative claim in E5p23s that the mind 'feels those things that it conceived in the understanding no less than those it has in memory' emphasizes the contrast between the intellectual feeling that 'our mind, insofar as it involves the essence of the body *sub species aeternitatis*, is eternal, and that the existence it has cannot be defined through time *or* explained through duration' and the imaginative sense of existing as endurance through time, which depends on 'the actual existence of the body' (E2p18s). To the extent or degree, then, that we are able to conceive the formal essence of our minds, we feel intellectually that we are eternal.

E5p29 demonstrates what E5p23s suggests: 'Whatever the Mind understands *sub specie aeternitatis*, it understands not from the fact that it conceives the Body's present actual existence, but from the fact that it conceives the Body's essence *sub specie aeternitatis*.' Put more simply, understanding *sub specie aeternitatis* ignores precisely what thinking *sub specie temporis seu durationis* requires. The demonstration is fairly straightforward. Spinoza argues that to conceive the 'present actual existence' of the Body is to locate it in time and measure its duration (E5p21 and 2p26). Since, however, E1d8 and its explanation instruct us that 'eternity cannot be explained by duration', to the extent that the Mind employs the apparatus of duration, it 'does not have the power of conceiving things *sub specie aeternitatis*'. To the extent that we think of things *sub specie aeternatitatis*, we think of them as involving 'the eternal and finite essence of God (as we have shown in 2p45 and p45s)' (5p29s), and that eternal and infinite essence of God is 'necessary existence' (E5p30dem). Hence our thinking can be only a meditation on one's life as the power of existing, i.e. on a singular mode as an immanent expression of the power of god or substance or nature (E1p25c, 5p36s). E5p36s further explains that we can know 'how our Mind, with respect to both essence and existence, follows from the divine nature' through either the second kind of knowledge or the third. While what Spinoza calls the 'universal' or rational knowledge of this idea is powerful, the excessive joy and *amor dei intellectualis* the intuitive knower experiences 'when this is inferred from the very essence of a singular thing which we say depends on God' are the very feeling of expressing the power of existing, which is eternal and necessary (E5p36s).

5 Conclusion: the inside and the outside

Thus far, I hope to have explicated Spinoza's senses of life and death and to have defended him against some critics. Against Matson's disappointment, I have

---

[54] See also CM II.1: 'Duration cannot in any way pertain to the essences of things. For no one will ever say that the essence of a circle or triangle, insofar as it is an eternal truth, has endured longer now than it has since the time of Adam.'

argued that Spinozan life, understood robustly for human beings as living under the guidance of reason and as *conatus intelligendi*, offers considerable joy. Consideration of the relative, scalar character of Spinoza's claims about knowledge and freedom, exemplified in his 'insofar as' (*quatenus*) and 'the more... the more' (*quamprimus... quamprimus*) formulations, ameliorates concerns that he counsels unachievable goals. Human beings can become more rational and active without becoming absolutely so. These resolutions notwithstanding, Spinoza's insistence on destruction by external forces remains problematic, for it conflicts with his metaphysical and physical affirmation of the causal co-constitution and inter-relation of singular things. In this concluding section, I suggest that our idea of bounded things or easily discernable individuals is imaginative and so provisional. Far from being unreal, it makes possible the very investigation that undermines it.[55]

As we saw, E3p4 argues that 'No thing can be destroyed except through an external cause.' Tempting as it might be to suppose that the proposition refers to really discrete individuals whose interior and exterior can be reliably determined, Spinoza's definition of singular things (E2d7) does not instruct us where to draw the boundaries of the causally concurring, complex assemblies. Nor for that matter does he inform us about the point at which accommodation and flexibility end, such that concurrence is transformed into difference and disagreement. By leaving the question of the *termini* of determinate things open, and indeed by specifying that individuals constitute a singular thing to the extent that they concur, E2d7 seems at the very least to defer our wish for clearly bounded individuals. It also indicates that we may predicate singularity at different scales and at different degrees of agreement.[56] How much and what kind, then, of concurrence need we perceive to discern a singular thing, and what differentiates one singular thing from another? When E3p4dem concludes, 'So while we attend only to the thing itself, and not to external causes, we shall not be able to find anything in it which destroys it', we need to know what it means to attend 'only to the thing itself, and not to external causes'. This question is all the more urgent in view of the way that the pivotal *conatus* propositions invoke the striving of 'each thing' (E3p6–8).

Returning to E1p28 and E2lemm3, which establish respectively, Spinoza's metaphysical and physical arguments that singular things exist in an infinite and dynamic causal network, complicates the question considerably. According to Spinoza, every singular thing, at whatever level of complexity or integration with other modes, is a determinate expression of the infinite power of nature.

---

[55] Oksenberg Rorty makes a similar point: 'The original limited point with which we begin— Hobbesian individuals endeavoring to preserve themselves—is meant both to be undermined *and* to be affirmed (Oksenberg Rorty 1987, 315).

[56] Sacksteder describes Spinoza's 'sliding scale of individuals' (Sacksteder 1977, 143) and coins the expression 'mid-region beings' (Sacksteder 1985).

150 SPINOZAN MEDITATIONS ON LIFE AND DEATH

As modes, Spinozan singular things are both determined and determining, and the regress of determination is infinite:

> Every singular thing, or any thing which is finite and has a determinate existence, can neither exist nor be determined to produce an effect unless it is determined to exist and produce an effect by another cause, which is also finite and has a determinate existence; and again, this cause also can neither exist nor be determined to produce an effect unless it is determined to exist and produce an effect by another, which is also finite and has a determinate existence, and so on, to infinity (E1p28).[57]

In the case of bodies,

> A body which moves or is at rest must be determined to motion or rest by another body, which has also been determined to motion or rest by another, and that again by another, and so on, to infinity (E2lemm3).

Considering the implications of E1p28 and in view of Spinoza's insistence on necessity in E1p29, Étienne Balibar has introduced the idea of transindividuation to distinguish the dynamic relations of co-constitution in Spinozan nature from an array of discrete, static things.[58] From a different but complementary perspective, Noa Shein has explicated E1p28 and its echo in E2lemm3 in terms of 'inter-determining relations'. Crucially, Balibar and Shein direct us to see the causal relations described in E1p29 as '*constitutive* of the individuation of finite modes rather than describing the interaction between already established finite singular things'.[59]

Shein uses Spinoza's physics to exhibit the constitutive character of causal relations. Given Spinoza's plenum physics, E2lemm3 requires that all motion be understood relationally and hence that bodies be understood as reciprocally involved, i.e. inter-determining. Any given body has its characteristic proportion of motion and rest amidst surrounding bodies, which it is simultaneously affecting and being affected by in the course of its persistence. Surrounding bodies in turn have surrounding bodies, and so on, such that any given body's causal relations occur both proximately and distally. As we saw in Section 2 above, Letter XXXII emphasized both local and larger-scale determination:

---

[57] Cf. E5p6dem: 'The Mind understands all things to be necessary (by 1p29), and to be determined by an infinite connection of causes to exist and produce effects (by 1p28).' TTP IV.4 (Giii 58) reiterates the theme. Spinoza's E1ax4 also captures the interconnected, mutually constitutive way singular things exist.

[58] Balibar 1997. Other helpful commentaries include Ravven 1998 and, Morfino 2006, and Sharp 2011, 21–54.

[59] Shein 2015, 335 [emphasis original] and 2017.

all bodies are surrounded by others, and are determined by one another to existing and producing an effect in a fixed and determinate way, the same ratio of motion to rest always being preserved in all of them at once, [that is, in the whole universe]. From this it follows that every body, insofar as it exists modified in a definite way, must be considered as a part of the whole universe, must agree with its whole and must cohere with the remaining bodies   (Giv 172–3a/Cii 19).

If no body is an island, with a clear line of demarcation and empty space between itself and others, it is hard to discern the boundary between its 'inside' and its 'outside', that is, between a thing and its causal environment. Indeed, the 'internal' motions of a thing and the 'external' motion of its others are one and the same motion, understood from different perspectives, not two motions. Thus, it seems we would search in vain for an intellectual idea of an ontologically discrete separate finite thing.[60] Letter XXXII acknowledges, further, that we can move from considering any given body as a whole to considering all bodies in their agreement as parts of a single whole, the universe. If one and the same thing can be conceived as a part and a whole, what explains the different scales at which we predicate part-whole relations?

Here the principal image of Letter XXXII, the 'worm in the blood', provides an answer. The Spinozan worm's location and restricted cognitive power model how we live in our 'part of the universe' (Giv171a/Cii19). Just as the worm sees a collection of different particles and their collisions but cannot grasp them as parts integrated into the nature of the blood as a whole, nor conceive anything outside the blood into which it is integrated as a part, so too human knowers take parts for wholes. We perceive—myopically—local discrepancy rather than more expansive relations of agreement and accommodation, and our perceptions of disagreement produce ideas of distinct wholes. If agreements signal parthood, disagreement signals wholeness. Insofar as things 'disagree with one another [*inter se discrepant*], to that extent each forms in our Mind an idea distinct from the others, and therefore it is considered as a whole and not as a part' (Giv 170a/Cii 18). Perceptions of disagreement themselves reflect cognitive limitation. The worm 'is capable of distinguishing' particles of the blood and 'capable of observing by reason how each particle, when it encounters another, either bounces back, or communicates a part of its motion, etc.', but its limited observations and its minimal power of making distinctions are not sufficient to generate knowledge. The worm 'could not know [*nec scire posset*] how all the parts of the blood are

---

[60] Balibar comments: 'Spinoza never actually says that anyone whose actions can be explained by his own or his sole nature (*per solam suam naturam intelligi*) is acting solely, or separately from the others' (1997, 24). Armstrong 2009 concurs and explores Spinoza as a theorist of relational autonomy; see also Tucker 2019. Still, many commentators find discrete individuals, e.g. Garrett (1994), Della Rocca (2008, 187) and (Viljanen 2011, 155).

regulated by the universal nature of the blood, and compelled to accommodate themselves to one another' (Giv 171a/Cii 19). The worm's experience is a cautionary tale: much as human abilities surpass the worm's, they are not unlimited. E1p33s1, for example, attributes the idea of contingency or possibility to 'a defect of our knowledge' according to which 'the order of causes is hidden to us'. TTP IV.4 notes that, given our ignorance 'of how things are really ordered and connected', considerations of practicality make it 'better, indeed necessary, to consider things as possible' (Giii 58).

In denying the worm knowledge, Letter XXXII indicates that ideas of the boundaries of things, as marks of the limits at which we can see the integration of things and differentiate 'internal' agreement from disagreement with some 'external' force, originate in imagination. Plainly put, they are artefacts of our position and powers. Turning back to the *Ethics*, the idea of free will is the example *par excellence* of imagined disconnection and self-enclosure.[61] Spinoza rejects free will precisely as a fantasy of causal independence, i.e. detachment and boundedness, rather than inter-determination: 'men are deceived in that they think themselves free [NS: i.e., they think that, of their own free will, they can either do a thing or forbear doing it], an opinion which consists only in this, that they are conscious of their actions and ignorant of the causes by which they are determined' (E5p35s; see also E1App).[62] At a lesser extreme, however, ideas of boundaries and distinctions between self and another can—but may not always—be clues for self-preservation and for connection. To the extent that I discern my own characteristic *ratio*, even inadequately, I can strive to act on what I take to be the requirements of my *ratio*. Looked at the other way round, my interactions can prod me to begin to discern, even inadequately, my *ratio*. If, in short, my path in nature has been for whatever reason relatively constructive, more congenial than disagreeable, those experiences and ideas of them may provide pointers to comprehending my nature and so to finding compatible others. Thus, the imaginative selections and projections that constitute separation can initiate useful commonality.

More specifically, while a collection of fortunate affections and connections does not automatically produce action, the commonality I can experience in encounters with congenial others and the way I manage to avoid dangers can enable the emergence of reason. Thus, even an imaginative idea of myself can be the beginning of living according to reason and not merely the source of

---

[61] E1p15s also suggests that the idea of discrete parts of substance is imaginative (Ci 423–425/Gii 59–60). While I cannot adequately defend the claim here, it is crucial to recognize that imaginative ideas are no less real than intellectual ideas. That they are incommensurable need not lead us to regard imaginative ideas as merely illusory.

[62] Cf. E3pref and TP I.2 for Spinoza's rejection of conceiving a human being as an *imperium in imperio*. Letter LVIII (Giv 266) and TP II.7 differentiate divine and human freedom.

destructive fantasies like free will.[63] My local awareness and my local self-image are, from this perspective, at the origin of my ability to understand myself as a mode among modes and an expression of the power of substance. In the presence of a constructive affective regime, imaginative ideas are starting points that may lead to reason, which may give rise to *amor dei intellectualis* and an intuitive apprehension of the relation of singular things to God (E2p40s2, 5p36, 5p36s; TTP IV.11 Giii 60).

From the standpoint of considering life and death, the connection to living is manifest most strongly in Spinoza's insistence that knowledge of the third kind is 'more powerful' (*potior*) than knowledge of the second kind (E5p36s). Given Spinoza's identification of life with *potentia*, we can say that *scientia intuitiva* is the most vivacious experience, an immediate apprehension of how our mind 'follows from the divine nature and continually depends on God' (E5p36s). Reason too, is indisputably powerful, even without leading to *scientia intuitiva*. The mind's actions 'arise from adequate ideas' (E3p3), and 'acting, living, and preserving our being' 'signify the same thing' (E4p24). Thus, the Spinozan free person 'thinks of nothing less than of death' and instead meditates on life, experiencing the power of nature as joy and love rather than fear and sadness. As all readers of Spinoza know, any human mind is an idea of its body (E2p11, 13), and the more the body can undergo, the more the mind can know and do (E2p14, 3p11,4p38, 5p39). Hence 'we strive especially that the infant's Body may change (as much as its nature allows and assists) into another, capable of a great many things and related to a Mind very much conscious of itself, of God, and of things' (E5p39s). In this light, the lives and deaths of natural and social bodies, are as relevant and interesting as the lives of minds. They provide clear illustrations of *rationes* as stable but flexible patterns of communicating force and of the processes of de- and re-configuration. Spinoza's analysis of death is perhaps particularly provocative in bringing to light the way he conceives individuation and identity in terms of scales, degrees, and respects.[64]

---

[63] James 2011 and 2012 provide the most sustained analysis of how imaginative regimes may lead to living according to the guidance of reason and actually coming to understand. Deleuze's discussion of more and less general common notions is helpful on this point (Deleuze 1990, 275–279).

[64] I thank the participants in the original London conference and subsequent readers, Susan James, Noa Shein, Mogens Laerke, and Michael Della Rocca foremost among them, for their immensely helpful comments on this essay.

PART IV
LEARNING TO DIE

7

Meditatio Mortis: Post-Cartesian Conceptions of Life and the Conjunction of Mind and Body

Michael Jaworzyn

According to one early Cartesian, Johannes Clauberg (1622–1665), the dissolution of what he calls the 'conjunction' of mind and body can come about in various ways. Like other Cartesians, Clauberg holds that the proximate cause of the most prominent form of dissolution, death itself, always lies in the body—more particularly, in 'a division or change of shape'.[1] But for Clauberg death is not the only way the conjunction of mind and body can dissolve, and the body is not its only cause. The mind can also bring about the dissolution of its conjunction with the body. In fact, in states of the most intense philosophical thought, that is exactly what occurs, giving rise to a form of ecstasy. 'That state of the mind,' Clauberg says, 'in which [the mind] exists while it most profoundly contemplates, entirely abstracted from the senses and the imagination, is called *Ecstasis*: of which all more than usually attentive metaphysical contemplation is a certain grade'.[2] In this respect, according to Clauberg, the Platonic definition of philosophy as *meditatio mortis* is apt, and this means philosophy involves the 'separation of the soul from the body'.[3] In this ecstatic state, the mind experiences 'pleasures of its own'; but there is a crucial qualification: 'at that time', Clauberg says, 'we would not perceive the sweetness of this life'.[4] Here he seems to confer on Cartesian thought what Rainer Specht has referred to as an 'ascetic sense'.[5]

---

[1] Clauberg 1691/1968, 683. Hereafter cited as OOP.

[2] OOP 262: 'Status autem ille mentis, in quo existit dum profundissime contemplatur, à sensibus & imaginatione prorsus abstractâ, *Ecstasis* appellatur: cujus gradus quidam est omnis Metaphysica contemplatio attentior solito.'

[3] References to *meditatio mortis* (or close variations) can be found at OOP 249, OOP 511, OOP 681, and OOP 1058, which is to say in works written in Clauberg's own name, works commenting on Descartes, and works defending Descartes against attacks by Jacob Revius and Cyriacus Lentulus (there is overlap between this last category and the first two).

[4] OOP 242: 'Ita anima suas delectations separatim habere potest, intelligibilium rerurm contemplation intentus & à corpore abstractus, licèt *vitae hujus* dulcedinum tunc temporis non percipiamus.'

[5] Specht 1966. It should not be forgotten, however, that Clauberg, presumably recognizing that this risks making our conjunction to the body undesirable in itself, hastens to add that for various reasons

---

Michael Jaworzyn, 'Meditatio Mortis': *Post-Cartesian Conceptions of Life and the Conjunction of Mind and Body* In: *Life and Death in Early Modern Philosophy.* Edited by: Susan James, Oxford University Press. © Michael Jaworzyn 2021. DOI: 10.1093/oso/9780192843616.003.0008

158 'MEDITATIO MORTIS': POST-CARTESIAN

This view certainly looks like something of a departure from Descartes' own philosophy.[6] At the very least, it requires an elaboration of Cartesian views, and involves making both subtle and overt changes to them. As far as *meditatio mortis* is concerned, Clauberg's most important departures from Descartes occur in his accounts of life and death, the mind-body conjunction, and the relation between sense perception and intellection. These reconfigurations of Cartesian thought are of interest not only from the perspective of how Clauberg himself is understood, but also in the context of the early reception of Cartesianism. There are reasons to suspect—based on what other contemporaneous thinkers took to be problematic about Cartesianism—that Clauberg's reference to *meditatio mortis* could have endangered any Cartesian claim to avoid the charge of Pelagianism, and also undermined the careful separation between philosophical and theological thought drawn by other Cartesians in the Dutch context. If, as is widely assumed, Clauberg was committed to the establishment of a Cartesian 'scholasticism' in the Dutch and German universities, it seems surprising that he should have made such theologically controversial modifications to Cartesianism. It is clear enough, however, that the objections to his view raised by anti-Cartesian opponents did not impress him. As he saw it, his position was compatible with Cartesianism and with religious orthodoxy.[7]

Although Clauberg does not seem to have taken *meditatio mortis* to have any direct bearing on questions regarding our salvation, he did take it to mean that philosophizing can involve the separation of the mind from the body. His account of this separation goes beyond the apparently similar claims made by Descartes, and the differences between them are the subject of the first part of this chapter. Clauberg provides a broader account of life and death than Descartes, and a subtly different analysis of the relation between the senses and the intellect. The second part of the chapter looks at Clauberg's account of life and the 'vital' conjunction of mind and body, and examines an objection raised by another influential Cartesian, Louis de La Forge (1632–1666). These steps in the argument make way for a reading of Clauberg's work according to which the conjunction of mind

---

being joined to a body is 'delectable' (and praiseworthy for God to have brought about). See, e.g., OOP 246–248. Nevertheless, that does not mean that the goods of the human composite and the goods of the soul might not actually coincide.

[6] Although compare Grigoropoulou 2012, 177–195. Grigoropoulou suggests that Plato's 'ambiguous' conception of death contributes to Descartes's philosophical understanding of the separation of soul and body (182); but even if this is conceded, Clauberg, as we will see, elaborates still further on the connection.

[7] It is difficult to say with any certainty what precisely motivated Clauberg in invoking *meditatio mortis*. Perhaps he took the Platonic authorities—he cites both Plato himself and Marsilio Ficino (1433–1499)—to be sufficiently persuasive of themselves; he certainly was not averse to making use of a great variety of sources from different traditions. Here I am interested primarily the question of what Clauberg needs to say in order to accommodate an understanding of philosophy as *meditatio mortis* in a broadly Cartesian context, which for various reasons is not obviously suited to it, rather than tracing the history of *meditatio mortis*.

and body can be dissolved by philosophical contemplation. The third part of the chapter considers this position in more detail, focusing on Clauberg's distinctive account of the relation between the confused sense perceptions that bind the mind to the body, and purely intellectual perception. The final part turns to the broader significance of Clauberg's *meditatio mortis*. Although the aspects of Clauberg's work at stake in this chapter clearly bear on some of the theological controversies of the period, I argue that, for Clauberg, the main issue at stake is the relationship between philosophical contemplation and the good health or vitality of the human being.

1 Clauberg's Cartesianism, *meditatio mortis*, and philosophy as the separation of the mind from the body

Clauberg often comes across as a wholly committed defender of Descartes, to the point where he could well be described as unoriginal.[8] It is true that a good deal of his work was intended both to defend Descartes against critics such as Jacob Revius (1586–1658) and Cyriacus Lentulus (1620–1678),[9] and to extend Cartesian principles into domains beyond those Descartes had written about. Clauberg's Cartesian logic and ontology, for example, and his attempts to consolidate the place of Cartesianism within Dutch and German education, contributed to the establishment of what Bohatec has referred to as a 'Cartesian scholasticism'.[10] As Bohatec indicates, Cartesian scholasticism was eclectic, even if its most recogniz-able characteristic was incorporating what would have been seen as primarily Aristotelian tendencies—just as more properly Aristotelian scholasticism had influences other than Aristotle.[11] But, given Clauberg's reputation as a dedicated Cartesian, it may still be surprising to find that he deviates from Descartes' conception of the conjunction of mind and body, and still more surprising that he appeals to a Platonic tradition in doing so.[12] As one would expect, much of what Clauberg says in the context of *meditatio mortis* is solidly grounded in

---

[8] For details of Clauberg's life and bibliography, see Verbeek 1999b, 181–199. Leibniz is responsible for one assertion regarding Clauberg's lack of originality with respect to Descartes (even if he found Clauberg the clearer of the two); Clauberg was included in a list he gave of Cartesians who had only paraphrased Descartes. On this, see Schmaltz 2016. 1–2.

[9] Strazzoni 2013, 123–149, examines one example of how Clauberg's works responded to polemics against Cartesianism; the numerous references throughout Clauberg's work to Revius and Lentulus indicate that this approach could help to explain Clauberg's choice of emphasis and terminology in many other instances too.

[10] See, e.g., Bohatec 1912, 18. The classic study of early Cartesianism in the Netherlands remains Verbeek 1992. For Descartes reception in Germany, Trevisani 2011.

[11] For a recent account of this movement outlining similarities and differences between Clauberg's and De Raey's respective attempts at a *philosophie novantique*, see Schmaltz 2016, 77–83.

[12] Clauberg's proximity to (neo-) Platonism has been noted by Spruit 1999, 75–93, particularly referring to its importance for Clauberg's theory of ideas. Here I address a different Platonic tendency

160   'MEDITATIO MORTIS': POST-CARTESIAN

Cartesian claims. The first question to consider is therefore how he departs from them.

Meditatio mortis, and the concomitant idea that philosophical meditation brings about a separation of mind and body, are mentioned on various occasions in Clauberg's work, and spelled out in a number of ways. Most often, Clauberg draws a connection between i) the different stages in a person's life, from infancy to old age and death; ii) the corresponding closeness of the bond between mind and body (or of the mind's dependence on the body, or its being mingled with it, as he variously puts it); and iii) the relative frequency and facility with which the mind can exercise the pure intellect, as opposed to exercising what Clauberg refers to as its sensitive operations (or even, when he talks in more Aristotelian terms, the operations pertaining to the vegetative life of a human being).[13] In brief, Clauberg suggests that the closer one is to the beginning of one's life, the more closely bound one's mind is to one's body, and the more one is subjected to the kinds of thoughts brought about by the sense organs. With time, the closeness of the bond is loosened, and with death it is finally entirely broken. Moreover, as this process occurs, the mind becomes 'freer' from its sense-related functions, and hence 'wiser'.[14]

Although Clauberg's use of the imagery related to *meditatio mortis* is evident in a way it is not in Descartes's work, the view that the mind can be separated from the body does find some precedent in Descartes' thought. For example, Clauberg's claim that the separation of the mind from the body is achieved when the operations of the intellect leave the senses behind is not far from Descartes's project in the *Meditations*. By the Fourth Meditation, Descartes has his meditator say, 'I have accustomed myself to leading the mind away from the senses.'[15] Descartes, however, is keen to emphasize not only the benefits, but also the dangers of this separation. In a famous passage, he tells Princess Elizabeth that although it is necessary at some stage ('once in a lifetime') to discover certain truths in metaphysics, he nevertheless thinks 'it would be very harmful to occupy one's intellect frequently in meditating upon them, since this would impede it from devoting itself to the functions of the imagination and the senses'.[16] He also expresses a similar view in his *Conversations with Burman*, at which Clauberg was present. Replying to Burman, Descartes again contends that the study of metaphysics leads the mind away from 'physical and observable things', which things, however, are 'most desirable to pursue, since they yield abundant benefits for life'.[17] Alison Simmons has pointed out that we—more recent scholars of Descartes—are 'used to Descartes insisting that the senses get in the way of our

---

in Clauberg's work, and sketch a slightly different, more intellectualistic view of Clauberg's account of perception. It is also worth emphasizing here that, as Spruit points out, Clauberg is also often close to various scholastic authors in his language.

[13] OOP 239.   [14] See, e.g., OOP 1058.   [15] CSMII 57, ATVII 52.
[16] CSMK 228, ATIII 695.   [17] CSMK 346–347, ATV 165.

intellectual pursuits. We're not used to him saying the intellect gets in the way of our sensory pursuits.'[18]

This point, and the questions it raises, do however seem to have been recognized by early readers of Descartes, including Clauberg. According to the latter, studying metaphysics too deeply or frequently not only interferes with the intellect's ability to understand those things for which it needs the co-operation of the senses or imagination. The use of the intellect can actually impede the functioning of the senses themselves. More precisely, it can bring about a state of affairs where particular movements in the body do not result in the perceptions of the intellect that Clauberg refers to as instances of the second grade of sense perception, such as perceptions of pain, pleasure, heat, cold or colour.[19] Here he seems to go beyond anything we find in Descartes. While Descartes does indeed worry that engaging too frequently in metaphysical contemplation may have a negative effect on the intellect's ability to make good use of the senses, he nevertheless maintains that 'as long as the mind is united to the body, it cannot withdraw itself from the senses whenever it is stimulated with great force by external or internal objects'.[20] To be sure, Clauberg sometimes seems to agree with Descartes on this point. One such case is in response to an objection that Clauberg recognizes could be raised against his view (and in fact was later raised by Louis de La Forge, despite Clauberg's attempt to avoid it). The objection is that, according to Clauberg's view, human beings die when they engage in deep metaphysical reflection; Clauberg responds that the mind cannot withdraw completely from the body. At the same time, however, he countenances the possibility that the mind can attain a state in which it does not perceive what is happening in the body—or at least does not perceive things that the relevant movements in the body would otherwise incite in the mind. Indeed, he appeals to this form of *ecstasis* as evidence that the mind alone senses [*sentire*] in the strict sense of the word.[21]

Clauberg therefore acknowledges that the disengagement of mind and body can have damaging or beneficial results. Focusing too much on intellectual pursuits may diminish the soul's ability to make use of what the senses give it, and thus diminish the power of the mind-body composite to survive. At the same time, however, the soul's disengagement from the body can free it to engage in the higher activities that philosophers aspire to. This latter claim indicates Clauberg's proximity to the tradition of *meditatio mortis*, in which the power to experience a special kind of insight or ecstasy is attributed to several different kinds of people, including prophets, the insane, enraptured lovers and those near to death. Clauberg alludes to this tradition when, in the course of explaining how the separation of mind and body works, he comments that 'the mortally ill feel a

---

[18] Simmons 2017, 1–36 (12).   [19] CSMII 294, ATVII 436–437.
[20] CSMK 356, ATV 219.   [21] OOP 744.

wonderful alleviation from the body & often have more sublime thoughts'.[22] Here
again we encounter a departure from Descartes, who mainly takes the contrary
view that illness, madness, and so on involve a greater, rather than a lesser
subjection to the body.[23] In the light of this difference, it is worth highlighting a
further point drawn from M. A. Screech's account of *mortis*. Screech observes that,
for the various thinkers he is concerned with, *meditatio mortis* primarily meant
'that philosophical striving to "practise dying" which results in one of the good
manias as the soul is loosened from its body—becoming in the process somewhat
like the ill-attached soul of the organic madman'.[24] This interpretation is to be
contrasted with an alternative view of *meditatio mortis*, captured in a different
Latin translation of the same Greek phrase. This latter translation, *commentatio
mortis*, refers to a 'diligent preparation for death'.[25] Clauberg, however, is clearly
talking about the former conception. The separation of the mind from the body is
not only a means of philosophizing correctly, but also refers to the state that
philosophical contemplation brings about: a kind of 'good mania'.[26]

2 The life of the human being and the conjunction of mind and body

Clauberg's references to the broadly Platonic idea that philosophizing in its purest
form is akin to dying are more than just passing allusions. His account of life and
death provides them with a philosophical grounding. Moreover, this account is
compatible with his acceptance of the Cartesian view that the proximate causes of
the death of a human being are bodily, while at the same time allowing him to say
that someone engaged solely in philosophical contemplation is not performing
any of the specifically human vital activities. In fact, it seems, as La Forge would
later point out, that on Clauberg's view someone who is solely engaged in
philosophical contemplation is no longer alive. Although Clauberg sometimes

---

[22] OOP 1058: 'Hinc lethaliter aegrotantes miram a corpore allevationem sentient & sublimiores
saepe habent cogitationes.'

[23] CSMK 356, ATV 219.

[24] Screech 1985, 29. Screech may exaggerate the extent to which all the authors he is concerned
with—from Plato, to Seneca, to Ficino, Rabelais, and Erasmus—had *meditatio* rather than *commentatio*, as he understands them, in mind, but the distinction is worth drawing.

[25] Screech 1985, 29.

[26] As Sarah Broadie has put it, in Plato's work the separation of the mind from the body amounts to
'an exercise in soul-saving'. Descartes, she goes on to say, could not subscribe to this Platonic
motivation for separating the soul from the body. The kinds of activities and goals Descartes has in
mind in his work do not fall under what she suggests might contribute, in varying combinations
depending on one's confessional commitments, to our salvation: faith and works. Broadie 2001,
296–308 (307). The suspicion that Cartesians were engaging in this 'exercise in soul-saving' is—
despite the history of Christian Platonism among thinkers such as Erasmus and Ficino—what makes
Clauberg's references of *meditatio mortis* surprising in the context. Of course, to advert to this kind of
separation of the mind from the body is not necessarily to say that we do so by our own powers.

seems willing to accept this way of putting things, he had in fact anticipated and pre-emptively responded to La Forge's criticism. Before we return to that point, though, we should first look at how Clauberg characterizes life and death more generally.

Descartes' conception of life, as it is interpreted in the most prominent recent discussions, is held to revolve around the life of the body and the beast-machine, while his conception of death is held to focus on the death of the body and of the human being.[27] Both these emphases are justified in the light of Descartes's own texts; but they should not lead us to ignore the fact that, for many Cartesians working in the wake of Descartes, the issues of life and death gave rise to a broader set of questions. For Clauberg, it was possible to say that a human being lives a threefold life on the basis of the different parts, so to speak, of which it is composed: the mind, the body, and the union of the two.[28] Clauberg's discussion of life, however, indicates that the notion of life itself was not only diverse in terms of what it was ascribed to, but could be understood in three further different ways in relation to each of its three objects.[29]

Clauberg's most explicit use of this latter threefold understanding of life is to be found in the discussions of life and death in his 1656 *Exercitationes Centum de Cognitione Dei et Nostri*. These are: i) simple existence [*existentia simplex*]; ii) active existence [*existentia actuosa*]; and iii) existence with another [*existentia cum alio*].[30] For each of these conceptions of life, Clauberg provides a corresponding account of death, and some argumentation as to why the soul ought to be considered immortal if life is understood in that way. Equally, although the sections discussing these conceptions of life are intended to prove the immortality or perpetual life of the soul in relation to each conception, Clauberg also considers their application to the body and the composite of soul and body. The issue of *meditatio mortis* arises when Clauberg discusses life as 'existence with another'; the life in question is the soul's existence with the body, and in certain

---

[27] For an example of the former, see Barnaby Hutchins in this volume, Chapter 13; for the latter, see Ablondi 1995, 47–53. Smith 2013, 105–123, notes that life has a broader application for Clauberg than Descartes, but Smith's purpose is primarily for the purpose of understanding corporeal life.

[28] OOP 676.

[29] He nevertheless warns in his *Logica* against running together different conceptions of the life and the soul and ascribing them indiscriminately to different objects in both metaphysics and physics (OOP 866–868); Smith 2013, is not wrong to characterize Clauberg's conception of life in terms of action, but Clauberg's reference to understanding life in terms of the action of the parts pertains to the mind and body, and not in the same way organic parts of the body; Clauberg's account of life and action is not univocal.

[30] OOP 676. This account was taken up by other Cartesians. Similar formulations can be found, among others, in La Forge 1997, 61, and Le Grand 1705, 231, and in modified form in a less well-known follower of Geulincx and commentator on Clauberg and La Forge, Flenderus 1731, 61. Because some of these texts were used in teaching, Clauberg's account of life would have been relatively well known, even if not necessarily recognized as his.

164 'MEDITATIO MORTIS': POST-CARTESIAN

contemplative states such life is absent.[31] The soul itself does not die in *meditatio mortis*, however. Consequently, the soul's life should still be understood according to the second conception of life, active existence, which for the soul is its continued thinking.

Because his focus in these sections of the *Exercitationes* is on the immortality of the soul, Clauberg does not say much about what he means by the soul's 'existence with another' when it and the body are conjoined. In the 1664 *Corporis et Animae Conjunctio*, however, there is a more developed account. In this work, Clauberg says that a human being is a composite of a mind and a body, and equates the life of a human being with the conjunction of the mind and body. 'The whole human lives,' he claims, 'as long as the soul and the body are conjoined: it dies when these two are entirely separated.'[32] Moreover, the conjunction of mind and body is solely constituted by vital acts; and life, Clauberg says at this point, consists in 'act and operation'.[33] Nevertheless, not all acts of body or mind are constitutive of the life of the composite. Following the standard scholastic terminology, Clauberg specifies that it is only by 'transeunt acts' that 'the body and soul are bound together [*colligantur*] in the human being'.[34] Transeunt acts are those acts of the body that terminate in the mind, and vice versa—or as Clauberg elsewhere puts it, acts which result in a change in the state of something else.[35] Immanent acts, by contrast, remain within the acting subject, which here means either the mind or the body. Although these latter acts can be said to make their subjects live [*vivificare*], they do not bind the mind and body into a single living composite. The human being only lives when the mind acts on the body and vice versa.

This account of the conjunction of mind and body seems to have some peculiar consequences, which were picked up by another Cartesian, Louis de La Forge. According to La Forge, Clauberg's account locates the 'essence' of the composite of body and mind in the 'actual concurrence' of the operations of the mind and body. But this means that 'as soon as the acts of the mind and body cease to concur and co-operate, as one could believe happens in lethargy, ecstasy, or very deep meditation, one would have to say that the mind is separated from the body human being dies every time they fall into one of these accidental conditions'.[36] For La Forge, this implication of Clauberg's position is unacceptable. One should take the essence of the union of mind and body to lie in their 'reciprocal dependence' rather than their actual interaction, where the dependence in question remains even when the interaction is (temporarily) halted.[37]

---

[31] OOP 681. Clauberg here refers to *contemplatio mortis*, and views it as a specifically Platonic view rather than endorsing it himself.

[32] OOP 216: 'Vivit autem Homo totus, quamdiu corpus & anima conjunguntur: moritur cum illa duo prorsus separantur.'

[33] OOP 216; see also OOP 273–274.

[34] OOP 217: 'Itaque transeuntes tantummodo sunt acts, quibus corpus atque animus in Homine colligantur.'

[35] OOP 217; OOP 322.   [36] La Forge 1997,123.   [37] Ibid.

Clauberg was, however, well aware that his view of the conjunction of body and mind might be construed this way. In fact, he had addressed a similar objection towards the end of the *Conjunctio*. This objection, he says, could throw his entire account of the conjunction of the mind and body into doubt. If Clauberg's account of the union holds, the objector says, and the life of the whole human being is situated in the 'concursus' of the transeunt acts by which mind and body affect one another, then the human being would have to be considered dead when the acts of mind and body cease to concur. But as Clauberg points out, the problem is not only that there might be the occasional accidental intermission in the life of a human being; the potential threat to his view is compounded by the fact that cessations of the transeunt acts which constitute this life seem to occur in more 'everyday' circumstances. Earlier in the treatise, in a preliminary discussion of the difficulties that the great dissimilarity between mind and body might pose for an account of their conjunction, Clauberg had mentioned that the mind is able 'not merely to exist and to live separated from the body, but is able to easily and constantly exercise the most noble operations concerning the most noble objects in such a state of separation'.[38] In this earlier passage it sounds as though he may well be referring primarily to the state of the soul after death. But when Clauberg later discusses the objection we are considering, he seems to be referring to philosophical activity in this life. A mind that is contemplating either itself, God, or some other intelligible object does not seem to be engaging in transeunt actions: it neither acts on the body nor does it undergo any change because of it. But if Clauberg's view is taken seriously, the objector would then say, someone exercising precisely those acts 'most worthy' of the human being 'will be either dead or at least cease to be a human'.[39]

Clauberg, however, does not altogether accept that this is the case. He confronts the objection in a chapter whose purpose is to show that the mind can be present to the body at times when it does not appear to be, and seems to consider two solutions. The first is that, when the mind appears to have withdrawn from the body, some interaction between them may remain. There may be 'mild and more languid acts, if not of the external senses, at least of the internal senses, or certain slower operations of the will in the body'.[40] As a Cartesian, we would expect Clauberg to accept that '*to think* is to have consciousness or perception of those things which are in you'.[41] But at this point he suggests that there can be

---

[38] OOP 211: 'Speciatim ad Mentem humanam quod attinet, eam non modo a corpore separatam existere ac vivere, sed etiam nobilissimas operationes circa objecta nobilissima in tali separationis statu facile & constanter exercere posse, aliunde notum est.'

[39] OOP 266: 'Tunc igitur temporis aut mortuus erit aut certè desinet effe homo, qui tamen actum eo ipso exercet homine dignissimum.'

[40] OOP 266: 'Posse remissos aliquos & languidiores si non externorum, saltem internorum sensuum actus aut voluntatis operationem quandam in corpus segniorem interea temporis concurrere.'

[41] OOP 637: 'Nam *cogitare* est eorum quae in te sunt conscientiam sive perceptionem habere.'

'functions' of the soul to which the soul does not attend.[42] In other words, while the soul seems to be engaged in the kind of acts that do not involve it being transeuntly acted on by the body it is in fact simply not attending to the less obvious perceptions of which it is (perhaps confusedly) conscious. The mind, for Clauberg, can be conscious of things arising in it as a result of transeunt, vital actions of the body, and to which it is not at that moment attending. Variations of attention therefore indicate at least one way in which the mind might be able to separate itself from the body without the death of the human being. We shall return to this suggestion below, p. C7.P26–C7.P27.

Taking up a second line of response, Clauberg also claims there can be interruptions in the conjunction of mind and body. Not only does he point out that it is possible for the mind to be present to the body when it seems not to be; he also proposes that, even if the interaction of mind and body were to be interrupted so that the mind was not present to the body at all, this would not constitute the death of the human being then and there. Elsewhere in the *Conjunctio* he puts it as follows: 'in a human life, which is the conjunction of the body and the soul, now more acts concur, now fewer, sometimes perhaps none at all. Nevertheless the same life remains.'[43] A human life, unlike a simple motion for example, can be interrupted and still remain the same life. The reason for this, Clauberg explains, is that the 'foundation of the identity' of this life can be found firstly in God's will, which maintains the conjunction even in the intervals of no interaction, and secondly in the disposition of the body.[44] Moreover, this applies to the cases that troubled La Forge—to people in states of ecstasy, to epileptics, and to those (habitually) engaged in deep meditation.[45] Their lives continue as long as their souls are able to return to their bodies; and they can do this provided that their bodies have not been somehow damaged or otherwise made unsuitable for the conjunction during the soul's absence.

According to Clauberg, then, there are two ways to explain the kinds of ecstatic states we are concerned with. Human life—the life of the composite—can remain the same life despite interruptions; and sometimes what appear to be interruptions are not interruptions after all. Death does not befall the human being in the cases raised by La Forge. So, what else does death involve? When discussing death proper, Clauberg adds two further conditions to the cessation of transeunt acts: the cessation must be total, and it must be final. When Clauberg suggests—however surprisingly—that the mind can be present to the body at times when

---

[42] OOP 266.

[43] OOP 269: 'Sic in vita humana, quae est corporis et animique conjunctio, jam plures actus, jam pauciores, aliquando forte nulli concurrunt. Attamen manet eadem vita.'

[44] OOP 269: 'Cujus identitatis fundamentum est, 1. Dei, ut vitae magistri, voluntas, qua continuari vult illam conjunctionem, mensurans interim animae a corpore absentiae, si qua sit, quasi Musici cujusdam silentii, intervallum: 2. corporis dispositio.'

[45] OOP 267.

it appears to be absent, this cannot amount to death, because real death only occurs when the interaction of body and mind totally ceases. In addition, death must be irreversible or final. As long as the body remains well disposed (and God remains willing), so that the soul is able to return to the body, death does not occur.

In addition to these conditions, which serve to distinguish real death from temporary cessations of the life of the composite, Clauberg also emphasizes that the true death of the human being always occurs as a result of something to do with the body, and never as a direct result of the mind's actions. But although the mind cannot be a direct cause of death, it can nevertheless be a remote one. When the separation of the mind from the body leads an individual to neglect their body, this can contribute to their death. Here Clauberg draws on the Cartesian view that the conjunction of mind and body is designed to preserve the human being. When the mind withdraws from the body so that the conjunction is, so to speak, dormant, the survival of the mind-body composite is also threatened.[46] Hence, according to Clauberg, someone such as St Paul who 'is wholly immersed in the contemplation and love of divine things' is exercising the 'most worthy actions of a human being, if you consider the mind alone'. But such absorption may lead to difficulties in exercising the actions 'which pertain to the composite, which make up the life of the whole, the animal life'.[47] Once again, it is clear that Clauberg has account of the 'dissolution' of the conjunction of mind and body according to which death is only one example. *Ecstasis* and profound meditation also bring about a species of dissolution, this time one caused by the soul. Although the mind cannot be the proximate cause of death, it can neglect the body, and thus be indirectly responsible for the death of the composite of which it is a part.

To summarize: Clauberg sometimes presents *meditatio mortis* not as an interruption in the life of the human being, but as involving a lack of attention to the vital acts of the human being. At other times, he presents it as a genuine interruption of the vital acts of the human being, but one that does not interrupt the continuity of a particular human life. Life, that is to say, is a flexible enough term to be applied to the interaction of the parts of the composite of mind and body as much as to the mind or the organic body itself, and to be interpreted in different ways in each case. Moreover, the two states in which the whole human being is alive, and the whole human being is dead, are not exhaustive. It is also

---

[46] OOP 197.
[47] OOP 267–268: 'Equidem actions exercet homine dignissimas (repete cap. LXII. 5.) si mentem solam respicias, qui rerum divinarum contemplation & amori totus immersus est. (sicuti S.Paulus in Paradisum raptus ineffábilia verba audivit, 2 Cor. 12.) sed facile accidit ut interea non exerceat eas, quae pertinent ad compositum, quae vitam totius, vitam animalem faciunt.' The latter sentence is interesting because it seems Clauberg is referring the functions of the mind and body and vice versa, where one might have expected a Cartesian to understand it as of the body alone. Animals, here, would not live the animal life: only composites of mind and body are animated, presumably in deference to the animating function of the soul in older traditions.

168 'MEDITATIO MORTIS': POST-CARTESIAN

possible for the body to be alive, the mind to be alive, and the whole human being neither alive nor dead. This state arises when, by means of philosophical contemplation, the mind withdraws from the body.

Here the term *meditatio mortis* is apt. The fact that actual death can result from careless excesses of philosophical contemplation is only a partial explanation of why philosophy is described as *meditatio mortis*, however. What has not yet been explained is how exactly philosophical contemplation might bring about the soul's withdrawal from the body. Clauberg's attempt to show how profound meditation can obstruct the transeunt acts of the body on the mind is the subject of the next section.

3 Intellectual perception and dissolving the conjunction of mind and body

According to Clauberg, philosophical contemplation involves a kind of ecstasy that resembles death, because the transeunt acts that constitute the life of a human being do not take place. Clauberg undoubtedly claims at various times that philosophical ecstasy involves an interruption of these vital acts. But why the interruption occurs is less clear. It should, after all, be possible for the vital acts that conjoin body and mind to take place without conscious attention, even if that does imply a certain amount of confusion in the mind. There are, however, some points that can give us an idea of how to explain Clauberg's ecstatic view of philosophical contemplation. First, some of the acts that join mind and body are confused sense perceptions—and confusion is precisely what philosophy aims to extirpate. Second, the very fact that we have sense perception at all presupposes not only that certain changes are occurring in the body, but also the attention of the mind to those changes. Without the requisite attention, we would not even have what Clauberg, after Descartes, refers to as the second stage of sense perception: the 'perception of the mind'.[48] In the right circumstances, however, attention is under our control.[49] Finally, Clauberg in many places denies that the

---

[48] OOP 196. As Clauberg reads it, the first stage is the movement in the body; the third is assent or dissent.

[49] There is not space here to provide a full outline of Clauberg's account of perception; I intend only to give an outline of how Clauberg's account of intellectual perception could have consequences consonant with *meditatio mortis*. This means I am setting aside the question of how to reconcile the various accounts Clauberg gives in different works. A more detailed account can be found in Spruit 1999'. For my purposes the differences between sense perceptions, sensations (e.g. pain) and passions in the strict sense (e.g. anger) can be set aside; all three can be subsumed under 'passion' in the broad sense, but I will continue to discuss sense perception primarily. It should also be noted that Clauberg does not seem to use various terms how they are taken in readings of Descartes nowadays; he only seems to use the terms idea and image in the context of intellectual perception—a sensation is not an idea, though if the associated act of the mind is to have an object, then a sensation must be accompanied by an idea of that object, albeit one that may not fully represent the object as it is in

body can in fact act on the mind at all. Instead, the mind produces the appropriate thoughts in itself, even when apparently being acted on by the body. Accordingly, although the vitality of the conjunction of mind and body must consist in the transeunt acts of one on the other, it is nevertheless possible to construe what we refer to as 'transeunt acts' to depend primarily on the kinds of thoughts the mind produces in itself. As paradoxical as this might sound, then, what is decisive in constituting the conjunction of mind and body—and hence the vitality of the human being as a whole—is something that happens in the mind.

On Clauberg's account, the conjunction of mind and body is primarily constituted by confused sense perceptions. He claims, in fact, that the confusion that joins the mind to the body is twofold: one form of confusion pertains to the perceiving subject, the other to the perceived object.[50] The first kind of confusion stems from the fact that 'we make our body itself and its parts participants of sense perception, when to perceive, however, is a proper function of the mind'.[51] For example, we locate pains in the body rather than the mind. The second form of confusion consists in the fact that, when we have sense perceptions, we do not perceive them as local motions in our body, but as something or other which is not motion—although Clauberg says that we do not know exactly what.[52] For now, I suggest that what Clauberg has in mind here is a very close tie between a non-representative sensation and a misrepresentation of the object of the perception, in which the object is represented according to how it affects the body rather than as it is in itself. For example, when our bodies are affected by external objects, we do not experience this as motion in the body, but as some combination of various sensations, such as colours, and a representation of the object itself (and not the motion in our body) from the perspective of the perceiving body (and hence not exactly as it is in itself).

The first of these two forms of confusion initially seems to be most crucial for understanding how sense perception results in the kind of conjunction of mind and body specific to the human being. This can be seen in the various cases where Clauberg points to sense perception as what distinguishes a human being from an angel. The angel is no more conjoined to its body than a pilot is to a ship, and does not feel 'for' its body any more than the pilot feels what goes on in the ship. By contrast, the conjunction of mind and body in a human being makes us feel what happens to the body as though the mind were itself somehow affected by what

---

itself. And it may also be surprising to note that because for Clauberg an image must bear a genuine resemblance to what it is an image of, the senses and the imagination do not directly make use of images, which are the preserve of the intellect—see OOP 243.

[50] OOP 242: 'Duplex autem in sensibus hisce confusio reperitur...altera ratione pericipientis subjecti, altera ratione objecti percepti.'

[51] OOP 242: 'in eo consistit, quod perceptionis sensualis ipsum corpus nostrum ejusque partes faciamus participes, cum tamen percipere...propria sit mentis functio'.

[52] OOP 242.

170 'MEDITATIO MORTIS': POST-CARTESIAN

affects the body.[53] Clauberg does not, however, spell out exactly how this first form of confusion is related to the second. My suggestion is that the first form of confusion, the mind's 'feeling for' the body, is to be explained as a consequence of the second form of confusion. When the mind is incited by the sense organs to produce an idea of an object, it does so according to the perspective of its body, rather than producing idea of the object as it is in itself. This, rather than any prior substantial union of body and mind, is why it feels 'for' the body.

If our confused feeling that our minds are joined to our bodies is grounded on our misrepresentation of the objects we perceive, the growth of our philosophical understanding will have implications for this relationship. As we overcome our confusion by understanding what the objects of our perception are really like, we cease to feel 'for' our bodies and undo one of the vital connections between the body and the mind. To give a more precise account of this process, it is worth putting it into the technical terminology that Clauberg takes over, in large part, from the scholastic tradition.[54] The perceptions of the pure intellect, Clauberg tells us, occur by means of 'formal signs' which 'truly represent things, insofar as images of them are depicted to the mind'.[55] Sensory perception, on the other hand, occurs by means of 'material signs', which 'indicate certain things … but do not represent them in the likeness of an image'.[56] The various qualities sensed in sense perception, such as heat, sounds, odours, 'and the rest', depend 'proximately' on the impression made by the object on the organs of our body. Describing this interaction, Clauberg refers to an earlier paragraph where he had said that the body 'excites' the mind to think 'this or that', or provides it with the occasion for thinking.[57] That is to say, an impression in the body leads the mind to form a sensation, which resembles neither the bodily impression nor the perceived object. The sensation in turn leads the mind to have an intellectual perception of the object; but the perception is distorted, since it depends on the impression the object has made on the body.[58]

---

[53] The denial that pilot or sailor in the ship is a crucial part of how Descartes and Clauberg reject what they refer to as a Platonic understanding of the unity of the human being. Clauberg, to be sure, agrees with Descartes in denying the appropriateness of the image of the sailor in the ship, but for Clauberg that does not mean that other closely connected, broadly Platonic imagery is impermissible— he accepts, if in a qualified way, the suggestion that the body is an (active) instrument of the soul (OOP 223). Whatever might be the case in Descartes's work, for Clauberg if there is any per se unity to the human being, it is constituted by the transeunt acts of mind and body on one another, rather than those acts presupposing such unity.

[54] In addition to Spruit 1999, 80–83, for further discussion of the scholastic and Cartesian background of Clauberg's references to signs, see Savini 2011, 248–258.

[55] OOP 243: 'Puri intellectus perceptio sit per *signa formalia*, quae res verè repraesentant, quatenus earum sunt imagines mente pictae.'

[56] OOP 243: 'Sensus sive sensualis perceptio sit per signa materialia, quae res quidem indicant, ut hedera suspensa monet vinum esse vendibile; sed eas non repraesentant instar imaginis.'

[57] OOP 233.

[58] There remains some ambiguity as to how directly the bodily impression determines the intellectual misrepresentation of the object indicated by a sensation. As I read it, the balance of evidence suggests that the bodily impression serves only as the occasional cause of a sensation, which in turn indicates an object to the intellect. This suggests that any misrepresentation by the intellect is

MICHAEL JAWORZYN 171

In sense perception, then, it is not that there is no object represented to the mind. There is an object in addition to the sensation. But, perhaps surprisingly for a Cartesian, Clauberg refers to this object as an image. The intellect produces the image in question, and without that image the sensations in the mind would have no bearing on any external object. According to Clauberg's account of perception, each perception is formally speaking an operation of the mind. But the thing perceived also has a kind of being in the mind, as the image of what is represented to the mind; this is the idea taken 'objectively', and it constitutes a certain, if 'diminished', reality. The mind itself produces this intramental image of the object according to an exemplar, namely the object as it is outside the mind—and not the impression made in our body. So, even in sense perception, when dealing with a 'material sign' that does not resemble the object, the intellect still has to do something.[59] As in the case of a purely intellectual perception, the mind looks to the object as exemplar to produce an image of that object in itself. But when incited to produce this image by the combination of mental and bodily factors involved in a 'material sign', namely the physical impression and the sensation of the object in the mind, it produces an image that represents the object according to the way it affects the body, rather than as it is in itself. This image is still an image of the object itself, distorted according to the perspective of the body, and not strictly speaking an image of the physical impression in the body. Clauberg puts it neatly in his commentary on Descartes's *Principles*: 'whatever our mind perceives by the intervention of a corporeal patient, is perceived not as it is in itself, but only relatively, in the way it can be represented to us'.[60]

The kinds of perceptions the mind produces in itself depend in turn on the way it attends to its objects. This is most evident in Clauberg's discussion of signs in his *Ontosophia*. Immediately after claiming that the only way something outside the mind can be present to or conjoined with the mind is by means of that external object's objective existence in the mind, Clauberg makes a crucial addition: 'the greater the affect with which we fix the attention of the will on it, the more closely we feel ourselves to be joined to the object which is present to the mind by means of an idea'.[61] Attention, in other words, is a matter of degree; it is not a case of

---

independent of the distortion of the bodily impression. The latter would provide a neat account of the precise character of the mind's misrepresentation, but Clauberg seems to want to have the sensation non-representational and the intellect to represent the object, rather than the impression. While there is no evidence that Clauberg took this view for the sake of being able to refer to *meditatio mortis*, it does complement it, by lessening the importance of any bodily occurrences for understanding the conflict between sensual and purely intellectual perception.

[59] Cf. OOP 336: 'patet signa non ad res mere corporeas, sed ad intellectu praeditas pertinere'.

[60] OOP 513: 'Ergo quicquid interventu patientis corporei mens nostra percipit, non quale in se est, sed relative tantum, quale repraesentari nobis potest, percipitur. At vero intellectus est, puras & sinceras rerum ideas percipere, & rerum realitatem repraesentare, quails ea est in se.'

[61] OOP 336: 'Nam praeter istam attingendi modum objectivum inter rem intelligentia praeditam & res quae extra eam sunt, nulla alia praesentiae vel conjunctionis ratio invenitur: nisi quod tanto propius objecto, quod menti per ideam presens est, nos jungi sentiamus, quanto majore voluntatis affect attentionem in eo figimus.'

either attending to, and hence representing, an object or not. In fact, the same exemplar can be imitated in various ways, depending on the kind of attention we give to it.[62] Ultimately, this means that sense perception and purely intellectual perception coexist uneasily at the same time in the same mind. It is certainly possible for the mind to have two simultaneous perceptions of the same thing. Referring to Descartes's example of the sun, Clauberg distinguishes the confused idea of the sun's distance from the earth, common to all people and 'connected' to movements of the bodily organs, and the clear and distinct idea of it, pertaining to the pure intellect, and possessed by very few people.[63] Both can be in our minds, but the two images compete, as it were, for our attention.

This account goes some way to explaining why philosophical contemplation—the use of the pure intellect—can be called *meditatio mortis*. According to some interpretations of Descartes, one of the primary purposes of his *Meditations* is to rid us of the systematized, Aristotelian misunderstanding of the world that we derive from sense perception.[64] According to Clauberg's analysis of sense perception, the same process that leads us away from a mistaken scholastic physics may also lead us to neglect our bodies, and eventually endanger our lives as human beings. Although our sense perceptions are too confused to be of use in the contemplation of truth, they do contribute to the 'good of the whole composite' and to its unity.[65] If the mind pays attention to the sensations occasioned by bodily movements, the ideas it produces will be useful for promoting the survival of the mind-body composite. But the more closely the mind attends to its object, the more closely the ideas it produces resemble their exemplar—and the less useful its ideas will be for practical purposes. Because our capacity for attention is limited, focusing on a purely intellectual image of an object reduces our capacity to form images of the world that will aid our survival. Both metaphysics and physics seek to understand things as they are in themselves, not as they appear to us. When our attention is given over to purely intelligible or divine things, the vital acts that constitute the conjunction of mind and body are liable to decrease.

So far, we have seen a way that, for Clauberg, profound philosophical contemplation can have a negative effect on the ability of the senses to play their proper role. The account reconstructed so far does not, however, fully explain Clauberg's claim that contemplative philosophers achieve a state akin to death. After all, even in contemplation, the body can continue to have some effect on the mind. To put

---

[62] OOP 339: 'Idem exemplar diversi diversis modis imitantur.'   [63] OOP 256.

[64] For a prominent example, see Hatfield 1986, 45–79.

[65] OOP 197. It is important that this is sense perception rather than sensation. It seems to me that for Clauberg a pure sensation without the accompanying intellectual representation would offer no advantages for survival over the mere mechanical reflexes of the body; the sensation serves to indicate an object in a certain way that is useful for life, but of itself it does not provide that kind of information. For the sensation to play the role of material sign, the mind must already be acquainted with what is supposed to be indicated by a sensation for it to amount to anything meaningful. This is what Spruit connects to a (broadly) Neoplatonic conception of the intelligibility of the world: Spruit 1999, 75–78.

the point differently, some transeunt acts of body on mind continue to occur, even if the mind does not attend to them in a way conducive to the survival of the composite. Why, then, does Clauberg not accept that they are enough to maintain the life of the composite and abandon his claim that philosophical contemplation can give rise to a genuine dissolution of the conjunction of mind and body? To answer this question, we need to return to his distinction between immanent and transeunt acts. Clauberg often draws this distinction in a traditional way, by contrasting an immanent act that brings about a change in state in the acting subject with a transeunt act that brings about a change in something other than the agent. In his discussion of the relation between body and mind, however, the distinction takes on an added complexity.

Because the ontological status of body is inferior to that the mind, Clauberg argues, the body does not actually exert any causal power on the mind, and there is consequently no real interaction or influx between them.[66] To be sure, the body does serve as what Clauberg calls a 'procatarctic' cause of mental events, by 'inciting' the mind to produce changes in itself. Whether or not the mind forms a corresponding idea, and how accurately it does so, is up to the mind itself. The mind, then, is always the cause of its own states.[67] In this connection, it is also worth noting that, in his *Theoria Corporum Viventium*, Clauberg seems to make the attentiveness of the mind a condition of all of the mind's states. Although in the other passages we have been considering attention plays a less prominent role in the production of thought, here the outcome is that even our involuntary sensations, which seem to be caused by motions in our bodies, depend on the mind's attentiveness for their production.[68]

It seems, then, that there are strictly speaking no transeunt acts of the body on the mind. We call certain acts transeunt, and hence vital, because they make us feel joined to the body, rather than because they are initiated by the body. When the mind produces a sensation in itself, it also produces a representation of an object, and can then identify a certain bodily movement as the foundation for the causal relation of which the sensation is taken to be the effect. So, although there is in practice something approaching a lawlike relation between bodily movements and sensations, a bodily movement is only designated as the cause of a sensation by the mind.

---

[66] Cf., e.g., OOP 221. There is, however, what Clauberg refers to as 'moral' causation.

[67] A further point which might corroborate this claim is that Clauberg does not seem to have clarified where the metaphysical status (i.e. reality) of sensations in the mind lies. If the distinction between the objective and formal reality Clauberg discusses in the case of representative ideas (see, e.g., OOP 623) is exhaustive, I would suggest a sensation is a characteristic of the operation (i.e. the formal or material reality of what Descartes would call an idea), rather than pertaining to the objective reality of the act of the mind, which is reserved for genuine representations. These appear to be the only two options, and the former Clauberg says we produce spontaneously, the latter necessarily (OOP 623).

[68] OOP 196.

174 'MEDITATIO MORTIS': POST-CARTESIAN

This account of Clauberg's work suggests that the vital conjunction of mind and body lies within the control of the mind. Most of the time, the mind maintains its conjunction with the body by producing the kinds of perceptions that join it to the body. But when it is engaged in deep philosophical contemplation, it ceases to produce these perceptions. Regardless of the bodily motions that may continue to occur, it temporarily dissolves its conjunction with the body. The fact that the mind possesses this power also suggests that, with the right kind of training, the mind may be able to learn to separate itself from the body and practise *meditatio mortis*.[69]

4 Philosophy, theology, and salvation

So far, we have seen that Clauberg's references to *meditatio mortis* involve a particular realignment of Cartesian views; but it seems to me that, within their historical and geographical context, their significance goes further. Taking philosophy to involve *meditatio mortis* would have been controversial among many of Clauberg's contemporaries. To suggest that philosophers could, as it were, anticipate a disembodied existence, and that philosophy itself might be able to produce a kind of virtuous understanding that anticipates eternal salvation, was to enter into contentious theological territory. In particular, one critic of Cartesianism, Jacob Revius, took issue with aspects of Descartes's work that he thought implied such claims. As we will see, however, Clauberg himself would not have drawn the conclusions Revius found in Descartes' work. In fact, my suggestion is that concerns of the kind raised by Revius would have been misplaced. Other concerns from other quarters, though, may be more to the point: Clauberg's account of *meditatio mortis* suggests that philosophical contemplation disrupts the basis of the careful separation of philosophy from theology—and from other 'practical' disciplines, including medicine—advocated by other leading Cartesians, such as Johannes De Raey (1622–1702).

Before we turn to this latter issue, it is worth looking at the question of the relation between salvation and the separation of the mind and body. Among Revius's many criticisms of Descartes, those most relevant to the Cartesian

---

[69] The actual process would be a longer term project, rather than something requiring a mere exertion of the will; thanks to the habits acquired in childhood, before we had the use of reason, we have many prejudices which we otherwise struggle to distinguish in perception; Clauberg distinguishes concurrences between the respective states of mind and body joined 'by nature' from those joined 'by habit', but really neither involve any 'natural relation' (OOP 237; OOP 219, respectively). See, e.g., Morris 1995, 290–306, for an account of Descartes's work which suggests both that confusion is key to Descartes's account of the union of mind and body, and that confusion should be overcome; the details, however, differ from Clauberg, and I suggest Clauberg's references to *meditatio mortis* indicate he is more positive about the prospects of a systematic removal of (natural) confusion—but also more negative about the consequences.

appropriation of *meditatio mortis* are Revius' accusations that Descartes had fallen into, and in fact 'exceeded', the heresy of Pelagianism. The basis of this charge was Descartes' view that we can have a clear and distinct idea of God by means our own natural faculties.[70] Pelagianism—while often functioning primarily as a term of abuse—was usually taken to involve the denial of original sin, and, more importantly for our purposes, the endorsement of the idea that our salvation is dependent on our own powers rather than God's grace. According to Revius, to say that we can have a clear and distinct idea of God by means of our own faculties goes against St. Paul's intimation that, in this life, we can only see God in a mirror darkly. Our having a clear and distinct idea of God would amount to seeing God face-to-face in this life, by means of our own powers.[71] It is true that Descartes had implicitly rejected this equivalence. As he says, and as Clauberg paraphrases, 'just as we believe through faith that the supreme happiness of the next life consists solely in the contemplation of the divine majesty, so experience tells us that this same contemplation, albeit much less perfect, enables us to know the greatest joy of which we are capable in this life'.[72] Our greatest earthly pleasures fall short of supreme happiness in the life to come. But for Revius, even to suggest that we could have an idea of God was improper; the implication, however qualified, that the contemplation of God in this life and the next could be 'the same' would have been unacceptable.[73]

One might expect that Clauberg would be careful to steer clear of inviting any comparable accusations. This is not the case. The examples and terminology he uses when he refers to *meditatio mortis* suggest that he is not only thinking of philosophical reflection, but also has religious *ecstasis* in mind. He not only associates the ecstasies of contemplation with the philosophical activities of Cartesian meditation, for example; he also compares them to the raptures of St. Paul.[74] Equally, his description of the activities of the pure intellect as the highest or 'most worthy operations' of a human being is, in the context, an allusion to a more-or-less perennial debate regarding the nature of happiness or beatitude,

---

[70] See Revius 2002, 175: 'Observent autem theologiae studiosi, quantopere haec a doctrina Spiritus S. divertant. Paulo enim si credimus, dum in via sumus, *ex parte cognoscimus, ut infantes loquimur, sapimus, ratiocinatur, per speculum et per aenigma cernimus*, 1 Cor. 13:9 *et seqq.* Si haec Apostolus de se, deque fidelibus reliquis profitetur, quantae arrogantiae est, claram et distinctam Dei cognitionem tribuere homini secundum se et naturales suas facultates considerato, prout hic facit Cartesius? Hic profecto plusquam sesquipelagianus est.' As Goudriaaen has pointed out, Pelagianism was one of various accusations aimed at Descartes from across confessional boundaries: Goudriaaen 2016, 533–549 (536). See also Lennon 2002, http://dx.doi.org/10.7710/1526–0569.1472.

[71] Revius 2002, 175; for Goudriaaen's discussion of this, see Revius 2002, 40. Revius does also make accusations of Pelagianism based on Descartes' ascription of infinite free will to humans, but for our purposes it is the role of contemplation that is of interest.

[72] CSMII 36, ATVII 52; OOP 416.

[73] Questions arising from our claiming to be able to see God in this life can be distinguished from those pertaining to Pelagianism, of course, even if Revius took them together.

[74] Cf. OOP 268. See Screech 1985, 25–39, for a discussion of the connection drawn between St. Paul and madness in the context of the kind of account of ecstasy and *meditatio mortis* Clauberg alludes to.

176 'MEDITATIO MORTIS': POST-CARTESIAN

and the question of what one has to do to attain it.[75] Here, too, theological questions are close at hand. In mentioning *meditatio mortis*, Clauberg would have been highlighting a tradition that regarded the ecstatic states brought on by philosophical contemplation as a likeness, prefiguration of, or even temporary access to, the afterlife of the blessed.[76] But if philosophical *meditatio mortis* provides us with an anticipation of the eternal blessedness of the next life, to say that it is attainable by means of philosophical contemplation is also to say that we can attain it by our own natural powers—that is, without grace.[77]

For Revius, any such claim would have been evidence of Pelagianism—hence his condemnation of Descartes. But there remains a significant difference between the imperfect knowledge of God that we may be able to attain by our own powers in this life, and the comprehensive vision of God that Christians hope to attain in the next, whatever Revius may have thought. Clauberg certainly takes *meditatio mortis* to be very closely related to the former, but it is less clear how he thinks it relates to the latter. Nevertheless, Revius' concerns may not have been wholly unjustified, in view of the fact that there were less orthodox Cartesians who did elide the distinction between the idea of God available to us in this life and that available to us in the life to come. In the work of Arnold Geulincx (1624–1669), for example, there are reasons to downplay the differences between philosophical separation of mind and body in this life and salvation and blessedness in the next. Although Geulincx himself never referred to *meditatio mortis* directly, his work makes use of many of images associated with it.[78] But it is a feature of Geulincx's metaphysics of time that leads him to the view that the separation of one's mind from body amounts to attaining salvation.

For Geulincx, only bodies have temporal existence; so, when the mind is separated from the body, it ceases to exist durationally and becomes eternal. Instead of experiencing its thought successively, thought exists all at once, *simul et semel*. Eternal things, moreover, are turned to God in 'perpetual felicity' (or else turned away in perpetual wretchedness).[79] Accordingly, to withdraw from the body and attain *ecstasis* is, for Geulincx, to achieve the eternity that souls possess

[75] The allusion is to a version of the Aristotelian argument which attempts to understand (human) happiness and supreme good in terms of what is taken to be the distinctively human function. Difficulties of course arise given the Christian view that the supreme good consists in the vision or enjoyment of God; one solution involves distinguishing between the imperfect happiness of this life and the perfect happiness of the next. See, e.g., Kraye 1988, 303–386, for a good outline of the situation just prior to Clauberg's time. Clauberg's familiarity with these debates is evident: see, e.g., OOP 1008–1010.

[76] See e.g. Van Ruler 2007, 57–80 (64).

[77] Clauberg's own references were in fact to Ficino and Plato himself rather than Erasmus, though he certainly was familiar with a number of works of the latter.

[78] See Van Ruler 2008, 159–175, for further discussion of Platonism in Geulincx, as well as Van Ruler 2007, 73, where he suggests that Geulincx relegates *meditatio mortis* to being of secondary importance compared to the attainment of beatitude in this life; it seems to me that for Geulincx the two come together—*meditatio mortis* here too does not mean preparation for death, but attempting to attain a post-death state in this life.

[79] Geulincx 1892, 157.

in the next life.[80] At whatever point the mind separates itself from the body, whether in this life or afterwards, it becomes eternal in the same way.

Geulincx himself seems to vacillate on the question of whether the mind can withdraw from the body by its own powers, or whether it requires some form of Divine assistance; if the mind can bring about such *ecstases* by its own powers, this goes some way to explaining why certain interpretations of *meditatio mortis* were theologically suspect. For some theorists, at least, claiming that the mind can withdraw from the body is tantamount to claiming that it is possible to attain salvation in this life. It is probably for the best, then, that Clauberg was more circumspect than Geulincx in his treatment of the mind's eternity. For Geulincx, the mind is not in time *per se* and hence is, as he puts at one stage, 'pure act'.[81] Clauberg, on the other hand, explicitly rules out the idea that the human mind can be described as pure act, precisely because this would imply that it had all its thoughts at once – '*simul et semel*'.[82] In contrast with Geulincx, Clauberg assigns the mind its own temporal succession, independent of bodily succession. The mind's separation from the body therefore does not imply that it has attained the state it will possess in the next life.

It does not seem, then, that Clauberg viewed the philosophical separation of mind from body as a genuine prefiguration of salvation. When he alludes to *meditatio mortis*, this is not what he has in mind. The significance of his reference to *meditatio mortis* is rather to be found in a more subtle deviation from other Cartesian views. Descartes himself certainly claimed at one stage that the knowledge of God that we derive from reasoning does not merit salvation, but merely serves as a preparation for faith.[83] Earlier on, moreover, he had simply denied that what he was saying about 'moral and natural' philosophy had anything to do with grace: as Lennon puts it, Descartes thinks that Pelagianism 'does not, and cannot arise in his work'.[84] A similar though still more general strategy was also often employed by certain Dutch Cartesians. For example, Clauberg's sometime teacher, Johannes De Raey, is a particularly clear case of a thinker who responded to these issues by attempting to draw a strict distinction between philosophy and theology.[85] Perhaps Clauberg, too, thought that claiming not to be engaged in theological speculation would be enough to divert the suspicions associated with his references to *meditatio mortis*. He sometimes explicitly distances himself from practical questions, including the kinds of theological issues at stake now. He warns, for example, that while his logic is designed to overcome some of 'the

---

[80] Strictly speaking, referring to it as the 'next life' may be an inappropriately temporal phrase. For Geulincx, unlike others of the period, eternity is not a form of duration, but wholly opposed to all of the various ways of referring to time (duration, succession, and so on).

[81] Geulincx 1892, vol. 2, 301.   [82] OOP 679.   [83] CSMK 211, ATIII 544.

[84] Lennon 2002, 195.

[85] For further discussion of the what has been termed the 'separation thesis', see Verbeek 1999a, 113–122, and Douglas 2015, 36–63.

178 'MEDITATIO MORTIS': POST-CARTESIAN

imperfections of the human mind', it does not aspire to overcome 'sins and moral vices'.[86] Clauberg would surely have seen, however, that such declarations on their own would not be enough to persuade his opponents, and even some of his friends, especially given his tendency to stray across the accepted boundary between philosophy and theology.

For De Raey—who was probably its most prominent defender of Cartesianism at the time—this division between philosophy and theology was part of a more general programme of separating philosophy in the strict sense from the practical disciplines, which pertain to everyday life. De Raey would have claimed that of all disciplines, philosophy alone makes use of purely intellectual understanding of things. The remainder—including theology—are supposed to be based on sense experience.[87] There were certainly times when De Raey himself was dissatisfied with the care Clauberg took to respect the division between philosophy and the practical disciplines. At one stage, for example, he felt the need to excuse Clauberg's failure to distinguish the logic required in philosophy from that used in everyday life, on the grounds that Clauberg had not attended his logic courses.[88] In fact, though, Clauberg's apparent lack of care could just as well have resulted from a desire to separate philosophy all the more sharply from the disciplines pertaining to daily life. De Raey's strategy of distinguishing theology from philosophy might help alleviate the fear that philosophers were speaking out of turn, but if philosophy really does result in something like death, it is not enough just to distinguish the respective domains of the two. Emphasizing the way that contemplation interferes with our sense perception only exacerbates the negative effect philosophy might have on the 'practical' disciplines, including theology. The implications of Clauberg's view of philosophy seem to be more wide-ranging than Revius, or even De Raey, might have anticipated, and extend beyond the concerns with salvation or theology.

Even if, on Clauberg's account, the separation of the mind from the body does not of itself bring the attainment of heavenly blessedness, striving towards that separation means striving to remove what for other Cartesians was foundational for other disciplines.[89] This much is evident in some of Clauberg's other concerns. Both De Raey and Clauberg sometimes refer to philosophy, and logic in particular, as a medicine of the mind [*medicina mentis*].[90] The 'sicknesses of the soul' [*morbi animi*] that Clauberg's *medicina mentis* is intended to cure include not only doubt and error, but also confusion and obscurity. As we have seen, *meditatio mortis* is

---

[86] OOP 769.   [87] See Douglas 2015, 51.   [88] See Verbeek 1999a, 119.

[89] One way of expanding on this is to say as follows: *pace* De Raey, it is not that Clauberg was not able to properly formulate the separation of philosophy and theology, it is that he thought that such a separation would not be possible in practice—that it was impossible to properly separate philosophy from the other disciplines without giving up on it. In any case, his references to *meditatio mortis* highlight this, even if it was not entirely Clauberg's intention.

[90] See Savini 2006, 73–88 for discussion of Clauberg's Cartesian (and Baconian) *medicina mentis*; Verbeek 1999a, 119, also briefly discusses *medicina mentis* in Clauberg.

one outcome of a medicine of the mind that attempts to remove confusion. Likewise, as recent scholars have mentioned, Clauberg argues that 'the infinite confusions & the most dense shadows in physics & medicine' arise from the fact that investigators confound the mind and body rather than considering them separately.[91] The issue is that even if the medicine of the mind can remove some forms and sources of confusion from the mind, there are some it might be better to maintain. Sense perception plays a role in our lives and in our survival, but always involves confused perceptions; that role differs from both whatever purely mechanical, automatic actions our bodies seem to perform without the mind's input and from the knowledge we can obtain purely intellectual observation of the body's states. But focusing greater attention on the fact that mind and body are separate things, which is involved in the medicine of the mind and a prerequisite of the medicine of the body, both weakens the very life of the human being doing so and precludes the possibility of studying that life in its own terms.

Clauberg undoubtedly had a genuine interest in what Smith has referred to as 'medical eudaimonism',[92] the regulation and cultivation of the health of the body as part of a good life. But he also thought that philosophers who have effected the separation of their minds from their bodies are in a state analogous to that of the 'mortally ill'. The resemblance of philosophical contemplation to death in Clauberg's work is an indication that the medicine of the mind does not always sit easily with what is necessary for the body's good health.[93]

5 Concluding remarks

In its most profound forms, Clauberg argues, philosophical contemplation involves the separation of mind and body, as the mind exercises its power to withdraw from the senses and focuses all its attention on its clear and distinct ideas. In contemplation of this kind, philosophers attain a condition that bears some resemblance to that of the soul after death. In this respect philosophy can rightly be called

---

[91] OOP 510: 'Et praecipua causa infinitarum confusionum & densissimarum tenebrarum in Physica & Medicina fuit hactenus, quod neque solius mentis proprietates sola mente seorsim considerant, sed quia perpetuo adhaerent sensibus & mentem cum corpore confundunt.' Quoted in Manning 2019, 219, quoting also Trevisani 2011, 94. The question of whether medicine was among the strictly philosophical, theoretical disciplines, or among the practical disciplines, was something De Raey changed his mind about in the course of his career; Clauberg here may have been under the influence of De Raey's earlier view.

[92] Smith 2013, 106.

[93] To put it another way: this 'medical eudaimonism' would have to not involve studying the distinctive life of the human being (or, if it does, that would presumably involve getting clear and distinct ideas of the contents of sense perception in the mind, because, as I have argued, Clauberg's view is that what is characteristic of the 'transeunt' vital acts that constitute the human composite is that the mind produces sensations in itself; in that sense, the human life would be a part of the life of the mind). In which case, it becomes harder to see why one would need to discuss the life of a human being as something over and above the respective lives of minds and bodies.

meditatio mortis. When philosophers withdraw their minds from their senses, they interrupt their lives as human beings or composites of body and mind.

But although for Clauberg it is possible to achieve this condition, we should not overestimate how easy it is to attain, or its benefits. It is possible to be mistaken, both about whether someone else has achieved it, and about whether one has achieved it oneself. Even when we appear to ourselves or others to be entirely absorbed in thought, some unnoticed residual confusion may continue to bind us to our bodies. The true separation of mind and body (and thus the interruption of the life of the mind-body composite) is not easy to achieve. Nor is it entirely free of risk. By interrupting the vital actions that constitute our human life, *meditatio mortis* can lead minds to neglect their bodily needs and threaten the survival of the composite.

Clauberg's account of *meditatio mortis* highlight an important strand of his thought, which both diverges from and draws on his Cartesian outlook. Whereas Descartes' analysis of life and death focuses on the operations of the body, Clauberg's approach allows for different senses of both life and death, and in turn these different senses apply in different ways to the mind, to the body and to the composite. As we have seen, the life of the mind-body composite is not an all or nothing affair. It can be interrupted when a mind withdraws from its body, and be restored when the mind once again starts to attend to its bodily perceptions. Equally, while the composite does not die when the mind withdraws, it undergoes something analogous to death. As well as departing from Descartes by providing these broader accounts of living and dying, Clauberg alters the balance of power between the body and the mind. For Descartes, the interaction of body and mind is such that the body imposes itself on a mind which cannot entirely ignore its promptings. For Clauberg, by contrast, there is no causal interaction between body and mind, and the capacity to respond to the body lies with the mind; it is up to the mind to produce the confused sensations that are constitutive of the life of the composite.

This crucial shift makes it easier for Clauberg to explain how the mind can withdraw from the body. But it also has implications for Clauberg's broader outlook and his place among his contemporaries. Engaging in philosophical contemplation can, in the longer term, weaken our habitual familiarity with foundations of the disciplines concerned with practical life. For some of his contemporaries, including his teacher Johannes De Raey, this would have included theology. Clauberg's references to *meditatio mortis* were not intended to suggest philosophy could have a role to play in salvation. They do, however, suggest not only that philosophical contemplation provides no guidance in the practical sphere, but that it could be detrimental to our everyday lives.[94]

---

[94] Thanks to Susan James, Andrea Robiglio, Lydia Azadpour, and participants at the Life and Death in Early Modern Philosophy conference for helpful comments and suggestions regarding various aspects of this essay. Research on this chapter was supported by the Research Foundation—Flanders.

8

Living Well, Dying Well

Life and Death in Spinoza's Philosophy and Biography

Piet Steenbakkers

In the reception and interpretation of the thought of Benedict de Spinoza, the substance of his works is inextricably linked with his biography and reputed character. What manner of life he led and how he died are questions that have fascinated friend and foe, and have played an important part in the assessment of his philosophy. Even Spinoza himself apparently found moral reputation a legitimate argument when he defended himself against Lambert van Velthuysen's accusation of atheism:

> [Van Velthuysen] says: *it's not important to know what my nation is, or what way of life I follow.* But of course if he had known, he would not so easily have persuaded himself that I teach atheism. For atheists are accustomed to seek honors and riches immoderately. But I have always scorned those things. Everyone who knows me knows that.
>
> (Letter 43, to Ostens, February 1671; Spinoza 2016, 386.)

It is not a coincidence that, in order to counter the charge of teaching atheism, Spinoza appeals to his way of life. As we shall see, the fascination displayed by his contemporaries, as well as later generations, in information about his life and—more particularly—the way he died, has always been connected with the question whether atheism reveals itself in a person's moral character, especially in the face of death. People were curious to hear if Spinoza died in line with his own philosophy: did he end his life as an unrepentant atheist?

In this chapter, I explore the meaning of the notions 'living well' and 'dying well' in Spinoza's philosophical system. The investigation starts from an intriguing concept with Platonic roots, which Spinoza touches on in the *Ethics*: that of a model of human nature. Next, I delineate how Spinoza's treatment of this idea compares with other views about a good life, and with the long tradition—explicitly renounced by Spinoza—of philosophy as a meditation on death. In that context I will also discuss a rumour about his own death that illustrates the interconnection between Spinoza's philosophy, biography, and reputation.

Piet Steenbakkers, *Living Well, Dying Well: Life and Death in Spinoza's Philosophy and Biography* In: *Life and Death in Early Modern Philosophy.* Edited by: Susan James, Oxford University Press. © Piet Steenbakkers 2021. DOI: 10.1093/oso/9780192843616.003.0009

182 LIVING WELL, DYING WELL

1 A good life: Spinoza's model

'A free man thinks of nothing less than of death, and his wisdom is a meditation on life, not on death.'[1] Thus Spinoza defiantly takes issue with a tradition that had prevailed since Antiquity, according to which philosophy is a preparation for death. His own philosophy is a celebration of life, and more particularly, of a human life worth living:

> When we say, then, that the best state is one where men pass their lives harmoniously, I mean that they pass a *human* life, one defined not merely by the circulation of the blood, and other things common to all animals, but mostly by reason, the true virtue and life of the mind.
>
> (*Political Treatise*, 5.5; Spinoza 2016, 530; adapted).

The defining feature of a human life, and the one that renders it worthy of that designation, is therefore that it affords an opportunity for reason to flourish.

This insistence on a rational life informs Spinoza's metaphysics, ethics, and political philosophy. The true life of the mind as a distinctive feature of a genuinely human life is embodied in his ideal or *model* of a fully rational human being, set forth in the preface to *Ethics* Part 4: 'I shall understand by good what we know certainly is a means by which we may approach nearer and nearer to the model of human nature that we set before ourselves. By evil, what we certainly know prevents us from becoming like that model (*exemplar*)' (Spinoza 1985, 545).[2]

It is only towards the end of Part 4 (from the scholium to proposition 66 onwards) that Spinoza returns to this model of human nature. There, however, he does not use the term *exemplar*, but refers instead to the 'free human being' (*homo liber*), that is, a person guided solely by reason. The opposite of the rational *homo liber* is the *homo servus*, the slave, or the *ignarus*, someone who is ignorant, and it is worth pausing to consider the source of this contrast. Although Spinoza explicitly distances himself from Stoicism in Part 5 of the *Ethics*, it is striking that he adopts the Stoic opposition between the sage (*sapiens*) and the ignorant (*ignarus*). He refers to it both in the preface to Part 5 and in its concluding

---

[1] *Ethics* Part 4, proposition 67; Spinoza 1985, 584. All quotations from Spinoza's works in English are taken from Edwin Curley's translations in *The Collected Works of Spinoza*, vol. I (Spinoza 1985) and vol. II (Spinoza 2016), though I do not always follow Curley's use of capitals and italics (for reasons explained in Steenbakkers 2018a). When the argument requires a detailed look at the exact formulations, I will quote the original texts in footnotes. There, too, I occasionally adapt capitals, accents, and punctuation. Spinoza's *Ethica* and *Tractatus Theologico-Politicus* are quoted from the recent critical editions (Spinoza 2020, Spinoza 1999), the other works from the Gebhardt edition (Spinoza 1925).

[2] 'Per bonum itaque...intelligam id, quod certo scimus medium esse, ut ad exemplar humanae naturae, quod nobis proponimus, magis magisque accedamus. Per malum autem id, quod certo scimus impedire, quo minus idem exemplar referamus' (Spinoza 2020, 344.27–30).

paragraph (*Ethics* 5, prop. 52, scholium), which is at the same time the resounding conclusion of the entire book. As these passages indicate, his ideal model of moral behaviour was at least partly inspired by the Stoic tradition.[3] The antitype of the wise and free human being—the model we should try to imitate—is someone who is ignorant.

When Spinoza first introduces the notion of a model of human nature in the preface to *Ethics* 4, he does so in the context of a discussion of the notions of perfection and imperfection. These concepts, he explains, are models (*exemplaria*) that we shape in our minds.

> If someone has decided to make something, and has finished it, then he will call his thing perfect—and so will anyone who rightly knows, or thinks he knows, the mind and purpose of the author of the work. For example, if someone sees a work (which I suppose to be not yet completed), and knows that the purpose of the author of that work is to build a house, he will say that it is imperfect. On the other hand, he will call it perfect as soon as he sees that the work has been carried through to the end which its author has decided to give it. But if someone sees a work whose like he has never seen, and does not know the mind of its maker, he will, of course, not be able to know whether that work is perfect or imperfect. And this seems to have been the first meaning of these words.

> But after men began to form universal ideas, and devise models of houses, buildings, towers, etc., and to prefer some models of things to others, it came about that each one called perfect what he saw agreed with the *universal idea* he had formed of this kind of thing, and imperfect, what he saw agreed less with the *model* he had conceived, even though its maker thought he had entirely finished it.

> Nor does there seem to be any other reason why men also commonly call perfect or imperfect natural things, which have not been made by human hand. For they are accustomed to form universal ideas of natural things as much as they do of artificial ones. They regard these *universal ideas as models of things*, and believe that *nature* (which they think does nothing except for the sake of some end) *looks to them, and sets them before itself as models.*

> (Spinoza 1985, 543; emphases mine)[4]

---

[3] There are, of course, differences as well: see Miller 2015, 126–132.

[4] 'Qui rem aliquam facere constituit eamque perfecit, rem suam perfectam esse non tantum ipse, sed etiam unusquisque, qui mentem auctoris illius operis et scopum recte noverit aut se novisse crediderit, dicet. Ex. gr. si quis aliquod opus (quod suppono nondum esse peractum) viderit, noveritque scopum auctoris illius operis esse domum aedificare, is domum imperfectam esse dicet, et contra perfectam, simulatque opus ad finem, quem ejus auctor eidem dare constituerat, perductum viderit. Verum si quis opus aliquod videt, cujus simile nunquam viderat, nec mentem opificis novit, is sane scire non poterit, opusne illud perfectum an imperfectum sit. Atque haec videtur prima fuisse horum vocabulorum

184 LIVING WELL, DYING WELL

Spinoza returns to this notion of *exemplar* at the end of the preface, no longer as a description of the way human thought produces models, but as an ideal that we can deliberately construct and use as a guide in our attempts to do what is good and avoid what is bad for us:

> As far as good and evil are concerned, they also indicate nothing positive in things, considered in themselves, nor are they anything other than modes of thinking, or notions we form because we compare things to one another.... But though this is so, still we must retain these words. For because we desire to form *an idea of man, as a model of human nature which we may look to*, it will be useful to us to retain these same words with the meaning I have indicated. In what follows, therefore, I shall understand by good what we know certainly is a means by which we may *approach nearer and nearer to the model of human nature that we set before ourselves*. By evil, what we certainly know prevents us from becoming like that model. Next, we shall say that men are more perfect or imperfect, insofar as they approach more or less near to this model.
>
> (Spinoza 1985, 545; emphases mine)[5]

In the *Ethics*, the model that concerns Spinoza is a philosophical construct of a rational and virtuous way of life; but as the above account suggests, models can be adapted to serve different ends and circumstances. It is therefore not surprising that, in the *Theologico-Political Treatise*, the model we are encouraged to set before ourselves is a model of God. This difference is a consequence of the divergent perspectives and strategies of the two books. The *Ethics* shows a philosophical road to salvation through reason. Yet it emphasizes at the same time that human beings are only partly rational, and that they will always be

---

significatio. Sed postquam homines ideas universales formare, et domuum, aedificiorum, turrium etc. exemplaria excogitare, et alia rerum exemplaria aliis praeferre inceperunt, factum est, ut unusquisque id perfectum vocaret, quod cum universali idea, quam ejusmodi rei formaverat, videret convenire, et id contra imperfectum, quod cum concepto suo exemplari minus convenire videret, quanquam ex opificis sententia consummatum plane esset. Nec alia videtur esse ratio, cur res naturales etiam, quae scilicet humana manu non sunt factae, perfectas aut imperfectas vulgo appellent; solent namque homines tam rerum naturalium quam artificialium ideas formare universales, quas rerum veluti exemplaria habent, et quas naturam (quam nihil nisi alicujus finis causa agree existimant) intueri credunt sibique exemplaria proponere' (Spinoza 2020, 340.13–342.10).

[5] 'Bonum et malum quod attinet, nihil etiam positivum in rebus, in se scilicet consideratis, indicant, nec aliud sunt praeter cogitandi modos seu notiones, quas formamus ex eo, quod res ad invicem comparamus.... Verum, quamvis se res ita habeat, nobis tamen haec vocabula retinenda sunt. Nam quia ideam hominis, tanquam naturae humanae exemplar, quod intueamur, formare cupimus, nobis ex usu erit haec eadem vocabula eo, quo dixi, sensu retinere. Per bonum itaque in seqq. intelligam id, quod certo scimus medium esse, ut ad exemplar humanae naturae, quod nobis proponimus, magis magisque accedamus. Per malum autem id, quod certo scimus impedire, quo minus idem exemplar referamus. Deinde hominess perfectiores aut imperfectiores dicemus, quatenus ad hoc idem exemplar magis aut minus accedent (Spinoza 2020, 344.19–346.1). Already in the early *Short Treatise* (Part 2, chapter 4), Spinoza develops a similar argument, stressing that this idea of a perfect human being is a 'being of reason', a construct (Spinoza 1925, I, 60.17–61.6).

under the sway of emotional forces they cannot control. The *Theological-Political Treatise* therefore shows an alternative way: true religion can also provide moral guidance, in that it teaches the fundamental divine law, that is: love God by loving your neigbour as yourself. This is also a model of the good life that we can set before ourselves. The difference is that the rule is here presented as a commandment to be obeyed, rather than as an insight to be grasped.

There is some disagreement among scholars as to whether Spinoza regards his model of the rational life as a state that humans can actually achieve. The almost general consensus that it is an *unattainable* ideal has been challenged by Steven Nadler, who has argued that the free man can and does indeed exist (Nadler 2015). I venture to disagree, for the following four reasons.

(i) In the *Short Treatise* (II, 4), Spinoza explicitly argues that the idea of a perfect man, as conceived by our intellect, is not a real being, but a 'being of reason' (*ens rationis*), in other words a mental construct. A good philosopher should not confuse these two types of being: 'I say, then, that I must conceive a perfect man, if I want to say anything regarding man's good and evil. For if I discussed the good and evil of, say, Adam, I would confuse a real being with a being of reason' (Spinoza 1985, 103). It could be argued that Spinoza is writing here about the ideal of the perfect man, rather than the free man, but as Nadler observes, there 'is general, but not universal, agreement that the free man is the "model of human nature" mentioned in the preface to Part Four' (Nadler 2015, 104). Nor does Spinoza distinguish between the two in the *Short Treatise*.

(ii) Models are perfect: they stand for the summit of achievement. That the free human being is an unattainable ideal is clear from Spinoza's insistence in the preface to part 4 of the *Ethics* that perfect models are human constructs that we may keep before our eyes to measure our advances *towards* this perfection.

(iii) The interpretation I am offering is entirely in line with Spinoza's picture of the free human being as someone guided *solely* by reason. As he emphasizes explicitly and categorically in propositions 2–4 of *Ethics* 4 (Spinoza 1985, 548–549), human beings can never be free in that absolute sense:

We are acted on, insofar as we are a part of nature, which cannot be conceived through itself, without the others (prop. 2).

The force by which a man perseveres in existing is limited, and infinitely surpassed by the power of external causes (prop. 3).

It is impossible that a man should not be a part of nature, and that he should be able to undergo no changes except those which can be understood through his own nature alone, and of which he is the adequate cause (prop. 4).

From this it follows that man is necessarily always subject to passions, that he follows and obeys the common order of nature, and accommodates himself to it as much as the nature of things requires (prop. 4, corollary).

186 LIVING WELL, DYING WELL

The formulation of proposition 4, in particular, excludes the real existence of free persons, i.e., *fully* rational human beings. If they were to exist, they would adequately cause *all* the changes they undergo, thereby proving proposition 4 false. This (in Spinoza's view) is absurd.

(iv) Finally, the fact that, in Spinoza's *Theological-Political Treatise*, God features as a model of true life again excludes the possibility that this place could be held by individual human beings.

As we have seen, the models to which Spinoza appeals are human constructs, designed to serve a practical, ethical end. (After all, he develops his argument in a book that is presented as an *ethics*.) They are a means of developing regulative rather than constitutive notions of good and bad. The terms 'regulative' and 'constitutive' are of course laden with Kantian associations, but I nevertheless use them advisedly. As I shall next go on to show, there are significant parallels between Spinoza's and Kant's appeals to the notion of a model. Why should this be? An explanation is at hand; in developing their conceptions of a model, both Spinoza and Kant draw on a common source. This insight is illuminating in at least two ways. As well as clarifying our understanding of the role played by the notion of a model in the ethical philosophies of each of the two authors, it draws our attention to one of the ways in which Spinoza radically departs from and transforms an established philosophical outlook.

1.1 The model of a good life in Spinoza and Kant

When Immanuel Kant discusses the notion of an *ideal* in the Transcendental Dialectic of the *Critique of Pure Reason*, he contrasts Plato with the Stoics.

> What is an ideal to us, was to *Plato* an *idea in the divine understanding*, an individual object in that understanding's pure intuition, the most perfect thing of each species of possible beings and the original ground of all its copies [*Urgrund aller Nachbilder*] in appearance.   (Kant 1998, 551)[6]
>
> Virtue, and with it human wisdom in its entire purity, are ideas. But the sage (of the Stoics) is an ideal, i.e., a human being who exists merely in thoughts, but who is fully congruent with the idea of wisdom. Thus just as the idea gives the *rule*, so the ideal in such a case serves as the *original image* [*Urbild*] for the thorough-going determination of the copy [*Nachbild*]; and we have in us no other standard for our actions than the conduct of this divine human being, with which we can

---

[6] 'Was uns ein Ideal ist, war dem *Plato* eine *Idee des göttlichen Verstandes*, ein einzelner Gegenstand in der reinen Anschauung desselben, das Vollkommenste einer jeden Art möglicher Wesen und der Urgrund aller Nachbilder in der Erscheinung' (KrV B 596; Kant 1900–1912, III, 383–384).

PIET STEENBAKKERS   187

compare ourselves, judging ourselves and thereby improving ourselves, even though we can never reach the standard   (Kant 1998, 552).[7]

The same notion of an ideal archetype of the perfectly virtuous human being is also invoked in the *Critique of Practical Reason*:

This holiness of will is nevertheless a practical *idea*, which must necessarily serve as a *model* [*Urbild*] to which all finite rational beings can only approximate without end and which the pure moral law, itself called holy because of this, constantly and rightly holds before their eyes; the utmost that finite practical reason can effect is to make sure of this unending progress of one's maxims toward this model and of their constancy in continual progress, that is, virtue; and virtue itself, in turn, at least as a naturally acquired ability, can never be completed.   (Kant 2015, 29–30)[8]

The German word Kant uses to express the notion variously rendered here as 'archetype', 'original image', and 'model', is *Urbild*. But in an early Latin text—his inaugural dissertation *De mundi sensibilis atque intelligibilis forma et principiis* of 1770—he uses the word *exemplar* (Kant 1900–1912, II, 394.33) to denote a model issuing from the general principles of the pure intellect. Kant equates this model with 'noumenal perfection', which is the highest being—God—when taken in a theoretical sense, and moral perfection when taken in a practical sense. He also observes that the maximum of perfection, which for Plato was an idea, is nowadays called an *ideal*.[9]

As we are now in a position to appreciate, there is a noticeable resemblance between Kant's view and the model of human nature that Spinoza offers in the preface to *Ethics*, Part 4. The similarities between them can be summarized in the following five points:

---

[7] 'Tugend und mit ihr menschliche Weisheit in ihrer ganzen Reinigkeit sind Ideen. Aber der Weise (des Stoikers) ist ein Ideal, d.i. ein Mensch, der bloß in Gedanken existirt, der aber mit der Idee der Weisheit völlig congruirt. So wie die Idee die *Regel* giebt, so dient das Ideal in solchem Falle zum *Urbilde* der durchgängigen Bestimmung des Nachbildes; und wir haben kein anderes Richtmaß unserer Handlungen, als das Verhalten dieses göttlichen Menschen in uns, womit wir uns vergleichen, beurtheilen und dadurch uns bessern, obgleich es niemals erreichen können' (KrV B 597; Kant 1900–1912, III, 384).

[8] 'Diese Heiligkeit des Willens ist gleichwohl eine praktische Idee, welche nothwendig zum *Urbilde* dienen muß, welchem sich ins Unendliche zu nähern das einzige ist, was allen endlichen vernünftigen Wesen zusteht, und welche das reine Sittengesetz, das darum selbst heilig heißt, ihnen beständig und richtig vor Augen hält, von welchem ins Unendliche gehenden Progressus seiner Maximen und Unwandelbarkeit derselben zum beständigen Fortschreiten sicher zu sein, d. i. Tugend, das Höchste ist, was endliche praktische Vernunft bewirken kann, die selbst wiederum wenigstens als natürlich erworbenes Vermögen nie vollendet sein kann' (KpV A 58; Kant 1900–1912, V, 32–33).

[9] 'principia generalia intellectus puri…exeunt in exemplar aliquod…, quod est *perfectio noumenon*. Haec autem est vel in sensu theoretico, vel practico talis. In priori est ens summum, *Deus*, in posteriori sensu *perfectio moralis*.…Maximum perfectionis vocatur nunc temporis ideale, Platoni idea' (Kant 1900–1912, II, 394.33–395.2).

188 LIVING WELL, DYING WELL

1. Ideas are human constructs, not the archetypal origins of the things that exist.
2. Though human beings can develop normative ideas of moral perfection, they can only keep these before their eyes in order to know what they are heading for.
3. The models, then, are no longer, as they were in Plato, the original reality from which all things derived their existence, but a projection of manmade ideals that we can strive for, without ever getting there.
4. There is in both cases a link with the Stoic ideal of the sage.
5. The summit of perfection, God, can also function as a model of true life, i.e., as a norm that shows us how to live and as a standard by which we can measure our conduct. Kant speaks of the divine man within us; for Spinoza, the authority of the prophets and of God's Word can fill in for philosophical insight.

How can these striking parallels be accounted for? There is no agreement among scholars about the extent of Spinoza's influence on Kant and it is unclear how much of Spinoza he read.[10] In this case, however, conspicuous features of the wording that the two philosophers use point to a common source rather than to direct influence. As Klaus Reich (2001) has shown, Kant's reception of the Platonic heritage was mediated here by Cicero's Latin rendering of the *Timaeus*, also known as *De Universitate*. It is not Plato's, but Cicero's notion of *idea* as an indispensable but unattainable ideal that inspired both Spinoza and Kant (and also modern everyday usage).[11]

There was also an additional and crucial influence on Kant that was not available to Spinoza: Jean-Jacques Rousseau's short treatise of 1764, *De l'imitation théatrale*, which draws on Plato's *Politeia*, book 10. Rousseau also adapts Plato to the Ciceronian interpretation of ideas. As Reich puts it, Kant appeals to Plato, seen through the glasses of Cicero with Rousseau's eyes.

Returning to Spinoza, it is obvious from the wording of the preface of *Ethica* part 4 that he knew and used Cicero's *Timaeus*.[12] Where Plato attributes the creation of the universe to the demiurge (29a), Cicero (*Tim.* 6) describes a

---

[10] See, e.g., Mason 2007; Boehm 2014; Bolduc 2015.

[11] As examples of unattainable ideals in Cicero that function as yardsticks Reich (2001, 307) cites the orator (*Orator* 10) and the *vir bonus* (*De officiis*, book 3). *Orator* 10 explicitly refers to Plato and the Platonic notion of ideas.

[12] There is no mention of this work in the inventory of the books Spinoza owned when he died, but the crucial passage about the *exemplar* is to be found, e.g. in the *Thesaurus Ciceronianus* compiled by Marius Nizolius, which was in Spinoza's library (see Te Winkel 1914, no. 7; Aler 1965, no. 102). Throughout his works, there are several veiled quotations which show that Spinoza was well acquainted with Cicero's works. A telling example—a quote from Cicero's *De amicitia*—will be discussed below (p. C8.P48 and note 23). The famous 'punchline' *omnia praeclara rara* with which Spinoza ends the *Ethics* also echoes *De amicitia* (79). Cicero is explicitly quoted in the explanation to def. 44 in the appendix to Part 3.

supreme Maker or Craftsman (*parens huius universitatis, fabricator, artifex*) who looks to an eternal type and holds it up to himself as a model that he imitates.[13] Let us compare this passage to Spinoza's text. People, Spinoza tells us, regard universal ideas as models of things; they also believe that nature looks to them, and sets them before itself as models (*ideas universales, quas rerum veluti exemplaria habent, et quas naturam intueri credunt sibique exemplaria proponere*).[14]

Cicero's phrase *intuebitur atque id sibi proponet exemplar* recurs conspicuously in both Spinoza's and Kant's texts.[15] Both are obviously inspired in similar ways by the specifically Ciceronian development of Plato's notion of *idea*: no longer a real being, but a rational construct. Both Spinoza's and Kant's treatment are instances of a radical shift in philosophical thought about the notion of an ideal. They prepare the ground for the current meaning of 'ideal' in non-philosophical, everyday usage, i.e., a perfect but unattainable standard or principle.

2 Spinoza's model: a textual emendation

Spinoza fills out his account of the ideal or *exemplar* we should try to imitate in the appendix to *Ethics*, part 4, his manual for the right way of living (*de recta vivendi ratione*, E4app, introduction). He begins (in *capita* or sections 1–3) by observing that we are driven by two kinds of desire, active and passive. We are the proximate cause of our active desires to the extent that our mind consists of adequate ideas. These are the rational drives, and they determine the extent to which we can have control over our own existence. Drives of the second kind, inadequate ideas, are determined by and explained through the power of things outside us. These external desires are indicative of our weakness and ignorance. It should be noted that this analysis does not come with a value judgement on Spinoza's part. Both kinds of desire follow from nature; they are manifestations of God's power and thereby necessary. And yet Spinoza qualifies our actions, which express our active desires, as 'good', and the passive desires as at least potentially 'evil' (section 3). The challenge he then faces is to show why our rational desires are to be preferred, and his answer focuses on the *practice of living*. 'In life, therefore, it is especially useful to perfect, as far as we can, our intellect, or reason. In this one

---

[13] *Tim.* 4: 'intuebitur atque id sibi proponet exemplar'; *Tim.* 6: 'videndum, ille fabricator huius tanti operis utrum sit imitatus exemplar'.

[14] See above, note 5, for the full quotation.

[15] In Kant's *Critique of Practical Reason* (A 58; Kant 1900–1912, V, 32–33), the pure moral law holds the model before the eyes of all finite rational beings. In Spinoza's *Ethics* the word *exemplar* also occurs in the second scholium to prop. 33 of part I, in what appears to be a paraphrase of Cicero's formula: 'those who maintain that God does all things for the sake of the good...seem to place something outside God, which does not depend on Go, *to which God attends, as a model (ad quod Deus tanquam ad exemplar in operando attendit)*, in what he does, and at which he aims, as at a certain goal' (Spinoza 1985, 438; Spinoza 2020, 148.4–6; emphases mine)—a view Spinoza rejects as absurd.

190 LIVING WELL, DYING WELL

thing consists man's highest happiness, or blessedness.'[16] So although externally determined desires are necessary and natural, only rational desires can really make us happy. Spinoza develops this argument in sections 4–8 of the appendix, and in sections 9–12 goes on to show that there is an essential social component to a rational way of life. From section 13 onwards he deals with the best way for a rational human being to accommodate to a society that will only be rational to a very limited degree.

In the course of this argument, we encounter four occurrences of a particular expression: *vita rationali frui*, i.e., 'enjoying a rational life'.[17] In all cases Spinoza uses this expression to strengthen and specify a preceding term:

1. (cap. 5) *rationem perficere et rationali vita frui* ('to perfect one's reason and enjoy the rational life')

2. (cap. 8) *existere et vita rationali frui* ('to exist and enjoy a rational life')

3. (cap. 8) *ad nostrum esse conservandum et vita rationali fruendum* ('for preserving our being and enjoying a rational life')

4. (cap. 9) *ad suum esse conservandum et vita rationali fruendum* ('preserving his being and enjoying a rational life')

These expressions, particularly the last three, drive home the point that mere self-preservation does not constitute a properly human life. To develop and flourish, humans also need to develop the rationality that Spinoza describes as the *true life of the mind*. Where this is absent, our existence does not deserve to be called a human life.[18]

So far, we have focused on the central place that enjoying a rational life occupies in the life of the free man. But while this is central to all four of the cases mentioned above, it is only part of the story. At this point, I must briefly recall the textual history of Spinoza's *Ethics*.[19] There are three sources for this work: the Latin text printed by his friends after he died in 1677 in the volume *B.d.S. Opera posthuma*; the Dutch translation by Jan Hendriksz Glazemaker, published simultaneously in 1677 in the parallel volume *De nagelate schriften van B.d.S.*; and a recently discovered manuscript, containing the entire Latin text, copied from the finished autograph (with Spinoza's agreement) by Pieter van Gent in 1675.[20]

---

[16] Cap. 4. (In vita itaque apprime utile est intellectum seu rationem, quantum possumus, perficere, et in hoc uno summa hominis felicitas seu beatitudo consistit.)

[17] Compare also: 'ut mentis vita fruatur, quae intelligentia definitur', cap. 5 ('to enjoy the life of the mind, which is defined by understanding').

[18] See also the definition in *Cogitata metaphysica* 2.6 (Spinoza 1925, I, 260): 'Quare nos per *vitam* intelligimus *vim, per quam res in suo esse perseverant*' ('So we understand by *life* the *force through which things persevere in their being*,' Spinoza 1985, 326).

[19] For a full account I refer to our Introduction to Spinoza 2020, 13–38.

[20] See Spruit and Totaro 2011.

There is, indeed, a fifth occurrence of the expression *vita rationalis*, but one that can only be found in the text of the *Ethics* in the *Opera posthuma*. What is striking about it is that here the verb *frui*, 'to enjoy', which accompanies the other occurrences,[21] is lacking:

5. (cap. 5) *Nulla igitur vita rationalis est sine intelligentia* ('No life, then, is rational without understanding')

But the only other source for the Latin text of this particular passage, the Vatican manuscript, offers a different reading: *Nulla igitur vita vitalis est sine intelligentia*. And what is more, that reading is corroborated by the contemporary Dutch translation in *De nagelate schriften*: *Dat leven, 't welk zonder kennis is, kan geen leven genoemt worden* ('A life without understanding cannot be called a life'). In establishing the correct Latin text for our new critical edition of the *Ethics*, we have decided to emend this passage in accordance with the reading in the Vatican manuscript, reading *vita vitalis* instead of *vita rationalis*.[22] Thus emended, the text throws new light on Spinoza's notion of living well. What it takes to make life worth living, as we can now more clearly see, is *an adequate understanding of our situation*. However weak the rational spark may be (and Spinoza again emphasizes its weakness in section 13 of the appendix), it is the only thing that will make human life worthy of that name. Everything else is merely persevering in one's existence, which, while it is of the utmost importance, does not distinguish human life from the life of other living things. Though weak in comparison with the infinity of forces that surround and affect us, this is the only power we can rely on, both individually and for social and political purposes. It is the power we need to cultivate if we are to approach Spinoza's model of perfection.

---

[21] *Frui* does occur in cap. 5 (quoted in note 18), but there it is without the expression *vita vitalis*.

[22] Fokke Akkerman recognized the admittedly curious expression *vita vitalis* as a veiled quotation from Cicero's *Laelius (de Amicitia)* 22. (By the way, this apparently goes for *all* occurrences of *vita vitalis* in Neo-Latin texts.) Even in Cicero, the expression is a most unusual one. It occurs only once, and it is presented by Cicero as a borrowing from the older poet Quintus Ennius. The exact source has not been identified; it may have been one of the works by Ennius that are now lost. The expression undoubtedly is a calque of the corresponding Greek expression, βίος βίωτος: much of Ennius' language reflects Greek models. Cicero's treatment of friendship here (in *Laelius* 22) owes a great deal to Aristotle's *Nicomachean Ethics*, book VIII, §1, but Aristotle himself does not employ the expression. It does, however, occur in several other Greek authors, in widely different contexts, often denoting something without which life will not or no longer be worth living, e.g. Aristophanes, *Plutus* 197: money; Sophocles, *Oedipus at Colonus*, 1690: parents; Plato *Apol.* 38a: self-examination; Plato, *Crito*, 47d-e: health; Demosthenes, *Against Meidias*, 21.120. So, the Greeks inspired Ennius, Ennius in turn inspired Cicero, and Cicero was Spinoza's source when he was searching for a very strong, startling expression to denote a life worth living.

192 LIVING WELL, DYING WELL

2.1 A model of how to die

The enjoyment that the free man experiences as he cultivates and exercises his understanding and increases the adequacy of his ideas extends to every aspect of his life, and even to his death.[23] According to Spinoza, those who have sufficient knowledge of themselves and of God will hardly fear death (*Ethica* part 5, proposition 39, scholium). Since the good life requires the right use of the mind, which in turn diminishes the fear of death, living well entails dying well. Precisely for that reason, people were curious to see whether Spinoza himself would remain steadfast in the face of death. Especially when thinkers were suspected of atheism, their demeanour at death's door was regarded as the ultimate test of their doctrines. Could they die in the manner they themselves recommended? The way a philosopher died thus acquired the status of an argument for or against his or her philosophy.

In a long letter written from Florence on 11 September 1675, Albert Burgh bombarded Spinoza with arguments for converting to Roman Catholicism, as he himself had done. His trump card was the horrible death awaiting atheists:

> Finally, reflect on how wretched and restless the life of atheists is. Sometimes they manifest great cheerfulness and try to seem to be leading a pleasant life, with the greatest internal peace of mind. But see what unfortunate and horrible deaths they experience. I myself have seen several examples of this, and I know, both from the accounts of others, and from history, a great many other, indeed, countless examples. Learn from the example of these men to be wise in time.
>
> (Letter 67; Spinoza 2016, 449–450)

Spinoza remained silent about this hideous paragraph, but what he would have thought of it may be deduced from the following remark in his reply to Burgh: 'I see, and your letter clearly indicates, that having become a slave of this church, you've been guided not so much by the love of God as by fear of hell, the only cause of superstition' (Letter 76; Spinoza 2016, 477).

In his *Ethics*—a work Burgh did not know—Spinoza occasionally mentions the fear of death. According to proposition 67 of part 4, 'A free man thinks of nothing less than of death, and his wisdom is a meditation on life, not on death.' The demonstration runs as follows:

> A free man, i.e., one who lives according to the dictate of reason alone, is not led by fear of death, but desires the good directly, i.e., acts, lives, and preserves his

---

[23] This section incorporates material from a publication in Dutch, on Spinoza's view of death and on the way he died (Steenbakkers 2013).

being from the foundation of seeking his own advantage. And so he thinks of nothing less than of death. Instead his wisdom is a meditation on life, q.e.d.

(Spinoza 1985, 584; adapted).

Here Spinoza emphatically rejects a long and influential tradition, according to which death is the object *par excellence* of philosophical reflection. Its origin lies in Plato's description of the way Socrates prepares for his imminent death (*Phaedo* 81a); Socrates longs for death, because he is convinced that it will allow his soul to return to its divine origin. However, since this can only occur once the soul has entirely disengaged itself from its perishable body, philosophy must bring about precisely that breaking away from matter and the senses.

— If at its release the soul is pure and carries with it no contamination of the body, because it has never willingly associated with it in life, but has shunned it and kept itself separate as its regular practice—in other words, if it has pursued philosophy in the right way and really practiced how to face death easily—this is what 'practicing death'[24] means, isn't it?
— Most decidedly.
— Very well, if this is its condition, then it departs to that place which is, like itself, invisible, divine, immortal, and wise, where, on its arrival, happiness awaits it, and release from uncertainty and folly, from fears and uncontrolled desires, and all other human evils, and where, as they say of the initiates in the Mysteries, it really spends the rest of the time with God. (*Phaedo*, 80e–81a; trans. Hugh Tredennick, Plato 1994, 640)

As Cicero put it, paraphrasing this passage in his *Tusculan Disputations*, 'the entire life of philosophers is a careful preparation for death'.[25]

Throughout the history of philosophy, we encounter traces of this view. Schopenhauer offers an impressive synthesis in a long chapter in Part II of *Die Welt als Wille und Vorstellung*, entitled 'Über den Tod und sein Verhältniß zur Unzerstörbarkeit unsers Wesens an sich' ('On death and its relationship to the imperturbability of our essence in itself'). It is true that, while this view of the relationship between philosophy and death has long been dominant, it has never gone unchallenged. 'Death', Epicurus wrote, 'is nothing to us: for that which is dissolved is without sensation; and that which lacks sensation is nothing to us.'[26] Again, as he explains in his *Letter to Menoeceus*: 'So death, the most terrifying of ills, is nothing to us; since so long as we exist, death is not with us; but when death comes, then we do not exist. It does not then concern

---

[24] 'Practicing death' translates μελέτη θανάτου.
[25] Cicero, *Tusculanae disputationes*, 1.75. His rendering of μελέτη θανάτου is *commentatio mortis*.
[26] *Principal Doctrines*, 2 (Epicurus 1926, ed./trans. Bailey, 95).

194 LIVING WELL, DYING WELL

either the living or the dead, since for the former it is not, and the latter are no more.'[27] However, Epicureanism has never displaced the view that life is a preparation for death. On account of its allegedly atheistic character (Obbink 1989), it has remained a relatively marginal phenomenon in the history of philosophy.

When Spinoza states that a free person thinks of nothing less than of death, he is clearly closer to Epicureanism than to the Platonic tradition. Even so, his conception of death cannot be equated with that of Epicurus. As Chantal Jaquet (2003) has convincingly argued, Spinoza's position is extraordinary in that he sees death as something *evil*. It is not, as Socrates and the Platonic tradition hold, something good and desirable, a transition to a higher form of being. Nor is it, as the Stoa and Epicureans claim, something indifferent that we ought to face with imperturbable equanimity. For Spinoza, death is the ultimate powerlessness, a transition to an existence that utterly destroys our present form. Of course, death cannot be called *evil* in an absolute sense; it is inevitable and follows from the laws of nature. However, since death triumphs over and cuts off our striving to persevere in our being, we are bound to *assess* it as evil for us.

Why, then, should we not fear death? According to Spinoza, free persons who live according to the precepts of reason are only guided by adequate knowledge. Since knowledge of death is inadequate (*Ethics* 4, prop. 64), it will not play a part in their efforts to be guided by Spinoza's model and live rationally. The more they manage to live on the basis of adequate ideas, the less will they fear death (*Ethics* 5, prop. 38); indeed, those who have an adequate knowledge of themselves and of God will hardly fear death at all (*Ethics* 4, prop. 39, scholium). However, the qualification 'hardly' is revealing here; because the free person as such does not exist, and because we are always subject to passions, we cannot expect to escape the fear of death entirely and can only expect to do so to some extent. As we become freer and more rational, our fear of death will decrease; but it will never disappear completely.

3 Spinoza's death

Unlike the Stoa or Epicureans, Spinoza did not promise that his philosophy would do away with the fear of death altogether; it would only make this fear more manageable. But how was the truth of this claim to be assessed? Ironically, the way Spinoza himself died was held to be a test of its validity and persuasiveness. Could he, the archetypal Spinozist philosopher, live up to his own model of the good life by dying accordingly? The question was particularly pressing for those of his

---

[27] *Letter to Menoeceus* (Epicurus 1926, ed./trans. Bailey, 85).

contemporaries who were convinced that he was an atheist. Spinoza denied, after all, that the soul was a substance and thus rejected the notion of an individual afterlife. Equally, he identified God with nature, thereby denying a personal God who functioned as Creator and Judge. Armed with these convictions, could he face death calmly?

These anxieties and curiosities are at work in contemporary rumours about Spinoza's death, which began to circulate immediately after his demise in 1677. Some are contained in a report of Spinoza's final days recorded in a notebook, kept in 1678–1679 by an anonymous young libertine from Utrecht. The notes it contains evince a strong interest in the way Spinoza's philosophy and his critique of religion related to his moral reputation and his death,[28] which is described (in one of the most substantial notes about Spinoza) in some detail. The wording of this entry suggests that the information in it came from the physician who assisted Spinoza in his final hours. But the physician's name is withheld. Since the manuscript's author habitually identifies his sources, this omission may indicate that he is passing on a rumour, rather than retailing inside information derived directly from Spinoza's doctor, the only person who had witnessed his demise. The entry contains some striking details that have so far not been found anywhere else. This is my translation of it:

> When death approached, Spinoza ordered medication and other vital necessities to be put by his bed, and he ordered the physician to withdraw, and the door to be closed and locked with a key. He lived there for three more days, as his personal physician testifies, who stayed awake on the storey above his head. And in that way he died; it is doubtful whether he repented.[29]

What are we to make of this? The most extensive account of Spinoza's death is given in the biography published by the Lutheran minister Johannes Colerus in 1705.[30] Colerus took special care to clear up the exact circumstances of the philosopher's death, and does his best to confront the many rumours surrounding it—of which the report in our notebook seems to be an example. He discusses five improbable stories, of which three are relevant here.

(1) Spinoza took precautions so as not to be disturbed by surprise visits.
(2) He had a supply of poppy juice, which he took when death approached, and, drawing the curtains of his bedstead, departed this life in a torpor.
(3) He asked his landlady to let no clergyman in, as he wanted to die without a dispute.

---

[28] For a full account and edition of this curious document see Steenbakkers et al. 2011.
[29] Steenbakkers et al. 2011, 307.
[30] See the edition (with translation) of Colerus's biography in Walther and Czelinski 2006, I, 98–171; comments: II, 62–79.

196 LIVING WELL, DYING WELL

Colerus explicitly denies that Spinoza kept to his room (let alone that he had himself locked in); that he ordered visitors to be refused admittance; and that he took any soporific to alleviate his suffering. While he allows that these rumours were rampant, Colerus insists they were all fabrications.

The notebook is the first documented evidence of such rumours, and indicates how they may have been transmitted. This makes the notebook entry about Spinoza's death historically significant, even if the details it relates are completely fictitious. The author presumably noted down the information about the death of a notorious freethinker because he deemed it an exciting story. At the same time, as his final sentence indicates, he expresses moral and religious concern about Spinoza's atheistical death: 'In that way he died; it is doubtful whether he repented.'

4 Conclusion

In the *Ethics*, Spinoza developed his thought as a closely knit system, in which each element is organically connected with the rest. His naturalistic ethical theory is embedded in a grand view of the place of human beings in the whole of nature. Unlike most other ethical theories in the history of Western philosophy, he lays great emphasis on the lust for life, or, as he prefers to call it, the striving (*conatus*) to persevere in one's being.[31] In the particular case of human beings, that striving is most successful when pursued under the guidance of reason. In this way, Spinoza ultimately derives his ethical prescriptions—his injunctions for the right way of living—from the metaphysical foundations of his philosophy. Thus, he solves the apparently impossible task he had set himself: to demonstrate how an ethics can be established without invoking a transcendent principle, starting from a philosophy that situates human beings in a fully determined, law-governed nature. Since for him nature conceived as a dynamic and all-embracing system coincides entirely with God, the rules of reason that constitute the right way of living are simultaneously the divine commands that tell us how to behave. Both perspectives reveal the depth and range of Spinoza's conception of a human life worth living. Unlike many of his contemporary and later critics (and admirers, too), I do not think that the way he himself lived and died conveys a deeper message about the validity or viability of his philosophy. That can perfectly well stand on its own.[32]

---

[31] *Ethics*, part 3, propositions 6–8; Spinoza 1985, 498–499.
[32] This chapter is an elaboration of the paper I presented at the 2016 London conference on 'Life and Death in Early Modern Philosophy'. The same ground was covered in a guest lecture I read at Ritsumeikan University in Kyoto in May 2018 (published in Japanese: Steenbakkers 2018b). It combines and develops themes I explored in unpublished papers that were presented in various seminars between January 2015 and July 2018.

9

Prevailing over Death

Democritus and the Myth of a Philosophical Death

Piero Schiavo

Historians of philosophy have often chronicled the deaths of prominent philosophers, in narratives that sometimes also outline a thinker's doctrine and appraise its veracity and integrity in the light of their demise.[1] Anecdotes about philosophers' deaths thus raise broader questions about the myth of a philosophical death as well as the place of death in philosophy. In this chapter I shall focus on a particular figure in the history of philosophy *sub specie mortis*: Democritus, whose learning was said to be so great that he was able to hold death at bay. I shall begin by commenting on several ancient accounts of his end, evaluating the extent to which they cohere with what we know of his doctrine, and assessing them in the light of contemporary narrations of his life and personality. I shall then go on to examine some of the ways in which early modern authors appealed to the story of Democritus' death for their own philosophical ends. In their hands, the legend serves many purposes. It offers a model for us to try to imitate, a counterweight to punitive theologies, a warning of the unreliability of historical data, and an opportunity to cut pretentious philosophers down to size. Each of these interpretations draws on different aspects of the legend and places it in a different context; but, as their sheer range indicates, the notion of an exemplary philosophical death remained central to philosophical thinking. To be a philosopher in the early modern era was, in part, to reflect on what philosophy can teach us about dying, and to live in the spirit of one's conclusions, whatever they turned out to be. Moreover, insofar as this project continued to be shaped by a series of historical exemplars, none was more resonant than Democritus.

1 The legend of Democritus' death

The portraits of Democritus that have come down to us straddle the boundary between history and legend. His life inspired many anecdotes that transform him

---

[1] See for example Critchley 2009. On Democritus himself, see in particular Chitwood 2004. See also Gori and Spallanzani, 2012.

Piero Schiavo, *Prevailing over Death: Democritus and the Myth of a Philosophical Death* In: *Life and Death in Early Modern Philosophy*. Edited by: Susan James, Oxford University Press. © Piero Schiavo 2021.
DOI: 10.1093/oso/9780192843616.003.0010

198 PREVAILING OVER DEATH

into a mythical figure and offer something for everyone. An icon of pensive melancholy in the visual arts, he is celebrated for his pioneering diagnosis of atrabilious diseases and their symptoms in the field of medicine. In the world of letters, the stance adopted by the 'laughing philosopher' in the face of human misery and vanity is often contrasted with that of the 'weeping Heraclitus', while in the field of moral philosophy, Democritus' satire on humankind attracted many followers until at least the eighteenth century.[2]

The fact that we have so little first-hand evidence about Democritus and that, aside from a handful of ethical maxims whose authenticity is a matter of debate,[3] his many writings have all been lost, undoubtedly makes it difficult for scholars to reconstruct his thought. There seems no alternative but to turn to the doxographic tradition for a fuller and more coherent picture of his doctrine. But although our lack of original sources makes it impossible for us to interpret his ideas without sifting through large numbers of second-hand accounts and fragments, this still does not explain why his life has generated a wealth of anecdotes, many of them decidedly fanciful. This myth making seems to have been spurred on by Democritus' reputation as a sage possessed of great learning. Known for the encyclopaedic knowledge he acquired during his youthful travels and studies, and for spending his mature years in solitary meditation, Democritus inspired reverence and even awe. Cicero, for example, called him a 'vir magnus in primis'.[4] Diogenes Laërtius reports that Socrates, 'says the philosopher resembles a pent-athlete'[5] and, quoting Aristoxenus, that Plato himself, fearing to be overshadowed, 'wanted to burn all the writings of Democritus he was able to collect'.[6] At the same time, as Aulus Gellius observes, Democritus' scholarly prestige enticed 'men lacking in intelligence' to shelter behind 'his celebrity and authority' and attribute to him 'marvels and delusions'.[7]

Feats of virtue and learning have often inspired extraordinary anecdotes, further magnifying the purported achievements of those to whom they were attributed, and Democritus us no exception. In Book 9 of *The Lives of Eminent Philosophers*, a work which to this day remains one of our best sources of information about the lives and doctrines of ancient philosophers, Laërtius reports Hermippus' account of the death of Democritus as follows:

> Hermippus says that Democritus died in the following way. When he was already very old, he was near the end. Then his sister became upset because he was going

---

[2] Richardot 2000, 197–212; Richardot 2002; Jehasse 1980, 41–64; Salem 1996a, 55–74; Salem 1996b; Lüthy 2000, 443–479; Starobinski 1984, 49–72.

[3] See Alfieri (ed.) 1936. Quotes from accounts and fragments of Democritus follow the Diels-Krantznumbering and AndréLaks' translation in Laks (ed. and trans.) 2016; henceforth Laks; I also refer to C. C. W. Taylor's 2016 translation of Luria 2016 (henceforth Luria).

[4] Cicerone 1951, I, 43 120; and also Cicero 1927, 'magnum illum quidem virum', I, 11 22.

[5] Laks, 45. [6] Laks, 363. See also Laërtius 1925, 9.7: 'Luria 2016', 447, 449.

[7] Laks, 489.

to die during the festival of the Thesmophoria and she would not be able to perform the proper honors for the goddess. He told her to cheer up and ordered her to bring him hot loaves of bread every day. By applying these to his nostrils he managed to stay alive until the end of the festival; and when the days had passed (there were three of them) he abandoned life without any suffering [...][8]

Laërtius then proceeds to quote the verses he himself composed in memory of the great philosopher:

Pray who was so wise, who wrought so vast a work as the omniscient Democritus achieved? When Death was near, for three days he kept him in his house and regaled him with the steam of hot loaves.[9]

This anecdote is almost certainly apocryphal. Indeed, we know, thanks to Diels, that Hermippus of Smyrna (200 BC) was himself the author of a book of lives that circulated widely, a compendium of parodic extracts accounting for the death of various philosophers in the light of their principles of physics.[10] There are, however, other similar accounts of Democritus' death, notably those by Caelius Aurelianus,[11] Athenaeus, and Asclepiades.[12] According to Asclepiades, Democritus did not die naturally but committed suicide, purposefully starving himself to death after postponing his demise for a few days because of the sacred festival. This opinion is shared by Athenaeus, who also attributes the philosopher's demise to suicide by fasting.[13] According to Athenaeus, however, Democritus did not keep himself going with the aroma of freshly baked loaves, but with the smell of honey. As Athenaeus reports, 'Democritus was always fond of honey, and when someone asked him how to keep healthy, he said: "Moisten the inside with honey and the outside with oil."'[14] The reference to honey probably derives from two of Democritus' doctrines, one praising honey for

---

[8] Laks, 55. See also Laërtius 1925, 9.7: 43, 453; Laërtius writes that Democritus lived for more than a century (9.7:39, 449) and that Hipparchus says he was 109 years old when he died (9.7: 43, 453). There are no reliable sources on this subject. See Alfieri (ed.) 1936, 59.

[9] Laërtius 1925, 9.7: 43, 453.   [10] See Alfieri (ed.) 1936, 52 and 69–70.

[11] In his account of Democritus' death, Caelius Aurelianus seems to confirm the legend of the hot loaves, although the details are not the same: 'So let there be prepared an infusion of barley and dry bread soaked in vinegar, or quinces or myrtle and similar things. For these preserve the failing strength of the body, as is shown by reason and by the celebrated story of the postponement of the death of Democritus' (Luria, DK68A28).

[12] 'And there he (i.e. Asclepiades) says that there is a story that Democritus had fasted for four days and was on the point of death when some women begged him to remain alive for a few days, so that the Thesmophoria, which were then being celebrated, should not be spoiled by an ill omen. He told them to go away, and sat by the loaves which were being baked, so that the vapour blew on him. And Democritus regained his strength by inhaling the vapours from the oven and so lived on for the remaining time' (Luria, DK68A28).

[13] 'It is reported that Democritus of Abdera *had decided to kill himself* because of his old age, and that he was reducing his food every day' (Laks, DK68A29).

[14] Luria DK68A29.

200 PREVAILING OVER DEATH

its health-giving properties (hence Athenaeus' comment), another extolling it as a preservative, useful among other things for preserving dead bodies.[15]

Diels suggests that, despite their discrepancies, these accounts of Democritus' death all allude to his view of the close connection between life and breath, and to his claim that breathing is what allows the body to retain and preserve the atoms of the soul. According to Democritean atomism, all living matter is composed of physical and spiritual atoms. These two types of atoms are not different entities, but a single entity with different characteristics and functions.[16] Aristotle echoes Democritus' position when, in *De Anima*, he describes the exceptionally small atoms of the soul as spherical and so perfectly smooth that nothing can slow them down. Hence their own perpetual motion, and their ability to permeate other bodies, thus setting them in motion.[17]

By virtue of these characteristics, the spherical atoms of the soul also endow bodies with the heat on which life depends, and this is why they are sometimes described as fiery. As Aristotle puts it, 'soul and heat are the same thing, and are the primary features of the spherical corpuscles'.[18] Indeed, for Democritus, still according to Aristotle, the soul 'is a certain kind of fire and heat',[19] and is the engine of life.

However, precisely because the smooth, spherical atoms of the soul move so fast, they have a tendency to scatter like 'the so-called motes (*xusmata*) that are visible in sunbeams'.[20] Indeed, the slightest pressure from the ambient atmosphere is enough to increase their speed and turbulence, making them prone to escape the body. According to Democritus, this is exactly what happens to the atoms of the soul, because 'what surrounds organic bodies [i.e. the ambient atmosphere] compresses them'.[21]

As a result of this compression, the already dynamic spherical atoms of the soul are ejected from the body.[22] Should this process go unchecked, death would be its logical, predictable, outcome. Here, however, respiration intervenes and stops the body from losing its life force. As Aristotle explains in *De Respiratione*, 'Democritus says that the effect of breath is to prevent the soul being extruded.'[23] This is because the spherical and fiery particles that make up the soul and keep us

---

[15] 'That is why Heraclides of Pontus, who advises that corpses should be burned, is more sensible than Democritus, who says that they should be preserved in honey' (Luria, DK68A161). On this point, Diels also quotes Lucretius. Alfieri attributes this doctrine to Bolus of Mendes, sometimes called Pseudo-Democritus (see Pseudo-Democritus 2009, 174). See also Berthelot 1983; Pseudo-Democritus 2009.

[16] Casertano 1984, vol. I: 347–353.

[17] See DK67A28 (Laks, 191–195) or Aristotle 2015, I, 2, 404a 6–8; see also Salem 2002, 188–193.

[18] DK67A28; Laks, 193.   [19] DK67A28; Laks.   [20] DK67A28; Laks.

[21] DK67A28; Laks, 195. The ambient atmosphere compresses the body because it is cooler, see Salem 2002, 199–204; see also Luria, DK68A106.

[22] See Luria, DK68A106. Luria also quotes passages from the sixth-century AD Byzantine John Philoponus that Diels-Kranz does not mention.

[23] Luria, DK68A106.

alive are also found all around us, in the ambient atmosphere. Every time we breathe in, they enter our bodies, taking the place of those that have escaped. Literally replacing the particles that have escaped the body under 'the expulsive action of the environment', they also stop more fiery atoms from exiting the body because of their heat and pressure.[24] This action, which is a direct consequence of breathing, is what keeps the spherical bodies in balance within the body, allowing it to stay alive. In other words, the actions of breathing in and breathing out are closely connected to life and death, and breathing involves a movement back and forth between life and death.[25]

To summarize, the soul is made up of fiery atoms. Breathing—'stimulated', in the case of Democritus' death, by the scent of the fresh bread or honey—is what keeps these spherical particles in balance within the body, allowing it to stay alive, and death occurs when these dynamic particles eventually leave the body. However whimsical they may seem, the surviving accounts of the last days of Democritus are intended as powerful demonstrations of the validity of his doctrine and the depth of his learning. Having discovered the hidden laws of nature, he made use of this knowledge to alter nature's course and mock death itself.[26]

Alongside these narrations of his successful attempt to forestall death, several other anecdotes attest to Democritus's willingness to laugh at it. Was he not known for sneering indiscriminately, some thought irresponsibly, at the sorrows and joys of others, and even at their deaths?[27] So much so, in fact, that his learning was mistaken for lunacy by his fellow Abderites. Blind to the depth of his insights, they failed to comprehend what Diderot would later describe as Democritus's attempt to 'disorientate' the course of nature in order to study, understand, and control it.[28] Was it not also Democritus who taught Epicurus that men have nothing to fear from death, which 'is nothing to us'?[29] Mortality and the afterlife hold no terror for those who understand that atoms are continually and inexorably engaged in a process of aggregation and disaggregation?[30]

In one of his letters, the emperor Julian writes that 'Democritus of Abdera, being unable to console Darius for the death of his beautiful wife, promised to

---

[24] 'When one breathes in these come in along with the air and, by resisting the pressure, prevent the soul which is in the animal from slipping out' (ibid.)

[25] See Salem 2002, 200. In the sixteenth and seventeenth centuries, chemical physicians tried to separate saltpetre from the surrounding atmosphere, considering it key to the lifeforce in the blood, and thus human life. This is why they advised against bloodletting, any loss of blood entailing a loss of life force. See Debus 1997, vol. 2: 37–59.

[26] See Salem 2002, 205. Alfieri also evokes the possibility that these accounts may have been influenced by the doctrine of the *aporroai* (DK68A135).

[27] See Hippocrates 1990 (letters 10–17 Hippocrate 1973; reprint of the Paris 1839 edition), vol. 9: 321, 339, 357–359.

[28] Article on 'Arbre' trans. 'Tree' in Diderot 1751–77.

[29] Epicurus, *Letter to Menoeceus*, quoted in Laërtius 1925, 10.124: 651.

[30] S. Zeppi 1971, 509 speaks of *athambia* in *Significato e posizione storica dell'etica di Democrito*. However, the passage from life to death is not an instant, but a digressive, process. See Salem 2002, 206 ff.

202 PREVAILING OVER DEATH

bring her back from the dead if the king was willing to provide everything necessary.' The king ordered that the philosopher should be given whatever he needed to accomplish this feat, but there was one request he could not fulfil:

> he [Democritus] said that everything necessary had been supplied, except one thing which he himself could not provide, but which Darius, the king of all Asia, could no doubt find without difficulty. And when Darius asked what this thing was which it was granted only to the king to know, Democritus replied that if he could inscribe on his wife's tomb the names of three people who had known no grief, she would immediately return to life, constrained by the ordinance of the rite. And when Darius, after long pondering, was unable to find anyone who had not suffered any misfortune, Democritus laughed in his characteristic way and said 'Why then, most foolish of men, do you grieve just as if you alone had such sorrow, when you cannot find one who has ever lived who is without his own grief?'[31]

In all these fictions constructed on the basis of his doctrine and reputation, Democritus is represented as laughing in the face of death. However, in Julian's anecdote, he does not so much scoff at death itself as at the irrational anguish that mortality and loss usually elicit from human beings. Even if we ignore the ancient and fiercely disputed notion that Democritus was able to bring the dead back to life,[32] Julian's account confirms that the philosopher stood above the common run of mortals. This superiority, which Democritus himself seems to ascribe in his ethical sentences to a difference *of nature*,[33] took the form of a different outlook on mortality. Democritus may have been short-sighted, but he could see very well that 'some people, ignorant of the dissolution of mortal nature, but aware of the adversity that affects life, suffer during their life from troubles and fears, fabricating false myths about the time after death'.[34] Fear of death is, however, deeply misguided; if 'thoughtless people live without enjoying life'[35] and yet wish to grow old, it is simply because 'they are afraid of death'.[36] Indeed, to live in fear of death is to live a living death: 'to live badly and not wisely [...] is to die over the course of a long time'.[37] In contrast, the philosopher exhibits his superiority through his clear awareness that 'all, even those in as good bodily condition as Milo, soon turn into skeletons, and are reduced finally to their original elements'.[38]

With these words, Democritus expresses the serenity and impassiveness in the face of death that shines through the accounts of his life that have come down to us. Living as a hermit cut off from civil life, and dedicating himself to the study of

---

[31] Luria, DK68A20.

[32] See Luria, DK68B1. This notion was still debated in the eighteenth century. See for example Anon 1744.

[33] See Lana 1951, 13–29.   [34] DK68B297; Laks, 293.   [35] DK68B200; Laks, 291.

[36] DK68B205; Laks, 291.   [37] DK68B160; Laks, 289.   [38] DK68B1a; Luria.

human madness, to the point where he seemed 'inattentive to everything, including himself',[39] he would only respond with mocking laughter when his fellow
Abderites demanded that he account for himself. Among those who challenged
him was Hippocrates, who asked him to explain why he scoffed at the folly of men
who, through a lack of sensitivity to the brevity of life, were too attached to their
material possessions. 'But what are you laughing at, Democritus? The good things
I mentioned, or the bad ones?'[40] Hippocrates describes his encounter with the
father of atomism in the longest and most famous of the epistles attributed to him,
the Letter to Damagetus, a veritable best seller of a text, which circulated widely in
the ancient world and played an important role in disseminating and consolidat-
ing Democritus' reputation as a sage. Accusing Democritus of laughing indiscriminately at all human experiences, including death, the Abderites believed
him to be insane; only a madman could be incapable of distinguishing good
from bad, and could fail to understand the value of life (and death)?[41] However,
as Hippocrates explains, these are the very values that Democritus uses philosophical reasoning to reverse. 'People who flee death are pursuing it,' Democritus
insists, both because 'their delusory hopes are irrational',[42] and because:

> It is necessary to recognize that human life is feeble and of short duration, and is
> mixed together with many sources of ruin and difficulties. One should therefore
> only desire to have moderate possessions, and measure suffering in relation to
> necessities.[43]

In other words, if the philosopher alone scoffs at death, it is because he alone
understands its value in the wider scheme of things.

The legend of Democritus' philosophical death has excited a great variety of
reactions and responses throughout the history of philosophy. As with any legend,
its existence, survival, and consolidation over time have depended on its continued transmission. Whether commentators have given it credit or rejected it as
mere fiction, what matters is that successive generations have continued to
consider it significant.

Laërtius' *Lives of Eminent Philosophers* was first translated from Greek into
Latin by the monk Ambrogio Traversari (also known as Ambrose of Camaldoli) in
1433, and by the eighteenth century had been retranslated several times. The
existence of these various editions undoubtedly contributed to the dissemination

---

[39] Hippocrates 1990, 57.   [40] Hippocrates 1990, 79.
[41] 'Don't you think you are outlandish to laugh at a man's death or illness, or delusion, or madness,
or melancholy, murder, or something still worse, or again at marriages, feasts, births, initiations, offices
and honors, or anything else wholly good? Things that demand grief you laugh at, and when things
should bring happiness, you laugh at them. There is no distinction between good and bad with you'
(Hippocrates 1990, 79).
[42] DK68B203; Laks, 291 and DK68B292; Laks, 297.   [43] DK68B285; Laks, 277.

204 PREVAILING OVER DEATH

of the legend of Democritus' death, but the enormous influence of the *Lives* is also due to the fact that, from the fifteenth century onwards, it appeared in many different formats. Through abridged versions, extracts, and numerous Latin and vernacular retellings, its influence spread beyond scholarly circles, to readers whose poor Latin did not stop them from seeking edification in the lives and sayings of ancient philosophers.

Laërtius's account of Democritus's death therefore appears in many forms. Sometimes, it is combined with other versions of the same anecdote and published in bilingual editions alongside erudite commentaries.[44] Sometimes, it is viewed with an understandable scepticism, for example by Giovanni Felice Astolfi who describes it in the commentary appended to his 1606 translation, as 'infinite di queste ciance [gossip] si trovano nelle Memorie de' Greci'.[45] Sometimes it is discussed in the light of Democritean atomism: Fénelon, for instance, suggests in his edition that the smell of warm bread made Democritus feel better and allowed him to maintain his natural heat.[46] However, regardless of these differences, the legend features in the index of almost all editions of Laërtius' *Lives*, where it is listed with other key passages. This is not insignificant, for these indexes were not simply useful tools designed to help readers locate particular items as speedily as possible. Rather, they were structured like independent rubrics and read like compendiums of maxims, listing the fundamental principles espoused by each philosopher alongside appropriate anecdotes. In other words, indexes were not simply neutral lists of words inventorying the contents of a book; they were also designed to guide the reader.[47] We find this, for example, in Henry Estienne's 1570 edition of Laërtius' *Lives*, where the index entry for Democritus includes a section entitled 'Eius obitus'. In Tommaso Aldobrandini's 1594 edition the index entry for Democritus mentions how the aroma of hot bread reached his nostrils, keeping him alive ('a pane calido naribus admoto vitam produxit'),[48] and this feature recurs in other editions including one from 1664 and a French edition from 1758. In short, the index to Laërtius' *Lives* became a quick and convenient source of information, sometimes richer and more complete than the text itself.[49]

While Laërtius' account of Democritus's death is pre-eminent as to its influence, he is not the only writer who played an important part in disseminating the legend. Among historians of philosophy who were concerned to transmit

---

[44] Casaubon (1593) and Ménage, for example, also quote Athenaeus' version in their notes. See Laërtius 1593, and Laërtius 1664. Indeed, Ménage also refers to other accounts, such as those of Lucretius and Marcus Aurelius.

[45] See Astolfi 1606, 60.

[46] Fénelon suggests that the smell of warm bread made Democritus feel better and allowed him to maintain his natural warmth ('lui faisoit du bien et *entretenoit sa chaleur naturelle*;' my emphasis); Fénelon 1848–1852, vol. 7, 36.

[47] On this subject, see Joukovsky 1969, 7–25.   [48] See Aldobrandini 1594.

[49] For example, when the index also refers the reader to material only found in the text's critical commentary.

knowledge of ancient philosophy as opposed to writing commentaries, several other figures also helped to spread it. Notable among these were Magnenus in his *Democritus reviviscens* (1646) and Thomas Stanley in his *History of Philosophy* (1655), a work of erudition rather than critical appraisal. Works of this kind circulated widely, and while they did not question the ancient narratives on which they drew, they nevertheless provided their readers with a wealth of information, presented in a certain evaluative light.

Early modern perceptions of Democritus were also stimulated by Richard Burton, author of the popular *Anatomy of Melancholy*, first published in 1621 and reprinted five times in less than twenty years.[50] Known to his readers as *Democritus Junior*, Burton seemed to identify with and even emulate Democritus, and his own somewhat mysterious death added to the aura surrounding his predecessor's end. According to Burton's first biographer, he seems to have successfully predicted the date of his death in January 1640, based on his horoscope, and as that date approached, he let a friend see the testament he had written in August 1639 while still in good health. The unsettling accuracy of his prediction spurred a number of theories. Perhaps he had committed suicide (a decision some writers attributed to Democritus before him) in order to avoid being mocked for his miscalculation and accused of false learning—a fitting end for a melancholy soul. Or perhaps he had simply sensed that his days were numbered; he was over sixty and suffering from various ailments relating to his age and way of life. It was also possible, of course, that he simply happened to die on the appointed day.[51] In any case, his death aroused a fascination for the idea that exceptionally learned people could not only read the future, but were able to defy, or even master, the vagaries of fate. Was it not thanks to his learning that the English Democritus had managed, if not to postpone, then at least to foretell, his demise? And had he not met a learned end, scoffing like Democritus before him at the torments of life? So suggests his delightfully ambiguous epitaph: 'Paucis notus, paucioribus ignotus, / Hic jacet / Democritus Junior / Cui vitam dedit et mortem / Melancholia'?[52] 'Known by few, unknown to even fewer—here lies Democritus Junior to whom melancholy gave life and death.'

The importance of meeting death lightheartedly is also emphasized by André-François Boureau-Deslandes, whose book, entitled *Réflexions sur les grands hommes qui sont morts en plaisantant* (1712; repr. 1714), reminds us that laughter in the face of death is the mark of a great man. Inspired by his reading of Michel de Montaigne to write a compendium of the most remarkable deaths in history,[53]

---

[50] The first edition came out in 1621 and the fifth in 1638. The posthumous edition published in 1651 is the one that publishers use today when reprinting this work.

[51] See Simon 1964, 53–55.   [52] Simon 1964, 56, 58.

[53] See Boureau-Deslandes 1712, 3–4.

206 PREVAILING OVER DEATH

Boureau-Deslandes includes Laërtius' account of Democritus' demise.[54] Observing in a critical spirit that the works of Laërtius, and indeed other historians of philosophy, are full of fables and falsehoods, and privilege a good read over historical accuracy, Boureau-Deslandes nevertheless admits to finding the story of Democritus' death strikingly congruent with the descriptions of his 'character' offered by Laërtius and other authors. They describe a man 'living outside society, in obscurity, entirely devoted to meditation who was consequently in a good position to discover the secrets of nature'.[55] They describe a philosopher who liked to laugh at humankind because he knew the relative value of things; a theoretician who understood that the existence of infinite worlds annulled any possibility of a privileged point of view from which to grasp reality. Above all, the fact that Democritus was a man who appreciated the ridiculousness of human behaviour, and who, unlike ordinary mortals, did not wait until he was on his deathbed before opening his eyes to the vanity of human life 'did him great honour'.[56]

Boureau-Deslandes thus paints Democritus as a sage whose insights into the natural world and human nature were so profound that he might well have been capable of the extraordinary death traditionally attributed to him. At the same time, he gives his doctrine a theological slant. As well as being unafraid of death, Democritus opposed theological commitments that encourage a fear of dying and cultivate a 'philosophy of sin and guilt'.[57] In short, Boureau-Deslandes' Democritus was a freethinker, whose laughter 'destabilized norms, upturning an established order, a hierarchy', and articulated a 'philosophy of life'.[58]

This aspect of Boureau-Deslandes' interpretation is in part a reply to certain 'overly credulous' critics[59] who had represented Democritus as a necromancer and accused him of practising magic. Their views had already been excoriated by Gabriel Naudé in his *Apologie* of 1625,[60] and Boureau-Deslandes concurs. He has no time for those who prefer legends to the truth, imagine that the lives of philosophers are full of wonders, and use their ignorance and conceit to sustain their *amour propre*.[61] Boureau-Deslandes concludes by returning to his opening theme, strengthening his argument by giving it circular structure. 'Democritus' century,' he comments, 'was similar to ours; by which I mean

---

[54] However, he also mentions Athenaeus' version of the philosopher's death, which is not mentioned by Laërtius.

[55] 'Retiré, obscur, et qui n'aimoit que la méditation; propre par conséquent à développer les secrets de la Nature' (Boureau-Deslandes 1712, 38).

[56] 'Des chimères et des sottises qui font l'occupation des hommes' (Boureau-Deslandes 1712, 4).

[57] 'Une philosophie du péché et plus generalement, de la culpabilité': (Markovits 2012, 24).

[58] 'Un discours qui déstabilise les normes, renverse un ordre, une hiérarchie,' 'philosophie de la vie' (Markovits 2012, 29).

[59] See Boureau-Deslandes 1712, 40.   [60] Naudé 1625, 271–289.

[61] 'Un raffinement de l'amour propre [...] l'ignorance s'en trouve soulagée en quelque façon' (Boureau-Deslandes 1712, 37–38).

that small minds felt free to attack those who soared above the prejudices of the common people.'[62]

Pierre Bayle was less keen on turning Democritus into a freethinker or *esprit fort* than in articulating a critical approach to erudition. Reading the anecdotes about Democritus' death through the lens of critical reason, he saw them as a posteriori demonstrations of the dubious veracity of historical sources and the need to develop a rigorous methodology for their evaluation. In his view, these anecdotes exemplified the ease with which facts could become distorted. Whether through involuntary error or, worse still, wilful manipulation, it was all too easy to generate false truths which then came to be accepted by the multitude.

In the entry on Democritus in Bayle's *Dictionnaire historique et critique* a brief but exhaustive account of Democritus' life and doctrines is followed by nineteen footnotes, analysing and discussing key passages of the article. Note 'E' focuses on Laërtius's account of Democritus's death, and opens with a characteristically ironic and shrewd observation:

> Democritus' sister was aggrieved, not because she understood that he was close to death, but because she knew that his death would make it impossible for her to attend the Ceres festival.[63]

After briefly but carefully reviewing various sources as to the duration of the Thesmophoria, and by implication as to the number of days Democritus was able to keep death at bay, Bayle concludes, taking his gloves off, that the legend of the philosopher's death 'reeks of an idle mind's invention'.[64]

Although it might seem logical to assume that Bayle's withering assessment of Laërtius would extend to Athenaeus, since their accounts of Democritus' death only differ on a couple of minor points,[65] Bayle also analyses Athenaeus' version of the legend. Far from skipping over its apparently less significant details, he harnesses them to illustrate the slippery, though commonplace, processes through which historical events can be distorted and transformed into myths, legends, and superstitions. The anecdotes surrounding Democritus' death thus provide Bayle with a pretext to develop a wider critique of the pernicious tendencies through which the historical record is falsified. Indeed, Bayle soon turns his attention to a 'modern' author who had the 'temerity' to criticize Athenaeus' narrative for including information that it does not actually provide, while also attempting to

---

[62] 'Le siècle où Démocrite vivoit étoit semblable au nôtre; je veux dire, que les petits esprits s'y donnoient la liberté d'attaquer ceux qui s'élevoient au dessus des préjugés du Vulgaire' (Boureau-Deslandes 1712, 40).

[63] 'Sa sœur s'attristait, non pas de voir qu'il allait mourir, mais de voir qu'à cause de cette mort elle n'assisterait pas aux fêtes de Cérès' (Bayle 1969, 463–464).

[64] 'Cela sent fort l'invention d'un esprit oiseux' (Bayle 1969).

[65] In Athenaeus' account, the smell of hot loaves becomes that of honey, and Democritus' sister, Abderite women.

208 PREVAILING OVER DEATH

discredit it by appealing to the irrelevant opinion of a sixteenth-century author, his compatriot Celius Rhodiginius. 'Who would not scoff at these lines?'[66] asks Bayle at the start of a withering four-part critique of the falsification of history. Does it not make a mockery of scholarship to quote 'Celius Rhodiginius on matters that happened more than two thousand years ago?'[67]

Although Boureau-Deslandes and Bayle were far from alone in commenting on Democritus' death, I have chosen to focus on them because they highlight both the enduring allure of the legend, and the propensity of historians of philosophy to interpret it freely, depending on their own concerns and priorities, without worrying too much about historical accuracy. However, their accounts also exhibit the fascination of philosophers (and indeed the rest of humankind) for death narratives. Historians of philosophy, in particular, have tended to privilege exemplary deaths over reports on the demise of anonymous figures. Their interest in the exceptional attitudes that great figures have adopted after years of meditation, in the face of mortality, may seem to suggest that living and dying wisely is the preserve of philosophers. Yet nothing be further from the truth, as Montaigne observes in one of his many meditations on death (rightly omitting any reference to Democritus' end, despite his familiarity with the anecdote):[68]

I never saw any countryman among my neighbours cogitate with what countenance and assurance he should pass over his last hour; *nature teaches him not to dream of death till he is dying; and then he does it with a better grace than Aristotle, upon whom death presses with a double weight, both of itself and of so long a premeditation.*[69, 70]

---

[66] 'Qui ne rirait en lisant cela?' (Bayle 1969).

[67] 'Un Célius Rhodiginius sur des faits qui se sont passés il y a plus de deux mille ans.'

[68] Montaigne was familiar with Lucretius' version of the anecdote. See Montaigne 1845, II, 12: 228; Montaigne 1992, II, XII, 496.

[69] Montaigne 1992, III, 12: 487 (my emphasis); 'Nature luy [au paysan] apprend à ne songer à la mort que quand il se meurt. Et lors, il y a meilleure grace qu'Aristote, lequel la mort presse doublement, et par elle, et par une si longue prevoyance Montaigne 1992, III, 12: 1052, 1039.

[70] I would like to thank Margaret Rigaud and Susan James for help with the translation and revision of this paper.

PART V
SUICIDE

10

When the Manner of Death Disagrees
with the Status of Life

The Intricate Question of Suicide
in Early Modern Philosophy

Sarah Tropper

Far from being ignored, the issue of suicide has always been a subject of philosophical reflection, and many arguments for and against its permissibility have been proposed. Following a medieval period of strict condemnation, debate about suicide gained in intensity during the Renaissance, when some thinkers defended its permissibility and even rationality. This phase of debate was also accompanied by an increased interest in suicide in art and literature, exemplified by Hamlet's famous deliberation about whether to be or not to be (Minois 1999: 86–115). But while the discussion of suicide in literature and in the socio-cultural as well as the judicial mores of the early modern period has received a significant amount of attention, the same cannot be said of its philosophical treatment in the era between Montaigne and Hume.[1] In this chapter, I examine what philosophers during this period have to say about the metaphysical foundations of suicide, and about what these foundations imply for its status and permissibility. I am not concerned with the issue of how suicide was in fact handled by the courts, or with the attitudes prevailing in states or social communities. (Social practices around suicide were in some respects and to some extent more lenient than the philosophical positions discussed here.[2])

In the mid-1750s, Hume writes: 'Let us here endeavour to restore men to their native liberty, by examining all the common arguments against Suicide, and shewing, that that action may be free from every imputation of guilt or blame, according to the sentiments of all the ancient philosophers. If Suicide be criminal, it must be a transgression of our duty, either to God, our neighbour, or ourselves.'

---

[1] Notable exceptions are Cahn (1998)'s book on the development of the discussion of suicide in France from Montesquieu to Cioran and a short treatise by Sprott 1961 on *The English Debate on Suicide. From Donne to Hume.* There are also overviews over various individual positions, e.g. Crocker (1952) and Crone (1996).

[2] There already exists a rich literature on those aspects, e.g., MacDonald/Murphy (1990: 77–143). For an overview of the recent literature, see Healy (2006).

Sarah Tropper, *When the Manner of Death Disagrees with the Status of Life: The Intricate Question of Suicide in Early Modern Philosophy* In: *Life and Death in Early Modern Philosophy.* Edited by: Susan James, Oxford University Press. © Sarah Tropper 2021. DOI: 10.1093/oso/9780192843616.003.0011

(Hume 1755/1980: 98) In his characteristically succinct manner, Hume refers to the main headings of a protracted series of philosophical-theological discussions regarding the moral character of suicide. At the same time, however, we need to remember that he stands at the end of a long philosophical debate about the role of the human being in society (Schneewind 1998). Out of this latter debate emerged a conception of the individual as an autonomous moral agent, whose ethical value is progressively less and less conceived as dependent on obedience to the divine law. While there is a general consensus that, by the time Hume was writing, the notions of autonomy and moral agency had undergone radical change and had come to occupy a more central position in philosophical discussion, this shift is not always taken into account when commentators turn to the issue of suicide. In his analysis of Hume's essay on suicide, for example, Thomas Beauchamp situates Hume in relation to Aquinas. Beauchamp's 'interpretative suggestion' is that 'the organization of the essay is that of a point-by-point reply to Thomas Aquinas' three arguments against the morality of suicide' (Beauchamp 1976: 73). There is undoubtedly some textual evidence in favour of this view. Since the three headings under which Hume's arguments proceed appear to have been taken straight from Aquinas, it is tempting to suppose that his defence of suicide is aimed at the most traditional and longstanding theological arguments against it. But this would be to ignore the way that other philosophical changes had reshaped debates about suicide in the intervening centuries. To grasp the implications of Hume's argument, it is not enough to focus on the superficial similarity in the way that Aquinas and Hume classify arguments about suicide. We also need to take account of the wider context in which Hume was writing. As a conspicuous social phenomenon, suicide is deeply embedded in metaphysical and moral considerations, and constitutes an important issue for early modern thinkers, whether they wish to oppose it or to advocate its permissibility. In its most general form, suicide's problematic character stems from the tension between the assumption that human beings are tied into a metaphysical system in which they are assigned a particular place and role, and the observation that ending one's life is an autonomous, highly individual, and deliberate decision to abandon that very place and role. During the early modern period, these conflicting claims underwent a transformation that enters into Hume's argument.

There are only a few self-contained treatises on suicide composed by philosophers during the early modern era. (Writing on the topic was still mainly the prerogative of practitioners of theology and law.) Nevertheless, the moral and metaphysical implications of suicide were never far from philosophers' minds, and many leading philosophers touched on these problems, even if they only expressed their views in remarks scattered throughout their works. In order to provide a preliminary systematization of the way philosophical discussion of suicide developed, I shall begin in Section 1 by outlining the medieval position as it is found in Augustine and Thomas Aquinas, before going on to discuss the resistance to their views mounted in the Renaissance by Erasmus, Thomas More, Michel de Montaigne, and John Donne. Section 2 turns to the canonical early modern thinkers, who—instead of following their Renaissance predecessors—often try to reinforce the impermissibility of suicide. As I shall show, it is their arguments, rather than those of Aquinas, that Hume opposes in his essay 'Of Suicide'.

1 Medieval Christian orthodoxy and the Renaissance backlash

Christianity's absolute and canonical prohibition of suicide has its origin in Augustine's *City of God*. While Augustine argues unambiguously that the commandment 'Thou shalt not kill' applies to oneself (Augustine 1998: 32–33; Book I, Chapter 20), and hence for the view that suicide is a sin, it is difficult to derive a direct argument for its impermissibility from sacred texts. There is no explicit prohibition of suicide in the Bible, and while we can find several instances of deeds that look suspiciously similar to suicide (such as the death of Samson in Judges 16:28–30, which seems, if anything, to be an act in worship of God), none of them are explicitly condemned. Against this objection, both Augustine and, following him, Aquinas respond that, in cases where the Bible appears to condone suicide, there must have been a divine call for self-sacrifice. They are therefore not cases of sinful behaviour. This reply seems hopelessly and irredeemably ad hoc. (As John Donne would later point out, God could have made his interventions clear in cases of legitimate suicide, as he does in other passages where he demands that men use violence against their bodies (Donne 1648: 197)). However, despite the ambiguity of the biblical evidence, the tradition follows Augustine in advocating a general prohibition of suicide, and enlarges on the reasons for it.

One of the most systematic expositions of these reasons is given by Thomas Aquinas:

> It is altogether unlawful to kill oneself, for three reasons. First, because everything naturally loves itself, the result being that everything naturally keeps itself in being, and resists corruptions so far as it can. Wherefore suicide is contrary to the inclination of nature, and to charity whereby every man should love himself. Hence suicide is always a mortal sin, as being contrary to the natural law and to charity. Secondly, because every part, as such, belongs to the whole. Now every man is part of the community, and so, as such, he belongs to the community. Hence by killing himself he injures the community, as the Philosopher declares (Ethic. v, 11). Thirdly, because life is God's gift to man, and is subject to His power, Who kills and makes to live.
>
> (Aquinas 1911: *Summa Theologica*, II–II, qu. 64, art. 5).

Aquinas invokes three reasons for the impermissibility of suicide: it violates our duties towards ourselves and our nature; towards the community of which we form a part; and towards God. Each of these duties is prescribed by the divinely ordained Law of Nature. First, since everything is inclined to persevere in its being, charity prescribes that every human should love themselves and express this love by continuing to exist. Second, the law requires us to play our part in communal human life. Finally, the law dictates that our life belongs to God, and that he alone has the right to end it.

Before assuming that, when Hume addresses these three claims, he is responding to Aquinas, we need to consider how a series of Renaissance philosophers changed the terms of debate about suicide. A first fundamental change was driven by the Renaissance recovery and renewed appreciation of classical authors who celebrated suicide, particularly in their accounts of the illustrious deaths of Lucretius, Cato, and Seneca. At the same time, a fresh interest in Stoicism gave currency to the suggestion that, under certain circumstances, one might have a moral obligation to end one's own life. This re-evaluation of classical philosophical arguments was accompanied by an increase in the popularity of theatrical presentations of suicide, especially as demanded by love or honour (Minois 1999: 63–66). But even at this time, when the philosophical and moral prescriptions of the medieval Christian thinkers were being questioned, there nonetheless remained a general reluctance to give outright support the idea that suicide might be permissible or even laudable.

A notable exception to this rule was Thomas More, whose Utopian islanders not only permitted and regulated suicide, but regarded it as in some circumstances praiseworthy. For them, ending one's own life could be a wise and pious act if it put an end to an existence in which there was no more pleasure to be had. Instead of reiterating the medieval view that one's obligation to the community or state militates against suicide, the Utopians hold that it is legitimate to end a life in which one has become 'unequal to any of life's duties, a burden to himself and to others' (More 1516/2002: 83–83). Rather than fulfilling one's duty to the community by merely staying alive, as Aquinas had demanded, More allows the Utopians to voice the view that one can only play one's part in communal life as long as one is healthy enough to do so. By implication, then, Aquinas's argument is not sufficient to rule suicide out. More also questions the Thomist position in a second way, by shifting the authority to judge whether suicide is permissible from God to priests. In Utopia, the task of deciding whether a particular person should be allowed to die falls to those whose profession it is to be the interpreters of God's will. If they deem the act permissible, it is pious to follow their judgement. The idea that we belong to God and that only he has the authority to decide when to end our lives is put in question.

Rather than owning these arguments, More attributes them to his fictional Utopians. The same rhetorical device is also employed by Erasmus, who allows a personified abstraction to voice a still broader argument for suicide. In Erasmus's eulogy to Folly, Folly not only argues that a state of incurable, painful disease licenses the ending of one's life. She also contends that, if men were not so foolish, they would see that life is permeated by evil and suffering from the moment of birth to that of death. The rational response is thus to commit suicide, the foolish one to stay alive and suffer (Erasmus 1511/2015: 40–41).

A third author who explores the legitimacy of suicide in voices other than his own is Michel de Montaigne. In his *Essays*, Montaigne samples many accounts of suicide from historical sources, along with a number of ancient arguments in their favour. The topic recurs in several of his essays (e.g. 'Of Cruelty', 'On the Cannibals'), but his most extensive and perhaps most famous treatment of the topic is to be found in 'A Custom of the Isle of Cea', where he echoes an argument from Cicero and Seneca:

> The saying goes that a wise man lives not as long as he can but as long as he should, and that the greatest favour that Nature has bestowed on us, and the one which removes all grounds for lamenting over our human condition, is the one which gives us the key to the garden-gate; Nature has ordained only one entrance to life but a hundred thousand exits.   (Montaigne 1580/1991: 393)

Montaigne's reasoning in this passage marks another significant departure from the assumptions we find in medieval writings: he not only emphasizes that we have the ability to rationally choose to end our lives, but also stresses that this ability is part of our human nature. The ability Montaigne directs attention to is traditionally regarded as one that sets man apart from other animals; one could even say that, as a capacity to act on a rational decision, the ability to end one's life is part of the *differentia specifica* that distinguishes humans from animals of other kinds. The inspiration for this piece of reasoning is clearly Seneca, who had argued that 'of all the things the eternal law has done for us, this is the best: we have one way into life, but many ways out'.[3] Seneca's view had virtually no influence on the philosophy of the Middle Ages—indeed, his outlook was very much at odds with it—but his ideas regained a prominent place within Renaissance thought. However, while Montaigne seems to share Seneca's positive attitude towards

---

[3] Seneca writes in the passage that was clearly the inspiration for Montaigne: 'You will find some people, even some committed philosophers, who say that one should never take violent measures against one's own life, feeling that it is wrong to become one's own murderer. They say one should wait for the end that nature has decreed. Those who say this do not realize that they are blocking the road to freedom. Of all the things the eternal law has done for us, this is the best: we have one way into life, but many ways out. Am I to wait for the cruel action of disease, or of a person, when I could pass through the midst of my torments, shake off my adversities, and depart? This is the one reason why we cannot complain about life: life does not hold anyone by force. The human condition is well situated in that no one is miserable except by his own fault. If it suits you, live; if not, you are allowed to return to where you came from.' (Seneca 2015: 211–212; Letter 70)

suicide, he is nonetheless more cautious in his estimation of the motives that can justify it. For Seneca, it seems enough to continue living 'if it suits you' and to end your life 'if not'. For Montaigne, by contrast, suicide is nature's solution to our ills, and we are only justified in ending our lives when they become burdensome.

During the sixteenth century there is therefore some pushback against the wholesale impermissibility of suicide upheld by the Christian churches. Prominent authors canvass and defend the view that suicide might be pious and wise (More), the suggestion that it is foolish not to commit suicide (Erasmus), and the claim that suicide is wise and natural (Montaigne). It is therefore not surprising that, at the turn of the seventeenth century, we should find a more extended discussion of arguments in favour of suicide. In his *Biathanatos* (completed in 1608, but only published posthumously in 1648), John Donne opposes every aspect of the Church's view that suicide is a sinful act. Donne's critique is much deeper and more far-reaching than any of the arguments we have so far considered. Whereas they are piecemeal, Donne attacks the idea that suicide is sinful on three fronts by arguing that it is neither against the law of nature, nor the law of reason, nor the law of God. His barrage of arguments includes, for example, historical reasons (a significant number of customs and laws have authorized suicide) and religious reasons (martyrdom is essentially suicide but there is no prohibition of it in the Bible). He also repeatedly appeals to the claim that, in certain situations, man is *sui juris*: laws concerning his liberty or conscience are only binding as long as there is a reason for them: 'and he whose conscience well tempred and dispassion'd, assures him that the reason of selfe-preservation ceases in him, may also presume that the law ceases too, and may doe that then which otherwise were against that law'. (Donne 1648: 47) Ultimately, the question as to whether suicide is permissible or not can only be answered by each individual, via a thorough investigation of their own motivation and conscience.

This argument marks an important shift towards the idea that virtuous action is autonomous. Rather than submitting to the law of nature, we ourselves must assess the reasons for and against an action and arrive at our own decisions. However, while this is undoubtedly one significant change in the way suicide comes to be viewed in the early modern period, it is not the only one. Another shift of outlook comes with an increasingly naturalistic approach to suicide,[4] exemplified in Robert Burton's *The Anatomy of Melancholy*. This work, written in the vernacular and first published in 1621, was reprinted four times within seventeen years. It presents itself as a comprehensive compendium of types of melancholy '*with all the Kinds causes, symptones, prognostickes & Severall cures of*

---

[4] In contrast to the classical philosophico-theological writings of the medieval era, in which suicide is unequivocally prohibited, early modern judicial practice was significantly more lenient. The plea that the suicide was insane was frequently accepted as a reason for judicial and moral absolution. (Lind 1999: 26–28, Murray 2000). Hence, in legal and social practice, there had—to a certain extent—always been a naturalization of the causes of suicide and thus a leniency in its treatment.

it. [...] *Philosophically, Medicinally. Historically, opened and cut up.*' Melancholy, Burton argues, can be expressed in suicidal tendencies (Burton 1632/1989: 437–438), and particularly affects persons of a scholarly nature or occupation. However, it is not a mere feeling, and is at least partially attributable to a physical trait—the presence of too much black bile. This idea is not original to Burton. The Greek term 'melancholia' means nothing other than 'black bile', and it was through their engagements with ancient writers such as Galen and Hippocrates that Renaissance and early modern thinkers came to conceive of melancholy as a medical condition. Nevertheless, Burton's presentation of it is important, since it proposes that the origin of melancholy, and thus the origin of suicide, is partly an innate or adventitious physical imbalance. To some extent, melancholy can be alleviated, for example by reading fewer books, diversifying one's activities, developing broader interests, changing one's diet or resorting to herbal remedies. But ultimately it cannot be cured. From our point of view, the main significance of Burton's account lies in the fact that it conceives suicide as much as an illness as a sin, and as a bodily problem instead of merely as an error of the soul. A suicidal person is therefore not so much in need of theological help as of medical or scientific assistance.[5]

We have traced a number of ways in which renewed access to classical texts and outlooks during the Renaissance changed the terms in which suicide was discussed. In a range of contexts, the adamant prohibition of suicide defended by Augustine and Aquinas was challenged by more concessive arguments as a theological approach to the issue came to be complemented by historical, imaginative, and medical considerations. However, although this more pluralist orientation undoubtedly formed an important intellectual and cultural setting for philosophical argument, it does not seem to have gained much traction within the thought of early modern philosophers. Many of these authors reiterate traditional arguments against suicide, as I shall show in the next section. Nevertheless, the debate had changed. The question of whether suicide can be rational and natural was there to stay.

2 The early modern philosophers on suicide

In a nutshell, two fundamental issues set the agenda for discussions of suicide from the mid-seventeenth century on. One, as we have seen, was an emerging conception of the virtuous individual who, rather than obeying God, governs themselves by making rational decisions based on considerations regarding the

---

[5] This is a significantly abbreviated account of Burton's book. Like Montaigne, he presents diverse and often opposing accounts and cures/prescribed by previous authors, without evaluating them. As a result, he leaves the reader with the impression that there is virtually nothing that has not at some point been considered to be a potential cause of melancholy.

218 WHEN THE MANNER OF DEATH DISAGREES WITH THE STATUS OF LIFE

good. The other more metaphysical issue concerned the place of human beings in nature. Here we still find remnants of the traditional idea that humans stand above animals, plants, and inanimate objects, because they possess certain mental faculties such as reason and free will. These traits determine their position in a comprehensive and hierarchical order of being; and because nature is the creation of a wise and omnipotent God, there is room for optimism about one's life and prospects.

This outlook allows for two different strands of reasoning about suicide. On the one hand, if the place allotted to humans in the natural order belongs to them as a species rather than as individuals, it is not obvious that suicide is prohibited. What matters is that the species, rather than any given individual, should continue to exist. So, while the suicide of all humans would be prohibited, it does not follow that the same is true of individual suicide. If, on the other hand, each individual is completely determined and thus forms its own lowest species, as we find in Leibniz and possibly Spinoza, vacating one's position is not permissible. Each individual, rather than each species, is irreplaceable in the grand scheme of things.

Defenders of this more rigorous hierarchical determination are open to the criticism that they have still not fully explained why an individual human being may not choose to vacate their place, since it might be part of its nature to decide to do so.[6] One response to this objection appeals to the claim that nature—that great structure comprising all beings—is inherently good. Because we do not always appreciate this fact, we often fail to grasp that a voluntary decision to end one's life can never be rational. In truth, however, suicide is irrational.

An influential advocate of this view is Descartes, for whom the goodness of this world—not just the goodness of the whole, but also the goodness of each of its parts—is the driving force of his argument against suicide. Here is what he writes to Elizabeth of Bohemia in January 1646:

> I think that even those who most give rein to their passions really judge deep down, even if they do not themselves perceive it, that there are more good things than evil in this life. Sometimes they may call upon death to help them when they feel great pain, but it is only to help them bear their burden, as in the fable, and for all that they do not want to lose their life. And if there are some who do want to lose it, and who kill themselves, it is due to an intellectual error and not to a well-reasoned judgement, or to an opinion imprinted on them by nature, like the one which makes a man prefer the goods of this life to its evils . . .
>
> (Descartes 1991: 283)

---

[6] Spinoza eliminates this option in his own system when he claims that the destruction of oneself can be caused only by external factors, even if we may mistakenly think that we ourselves are the driving force. (Spinoza 1985: 556; i.e. *Ethics* Book 4, Proposition 18, Scholium). Hence, the conception of suicide as discussed in this paper seems to be excluded from Spinoza's metaphysics as an impossibility.

Descartes assumes here that this world contains more good than evil, not only with respect to the whole, but also for each individual human being. Moreover, if even the most desperate and suicidal person were to form a reasoned judgement, they would come to this conclusion. Hence, taking one's own life can never be a rational act, but can only result from intellectual error and faulty judgement. In this assessment of suicide, Descartes does not appeal to any of Aquinas's arguments. He is not moved by any obligation towards God or community or even oneself, but rather by the overall goodness of each human life.

Descartes is not alone in arriving at this view. A similar stretch of reasoning, albeit not explicitly aimed at suicide, can be found in Leibniz's *Theodicy*:

> §13. But it will be said that evils are great and many in number in comparison with the good: that is erroneous. It is only want of attention that diminishes our good, and this attention must be given to us through some admixture of evils. [...] Had we not the knowledge of the life to come, I believe there would be few persons who, being at the point of death, were not content to take up life again, on condition of passing through the same amount of good and evil, provided always that it were not the same kind: one would be content with variety, without requiring a better condition than that wherein one had been.
>
> (Leibniz 1710/1985: 130)

In this argument Leibniz goes further than Descartes, not only by asserting the overall goodness of each life, but also by defending evil as required for and even conducive to this overall goodness.[7] But his conclusion nevertheless aligns with the Cartesian one: since life is good overall, the only reasonable stance is to prefer living to not living. To phrase the point differently: to decide to end one's life, even in the face of present and future suffering, is irrational.

The conclusion upheld by Descartes and Leibniz is not only far removed from Aquinas's reasoning, but also in stark opposition to that of Montaigne. For Montaigne, the wise man lives only as long as he should and can reasonably end his life before his time naturally runs out; but Descartes and Leibniz contend that the two durations coincide: A man should live as long as he is naturally determined to and it can never be rational for him to cut short his own life. In addition, this view looks like an attempt to refute the claim made by Erasmus's Folly, to the effect that, if people were wise, they would not let the small moments of happiness that earthly life provides fool them into overlooking its greater miseries. The rational course, Folly contends, is to end one's life rather than pinning one's hope on the minor moments of happiness it provides, because, taken overall, life contains more evil and misery than goodness. Descartes and Leibniz, by contrast,

---

[7] For the relevance of the notion of 'evil' in Leibniz's metaphysics, see Antognazza (2014).

appeal to a divinely ordered nature to show that reasoning prevents us from committing suicide by providing insight into the overall goodness of each of our lives.

A related yet distinct reason for opposing suicide can be found in the works of philosophers who are less strongly attached to the idea of a necessary order of beings and appeal instead to the Law of Nature. For these authors, the decisive factor is not the overall balance of good within each individual life, but the mutually beneficial relationship between individual and society. Among the philosophers who take this approach, one of the most prominent is John Locke who, in his *Two Treatise of Government*, discusses suicide in the context of his political philosophy. Locke's reasoning follows from his conception of the natural state of men and the contractual basis of society. As Crone puts it, 'Locke derived both the prohibition of suicide and the idea of limited government from one and the same source, natural law. In Locke's writings, the limitations on the liberty to dispose of oneself were closely linked with limitations on the government's authority to dispose of the individual's affairs' (Crone 1996: 34).

Locke's reasons for claiming that suicide is impermissible are discussed at several points in his 'Second Treatise of Government', where he argues that, under the Law of Nature, all men are free and possess equal natural rights. For a legitimate state to come into being, individuals must agree to transfer some of these rights by entering into a social contract. But the Law of Nature also imposes some limits on the form such a contract can take.

> But though [the State of Nature] be a *State of Liberty*, yet it is *not a State of Licence*: though Man in that State have an uncontroleable Liberty, to dispose of his Person or Possessions, yet he has not Liberty to destroy himself, or so much as any Creature in his Possession, but where some nobler use, than its bare Preservation calls for it. The *State of Nature* has a Law of Nature to govern it, which obliges every one: and Reason, which is that Law, teaches all Mankind, who will but consult it, that being all equal and independent, no one ought to harm another in his Life, Health, Liberty, or Possessions. For men being all the Workmanship of one Omnipotent, and infinitely wise Maker; All the Servants of one Sovereign Master, sent into the World by his order and about his business, they are his Property, whose Workmanship they are, made to last during his, not one anothers Pleasure. [...] Every one as he is *bound to preserve himself*, and not to quit his Station wilfully [...].
>
> (Locke 1689/1960: 270–271, Book II, Chapter IV, §6)

Like the rationalists we have already considered, Locke appeals to reason. This time, however, the rational insight we need does not concern the goodness of the world, but focuses instead on our duty to *contribute* to the good of the divine order. Locke's prohibition of suicide is on the same level as the demand that we should save the lives of others when we can do so without endangering ourselves. Both are requirements of the Law of Nature. But Locke's key premise is his claim that humans are the property of God, who has right of ownership over our earthly existence. As a member of a single community that includes all human beings, no individual is entitled to quit their station by voluntarily ending their life. The natural law that is reason endows each human with an inalienable right to life and leaves no latitude for individual deliberation. Furthermore, although some of one's rights are transferred to the sovereign when one contracts into the state, the inalienability of one's right to life remains intact:

> This *Freedom* from Absolute, Arbitrary Power, is so necessary to, and closely joyned with a Man's Preservation, that he cannot part with it, but by what forfeits his Preservation and Life together. For a Man, not having the Power of his own Life, *cannot*, by Compact, or his own Consent, *enslave himself* to any one, nor put himself under the Absolute, Arbitrary Power of another, to take away his Life, when he pleases.   (Locke 1689/1960: 284, Book II, Chapter IV, §23)

Despite the differences between the two arguments we have considered—one defended by Descartes and Leibniz, the other by Locke—there is something that unites them with respect to suicide: both assume that each individual occupies a determined place in a greater structure, and has no right to leave it of their own accord. Suicide is therefore prohibited. Moreover, by contrast with the medieval view, the basis of this prohibition is not merely a divine decree that individuals are obliged to obey. Instead, the impermissibility of suicide is presented as a rational conclusion that individuals can arrive at for themselves. We can understand the reasons against suicide by understanding the divinely created world we live in and the divinely ordained laws by which it is governed.

While this appeal to reason plays an influential part in seventeenth-century discussions of suicide, not all philosophers take such an uncloudedly optimistic view of reason's potential. A different position, closer to the medieval heritage, is upheld by Malebranche, who derives the conclusion that we are not permitted to kill ourselves from God's ownership of our bodies, together with our concomitant duty to use our bodies to further our earthly obligations. In Malebranche's view, our striving for rationality can obscure this duty. Motivated by a strong desire for a more rational understanding of God, we may come to feel that '[w]e must break off the dangerous commerce we have with [the world] by way of our bodies, if we want to augment the union we have with God by way of Reason'. Malebranche feels forced to point out this danger and discourage us from falling into it; we should not try to leave our earthly life in anticipation of a better state. But he stops short of the Lockean view that our overarching duty under the Law of Nature is to

222 WHEN THE MANNER OF DEATH DISAGREES WITH THE STATUS OF LIFE

preserve ourselves. Rather, he claims, we are obliged to expose our earthly life to certain risks for the good of society and the good of the divine order:

> [I]t would [not] be permissible for us to take our own life, nor even to ruin our health. For our body is not ours – it is God's, it is the state's, our family's, our friends'. We ought to conserve it in its strength and vigor, according to the use we are obliged to make of it. But we ought not to conserve it against the order of God and at the expense of other men. We must expose it to danger for the good of the state, and not fear to weaken it, ruin it, or destroy it in order to carry out the orders of God. […] All is for God and for charity, and ought to be conserved, employed, and sacrificed in honor of and through reliance on the divine law, immutable and necessary order.   (Malebranche 1684/1993: 222)

Some 'suicidal' actions, such as risking one's life in battle on behalf of the state, or working oneself to death to promote faith therefore seem to be permissible.

According to Malebranche, all our social duties are fundamentally duties to God. It is only because God decrees it that we possess duties to other people. But we find a less theologically grounded commitment to community in the work of Rousseau, who also argues that our duty to other people overrides any right to commit suicide. In *Émile*, written a few years after Hume's essay on suicide, Rousseau calls on his readers to accept their allotted lifespan and '[r]emain in the place which nature assigns to you in the chain of being. Nothing will be able to make you leave it' (Rousseau 1762/2010: 30). However, as he stresses elsewhere, the objection to abandoning one's place is not that doing so is contrary to reason or violates our duty to ourselves. Rather, it stems from the fact that we are duty-bound to be of use to humanity:

> But you, who are you? What have you done? Do you think your obscurity is an excuse? Does your weakness exempt you from your duties, and does having neither name nor rank in your Fatherland make you less subject to its laws? Some right you have to dare speak of dying while you owe the use of your life to your fellow men! Know that a death such as you contemplate is dishonourable and devious. It is a larceny committed against mankind. Before you take your leave of it, give it back what it has done for you. But I have no attachments? I am of no use to the world? Philosopher for a day! Have you not learned that you could not take a step on earth without finding some duty to fulfil, and that every man is useful to humanity, by the very fact that he exists?   (Rousseau 1761/1997: 322–323)[8]

---

[8] It should also be mentioned that caution must be exercised if one wishes to ascribe a particular stance on this issue to Rousseau, since his arguments might not be motivated solely by his philosophical convictions, but driven, at least in part, also by his opposition to the philosophers of the French Enlightenment, especially to the lenient stance of some of its members took towards it (see Crocker 1952: 67–69).

In this section we have so far surveyed a range of philosophical arguments against suicide. Despite the differences between them, they all rest on some version of the idea that an individual human is allotted a particular station in the overarching order of nature, and is not permitted to leave it until their lifespan reaches its natural end. While people can risk their lives in certain circumstances, no one can legitimately decide to kill themselves. To do so would be to violate the terms of the natural order and disobey God. The philosophers we have discussed therefore demand that we humans should submit to a supra-human moral order. In doing so, however, they turn their backs on a capacity that many of them also value—our human ability to act autonomously. Regardless of how suicidal you feel, they argue, and regardless of your reasons for ending your life, you must refrain from doing so. But if autonomous suicide is blameworthy, individual autonomy— usually one of the reasons to assign humans a privileged position, while denying it to other animals—seems to be subordinated to the natural order. Indeed, the more important an individual is to the structure, the less they have the right to exercise an autonomous decision to end their life.

The paradoxical flavour of this position is exposed at the beginning of the eighteenth century by Bayle, who argues against the dominance of Christian assumptions and thus against the universal moral impermissibility of suicide. Half a century later, Hume will criticize the reasonings of his predecessors and contemporaries still more radically, by pointing to the impossibility of intervening in God's order in the first place.

Bayle discusses the tension we have identified in the entry in his *Dictionary* on 'Lucretia', where he proposes that we should distinguish the general and unwavering Christian prohibition of suicide from the question of whether it is permissible in individual cases. Discussing Augustine's condemnation of Lucretia's suicide, he concludes, quoting the Jesuit Pierre Le Moyne, that when it comes to the evaluation of a particular case, we have to differentiate between a Christian perspective and a perspective that focuses on an individual and their beliefs:

> [I]f she [i.e. Lucretia] were to be judged by the Christian law, and the rules of the gospel, she would find it very difficult to justify her innocence. But if she be removed from this severe tribunal where Pagan virtue finds no footing, she is out of danger of being condemned. If she be judged by the laws of her own country, and the religion of her time, she will be found to be the chastest of those who then lived, and the most resolute of all the Heathens. (Bayle 1702/1826: 236)

Bayle contends that Augustine's condemnation of Lucretia is misplaced, since he judges her by a Christian standard that was not available in her time and which she would not have applied to herself. He points to the gap between a strict Christian view and the acceptance of suicide in other cultures. When assessing a case of socially permitted suicide, we ought to take a more lenient attitude. Bayle thus opposes the idea that the problem of suicide has a one-fits-all solution and can only be assessed by appealing to a single perspective. Since an individual may have good reasons for ending their life, the irrationality of suicide cannot be taken for granted. Judged from the eternal perspective of the divine order, it may seem that suicide is always impermissible, but for Bayle there is also room for a justification from the perspective of the individual agent.

While Bayle bases his sceptical outlook on the contention that the divine order is not the only standard by which the rationality of suicide can be assessed, Hume challenges the very supposition that such an order could be violated by human action. Since all our actions are the result of powers and faculties we receive from God, they cannot but contribute to the order God has ordained. The idea that an action—in this case a suicide—could introduce disorder into the universe is consequently a mistake. Moreover, if suicide were a violation of order, what would this imply for the creation of artefacts? When someone builds a house or harvests a field, for example, they interfere with nature and change the overall structure in which they are embedded. Do they violate of the natural order? Should their actions be prohibited? Is the house builder or the harvester at fault? If the answer to these questions is no, why is suicide any different? Why should we not change the natural order by ending our own lives, just as we change the order every time we build a dwelling—if that even constitutes a change to the natural order at all?

Hume's argument is not directed against Aquinas's claim that suicide is prohibited by a God to whose will we are bound to submit. Rather, he aims to discredit those of his early modern predecessors who had tried to outlaw suicide by appealing to the divinely ordained order of the world, and had contended that ending one's own life was unnatural and irrational. His riposte specifically addresses this argument: since all our actions must accord with the divinely decreed order, he claims, and since we are capable of ending our lives, acts of suicide must be part of this order. They therefore cannot be condemned on the grounds that they are unnatural or involve a fundamental misunderstanding of what the order of nature requires.

Hume also challenges the view that suicide violates our duties to other people, and thus our duties to the communities in which we live. As we have seen, early modern philosophers appealed to this line of argument to condemn suicide as impermissible, and here again, they are the opponents Hume is addressing. People who end their lives, he argues, do not always forsake their obligations, because the obligation to do good within society is reciprocal. One enters a community not only to contribute to it, but also to gain certain benefits. As soon as these benefits cease, or are outweighed by the pain and suffering of one's life, one's obligation to contribute lapses and the contract through which one entered society is void. Again, this argument is not primarily directed against the Thomist claim that our duty to society forbids suicide. Aquinas grounds this duty on the virtue of charity;

we are bound to express our charitableness by loving our neighbours and thus by contributing to society. Hume, by contrast, construes our duty to society conditionally, in terms of a balance of costs and benefits. Once the costs to an individual outweigh the benefits, the duty comes to an end. In fact, looking ahead a little, we can see that Hume pre-emptively challenges Rousseau's claim that we have an unconditional obligation to society. When society ceases to benefit us, Hume argues, we are no longer obliged to be part of it. Moreover, in the absence of a bond that, according to his opponents, brought with it a prohibition on suicide, we are no longer under an obligation to go on living.

3 Concluding remarks

Despite outward appearances, it is a misunderstanding to think of Hume's opposition to the prohibition of suicide as targeting the medieval tradition, and in particular the three arguments against suicide given by Thomas Aquinas. Rather, as we have seen, Hume argues against the position of canonical early modern philosophers who reject the legitimacy of suicide by claiming either that it violates the natural order, or violates a natural obligation to society. In tracing the development of several arguments for and against suicide, we have seen that the medieval phase of a blanket prohibition met some resistance in the Renaissance. Thinkers such as More, Erasmus, and Montaigne crafted fictional accounts or drew on Roman sources to introduce the suggestion that suicide might not only be rational, but even pious. Contrary to what one might expect, early modern philosophers neither absorbed nor countered those arguments. Rather, they returned to a prohibitionist stance of the medieval tradition, albeit on different grounds. Their arguments were based on assertions about the rights and duties bestowed on us by the Law of Nature (Locke, to some extent Rousseau) or on the claim that in the world God has created, good outweighs evil (Descartes, Leibniz). However, both approaches share the view that we can understand why suicide is prohibited by reasoning. This view is initially attacked by Bayle, who cautions us not to put too much faith in our ability to judge from the perspective of a divine order.

Bayle's attack is then taken further by Hume. According to Hume, to suppose that we could violate a divinely ordained order is to underestimate God's power. In fact, since each of our actions necessarily accords with the order God has put in place, nothing we do can be contrary to it. The changes we bring about—for example by ending our lives—are therefore entirely natural and do not reflect any misunderstanding of the nature of the divine order. The only way to construe suicide as unnatural and consequently impermissible is thus to single it out on an ad hoc basis, and make it an exception to the rule.

Hume does not go as far as Erasmus's Folly by claiming that it is irrational *not* to end one's life, nor does he agree with Descartes and Leibniz that every suicide is based on intellectual error. Rather, he places suicide on a par with all other human actions that manipulate the material of the world and challenges his opponents to accept that either all or none of them are impermissible. In general, Hume's arguments suggest that, if his early predecessors had taken their own metaphysical commitments seriously, they would not have been entitled to condemn suicide.[9]

---

[9] I am indebted to Susan James for her careful reading of as well as insightful comments and suggestions on earlier drafts.

11

David Hume's Philosophical Approach to Suicide

Teresa Tato Lima

Thinking about suicide is directly related to the principles on which life and death are based, and David Hume's *Of Suicide* is no exception. Hume's essay serves as a common point of reference within contemporary philosophical discussions about the morality of ending one's own life.[1] Indeed, his criticisms of three longstanding and influential arguments against suicide are often presented as a turning point in the debate surrounding the topic. In this paper I examine the role of philosophy within Hume's conception of morality, and attempt to understand it implications for his view of the morality of suicide.

In *Of Suicide*, Hume seems to adopt a novel approach to the problem of how suicide should be faced. He starts by presenting the objections[2] that are usually made against suicide and distinguishes them into three categories: suicide can be analysed in terms of God's plans, society, or oneself. Considering each of these positions, Hume is keen to prove that none of them sustain the supposition that the act of killing oneself is immoral. In fact, Hume's chief object in this essay is to show how suicide need not be regarded as immoral. In Hume's words: 'Let us here endeavour to restore men to their native liberty, by examining all the common arguments against Suicide, and shewing that that action may be free from every imputation of guilt or blame.'[3]

Although he discusses three lines of argument against this position, Hume gives special attention to arguments related to the religious aspects of suicide. He aims to show, in his own words, that 'Suicide is no transgression of our duty to God.'[4]

When Hume comes to defend this point, it is particularly noticeable that philosophy is the protagonist in his arguments. This fact raises many questions. How does one explain the importance of philosophy in this enterprise? What role does philosophy play in other aspects of the discussion on the morality of suicide? The aim of this chapter is to focus on the role of philosophy in Hume's discussion

---

[1] Many authors hold that *Of Suicide* is an important reference point for modern discussions of life-limiting topics. For example: Frey 1999, 336–51; Holden 2005, 189–210; Mower 2013, 563–575.
[2] Thomas Beauchamp identified Hume's essay as an alternative to Christian and Thomistic perspectives on the topic. See Beauchamp 1976, 73–95. See also, McLean 2001, 99–111.
[3] Hume 1985, 'Of Suicide'. Henceforth *Su*, para. 3, p. 580.   [4] Hume 1985, *Su*, para. 4 p. 580.

Teresa Tato Lima, *David Hume's Philosophical Approach to Suicide* In: *Life and Death in Early Modern Philosophy*. Edited by: Susan James, Oxford University Press. © Teresa Tato Lima 2021. DOI: 10.1093/oso/9780192843616.003.0012

228 DAVID HUME'S PHILOSOPHICAL APPROACH TO SUICIDE

of suicide. The chapter has two parts. First, we will distinguish two types of arguments that Hume addresses when considering whether suicide is blameworthy: arguments about our duty to God and arguments about our duty to Society. In this first part we focus on the importance of philosophy in relation to one specific type of objection—superstition.

In the second part, we consider the case of suicide respecting oneself, as a different kind of arguments which requires a different kind of philosophical approach. This section will consider Hume's other works to describe his view of some of the characteristics of philosophy so that we get to know if it could give a response to the morality of acts and, specifically, to suicide.

1 Native liberty and artificial duties

'Let us here endeavour to restore men to their native liberty, by examining all the common arguments against Suicide, and shewing that that action may be free from every imputation of guilt or blame.'[5] These words provide a precise summary of the objectives of Hume's essay. On the one hand, it aims to free men from constraints that could prevent them from acting according to their native liberty. On the other hand, it suggests that the act of suicide is not necessarily immoral in itself.

When Hume speaks of 'native liberty', he is referring to the original power of decision-making that belongs to a human being. By 'native' liberty, Hume therefore means a liberty that a human being *naturally* possesses. What, however, does Hume understand by *natural*? Despite Hume's depressing claim that among words 'there is none more ambiguous and equivocal'[6] than nature, he says in Book 3 of the *Treatise* that the natural is opposed to the artificial: '*nature* may also be opposed to artifice, (...) and in this sense it may be disputed, whether the notions of virtue be natural or not'.[7] In fact, Hume maintains that actions are sometimes naturally virtuous or moral and sometimes artificially virtuous or moral. In general 'the end of all moral speculations is to teach us our duty'.[8]

Hume explicitly states that moral duties may be natural or artificial. 'By the *natural Virtues* he plainly understands *Compassion* and *Generosity*, and such as we are immediately carried to by a *natural Instinct*; and by the *artificial Virtues* he means *Justice, Loyalty*, and such as require, along with a *natural Instinct*, a certain Reflection on the general Interests of Human Society, and a Combination with others. In the same Sense, Sucking is an Action natural to Man, and Speech is artificial.'[9] Elsewhere Hume says: 'All *moral* duties may be divided into two kinds.

---

[5] Ibid., 580.   [6] Hume, 2011a, vol. I, bk. 3.1.2.7, p. 304.
[7] Hume, 2011a, vol. I, bk. 3.1.2.9, p. 305.   [8] Hume, 2006b, sec. 1.7, p. 5.
[9] Hume 2011b, vol. I, *A letter from a Gentleman*, para. 38, p. 430.

The *first* [natural duties] are those, to which men are impelled by a natural instinct or immediate propensity, which operates on them, independent of all ideas of obligation, and of all views, either to public or private utility.'[10] In turn: 'The *second* kind of moral duties [the artificial] are such as are not supported by any original instinct of nature, but are performed entirely from a sense of obligation, when we consider the necessities of human society, and the impossibility of supporting it, if these duties were neglected.'[11]

According to Hume, a virtuous act is artificial as long as it results from the imposition of a duty that is extrinsic to the individual. In spite of being performed by an individual author, an artificially virtuous act does not spring directly from a natural desire or human tendency. Artificial acts are therefore defined as actions that the individual is led to pursue by principles imposed on them by something or somebody. For instance, traffic signs are often irksome measures, but even so everybody easily agrees to them. Why should an individual 'humble himself' to such unappealing obligations? From Hume's perspective, two things make this reasonable. First, artificial rules are sometimes the only way to create particular liberties. Second, artificial rules promote the general welfare (even if in an artificial, utilitarian way), where this includes—directly or indirectly—one's own welfare and wellbeing.

By contrast, natural virtues are those that result from an individual desire or impulse. As Hume explains, 'NATURAL may be opposed, either to what is *unusual, miraculous,* or ***artificial.*'* In the two former senses, justice and property are undoubtedly natural. But as they presuppose reason, forethought, design, and a social union and confederacy among men, they are perhaps not entirely free of artificiality. 'Had men lived without society, property had never been known, and neither justice nor injustice had ever existed. But society among human creatures, had been impossible, without reason, and forethought. Inferior animals, that unite, are guided by instinct, which supplies the place of reason.'[12] We should notice that natural virtues should be seen, specifically, only in contrast to artificial virtues: those virtues that man displays willingly, as it were, *if* nothing prevents him from doing so.[13]

In *Of Suicide*, Hume's concern is to establish clearly which kinds of moral duties cover the specific case of suicide, so that it will be easy to determine whether or not the act of suicide breaches them.

---

[10] Hume, 1985, 'Of the Original Contract', henceforth *OC*, para. 33, p. 479.

[11] Hume, 1985, *OC*, para. 34, p. 480.

[12] Hume, 2006b, App 3.9 (footnote 64), p. 99 (emphasis added).

[13] By this is meant, in Hume's perspective, that justice could not be a natural virtue, because its content does not result from an immediate impulse or tendency of the individual. On the contrary, if justice did not exist, each individual could act more freely than when he lives with justice, were justice not necessary to make it possible for different individual liberties to live together.

230 DAVID HUME'S PHILOSOPHICAL APPROACH TO SUICIDE

1.1 God and society

Hume asserts that the arguments commonly given in discussions of this topic are not adequate. This is because at least two kinds of argument—those involving our duty to God and our duty to society—rest on unpersuasive premises. In the latter case, Hume argues that the individual does no damage to anyone else by killing himself; he just 'ceases to do good'[14] to the society to which he belongs, because he stops contributing to the welfare of other people. Hence, the individual's duty concerning society (understood in an artificial sense), ceases to exist when his life ends.

In the case of our duty to God, Hume's analysis is more extensive. First, we need to notice that in *Of Suicide* he distinguishes religious arguments of two kinds: arguments concerning divine providence, or God as creator, and arguments against superstition. Respecting divine providence, Hume's response is essentially based on two elements. He first maintains that, since God determines every event that occurs in the world, he must determine the occurrence of suicides: 'Every event is alike important in the eyes of that infinite being, who takes in, at one glance, the most distant regions of space and remotest periods of time. There is no one event, however important to us, which he has exempted from the general laws that govern the universe, or which he has peculiarly reserved for his own imme-diate action and operation.'[15] It follows that, before God, every action is part of the divine order.[16] Second, one of the powers God has bestowed on us by giving us free will is the power to 'put a period to life'.[17] People who kill themselves are therefore simply exercising a God-given power. One could even say that suicide, as well as failing to violate divine providence, exalts it, because the individual concerned is using a power entrusted to him by God.

Hume also claims that the belief that suicide violates our duty to God is often superstitious, and is therefore grounded on a particular type of misunderstanding. Superstitious attitudes and behaviour are responses or reactions to a difficult 'state of mind'[18] that can in turn have many causes. As Hume describes them, 'The mind of man is subject to certain unaccountable terrors and apprehensions, proceeding either from the unhappy situation of private or public affairs, from ill health, from

---

[14] Hume, 1985, 'A man, who retires from life, does no harm to society. He only ceases to do good; which, if it be an injury, is of the lowest kind.' *Su*, para. 22, p. 586.

[15] Hume, 1985, *Su*, para. 7, p. 581.

[16] As Hume claims: 'It would be no crime in me to divert the *Nile* or *Danube* from its course, were I able to effect such purposes. Where then is the crime of turning a few ounces of blood from their natural channel!' (Hume, 1985, *Su*, para. 12, p. 583). This kind of 'moral indifference' has been discussed and problematized by many authors. See, for example, Holden 2005, 189–210 and Holden 2012.

[17] Hume, 1985, *Su*, para. 10, p. 583.

[18] Hume, 1985 'Of Superstition and Enthusiasm' henceforth *SE*, para. 2, p. 73.

a gloomy and melancholy disposition, or from the concurrence of all these circumstances.'[19] In these circumstances, individuals often alleviate their terrors and apprehensions by imagining a being with the power to cause or calm them. As Hume puts it, 'where real objects of terror are wanting, the soul, active to its own prejudice, and fostering its predominant inclination, finds imaginary ones, to whose power and malevolence it sets no limits'.[20] The individual comes to believe that a supreme, invincible power controls all things, and sees no alternative but to surrender himself—and all his rational faculties—to that power. Suicide, as Hume presents it, is a miserable condition; by overwhelming a person's capacity for autonomous action, it 'renders men tame and abject, and fits them for slavery'.[21] Regarding suicide specifically, an individual trapped by superstition is prevented from exercising and acting on his own judgement, because an imaginary being has a kind of power over him.

So far, we have examined Hume's responses to two arguments against suicide: the view that suicide violates a duty to our neighbours, and the view that it violates a duty to God. As our investigation shows, his objections to the views that suicide is contrary to our duties to God or to society have one thing in common: the moral duties concerned are artificial, and suicide does not in fact violate them. On the contrary, the moral duties themselves seem to be the problem. In fact, Hume appears to maintain that these 'moral duties' sometimes prevent us from making free subjective decisions, that is, exercising our 'native liberty'.[22] The arguments Hume is contesting do not prioritize the individual's will or feeling. If a person is prevented from killing himself because he fears his act will be unpleasant to God or will damage society, he is not acting on behalf of himself but on behalf of God or others. In other words, the extrinsic reasons that constitute our artificial duties prevent him from using his 'native liberty'.[23]

'Native liberty' is therefore central to Hume's discussion of the morality of suicide. Since the artificial reasons that stand in the way of committing suicide seem to be irrelevant to judging the moral status of the action, it is vital to judge it by appealing to *individual* reasons, or to an individual's autonomy.[24] If God and society provide only artificial reasons against suicide, and these reasons are not persuasive, natural reasons seem to be the most acceptable arbitrators of morality. Suicide's morality therefore directly depends on whether or not it is founded on a perfect 'native liberty', that is to say, on whether it is the effect of 'a natural instinct or immediate propensity'.[25]

---

[19] Ibid.   [20] Ibid.   [21] Ibid., para. 9, p. 78.   [22] Hume, 1985, *Su*, para. 3, p. 580.
[23] Ibid.
[24] Authors have frequently maintained that Hume introduced a different key topic to the question of suicide: autonomy. Although this expression was not used by Hume, 'native liberty' seems to be a kind of synonym for it. See, Frey 1999, 336–351 and Beauchamp 2005.
[25] Hume, 1985., *OC*, para. 33, p. 479.

232 DAVID HUME'S PHILOSOPHICAL APPROACH TO SUICIDE

1.2 Philosophy as a clue

Philosophy is initially introduced as the great hope in Hume's 'endeavour to restore men to their native liberty'.[26] He describes philosophy as a kind of solution or cure to the danger posed by extrinsic moral reasons or obligations. Specifically, philosophy is the only 'remedy' for superstition, which is nothing but an effect of 'weakness, fear, melancholy, together with ignorance'.[27]

Unlike 'good sense', which is perfectly compatible with a superstitious outlook, philosophy is the 'sovereign antidote' to superstition and false religion.[28] 'Superstition, being founded on false opinion, must immediately vanish when philosophy has inspired juster sentiments of superior powers.'[29] How does philosophy vanquish superstition? By enabling people to recognize that the entities to which they think themselves beholden are merely projections of their own minds and creations of their own fantasies, thus prompting them to examine their motives for emotionally investing in them. Once the philosopher comes to see that superstitious attitudes are an ineffectual response to fear, sadness, weakness, and ignorance—that is, to every kind of frailty of the mind—he puts himself in a position to reject superstitious beliefs, including superstitious beliefs about the existence of artificial duties. In short, philosophical arguments of the very kind Hume offers can liberate us from superstition. Thanks to 'sound philosophy',[30] the individual is able to see clearly that his mind has been dominated by extrinsic and artificial powers. It finally becomes easier to release the spirit from this oppressive weight and freely decide what to do.

We have explored the efficacy of philosophy in restoring our original liberty and releasing us from the idea that we are bound to by our duty to God to refrain from suicide. But this is only one aspect of Hume's investigation. What should we say about the view that we are prevented from committing suicide by our duty to ourselves? If philosophy was successful in answering the claims that suicide is contrary to our duties to God and society, can it have the same success in overturning the view that our duty to ourselves makes suicide impermissible?

---

[26] Ibid.

[27] Hume, 1985. *SE*, para. 2, p. 73. 'The mind of man is subject to certain unaccountable terrors and apprehensions, proceeding either from the unhappy situation of private or public affairs, from ill health, from a gloomy and melancholy disposition, or from the concurrence of all these circumstances. In such a state of mind, infinite unknown evils are dreaded from unknown agents; and where real objects of terror are wanting, the soul, active to its own prejudice, and fostering its predominant inclination, finds imaginary ones, to whose power and malevolence it sets no limits. As these enemies are entirely invisible and unknown, the methods taken to appease them are equally unaccountable, and consist in ceremonies, observances, mortifications, sacrifices, presents, or in any practice, however absurd or frivolous, which either folly or knavery recommends to a blind and terrified credulity. Weakness, fear, melancholy, together with ignorance, are, therefore, the true sources of *Superstition*.'

[28] Hume, 1985, *Su*, para. 1, p. 577.   [29] Ibid., p. 579.

[30] 'But when sound philosophy has once gained possession of the mind, superstition is effectually excluded.' Hume, 1985, *Su*, para. 1, p. 579.

2 Suicide respecting oneself

Here Hume's argument takes a quite different direction from those we have so far considered. As he sets out his position: 'That Suicide may often be consistent with interest and with our duty to *ourselves*, no one can question, who allows, that age, sickness, or misfortune may render life a burthen, and make it worse even than annihilation.'[31] Since we are dealing with an individual who does not want to live—whose '[existence] becomes a burthen'[32]—we could say that their natural duty or original liberty is already ensured. To ascertain whether their suicide would be morally permissible we have to consider how this original liberty should be used. We need to ask: in what circumstances is suicide 'consistent' with our duty to ourselves?[33] Can philosophy pronounce in this regard? We could also ask: if philosophy can enable individuals to overcome their superstitious attitudes and release themselves from the false belief that suicide contravenes their duty to God, can it also undermine an individual's conviction that they have a duty to themselves to stay alive?

When Hume defends the compatibility of suicide with our duties to ourselves, he uses a conditional form: the one 'may often be consistent' with the other.[34] We comprehend then that sometimes suicide is morally acceptable and sometimes not; it depends on the conditions under which the act occurs. What then determines the legitimacy of suicide? To answer this question, one must consider Hume's moral theory.

Virtue, Hume tells us in his *Treatise*, 'is distinguished by the pleasure, and vice by the pain, that any action, sentiment or character gives us by the mere view and contemplation'.[35] Furthermore, 'some objects produce immediately an agreeable sensation, by the original structure of our organs, and are thence denominated Good; as others, from their immediate disagreeable sensation, acquire the appellation of Evil'.[36] The morality of an act—that is, its virtuous or vicious character—depends on the sentiment of pleasure or pain that it provokes in the individual.

Here philosophy or reasoning may play an important role in identifying the presence of pleasure in an act. 'Reason', Hume tells us, 'is the discovery of truth or falsehood.'[37] Through philosophical reflection, one may be able to clarify one's authentic understanding of the pleasures and pains that a course of action will produce, thereby refining one's assessment of whether it will be pleasurable and thus moral. If one finds, for example, that suicide will overcome extreme pain, the morality of the act will be vindicated. In the case in question, suicide will be compatible with our duty to ourselves.

---

[31] Hume, 1985, *Su*, para. 28, p. 588.   [32] Hume, 1985, *Su*, para. 29, p. 588.
[33] Hume, 1985, *Su*, para. 28, p. 588.   [34] Ibid. (emphasis added).
[35] Hume, 2011a, 3.1.2.11, p. 305.   [36] Hume, 2009, 1.1, p. 3.
[37] Hume, 2011a, 3.1.1.9, p. 295. Also, in the *Dissertation on the Passions* for instance, Hume defines reason as 'the judgment of truth and falsehood'. Hume, 2009 5.1, p. 24.

234 DAVID HUME'S PHILOSOPHICAL APPROACH TO SUICIDE

Taking into account philosophy's capacity to diagnose and review the consistency between someone's motivation to commit suicide and their duties, could philosophy also modify the passions of an individual who is considering killing themselves? Sometimes philosophy as Hume describes it seems to promote certain kinds of sentiments. As he observes, it 'refines the temper, it points out to us those dispositions which should endeavour to attain, by a constant bent of mind, and by repeated habit'.[38] Or as he adds elsewhere, 'in many orders of beauty, particularly those of the finer arts, it is requisite to employ much reasoning, in order to feel the proper sentiment; and a false relish may frequently be corrected by argument and reflection. There are just grounds to conclude, that moral beauty partakes much of this latter species, and demands the assistance of our intellectual faculties, in order to give it a suitable influence on the human mind.'[39] In these passages, Hume suggests that philosophy has the power to shape one's character, at least to some extent. When one knows how one is—how one reacts to things, for example, or whether one has a peaceful or an explosive temper—one realizes how that way of being is either pleasant or painful. To put it another way, one discovers which natural emotions contribute to a pleasurable life and which do not. This kind of philosophical 'exercise' or 'endeavour'[40] may 'suggest particular views, and considerations, and circumstances, which otherwise would have escaped us'.[41] Should we not therefore say that philosophical reasoning might produce a change of attitude respecting suicide?

Although, as we have seen, philosophy can help to shape our characters, it, cannot cause this kind of change. This conclusion emerges from three essential aspects of Hume's theory. First, Hume talks about the most important principle discovered by philosophy; 'If we can depend upon any principle, which we learn from philosophy, this, I think, may be considered as certain and undoubted, that there is nothing, *in itself*, valuable or despicable, desirable or hateful, beautiful or deformed.'[42] Hume makes this claim in *The Sceptic*, where he argues that the passions that objects provoke in our minds are the product of our own emotional dispositions. As he puts it, 'these attributes arise from the particular constitution and fabric of human sentiment and affection'.[43]

Thus far, good and evil[44] seem to be entirely subjective qualities, and if someone were to object that this judgement is excessive, Hume would quickly respond that

---

[38] Hume, 1985, 'The Sceptic', henceforth *Sc*, para. 33, p. 171. [39] Hume, 2006b, para. 1.9, p. 5.
[40] Hume, 1985, *Sc*, para. 33, p. 171. [41] Hume, 1985, *Sc*, para. 35, p. 172.
[42] Hume, 1985, *Sc*, para. 8, p. 162 (emphasis added). [43] Ibid.
[44] This essential feature of philosophy is better understood if we observe Hume's epistemological theory of comparison. In the first book of *Treatise*, we could read: '*All* kinds of reasoning consist in nothing but a *comparison*, and a discovery of those relations, either constant or inconstant, which two or more objects bear to each other' (Hume, 2011a, 1.3.2.2, p. 52). Hume's knowledge theory is based on the 'irrecusable' principle that every idea we have comes from experience. For, everything one knows arises from one's experience of elements of things that are frequently and constantly combined. From this experience one may conclude that those elements probably belong to that thing and, from this probability one can say that 'that thing is like that'. For instance, the very first time we see a dog barking,

it is just as excessive to locate good and evil in external objects. In fact, the latter 'excess' is the less reasonable, because it is based on a non-experimental presupposition: we have no access to objects besides our own way of knowing them. Thus, 'even when the mind operates alone, and feeling the sentiment of blame or approbation, pronounces one object deformed and odious, another beautiful and amiable; I say, that, even in this case, those qualities are not really in the objects, but belong entirely to the sentiment of that mind which blames or praises'.[45] In short, 'it is not from the value or worth of the object, which any person pursues, that we can determine his enjoyment, but merely from the passion with which he pursues it, and the success which he meets with in his pursuit. Objects have absolutely no worth or value in themselves. They derive their worth merely from the passion.'[46]

If one applies this principle to the case of suicide, it appears to lead to the conclusion that philosophy has no power to show that suicide is contrary to the demands of our moral duties to ourselves. If no object is good or bad in itself, then we must say that life, too, does not have an objective value.[47] If, in turn, life seems to be 'a burden', that is to say, it seems (at that moment, at least), to be of negative value to an individual, and if this sentiment is authentic, philosophy cannot deny it. No man, Hume tells us, 'ever threw away life, while it was worth keeping'.[48]

Second, action for Hume can only be motivated by sentiment and never by reflection. As he says, 'the ultimate ends of human actions can never, in any case, be accounted for by *reason*, but recommend themselves entirely to the sentiments and affections of mankind, without any dependence on the intellectual faculties'.[49] Sentiment alone is the cause of action: 'Ask a man, *why he uses exercise*; he will answer, *because he desires to keep his health*. If you then enquire, *why he desires health*, he will readily reply, *because sickness is painful*. If you push your enquiries farther, and desire a reason, *why he hates pain*, it is impossible he can ever give any. This is an ultimate end, and is never referred to any other object.'[50] We therefore cannot assign the cause of any action to philosophy.

---

we could not recognize it as a dog, as this is a concept that arises only from the repetition of some elements. Hence, we could state the general rule that 'a dog barks' only if we have seen many particular dogs barking and then we could recognize it as an essential characteristic of dogs. But what is important to observe is that that 'judgement' (dogs bark) arises from a probability, founded on comparison between similar elements.

[45] Hume, 1985, *Sc*, para. 11, p. 163.   [46] Hume, 1985, *Sc*, para. 18, p. 166.

[47] In fact, Hume claims: 'the life of man is of no greater importance to the universe than that of an oyster. And were it of ever so great importance, the order of nature has actually submitted it to human prudence, and reduced us to a necessity, in every incident, of determining concerning it,' (Hume, 1985, *Su*, para. 9, p. 583).

[48] Hume, 1985, *Su*, para. 28, p. 588.

[49] Hume, 2006b, app. 1.18, p. 88. We could find this idea in many excerpts of the works of Hume. For example: 'that reason has no influence on our passions and actions, 'tis in vain to pretend, that morality is discover'd only by a deduction of reason' (Hume, 2011, 3.1.1.7, p. 294).

[50] Hume, 2006b, app. 1.18, p. 88.

Third, Hume considers that philosophy cannot interfere with nature. As he eloquently puts it, 'it may seem unreasonable absolutely to deny the authority of philosophy in this respect: But it must be confessed, that there lies this strong presumption against it, that, if these views be natural and obvious, they would have occurred of themselves, without the assistance of philosophy; if they be not natural, they never can have any influence on the affections'.[51] Besides, philosophy occupies a role like that of a spectator who watches a play, criticizes it, and afterwards forgets it. '[The topics] of disdain towards human affairs, (...) occur to a philosopher; but being, in some measure, disproportioned to human capacity, and not being fortified by the experience of any thing better, they make not a full impression on him. He sees, but he feels not sufficiently their truth; and is always a sublime philosopher, when he needs not; that is, as long as nothing disturbs him, or rouzes his affections.'[52]

Philosophy is therefore powerless in the face of extreme passions; to detect or recognize these passions is not sufficient to avoid them. 'Where one is born of so perverse a frame of mind, of so callous and insensible a disposition, as to have no relish for virtue and humanity, no sympathy with his fellow-creatures, no desire of esteem and applause; such a one must be allowed entirely incurable, nor is there any remedy in philosophy.'[53] Philosophy therefore seems to be useless concerning violent or extreme natural passions. Moreover, a similar situation obtains in relation to moderate passions. If somebody is naturally serene, moderate and stable, philosophy also has no work to do: 'If a man have a lively sense of honour and virtue, with moderate passions, his conduct will always be conformable to the rules of morality; or if he depart from them, his return will be easy and expeditious.'[54]

Philosophy therefore lacks the power to change our desires, including the desire to commit suicide. Indeed, this may be why, when Hume turns to our duties to ourselves in *Of Suicide*, philosophy suddenly falls silent; once he stops talking about superstition he says no more about it. This silence appears to be eloquent. At the beginning of the essay, Hume proposed that the morality of suicide should be discussed with regards to our 'native liberty',[55] that is, our view of the matter should be freed from artificial objections. He now seems to have gained his objective. Discussion of suicide has been liberated from unfounded reasons (i.e. superstition). Once that has been done, however, any remaining moral judgements about suicide flow from our authentic sentiments rather than from philosophical argument. Philosophy cannot take a position. It is therefore appropriate that it should remain silent.[56] Taking these reasons into account, we should

---

[51] Hume, 1985, *Sc*, para. 36, 172. [52] Ibid., para. 48, p. 175.
[53] Hume, 1985, *Sc*, para. 29, p. 169. [54] Ibid. [55] Hume, 1985, *Su*, para. 3, p. 580.
[56] Regarding this, Kenneth Merrill maintains that, despite Hume's view that philosophy frees man from superstition, that does not mean that philosophy provides a justification for suicide. See Merrill 1999, 395–412.

conclude that, for Hume, philosophy has no power to motivate or demotivate an action, even if that action is suicide.

There is, however, another conclusion to be considered. Suicide is, after all, an individual act performed in a particular situation. Killing oneself is something one does in a difficult or dramatic context, where the 'fact' of living is experienced as a heavy burden. In some cases, a person's reasons for ending their life may be readily intelligible—they may be suffering from 'age, sickness, or misfortune'.[57] But even where this is not the case, a philosopher should conclude that the reasons for the action are authentic and natural. In Hume's words, 'tho' perhaps the situation of a man's health or fortune did not seem to require this remedy, we may at least be assured, that any one, who, without apparent reason, has had recourse to it, was curst with such an incurable depravity or gloominess of temper, as must poison all enjoyment, and render him equally miserable as if he had been loaded with the most grievous misfortunes'.[58]

Philosophy makes it possible to discover the originality or authenticity of the motivation for an action, therefore philosophy can also confirm the originality or authenticity of a sentiment amenable to suicide.

3 Conclusion

In conclusion, one can say that philosophy may qualify suicide as an immoral or moral act depending on the individual's feeling concerning the action. However, philosophy has no power to achieve more than that. Philosophy cannot create a different sentiment towards human life: 'if we confine ourselves to a general and distant reflection on the ills of human life, *that* can have no effect to prepare us for them'.[59] From Hume's perspective, philosophy cannot change an individual's natural desire to commit suicide or refrain from doing so.

If a person changes his or her mind about life, this will not be due to philosophy, but rather to a change of feeling towards life. Nor are difficult circumstances in themselves a sufficient motivation for suicide; 'perhaps the situation of a man's health or fortune did not seem to require this remedy'.[60] Hume confirmed this perspective through his own example. He died from an abdominal cancer, and during his last months, which were extremely painful, suffered so much that he claimed 'my life has become rather a Burden to me'.[61] However, being perfectly conscious of his 'mortal and incurable'[62] illness—his 'tedious illness'[63]—Hume

---

[57] Hume, 1985, *Su*, para. 28, p. 588.   [58] Ibid.   [59] Hume, 1985, *Sc*, para. 42, p. 174.
[60] Hume, 1985, *Su*, para. 28, p. 588.
[61] Hume 2011b, n. 534, letter to William Strahan, on 12 August 1776.
[62] Hume, 2011a, vol. I, *My own life*, para. 20.
[63] Hume, 2011b, vol. II, n. 540, letter to Adam Smith, on 23 August 1776.

maintained a 'great moderation in all his passions'.[64] Contemporary descriptions of his last days are touchingly eloquent, and 'public interest in the death of Hume centred around the philosophical tranquillity he had displayed in the last weeks of life'.[65]

We could end with this his own advice: 'Propose not a happiness too complicated. But does that depend on me? Yes: The first choice does. Life is like a game: One may choose the game: And passion, by degrees, seizes the proper object.'[66]

---

[64] Hume, 2011a, vol. I, *My own life*, para. 21.   [65] Mossner 1980, chap. 40.
[66] Hume, 1985, *Sc*, para. 51, n. 9.

12

Less than Zero

Kant's Opposition to Suicide

John J. Callanan

1 Suicide in the *Groundwork*

In his *European Thought in the Eighteenth Century*, Paul Hazard cites suicide as a typical instance of the contradictions inherent in the Enlightenment's newly naturalized worldview. Replacing transcendent authorities with appeals to nature perhaps avoided rigid dogma, but new problems emerged in its place, not least in the case of the ethical question of whether one may non-culpably end one's own life:

> The truth was that when you came to consult Nature on any specific matter, she answered both 'yea' and 'nay'. Was it lawful to commit suicide? Yes, because Nature permitted it. If anyone found that existence had become so hateful to him as to be tolerable no longer, and if he consequently did away with himself, he was but obeying a power which, having imposed this suffering upon him, had furnished him with a means of putting an end to it .... Again, was suicide lawful? No, for Nature's business was the maintenance of the species, and the individual who destroys himself contravenes Nature's law.[1]

Hazard would not have had to look far to find evidence of this kind of sentiment. The Savoyard Vicar in Rousseau's *Émile* explains that, with regard to suicide, we can eschew rational guidance, since while 'nature makes us sense our needs' for the aim of self-preservation it also insists that '[d]eath is the remedy for the evils you do to yourselves; nature did not want you to suffer forever'.[2] Rousseau embraces the idea that the same natural voice can provide guidance by speaking for or against the preservation of one's own life.

As the familiar story has it, Kant aimed to rescue the Enlightenment project by establishing that, with a few concessions to its critics, a chastened conception of

---

[1] Hazard 1965, 365.   [2] Rousseau 1979, 281.

John J. Callanan, *Less than Zero: Kant's Opposition to Suicide* In: *Life and Death in Early Modern Philosophy*. Edited by: Susan James, Oxford University Press. © John J. Callanan 2021. DOI: 10.1093/oso/9780192843616.003.0013

240 LESS THAN ZERO

rationality could in fact be shown to govern both nature and human conduct.[3] The universalization procedure of the Categorical Imperative test, set out in the *Groundwork of the Metaphysics of Morals*, is Kant's means of showing that lawlike reason rules within ordinary moral psychology.[4] Kant famously set the test to work on four examples, the first of which was the case of suicide, showing that it *was* in fact contradictory to think that nature might recommend both the preservation and the cessation of a human being's life.

Despite the clear evidence of Kant's implacable personal opposition to suicide, his choice of it as an example in the *Groundwork* is nevertheless unusual for at least two reasons.[5] First, suicide was a case where it was commonly held to be obvious that there *are* exceptions to the rule, i.e. non-culpable acts of ending one's own life. Moreover, Kant in fact *agrees* with this; in the later *Metaphysics of Morals* he sets out a range of difficult cases that raise 'casuistical questions'.[6] Acts of knowing self-sacrifice in combat or indeed on points of principle, or acts of taking one's life so as to prevent danger to others, are all included in the questions that Kant raises but fails to answer. In this matter, he implicitly acknowledges, there will inevitably be cases and cases. In the *Groundwork* his aim is only to show that suicide is prohibited in a restricted set of cases, i.e. when it is contemplated from the motive of 'self-love'. Yet, given that the Critical Philosophy aims to demonstrate the unrestricted lawfulness of moral commands, suicide is an odd test case to choose. Why demonstrate the exceptionless nature of moral commands by appealing to a general action type where the existence of morally justifiable exceptions is already universally acknowledged?

Second, Kant's use of his co-called 'universalization test' argument against suicide in the *Groundwork* seems peculiarly weak. Allison claims that '[o]ne of the few truly non-contentious claims in Kant scholarship and interpretation is that this argument is unsuccessful'.[7] To appreciate its unpromising character, one

---

[3] For standard accounts see Ameriks 2012b; Beck 1969; Beiser 2017; 2002; 1992; 1987; Cassirer 1983; 1951; Pinkard 2008.

[4] Unless otherwise specified, references to Kant's writings are to the *Groundwork* Kant (1786) 2011. References to Kant's other writings are to the Cambridge Edition series. Page references to Kant's writings in general are to the standard *Akademie* edition of Kant's works, *Kants Gesammelte Schriften*, ed. Königlich Preussische Akademie der Wissenschaften, vols. 1–29 (Berlin: de Gruyter, 1902–). Abbreviations used are as follows:

A/B: *Critique of Pure Reason*
Anthropology: Lectures on Anthropology
CPJ: *Critique of the Power of Judgment*
CPrR: *Critique of Practical Reason*
Ethics: Lectures on Ethics
Inquiry: 'Inquiry concerning the distinctness of the principles of natural theology and morality.'
MM: *Metaphysics of Morals*
Negative Magnitudes: 'Attempt to Introduce the Concept of Negative Magnitudes into Philosophy.'
Notes: Notes and Fragments

[5] For Kant's general opposition to suicide, see *CPrR*, 5: 44, *MM*, 4: 422–423, *Ethics*, 3: 373, 375.
[6] *MM*, 6: 423–424.   [7] Allison 2011, 184—though an exception can be found in Uleman 2016.

might contrast it with the subsequent defence of the universalization test in the *Groundwork*, where Kant takes the example of someone who makes a false promise to repay money to secure a loan. His argument—I would claim—runs roughly as follows: if we universalize the maxim 'one should always promise sincerely *except* when making a false promise is to one's great advantage', then it tends to undermine itself by generating a logical contradiction, a 'contradiction in conception' as it is sometimes called.[8] In the possible world imagined—one where *everyone* makes and receives promises with this exception clause always kept in mind—the result is that no one in such a world could now view there being even a default norm in place such that the occasion of making a promise is ever indicative of a subject binding themselves to another.[9] In a possible world where *everyone* is operating with the rule 'make promises sincerely unless it's a case where it's to one's advantage to make them insincerely' the very practice of promising—it is argued—would lose its currency and the very idea of promising its coherence.

The parallel argument against suicide seems far less compelling, despite the fact that it also seems to be a case of a 'perfect duty', formed through seeing that suicide-approving maxims generate clear contradictions in conception. Here the idea is that one is considering the following maxim: 'from self-love I make it my principle to shorten my life if, when protracted any longer, it threatens more ill that it promises agreeableness' (4: 422). Kant claims that a contradiction immediately and obviously arises:

> But then one sees that a nature whose law it were to destroy life itself by means of the same sensation the function of which is to impel towards the advancement of life, would contradict itself and would thus not subsist as a nature, hence that maxim could not possible take the place of a universal law of nature... (4: 422).

What is the argument here? The contradiction Kant points to cannot be a logical one, since by universalizing the maxim we don't get the result that *the very idea* of a drive to life would annihilate itself or utterly lose its meaning. Rather, as Allison puts it '[a] world in which there was a law of nature specifying that everyone act on this maxim would be significantly depopulated, but there is no contradiction in that'.[10] A familiar thought is that Kant's argument must hinge instead on an implausible teleological premise regarding the natural 'function' [*Bestimmung*] of

---

[8] O'Neill 1975, 139.

[9] I suggest this way of understanding the test, i.e. in terms of generating a conflict between a 'default norm' and an 'exception clause', and which is broadly in the 'logical contradiction' interpretative tradition, in Callanan 2013. For alternative readings see Galvin 2009; Korsgaard 1996; Paton 1946.

[10] Allison 2011, 183.

242 LESS THAN ZERO

'self-love' to promote life.[11] Here the idea is that the end of self-preservation might be somehow shown to be self-stultifying when universalized. Yet if this is Kant's intention one must rely more upon a natural teleology than on universalization to get the whole argument going.[12]

Even if we were to accept this interpretation, there is still, as Rousseau pointed out, no *prima facie* contradiction in saying that the same 'sensation' might have the natural end of speaking for the continuance of one's life on one occasion and yet on another occasion might speak against it. If all that one's future life offers are pains, then all that sensation will recommend will be the cessation of one's life. As Paton elegantly puts it '[w]hy should it not be a merciful dispensation of Providence that the same instinct which ordinarily leads to life might lead to death when life offered nothing but continuous pain?'[13] Even more worryingly perhaps for the Kantian project is that it is not at all clear how appeals to *universalization* bring any new insight. That a drive for the beneficial maintenance of one's life might speak for continuing it or ceasing it on different occasions is not rendered any more peculiar—let alone contradictory—when imagined as a law of nature.[14] It certainly doesn't seem to be the case that imagining the drive to preserve oneself as a universal law suddenly reveals to our consciousness that it could not conceivably 'subsist as a nature'. The case of suicide appears both ad hoc and yet for all that miserably ill-chosen as the primary example of how the Categorical Imperative test can reveal our moral obligations.

My aim here is not to defend Kant's argument but rather to explain it. I am primarily concerned to explain why Kant chose suicide as a test case in the first place, given the obvious suasive disadvantages the example affords for the end of promoting his moral philosophy. Discussions of the historical context of Kant's discussion reasonably appeal to the context of Hume's 'On Suicide'.[15] However, I shall argue that a more thorough consideration of the historical context of Kant's writing shows that he likely had in mind a different opponent, who nevertheless had a wide audience in eighteenth century educated culture.[16] Philosophically inspired novels and plays had a well-publicized effect in promoting the idea that suicide was a personal choice determined by the strength of one's passions; *feeling* was promoted as a normative source that was not to be outweighed by external and dogmatic rational authorities. This line of argument was sometimes voiced by

---

[11] See Allison 2011; Korsgaard 1996, 158, fn. 20; Paton 1946; Schonecker and Wood 2015; Timmermann 2007; Wood 1999. It has seemed to many commentators that Kant's hasty re-phrasing of the just-introduced universal law formulation in terms of imagining maxims as 'laws of nature' (4: 421) was made just for the purpose of accepting the implausible teleological premise in the example that immediately follows.

[12] Allison 2011, 184; Feldman 1978, 108; Timmermann 2009, 81–82.   [13] Paton 1946, 181.

[14] This is alluded to in Schonecker and Wood 2015, 133.

[15] Cholbi 2000; Uleman 2016, though Cholbi is non-committal about the influence here. For Hume's essay see Hume (1777) 2008, 315–324.

[16] As for example discussed in Crocker 1952 An important exception and one I have drawn upon for this essay is Cassirer 1951.

authors who later committed suicide themselves, and sometimes seems to have given rise to suicide among their appreciative audiences. Kant's motive for including suicide among his examples of the Categorical Imperative was to offer a cultural corrective to what he saw as a new and particularly pernicious social phenomenon that was directly influenced by philosophy.

Tackling the issues of how the value of one's life was conceptualized and how to consider the issue of when life 'threatens more ill' than pleasure was of crucial rhetorical importance to Kant, who was defending the Enlightenment project on two fronts. On the one hand, he sought to oppose Rousseauian appeals to nature as the judge of whether suicide was justified, and to validate reason as 'the supreme court of justice' (A740/B768). This conception of reason had found its authority in the sciences, and a crucial aspect of Kant's project was to extend it to the practical domain. On the other hand, Kant was no less concerned with a threat that came from within the Enlightenment project and threatened to destabilize the aspiration to institute a 'culture of reason' (B*xxx*) by uncritically adopting a *mathematical* conception of rationality and applying it to moral matters. Kant saw the issue of suicide as one where both these destructive strands—counter-Enlightenment anti-rationalism and Enlightenment hyper-rationalism—had manifested an egregious influence. By including suicide as the first example in the *Groundwork*, he sought to show how his own philosophy could resolve the damage they had done. His conception of a non-mathematical form of reasoning at work in the moral psychology of ordinary subjects offered a means to oppose both irrationalism and mathematical rationalism alike. Moreover, it provided a basis for paying due deference to the era's demand for a form of methodological subjectivism—whereby a subject can reliably rely upon their own internal deliberation as a source of practical guidance—without collapsing into a full-blown ethical subjectivism.

In Section 2 I roughly sketch Kant's understanding of the history of moral philosophy, laid out in a famous table in the *Critique of Practical Reason*. Among Kant's reasons for opposing feeling-based moral systems was their tendency to rely on a conception of rationality considered primarily as a function for calculating the expected intensity and duration of feeling. In Section 3, I explain how this application of mathematical reasoning was energetically applied, in the writings of Mendelssohn and Maupertuis, to the question of the value of continuing one's life. In Section 4, I examine Kant's pre-Critical resistance to Maupertuis, itself a manifestation of his anxiety about the relationship between mathematics and philosophy. In Section 5, I show how this anxiety was specifically fed by Kant's encounter with Rousseau's counter-Enlightenment writings and the latter's ambivalent attitude to suicide. In Section 6, I finally return to Kant's argument against suicide in the *Groundwork*. I contend that the historical context suggests that Maupertuis and Rousseau, rather than Hume, are the targets Kant has in mind. I then go on to show that, once this rhetorical context is illuminated, we can

244   LESS THAN ZERO

arrive at a new and previously unnoticed reading of Kant's argument to the effect
that a pro-suicide maxim cannot be universalized.

2 Love of life and love of self

Kant's argument focuses on the claim that he sets the problem up by presupposing
a natural drive towards self-preservation. That there was a default normative
recommendation in favour of life was rarely challenged among Kant's opponents.
Few would disagree with Cicero's claim in the widely read *De Officiis* that '[f]rom
the beginning nature has assigned to every type of creature the tendency to
preserve itself, its life and body, and to reject anything that seems likely to harm
them . . .'.[17] This conception of self-preservation implies, however, that the general
recommendation in favour of maintaining one's life is a by-product of a trait that
nature has assigned to us, which is in turn manifested in our *desires* for particular
objects. This default norm in favour of living is dependent on the continual
movement from realized to as-of-yet-unrealized desires. Kant was fundamentally
opposed to any such subjective account of the source of such norms, whereby the
warrant for our moral behaviour might be conditional on the presence or absences
of a relevant desire. When Kant came to compose his famous table of the varieties
of subjectivist moral principles in the *Critique of Practical Reason*, he does not
mention Hume but does mention figures such as Montaigne, Mandeville,
Epicurus, and Hutcheson.[18] My contention is that, in Kant's history of moral
philosophy, the theme of the justification of life (and death) was intertwined with
three quite different issues relating to moral subjectivism. First, there is the issue of
how one accounts for the plentiful empirical evidence suggesting that the warrant
for actions is merely subjective; second, there is the question of how to elucidate
the difference between the motivational and explanatory dimensions of morality
on such accounts; third, there is a question of how then to understand the role of
scientific rationality in regulating or aiding personal moral guidance. I'll address
the first two issues in this section before turning to the third in Section 3.

By the time Kant was writing, Montaigne's A *Custom* of the *Isle* of *Cea* had
become a standard reference point for discussions of suicide, but here the presentation had clearly implied that the variability of custom exposed the subjective
nature of the warrant for suicide and the conventional status of its prohibition.[19]
Furthermore, Montaigne's discussion of the canonical cases of putatively virtuous
suicides raised additional sceptical questions. When commenting on Cato's

---

[17] Cicero 1991, 6, Bk. I. As is well-known, Christian Garve's translation of and commentary upon *De
Officiis* was of some importance for Kant's composition of the *Groundwork*—see Allison 2011;
Kuehn 2001.
[18] *CPrR*, 5: 40.
[19] Montaigne (1580) 2003, Bk II, Ch. 3. For a helpful examination see Henry 1984.

suicide in 'On Cruelty', Montaigne wonders whether we can plausibly identify his motive as a virtuous one:

> Witness the younger Cato: When I see him die, and tearing out his own bowels, I am not satisfied simply to believe that he had then his soul totally exempt from all trouble and horror: I cannot think that he only maintained himself in the steadiness that the Stoical rules prescribed him; temperate, without emotion, and imperturbed. There was, methinks, something in the virtue of this man too sprightly and fresh to stop there; I believe that, without doubt, he felt a pleasure and delight in so noble an action, and was more pleased in it than in any other of his life...[20]

Mandeville followed Montaigne in problematizing the case of Cato. Behind Cato's action, Mandeville claimed, lay pride, that positive manifestation of the fundamental passion of 'self-liking', the ancestor of Rousseau's *amour-propre*. For Mandeville, self-liking is a fundamental passion that motivates us to assign an inaccurate value to our own desires so as to produce a stronger manifestation of the drive to self-preservation. This self-valuing response usually manifests itself immediately, non-reflectively, and very often subpersonally. For these very reasons Mandeville identifies it as thoroughly non-rational in nature and as easy to misidentify.

In an ironic cultural development, Mandeville goes on, self-love has garnered an overweening dominance over all other passions. Our concern with pride and status is now considered to be so strong that it can overpower the drive to self-preservation of which it was originally held to be a manifestation. Nowadays, Mandeville remarks, 'no one can resolve upon suicide, whilst self-liking lasts'.[21] But both pride and shame—the latter being self-liking's negatively valued output—are more than sufficient to warrant such a resolution. Moreover, in modern society, Mandeville claims, the self-interest generated by pride is a more powerful 'natural' instinct than the instinctual drive towards life. A human being has 'as much horror against shame, as nature has given him against death; and there are things to which man has, or may have, a stronger aversion than he has to death'.[22] Cato's suicide, for example, had been motivated by pride; so, apparently, had Lucretia's, albeit in her case pride mixed with grief, rage, and desire for revenge. The strength of shame was also evident in more everyday circumstances, Mandeville claimed, for example when it triumphed over maternal instinct in cases of the infanticide of children born out of wedlock.[23]

---

[20] Montaigne (1580) 2003, Bk II, Ch. 11, 475.
[21] Mandeville (1732) 1988, II: 136, Third Dialogue.   [22] Mandeville [1724] 1988, I: 209.
[23] Mandeville (1724) 1988,I, Remark H.

246 LESS THAN ZERO

Mandeville complicates the picture by presenting the drive to life as conditional on passions that are socially generated and subtly internalized within our moral psychology. Kant's own suspicions over the true motivations for Cato's and Lucretia's suicides indicate a certain cynicism resonant of Montaigne and Mandeville.[24] In fact, by the Critical period, Kant had thoroughly integrated Mandeville's French Augustinian scepticism with regard to motivational self-knowledge. Later on, in the *Groundwork* he would deny that we possess the cognitive resources to identify the motivational bases of our own behaviour, and claim that what passes as a moral motivation might always turn out to be a 'covert impulse of self-love' (4: 407).

Kant therefore conceded epistemological ground with the problem of the infallible identification of our motives via introspection; his target was establishing the mere metaphysical possibility of purely rational motivation. Such rational motivation was required, he thought, in order to address a second problem attached to subjectivist theories, namely that of giving a plausible account of the *explanation* of morality. This problem was pronounced with regard to another group of 'subjective' theories on Kant's list—those according to which the source of moral value lay either in natural or in socially conditioned feeling-based responses. Such responses, Kant claims, are 'obviously not at all qualified for the universal principle of morality' (*CPrR*, 5: 41).

One of the most prominent exponents of this type of view whose position Kant discusses is Hutcheson. Hutcheson was sensitive to the difficulty of giving a phenomenologically plausible account of the responses of ordinary subjects—responses that were unreflective and immediate and yet nevertheless possessed a distinctive moral character. He recognized that, among the challenges he faced, was the problem of distinguishing what one might call the *epistemic* and *motivating* bases of our moral responses from their *explanatory* basis. By an 'epistemic basis', I mean the actual ground of our *knowing* that φ is the right thing to do; a 'motivating basis' is the actual ground of our being *moved to act* in accordance with φ; and an 'explanatory basis' is the actual account of why *it is true* that φ is the right thing to do (if it is). Needless to say, these things can come apart. While it might be plausible that our having a *feeling* that we ought to φ is the source of our knowledge as well as our motivation that we ought to φ, it cannot serve as a plausible candidate for *why it's the case* that φ is the right thing to do. However, Kant would later comment that Hutcheson fails to keep these things apart. 'Hutcheson's principle is unphilosophical, first because it introduces a new feeling as a ground of explanation, and second because it sees objective grounds in the laws of sensibility.'[25] Somewhat more harshly, Kant criticizes the moral sentimentalist movement in general:

---

[24] For Cato and Lucretia see *Ethics*, 27: 370–374.   [25] *Notes*, 19: 120.

If someone says that he feels the truth, then the other can do nothing with him. It is a refuge of idiots to say that they feel it to be true. Morality must be based on *a priori* grounds.[26]

For these reasons, Kant places Hutcheson alongside Mandeville and Montaigne as advocates of subjective principles of morality.

3 Maths and morals

The popularity of subjectivist accounts of the motivating basis of moral action raised a demand to see whether and how Enlightenment scientific rationality might provide an account of the explanatory basis of right action, one to which a subject might then avail to regulate or guide their unprincipled desires. Yet these appeals to science brought a further third problem, one with which Kant was very familiar, which is that the misapplication of scientific methods, specifically those of mathematics, threatened to undermine rather than reinforce rationality's authority within practical life. Kant may have been unaware that Hutcheson had in fact endeavoured to separate out the question of the motivating and explanatory bases for our moral attitudes. Hutcheson's motivational account made appeal to a moral sense; but he offered to explain our moral attitudes when he went on to claim that the outputs of this sense could be vindicated by a mathematically calculable utilitarianism.[27] Hopes for a moral calculus of this nature were, however, quite short-lived. Apart from the question as to whether and why the outputs of ordinary subjects' first-order moral sense tallied with the results of such a calculus, there was also general scepticism about whether there is an adequate mode of measurement for the pleasures and pains that were to be its basic units. By the time Mandeville wrote the second part of the *Fable of the Bees* in 1729, he was mockingly dismissive of a Hutchesonian account of virtues such as patriotism:

> Mr. Hutcheson, who wrote the *Inquiry into the Original of our Ideas of Beauty and Virtue*, seems to be very expert at weighing and measuring the Quantities of Affection, Benevolence, *etc.* I wish that curious Metaphysician would give himself the Trouble, at his Leisure, to weigh ... the real Love Men have for their country, abstracted from Selfishness.[28]

Kant was also critical of the suggestion that there could be calculus of moral pains and pleasures, but his philosophical reservations about it were different from Mandeville's and more metaphysical in character. He wanted to understand the

---

[26] *Ethics*, 29: 626.   [27] For discussion see Brooks and Aalto 1981.
[28] Mandeville (1732) 1988, II: 345–346, Sixth Dialogue.

248   LESS THAN ZERO

very possibility of a genuinely moral basis for action, such that it could—unlike Hutcheson's calculus—possess a plausible explanatory connection with our ordinary moral psychology.

Kant had long been sceptical of using mathematics to supply such a connection, and had considered this point with regard to the justifiability of suicide. Commenting on national characteristics in his lectures in anthropology, he remarks somewhat bizarrely on a characteristic of the English:

> One effect of their temper (of the English) is also suicide. Nowhere do such rich, distinguished, and high-ranking persons commit suicide due to temper, as in England.   (*Anthropology*, 25: 660)

Kant is most likely referring to Charles Blount, whose suicide Charles Gildon (writing under the pseudonym 'Lindamour') had attempted to defend. 'Lindamour', author of one of the best-known defences of suicide prior to the publication of Hume's essay on the topic, had claimed that 'the preservation of ourselves is not a law so universal as some faint-hearted philosophers would imagine it to be', and had gone on to defend his view in mathematical terms. His use of mathematics had, however, been challenged by Moses Mendelssohn in an early and extremely popular work, 'On Sentiments'. 'Lindamour' had claimed that a clear rational justification for suicide could be constructed in the following way:

> Death, people say, is a complete annihilation; of all possible evils it is the greatest and must necessarily lose in their comparison. Oh, no, as far as our thinking self is concerned, the greatest evil, if we do not feel it, is far more desirable than a condition of consciousness in which evil outweighs the little good that there is. An algebraist would compare the good in his life with positive quantities, the evil with negative ones, and death with zero. If in the mixture of good and evil, after reckoning them relative to one another, a positive quantity remains, then the condition [of continued life] is to be wished for rather than death. If they cancel each other out, then the condition is comparable to zero. If a negative quantity remains, what prevents someone from preferring zero to it?[29]

To oppose this view, Mendelssohn's own representative in his dialogue homes in on the use of negative numbers. He denies that negative numbers can refer to anything real in any meaningful sense, claiming that they can at best be viewed as operations of subtraction from an existing creature's stock of positive conscious feelings. Since zero represents the annihilation of consciousness, Mendelssohn

---

[29] Blount and Gildon 1695, quoted in 'On Sentiments' [1755] in Mendelssohn 1997, 41.

denies that we can make sense of an *existing* consciousness whose states have tipped over into possessing a negative value. Mendelssohn's ultimate reason for opposing 'Lindamour' is ultimately the familiar one that a non-existing being cannot coherently benefit from its non-existence, so that '[n]othing is more absurd than a sanction for suicide, an ethical capacity to prefer death, if it is annihilation, to life. Merit, choice, freedom, all these concepts vanish as soon as a decision is to be made between being and nonbeing.[30] 'Lindamour' had argued for the appropriateness of applying mathematics to determine the value of a subject's conscious states so as to buttress the rational respectability of a possible choice in favour of suicide. Mendelssohn claims the very idea of the use of mathematics in this domain is misguided and in particular rejects the conceptual coherence of a consciousness whose value might ever be measured as being 'less than zero'.[31]

Mendelssohn had originally written 'On Sentiments' in 1755; in 1771 he accompanied it with 'Rhapsody or additions to the letters on sentiments'. Here he took aim at another thinker—Maupertuis—who had attempted to bring mathematics to bear on the question of the value of continuing one's existence. At issue in this exchange is the question of whether it is possible to integrate sentiments into a mathematical calculus. Mendelssohn had already argued that human sentiments more often than not possess a mixed character, with both positive and negative elements:

> Given the astonishing mixture of pleasant and unpleasant sentiments which are interwoven in a way infinitely more refined than that of the most delicate network of fibers in the human body, one must surely wonder at philosophers who have wanted to compute the sums of pleasant and unpleasant sentiments in human life and compare them. The author of the 'Essay on Moral Philosophy' [viz: Maupertuis] imagined this consideration in a very facile manner. He calls the product of the strength of a pleasant sentiment as long as it persists 'the moment of happiness' and the sum of these moments 'human happiness.' He subtracts from this sum the sum of the moments of unpleasant sentiments, and so forth.[32]

Due to his stature as both a scientist and a representative of the *Encyclopedie* project, Maupertuis's *Essai de Philosophie Morale* (1750) was one of those works that invited responses from a range of European writers.[33] Maupertuis had attempted to provide a hedonic calculus precisely for the purpose of determining the question of the value of continuing one's existence. Pleasures and pains could

---

[30] 'On Sentiments' [1755] in Mendelssohn 1997, 60.
[31] 'On Sentiments' [1755] in Mendelssohn 1997, 59.
[32] 'Rhapsody or additions to the letters of the sentiments' [1771] in Mendelssohn 1997, 147–148.
[33] Maupertuis 1751—a copy of which was possessed by Kant, Warda 1922. For the subsequent analysis I am indebted to Cassirer 1951 and especially to Kelly 2017.

250 LESS THAN ZERO

be calculated according to two axes: intensity and duration. Giving a value to both, one could perform some actuarial reflections on the likelihood of the pleasures that were both intense and long-lasting being more frequent than the pains that were similarly intense and long-lasting. Alas, Maupertuis noted, the human condition is such that pleasures that are intense and long-lasting are rare throughout one's life; chronic pain, on the other hand, was a more common occurrence. Mathematical analysis made available conclusions that one might not have previously countenanced. Even if one's pleasures were frequent, they would likely not be intense; if one's pleasures were intense, they would most likely not be frequent (or of great duration). If this is right, then a persistent low level of negative sensation (perhaps even boredom might qualify) throughout one's conscious hours would quickly secure a far higher numerical value than rare ecstasies. There was consequently no mathematically justifiable reason for prolonging one's life. At *any* point at which one might perform the calculation, life threatened a greater quantity of pain than pleasure. Maupertuis therefore concluded that faith was the only adequate motivational basis for continuing to live.[34]

4 Negative magnitudes of feeling

Mendelssohn was firmly opposed, both to Maupertuis' argument and to his conclusion. His most fundamental objection focused on Maupertuis's foundational assumption that the targets of his moral accounting system, namely the experience of pleasures and pains, were of sufficiently undiluted purity to be treated as homogenous units with which one might perform calculations. Mendelssohn made this accusation in 1771, when he wrote the 'Rhapsody' for the publication of the second volume of his *Philosophische Schriften*. Yet a different technical challenge had already been raised against both Mendelssohn and Maupertuis in 1763. In his essay *Attempt to Introduce the Concept of Negative Magnitudes into Philosophy*, Kant had pushed the idea that a negative magnitude *is* in fact 'something truly positive in itself, albeit something opposed to the positive magnitude' (*Negative Magnitudes*, 2: 169). In doing so, he directly opposed another of Mendelssohn's objections to Maupertuis—Mendelssohn's claim that a negative value was just shorthand for an operation of subtraction from a given value.

Kant's target in his discussion of negative magnitude is primarily the Leibnizean metaphysician who holds that all opposed forces can be given a logical

---

[34] Whether that appeal to faith was sincere or not I don't attempt to answer here. Maupertuis was likely to have been aware that the negative calculation life's pleasures and pains had been made by Bayle. In the 'Xenophanes' entry in the *Critical Dictionary*, Bayle had raised the point of the likely preponderance of physical evil in the world, which had in turn instigated Leibniz's famous response in the *Theodicy*. For discussion see Wootton 2018, 118–121.

analysis in terms of identity and contradiction. Not so, Kant maintains: sometimes the minus symbol indicates a 'real' opposing force, as when a west wind carries a ship a certain distance while an east wind pushes in the opposite direction. These relations are not relations of logical opposition. Arguing against Mendelssohn, Kant claims that the idea of a negative magnitude has a place in our understanding of the relation between pleasure and displeasure. Imagine, he suggests, that a Spartan mother is first informed of her son's bravery in battle but subsequently informed of his death. Her overall state, Kant claims, would be of one of pleasure from the honour accrued, but the pleasure would be 'really' diminished by displeasure at her loss.[35] Her grief is a negative magnitude of feeling, which possesses a positive reality of its own.

Lest his use of this example be misunderstood, Kant also comments on Maupertuis's use of the concept of negative magnitude. Although Kant is petitioning to introduce the concept in limited cases of philosophical inquiry, he nevertheless opposes the way Maupertuis uses it in the *Essai*:

> *Maupertuis*, employing concepts such as these, attempts in his essay on moral philosophy, to calculate the sum of human happiness. And, indeed, his would be the only way in which it could be calculated; but, unfortunately, the calculation is not humanly possible, for it is only feelings of the same kind which can feature in such calculations. But the feelings which we experience in the highly complex circumstances of life appear to vary a great deal, according to the variety of ways in which our emotions are affected. The calculations performed by this learned man yielded a negative balance, a result with which, however, I do not concur.
>
> (*Negative Magnitudes*, 2: 181–182)

Kant contends that feelings manifest so differently for different people (and even for the same person on different occasions) that a reliable prediction of how we would be affected by future hardship (for example) cannot be made. It is worth noting Kant's stance here. When he says that he does 'not concur' with Maupertuis's result, his objection cannot be that a calculation of pleasures and pains must produce a *positive* balance, since Kant thinks at this point that no such calculation is possible. It is more likely that Kant is expressing his disagreement with Maupertuis's claim to have shown that life is not worth living. Since feelings are not adapted to mathematical calculation, Maupertuis's argument for this conclusion fails. Kant might still have endorsed the counterfactual claim that, *were* such a mathematical calculation possible, it *would* in fact yield a negative balance.

---

[35] Kant was likely influenced by Plutarch's 'Sayings of Spartan Women' concerning Spartan mothers' attitude to their sons' performance in battle—see Plutarch 2005, 183–188.

252 LESS THAN ZERO

At this stage in his intellectual development, Kant had yet to formulate the deontological conception of morality expressed in the *Groundwork* that would sever the basis of moral response from considerations of happiness conceived as the 'idea that all inclinations unite in one sum [*Summe*]' (4: 399).[36] When Kant comes to break that connection, he argues that considerations of terrestrial happiness are altogether irrelevant to the agent possessed of a good will. In 1763, however, he was still unaware that he did not need to question the viability of Maupertuis's calculus in order to defend the value of remaining alive.

5 Rousseau's critique of philosophy

Although, as we have seen, Kant entered into an ongoing debate about the nature of negative magnitudes, his main attitude concerning the relevance of mathematics to philosophy was decidedly negative. *Negative Magnitudes* begins with a warning regarding the use of mathematical methods in philosophy. In this respect, it echoes a view Kant had expressed more fully in a Prize Essay submission drafted the previous year. His *Inquiry concerning the distinctness of the principles of natural theology and morality* (1763), had offered a pessimistic picture of current progress in philosophy. Not only had no metaphysics been written to date, he claimed, but it was hard to see how philosophy could ever equal the achievements of mathematics. The latter had its own *sui generis* methods, and mimicking them could only produce monsters.[37] Given the proximity of the *Inquiry* to the essay on *Negative Magnitudes*, where Kant explicitly takes issue with Maupertuis, it is plausible to think that, when he wrote the *Inquiry*, he also had Maupertuis's conclusion in mind.

Kant spends most of the *Inquiry* discussing the differences between mathematical and philosophical method, and says relatively little about the state of moral philosophy. But his reflections raise a further and seemingly insuperable problem related to the explanatory and motivational bases of morality. Moral understanding, if it is possible at all, is motivationally efficacious. For Kant this entails that it must be related to *feelings* of some kind. Yet it is then hard to see how moral understanding is possible, since as he puts it 'the faculty of representing the *true* is *cognition*, while the faculty of experiencing the *good* is *feeling*'. If understanding requires some representation of truth, but motivational sensitivity requires an entirely different capacity, it is hard to see how representation of *moral truth* is to be had. If the relevant state is noncognitive, it cannot be truth-evaluable; if it is cognitive and truth-evaluable, it cannot be motivational. Here Kant leans towards the view that moral goodness is 'indemonstrable': he thinks that registering the

---

[36] For discussion see Kuehn 2001; Schönfeld 2000; Ward 1972.
[37] For discussion see Beiser 2010; Callanan 2014; Carson 2004; 1999; Hintikka 1967.

appropriate moral bindingness in a judgement like 'this is good' requires a kind of non-reflective responsiveness, or as he puts it 'an immediate effect of the consciousness of the feeling of pleasure combined with the representation of the object' (*Inquiry*, 2: 299). He is convinced, however, that the essential immediacy of the feeling is antithetical to the kind of awareness constitutive of moral cognition. His complaint against Hutcheson notwithstanding, Kant praises Hutcheson for having focused on the issue of registering immediate moral responses. Hutcheson, Kant claims, had thereby 'provided us with a starting point from which to develop some excellent observations' (*Inquiry*, 2: 300). For Kant, the difficulty that lay ahead concerned just how to connect morality with rationality if the former was not mathematizable. He cannot have been unaware of Hobbes's contention in *Leviathan* that 'in what matter soever there is place for *addition* and *substraction* [sic], there is also place for *Reason*, and where these have no place, there *Reason* has nothing at all to do'.[38]

The timing of Kant's expression of these two thoughts—that the application of mathematics to every domain of human experience is wrong-headed and that the common moral experience of ordinary subjects must be prioritized as a methodological constraint—is not insignificant. Sometime in the 1760s Kant became committed to several key claims expressed in the writings of Rousseau.[39] A crucial element in Rousseau's position is that the natural sentiments of sympathy and pity are to be trusted as reliable first-order moral responses. To this extent Kant would have seen in Rousseau an appreciation of Hutcheson's moral sense. Theories that prioritize moral feelings, sentiments, senses, etc., all have the advantage that they treat the first-order moral responses of ordinary subjects as typically reliable. They also have the advantage that our epistemic access to our own moral judgements is prima facie superior to that of purported moral experts. In the *First Discourse*, Rousseau makes the latter aspect of his position part of his critique of philosophy. Philosophers are presented as sophists primarily motivated by pride (again) and reputational profit and are also presented as de-stabilizers of society (Hobbes and Spinoza are marked out as advocates for vice and atheism respectively). What makes them dangerous, moreover, is that even when their motives are good, they suffer from the Enlightenment affliction of a fetishization of scientifically modelled rationality, thinking themselves warranted in applying it to any subject matter whatsoever, even when the results contradict what any ordinary person knows in their heart.

In the *Second Discourse*, Rousseau picks out a particularly egregious example of this fault:

---

[38] Hobbes (1651) 1996, 32, Part I, Ch. V, 'Of Reason and Science'.
[39] On this influence see Ameriks 2012a; Cassirer 1983; Henrich 1992; Shell 2009; Velkley 1989; Zammito 2002.

254   LESS THAN ZERO

> A famous author, calculating the goods and evils of human life and comparing
> the two sums, found the last greatly exceeded the first and that, all things
> considered, life was a rather poor gift for man. I am not at all surprised by his
> conclusion: he drew all his arguments from the constitution of Civil man....[40]

Maupertuis's conclusion is for Rousseau the paradigmatic case of Enlightenment
rationality run amok. It assumes the priority of mathematical reasoning over all
other forms of rationality; it presumes that a subject matter like the 'goods and
evils of human life' is appropriate for rational analysis, and therefore concludes
that the question of the value of human life must be apt for mathematical
treatment. Rousseau has no quibble with the first premise but takes aim at the
second. The overarching assumption that human beings are appropriately guided
by abstract rational reflection is just another commodified self-image of the
'civilized' man in modern society. It is also crucially the case that the application
of cultivated rationality to civilized man's existential condition generates results
that would never be tolerated by the 'natural' sentiments of his uncivilized
counterpart:

> Almost all the People we see around us complain of their existence, and some
> even deprive themselves of it as far as they are able, and the combination of
> divine and human Laws hardly suffices to stop this disorder: I ask whether
> anyone has ever heard tell that it so much as occurred to a Savage, who is free,
> to complain of life and to kill himself?[41]

Kant's writings throughout the 1760s—*Negative Magnitudes* and the *Inquiry*, but
most of all his satirical *Dreams of a Spirit-Seer* (1766)—manifest a sometimes
mitigated, sometimes despondent scepticism regarding the prospects for philosophy and the inauguration of an Enlightenment 'culture of reason'. By the end of
the decade, and with the publication of his *Inaugural Dissertation* (1770), he had
regained his optimism, but that optimism is best understood as operating within
the philosophical constraints set out by Rousseau. The Kant of the Critical period
remains committed to what I will call *Rousseau's premise*: that the primary reliable
data for moral philosophy ought to be the immediate responses of ordinary
uneducated subjects. The challenge of the Critical period is to retain this premise
whilst avoiding *Rousseau's conclusion*: that rational reflection is paradigmatically
harmful for the guidance of a human being's life.

Kant could not accept what he, like many others, saw as the misanthropy of
Rousseau's anti-rationalism, not least with regard to the question of suicide.
Perhaps uncivilized human beings would not even consider killing themselves,

---

[40] Rousseau, Second Discourse, Part I, Note IX, *OC* III: 202.
[41] Rousseau, Second Discourse, Part I, *OC* III: 152.

but Rousseau's phenomenally successful *Julie* seemed to be strikingly ambivalent as to whether suicide from self-love is always prohibited. Saint-Preux's debate with Bomston in Part III of *Julie* had struck many readers as presenting a clear indication of where philosophical rationality gives out. At the very least, it showed that reasoning *ad utramque partem* can provide equally compelling grounds for each of the two sides of a case, even if it so happened that, in the instance in question, Saint-Preux's will aligned with the arguments against suicide. In *Émile*, the Savoyard Vicar sums up his anti-philosophy with a compelling plea that human beings should remain piously grateful for their existing cognitive bequest. In moral affairs, all that matters is to recognize that the deity '[gave] me conscience for loving the good, reason for knowing it, and liberty for choosing it'.[42] Kant and fellow obsessive readers of Rousseau's writings would not have missed the fact that the very same pieties had also been expressed in *Julie*, though this time as part of Saint-Preux's case *in favour* of suicide:

> But [God] has given [man] freedom to do the good, conscience to will it, and reason to choose it. He has constituted him sole judge of his own acts. He has written in his heart: do what is good for you and harmful to no one. If I feel it is right for me to die, I resist his command by clinging obstinately to life; for by making my death desirable, he instructs me to seek it.[43]

The worry was not just that Rousseau had left open the possibility of justified suicide, or even that he might have implicitly recommended it. What would have particularly agitated Kant was that the language put to such important philosophical work in *Émile* could be co-opted to defend such appalling conclusions. Kant's concern was that our dispositions to judge in accordance with our feelings of conscience, pity, and the like are orthogonal to the disposition to judge rightly with regard to moral truths. That Rousseau could deploy the same resources to argue in favour of life, and against it, emphasized the philosophical poverty of Enlightenment sentimentalism and its concomitant anti-rationalism.

By the time Kant came to write the *Groundwork* in defence of rationality, philosophy, and what he now called 'common moral cognition', the question of suicide had if anything gained still greater cultural significance. In 1755, Mendelssohn had complained of Lessing's popular play *Miss Sara Sampson* in which a lead character kills himself,[44] on the grounds that it was vital to combat the 'madness that has broken out in our country'.[45] The madness in question was a rash of suicides, and the worry Mendelssohn expresses concerned the possibility that intellectual arguments such as those expressed in Rousseau's *Julie* and

---

[42] Rousseau, *Émile*, Bk IV, 294.   [43] Rousseau, *Julie*, Letter XXI, 315.
[44] 'On Sentiments' [1755] in Mendelssohn 1997, 42.
[45] 'On Sentiments' [1755] in Mendelssohn 1997, 55.

256 LESS THAN ZERO

Hume's 'On Suicide' were infecting ordinary society and encouraging people to end their lives.[46] The intellectual aspect of this debate was lively. Mendelssohn's attack on 'Lindamour' was in turn the subject of an attack by Karl Wilhelm Jerusalem, whose defence of suicide was later published with other essays by Lessing as *Philosophische Aufsätze* (1776). Jerusalem had killed himself in 1772. His suicide, perceived by Goethe as motivated by sentimentalism following an impossible love interest, has been recognized as a formative influence on the description of suicide in Goethe's *The Sorrows of Young Werther* (1774). That work was in turn a European literary sensation, comparable to *Julie*, and famously *did* inaugurate—despite Goethe's intentions—a rash of copycat suicides among impassioned but despondent young men (the so-called 'Werther Effect').

6 The argument of the *Groundwork* again

There can be no doubt then that when Kant wrote the *Groundwork* in 1785, he was aware that the provision of romantic grounds for suicide had spread from the study to the street. I hope to have shown that there is good reason to think that Kant would have seen this cultural phenomenon as one that had its intellectual roots in moral sentimentalism's inherently unprincipled character, leaving it open to be deployed for or against the default norm supporting the preservation of life. Still worse, Rousseau's advocacy of uncomprehending sentiment had gained support from a critique of the application of mathematical reasoning to matters of value, with which Kant strongly sympathized. How, then, was a non-mathematical form of philosophical reasoning to oppose sentimentalism, and with it, sentimentalist arguments for suicide?

In the *Groundwork*, Kant sets out to defend the implicit rationality of ordinary moral experiences and it is to this end that he famously deploys an essentially *nomological*, rather than mathematical, conception of rationality. What determines whether or not an action is rational is whether it possess *lawlikeness* [*Gesetzmassigkeit*] (4: 402). This is the feature Kant identifies as the essential mark of rationality, and distinguishes from the question of whether or not an issue is apt for mathematical characterization. Some problems are both lawlike and inherently mathematizable and these belong to physics. Others are non-mathematizable yet still lawlike and these are treated in ethics. In this way, Kant endorses Rousseau's claim that mathematical rationality has limited scope, without rejecting the scientific self-conception of Enlightenment philosophy. It is true that applying mathematics to questions about the value of human life generates

---

[46] On the contemporary anxiety of suicide's cultural contagion from the influence of *Julie* see Faubert 2015.

repugnant conclusions; but it does not follow that these questions are not essentially determined by rational principles.

According to Kant, the nomological conception of reason can also help to explain Rousseau's premise—that the primary reliable data for moral philosophy ought to be the immediate responses of ordinary uneducated subjects. In the First *Critique*, Kant had claimed that strict universality was equivalent to necessity (B4). This he thinks can explain the phenomenology of our moral psychology. When an ordinary uneducated subject is rationally accessing a universal practical principle, the operation manifests within their consciousness in terms of its modal profile. This modal profile is experienced in terms of the *bindingness* that characterizes the representation of obligation. In Kant's view, this feature of the moral law—the phenomenological experience of *Gesetzmassigkeit*—enables it to accommodate the data that originally motivated moral sense theories. Ordinary human beings register this feeling immediately, non-reflectively (and perhaps even on occasion subpersonally). Kant provides an analysis that explains this process as rationality itself, operating under a feeling-like mode of presentation. In this way, he avoids the criticism he had raised against moral sense theories—that they cannot bridge the gap between the way an individual is motivated to perform a certain act, and the explanation of why that act is the right thing to do. In the Kantian system, reason (under its feeling-like mode of presentation) motivates the action, and reason (under its reflective mode of presentation) explains why it is the right thing to do. The immediate and non-reflective push towards some actions and away from others is just an implicit registering of rational rules that the philosopher can subsequently make explicit through abstract reflection.[47] In this way, the universalization procedure outlined in the *Groundwork* is supposed to vindicate the first-order responses of ordinary folk.

These contextual features can also help us to understand, if perhaps not defend, Kant's opposition to suicide in the *Groundwork*. Here is how Kant imagines an individual contemplating suicide:

> Someone who feels weary of life because of a series of ills that has grown to the point of hopelessness is still so far in possession of his reason that he can ask himself whether it is not perhaps contrary to a duty to oneself to take one's own life. Now he tries out: whether the maxim of his action could possibly become a universal law of nature. But his maxim is: from self-love I make it my principle to shorten my life if, when protracted any longer, it threatens more ill than it promises agreeableness. The only further question is whether this principle of self-love could become a universal law of nature. (4: 421–422).

---

[47] For this Brandomian reading of Kant's approach see Geiger 2010.

258 LESS THAN ZERO

An important but infrequently noted aspect of Kant's argument is that he is clearly assuming an interlocutor who already has a general concern for moral uprightness and moreover has a general concern for the default uprightness of maintaining one's life. The subject under consideration is asking whether or not there are morally acceptable defeating conditions for this default norm. Without this prior commitment to the general wrongness of suicide, the subject would lack any reason to worry about the wrongness of suicide in his particular case.[48]

Kant goes on to claim that, when the maxim in question is universalized as an imagined law of nature, the individual finds himself imagining a nature 'whose law it were to destroy life itself by means of the same sensation the function of which it is to impel towards the advancement of life'. Immediately grasping this contradiction, he sees that the maxim 'conflicts entirely with the supreme principle of all duty' (4: 422). Bearing in mind the historical context we have traced, it is striking that the subject in question is considering a cost/benefit calculation of the reasonableness of continuing one's life. It is possible, then, that by the time of the *Groundwork*, Kant's objection to Maupertuis's conclusion was not that it was a miscalculation, but rather that it was an *accurate* calculation. If one applied mathematical methods to pleasure and pain one would be driven to accept that there will *always* be an available justification for ending one's life *whenever* one attempts to calculate it, since a calculation will always 'yield a negative balance'. One might imagine the possibility that, if one of the functions of life is to respond differentially to predicted results, and if one now includes Maupertuis's conclusion in one's considerations, it *would* follow in this possible world that, for *any* given consultation of a principle of self-love with regard to life, the answer would *always* be that we are rationally recommended to end our lives.

In such a world it *is* incoherent to speak of there being a default norm in favour of life. This is arguably what Kant has in mind when he complains, in the *Critique of Practical Reason*, that a suicide maxim, when elevated to the status of a law of nature, would entail that someone 'could end his life *at will* [*willkürlich*]' (*CPrR*, 5: 44). The implication here is that if the maxim were universalized it would warrant suicide promiscuously on any occasion of one's behest. On the reading I have been suggesting, Kant's universalization test functions to make explicit a kind of logical contradiction when one attempts to conjoin a general moral norm with a clause specifying circumstances when exceptions from that norm are permitted. In the suicide case we are envisioning just such a contradiction: the principle of ending one's life out of self-interest was introduced as the exception clause, to be cited in extreme circumstances, to a default norm in favour of the beneficial maintenance

---

[48] As Kant makes clear when he re-presents the case in the context of the Humanity Formulation of the Categorical Imperative, the subject is precisely considering whether this particular act of self-love is consistent with their pre-existing moral commitments as 'someone who is contemplating self-murder will ask himself whether his action can be consistent with the idea of humanity, as an end in itself' (4: 429).

of one's life. If that exception clause were viewed as constantly available, however, the norm would be defeated whenever challenged. The very idea of that drive is plausibly interpreted as a default basis for persisting in one's existence in the face of some of life's quotidian challenges. As such, the very idea of the default norm is that it might withstand some occasional challenges. In the possible world that Kant is imagining this meaning is lost.

On the reading I have been offering, the individual considering the suicide maxim is confronted with the conclusion that life is not worth living if they mathematically calculate the duration and intensity of life's pleasures and pains. Five years after the publication of the *Groundwork*, Kant stated this very result in the *Critique of the Power of Judgment*:

> It is easy to decide what sort of value life has for us if it is assessed merely by **what one enjoys** (the natural end of the sum of all inclinations, happiness). Less than zero: for who would start life anew under the same conditions, or even according to a new and self-designed plan (but one still in accord with the course of nature), which would, however, still be aimed merely at enjoyment?
>
> (CPJ, 5: 434, note—emphasis in original)[49]

The context here is Kant's consideration of aesthetic experiences as revelatory of the moral dimension of the value of human existence. Here he states that were one to 'start life anew' by estimating one's overall balance of expected pleasures and pains, the answer would be 'less than zero'. This mathematical expression is used in the *Groundwork* too, again in the context of a discussion of the relation between the value of life and the role of rationality:

> ... [O]ne must admit that the judgment of those who greatly moderate and even reduce below zero the vainglorious eulogies extolling the advantages that reason was supposed to obtain for us with regard to the happiness and contentment of life, is by no means sullen, or ungrateful to the kindliness of the government of the world; but that these judgments are covertly founded on the idea of another and far worthier purpose of their existence, to which, and not to happiness, reason is quite properly destined.... (4: 396)[50]

---

[49] I am very grateful for Bernd Ludwig for drawing my attention to this passage. See also (*Anthropology*, 25: 1319) for the same thought. Kant here is in the end affirming Bayle's view that 'it might be believed that everyone, all things considered, finds that the pleasures which he enjoys do not equal the pain and suffering with which he is afflicted'—Bayle approvingly mentions the view of 'La Mothe le Vayer, who had no wish to pass again through the bad times or the good that he had known in his life' ('Xenophanes', Remark F, in Bayle, 2000, 295).

[50] See also 4: 442, where Kant objects to happiness considered as the ground of moral laws on the basis that it eliminates the very distinction between specifically moral and immoral motives and instead it can 'only teach us to improve our calculations'.

260 LESS THAN ZERO

When this passage is understood in its context, Kant can be seen to be subtly alluding both to the idea of happiness as the proper end of the ethical life and to Rousseau's critique of mathematical reason as the proper means of determining it. Once happiness is dropped as the proper end of human beings' lives, Kant argues, reason's role can also be rehabilitated. It was the very idea that the proper end of human beings' lives could be articulated as the 'idea that all inclinations unite in one sum' (4: 399) that suggested that reason be co-opted to calculate that sum. But mathematical reason turned against human beings. Rather than forsake rationality, Kant re-conceived it as having a paradigmatically non-mathematical function, that of universalization. This re-conceptualization was necessary, Kant thought, if we are to see how scientific rationality might be practically relevant to life, not least in providing reasons for continuing it.[51]

[51] I am grateful to feedback from the audience at the Life and Death in the Early Modern Period conference held in Birkbeck and to Susan James for the opportunity to write this chapter. I benefitted also from assistance from Susan James, Christopher Kelly, Bernd Ludwig, and David Wootton.

PART VI
INANIMATE AND ANIMATE

13

'Everyone Knows What Life is'

Life as an Irreducible in and outside of Descartes's Metaphysics and Biology

Barnaby R. Hutchins

If Cartesian knowledge in natural philosophy can only be reductionist—that is, if all knowledge of the natural world must come down to 'the size, shape, and motion of the tiny parts that make it up' (Garber 2001: 112)—then Descartes has a problem in accounting for life. The problem is that, if the only resources available to him are the basic properties of homogeneous matter, he seems to have no well-grounded way of distinguishing between artificial machines and living creatures. All that is available in Descartes's dualist ontology is body (extended substance) and soul (thinking substance). He explicitly rules out the view that life pertains to the soul, not least because the Cartesian soul is nothing but thought—and he is perfectly clear that living is not a kind of thought (to Regius, May 1641; ATIII: 371[1]). That leaves just extended substance. Change within extended substance occurs mechanically, and, on Descartes's account, animals, plants, and the bodies of humans are nothing but machines (ATXI: 120). As machines, they are ultimately made from the same stuff as clocks or automata or fountains, and work on the same bases, even if living things happen to be rather more intricately constructed than any machine humans had, at that time, been able to build (ATIII: 163–164; ATVI: 56; ATXI: 120). Given this, it is difficult to see how there could be any principled way for Descartes to distinguish living things from artificial machines. A duck is no more alive than a clock, and a clock no more inanimate than a duck.

Several attempts to provide Descartes with a principled, reductionist account of life have been made in the literature. The obvious candidate for such an account— that life can be reduced to heat—is a non-starter. Although Descartes regularly associates the phenomena of life with heat, heat is too inclusive to provide a reductionist concept of life by itself, because it does not exclude heat-driven

---

[1] In this chapter, the following abbreviations are used for the standard editions of Descartes's work: AT for *Œuvres de Descartes* (Descartes 1996); CSM for the first two volumes of *The Philosophical Writings of Descartes* (Descartes 1984–85); and CSMK for the third volume of the latter (Descartes 1991).

Barnaby R. Hutchins, *'Everyone Knows What Life is': Life as an Irreducible in and outside of Descartes's Metaphysics and Biology* In: *Life and Death in Early Modern Philosophy*. Edited by: Susan James, Oxford University Press.
© Barnaby R. Hutchins 2021. DOI: 10.1093/oso/9780192843616.003.0014

264 'EVERYONE KNOWS WHAT LIFE IS'

machines that we would want to classify as non-living. Thus, in his reading, Hall goes a little further and suggests that life, for Descartes, consists in a set of functions that 'have their kinetic origin in heat' (Hall 1970: 61). MacKenzie 1975 notes the problems with heat and argues instead that life reduces to specific functions, while Ablondi 1998 tries to locate Descartes's conception of life in a certain kind of complexity (the kind of complexity that only God can create). More recently, Detlefsen 2016 has argued that Cartesian mechanism alone cannot support a coherent conception of life; it needs to be augmented with some teleology, which, as Detlefsen is aware, is inconsistent with Descartes's epistemo- logical and ontological commitments.

I argued in Hutchins 2016a, that none of these accounts works, ultimately for the reasons outlined above. I concluded that Descartes has no need for such an account, and is fully eliminativist about life itself. The trouble with the elimina- tivist reading, though, is that it struggles to make sense of Descartes's frequent references to life. He explicitly distinguishes between living and dead bodies in general (ATxi: 330–331) and, in an experimental context, between living and dead eels in particular (ATii: 66). He classifies animals as living (e.g. ATv: 278), but severed animal heads that are still active enough to 'bite the earth' as non-living (ATvi: 55). Perhaps most tellingly, in a letter to Regius, Descartes explicitly affirms 'life' as the 'category which includes the forms of all living things' (ATiii: 556). On a reductionist reading, this would seem strangely tauto- logical. On an eliminativist reading, it looks nonsensical. On the reading I give in this chapter, the reason Descartes readily refers to life and identifies it as an existent category is that he does indeed recognize a genuine distinction between the living and the non-living. However, the conception of life this involves will have to be irreducible to the terms of Descartes's dualist system. In the following, I argue that Descartes does not need a reductionist account of life in order to know that there is such a thing as life. Despite its irreducibility, he has a means of identifying life as a category that includes all living things. This constitutes a weak ontological commitment to life, which we might interpret as a kind of vitalism.

1 Life and indefinability

In a paper on the definition of life, the biochemist Daniel Koshland Jr recounts an anecdote from a conference dedicated to the subject:

> After many hours of launching promising balloons that defined life in a sentence, followed by equally conclusive punctures of these balloons, a solution seemed at hand: 'The ability to reproduce—that is the essential characteristic of life,' said one statesman of science. Everyone nodded in agreement that the essential of a life was the ability to reproduce, until one small voice was heard. 'Then one rabbit

is dead. Two rabbits—a male and female—are alive but either one alone is dead.'
At that point, we all became convinced that although everyone knows what life is
there is no simple definition of life. (Koshland 2002: 2215)

Koshland takes the lesson here to be that we need a non-simple definition of life.
Since we all know what life is, there must be some definition available. But simple
definitions—by which, he seems to mean those that reduce life to a single
characteristic, such as the ability to reproduce—are not going to do the job.
What he proposes instead is the reduction of life to multiple basic principles,
which can be instantiated in various ways.[2]

There is a different lesson to be drawn from Koshland's anecdote: the story
shows, succinctly, that being unable to define life is not inconsistent with knowing
what life is. We can all know what life is and still not be able to say, in any
principled way, what life consists in. We can consistently distinguish living from
non-living even if we cannot definitively point to specific features on which that
distinction depends—that is, even if we cannot find a reductive analysis of life or
turn it into a natural kind (at least, not under a physicalist conception of nature).
The present chapter rejects Koshland's assumption that our recognition of life
implies that there is still a definition to be found: Descartes knows what life is even
though he treats life as entirely indefinable.

In Hutchins 2016a, I argued that Descartes's frequent references to life, and
his explicit use of it as a category, are not incompatible with eliminativism about
life for two reasons. First, because he uses 'life' as a folk term, where doing otherwise
would be inefficient. Second, because he uses it as an Aristotelian term, with the
intention of showing that he can explain everything the Aristotelians take to be
encompassed by life without requiring the addition of souls. Both these reasons
stand, up to a point. But there is a problem with this approach: Descartes never
writes as though he takes the term 'life' to be merely some sort of colloquial
shorthand, as we might expect him to do if he holds that what others call 'life'
fails to refer to anything within his ontology. He never claims that, while he can
account for all the phenomena others have associated with life, 'life' itself is
fictitious; he simply talks of life as anyone who takes the category to be real would
do. And while Descartes does have a habit of appropriating established terms for
his own, very different, purposes, he is not one to suffer false concepts silently.

Take, for instance, his rejection of forms and qualities in *The World*:

[o]thers may, if they wish, imagine the form of fire, the quality of heat, and the
process of burning to be completely different things in the wood. For my part,
I am afraid of mistakenly supposing there is anything more in the wood than

---

[2] This suffers from some degree of arbitrariness, amongst other issues. See Ruiz-Mirazo, Peretó, and
Moreno 2004: 326, Cleland and Chyba 2002: 388, and Zhuravlev and Avetisov 2006: 282.

266 'EVERYONE KNOWS WHAT LIFE IS'

what I see must necessarily be in it, and so I am content to limit my conception to the motion of its parts. For you may posit 'fire' and 'heat' in the wood, and make it burn as much as you please: but if you do not suppose in addition that some of its parts move about and detach themselves from their neighbours, I cannot imagine it undergoing any alteration or change. On the other hand, if you take away the 'fire', take away the 'heat', and keep the wood from 'burning'; then, provided only that you grant me there is some power which puts its finer parts into violent motion and separates them from the coarser parts, I consider that this power alone will be able to bring about all the same changes that we observe in the wood when it burns.   (ATxi: 7; CSMi: 83)

As things in their own right, distinct from the mechanical activity of material corpuscles, fire and heat are excised as superfluous. Descartes tells us, with some condescension, that we can talk about fire and heat if we want, but would be wasting our time: there is no fire as such and no heat as such; there is only the activity of corpuscles. Similarly (and not unironically, given the present context), Descartes's rejection of the soul as the principle of life is both vociferous and explicit. He considers vegetative souls to be redundant (e.g. ATi: 523; ATiii: 371) and regards the view that the soul is the source of life as a 'very serious error' (CSMi: 329; ATi: 330).

So why is the attribution of life to humans, animals, and plants not also an error? If Descartes expressly rejects forms, qualities, and vegetative souls as superfluous, it seems he should also reject any need to appeal to life. We might expect him to note the bankruptcy of the term and flag his own use of it as purely pragmatic, as with his occasional use of terms such as 'form'.[3] If he has good reason to distance himself from the term—and it seems that he does—why does he not do so? This is, perhaps, only a small puzzle, but it is a puzzle lacking an entirely satisfactory resolution. At least, it is hard to see how it could be resolved if Cartesian knowledge is taken to be purely reductionist.

2 Indefinability and irreducibility

That Descartes does not attempt to distance himself from his own use of 'life' could just be an oversight on his part. It is, of course, possible that he simply made use of the term without fully thinking through the consequences. But Descartes is rarely, if ever, careless with his language, and he certainly put a great deal of

---

[3] For instance, in the *Description of the Human Body*, Descartes describes the blood particles in the heart that start the fermentation-like process responsible for cardiac heat and motion (see Hutchins 2015: 681–684) as separating particles of new blood 'from one another, and in separating thus they acquire the form of fire' (Descartes 1998: 203; ATxi: 282).

thought into matters of biology. With that in mind, simple negligence does not seem a promising answer to the puzzle at hand. So, let's take Descartes seriously when he claims that he does not deny life to animals (ATv: 278). Let's assume that, when he talks about 'life', he knows what it is. The problem then is how we can reconcile Descartes's knowledge of what life is with his inability to account for it reductively. This is a significant problem for Descartes as long as we take all Cartesian knowledge to be reductionist. But, Cartesian knowledge need not be reductionist—or, at least, it need not bottom out in the terms of his dualist ontology. We can say as much because Descartes provides a clear example of knowledge of this kind: on his account, the union of mind and body is explanatorily irreducible within the dualist system, but is nevertheless known 'very clearly' (CSMK: 227; ATIII: 692).

Descartes's most extensive treatment of the union occurs in his correspondence with Elisabeth, whose stated motivation for writing to Descartes in the first place was to raise the problem of mind–body interaction (ATIII: 661). In his first reply, Descartes addresses the problem in terms of primitive notions, of which three in particular are relevant: thought, extension, and union.

> First, I consider that there are in us certain primitive notions which are as it were the patterns on the basis of which we form all our other conceptions. There are very few such notions. First, there are the most general—those of being, number, duration, etc.—which apply to everything we can conceive. Then, as regards body in particular, we have only the notion of extension, which entails the notions of shape and motion; and as regards the soul on its own, we have only the notion of thought, which includes the perceptions of the intellect and the inclinations of the will. Lastly, as regards the soul and the body together, we have only the notion of their union, on which depends our notion of the soul's power to move the body, and the body's power to act on the soul and cause its sensations and passions.   (CSMK: 218; ATIII: 665)

That mind and body should be primitive notions is something we should expect. Within Descartes's dualist ontology, everything in the material world is a modification of extension, while everything in the mind is a modification of thought. Necessarily, then, when we conceive of something material, we conceive of it through extension, and when we conceive of something mental, we conceive of it through thought. Since Descartes's (standard) ontology contains nothing but thought and extension, our only options for conceiving of thought and extension are thought and extension themselves. And because substances can depend only on themselves,[4] extension can tell us nothing about thought,

---

[4] And, in the case of created substances, on God (*Principles of Philosophy*, 1/52; ATvIIIA: 24–25; CSMI: 210).

and thought nothing about extension. We therefore cannot conceive of the one through the other, and thought and extension must be primitive.

Within this framework, treating the union as a further primitive notion seems counterintuitive.[5] After all, the union is meant to be a union of mind and body. On the face of things, it would seem perfectly natural to take the union to be, if anything, a composite notion, conceived through both thought and extension. Given Descartes's famous dualism, given his famous ontological and explanatory parsimony, and given that the union is precisely a union of his two fundamental substances, we might reasonably expect it to be conceived through those two substances—and this is precisely what Elisabeth is looking for as well.

However, while it would be consistent with some of his wider commitments for Descartes to characterize the union as a composite notion, he takes it to be a primitive notion in its own right. Why this ultimately has to be his position is fairly straightforward: if extension can tell us nothing about thought, and thought can tell us nothing about extension, then neither thought nor extension can tell us anything about their union. This is because the union has properties that are present in neither the mind nor the body taken by themselves.[6] So whatever we want to know about the union is not going to be conceivable through the notions of either thought or extension. And it cannot be conceivable through the notions of both thought and extension simultaneously, because thought and extension are conceptually isolated from each other: the notion of both thought and extension simultaneously is not covered by the individual notions of thought and extension. Put another way, to appeal to thought and extension simultaneously is just to restate the problem of the union itself.

Necessarily, then, the union needs a primitive notion of its own. Neither thought nor extension is going to do the job. And since the other primitive notions that Descartes mentions ('being, number, duration, etc.') 'apply to everything we can conceive', they are not going to pick out anything specific to the union. Our only means of conceiving of the soul and the body together is therefore through the notion of their union. And, Descartes claims, it is on this notion that our conception of mind–body interaction depends.

This is in no way a trivial result. It means that thought and extension, which are supposed to be the fundamental elements of Descartes's philosophy, can tell us nothing at all about the union. It means that the union is not reducible to the terms of the dualist system. This is not just a matter of epistemic uncertainty. Descartes's claim is explicitly *not* that he simply does not yet have a good explanation of the union in terms of thought or extension. His claim is rather

---

[5] Trialist readings are, of course, a notable exception, see e.g. Cottingham 1985.

[6] On properties specific to the union, see Simmons 2011: 9–10 and Brown 2014: 248, who writes, 'the special subject of these irreducible modes is not one that Descartes can draw from his official ontology of basic substances, and hence he needs to conceive of the union as *sui generis*'.

that there can be no explanation of the union in terms of thought or extension, for the reasons given above. The union requires a primitive (i.e. irreducible) notion of its own.[7]

Descartes is explicit that the union exists, is known very clearly, and can only be conceived through an irreducible, primitive notion of its own. If we take this position seriously, it seems that Descartes allows for nonreductionist knowledge; consequently, his system's inability to support a reductionist account of life need not require him to deny the existence of life. He can allow for an irreducible notion of life.

3 Nonreductionist knowledge and life

Descartes provides a relatively strong statement that there is indeed such a thing as life in the letter to Regius mentioned above: '[s]ince "self-moving" is a category with respect to all machines that move of their own accord, which excludes others that are not self-moving, so "life" can be taken as the category [*vita sumi potest pro genere*] which includes the forms of all living things' (to Regius, June 1642; CSMK: 214, translation adjusted; ATIII: 566).

The letter compares the existence of 'life' as a category with that of 'self-moving' as a category; the former encompasses all living things just as the latter encompasses all self-moving things. But the analogy is not exact. On the one hand, the property of being self-moving is reducible and therefore definable within Descartes's ontology. A self-moving thing is something that contains its own principle of movement, rather than being moved by external causes. And since Descartes takes movement to be a mode of extended substance, a body's self-movement reduces to a fundamental property of extension. Specifying the category of self-moving things therefore requires no additional metaphysical commitments from Descartes; his commitment to extended substance already gives him everything he needs. It therefore makes good sense for 'self-moving' to be an existent category: it is both a category we recognize and one for which we can access well defined conditions of membership. For life, on the other hand, the situation is different. While we recognize the category, the conditions of membership are not reductively definable. To belong to the category 'life' is just to be alive, but we can say nothing further or definitive about *what it is* for a member of the category to be alive.

According to Descartes, then, 'life' is an existent category encompassing everything that is alive, but its membership conditions are not reductively definable. This is entirely consistent with his account of the union, which we also know to

[7] Cf. Brown & Normore 2019: ch. 6.

exist, but which is also is indefinable (in the terms of the dualism). If Descartes's system can allow for irreducible knowledge of the mind–body union, there seems nothing to prevent it from likewise allowing for irreducible knowledge of life. Moreover, if we allow Descartes a primitive notion of life, we can make sense of his unapologetic endorsement of the category and use of the term. On this reading, even though life is irreducible within his ontology, the category of living things is just as real as the category of self-moving things. Descartes can meaningfully and legitimately describe animals, people and plants as 'living', distinguish between living and dead eels (AT II: 66), or even claim that life ends when any of the principle parts of the body stops working (ATxi: 330; see Hutchins 2016b: 762–764). And he can do all this without being able to say what it is to be alive, in what the distinction between living and dead eels consists, or what it is that ends when the body breaks down. In all these cases, Descartes can do no more than appeal to life itself.

In her paper on Descartes's conception of life, MacKenzie asks for a definition in terms of 'what is asserted by the whole sentence "x is alive"' (MacKenzie 1975: 2). If my reading here holds, it seems that the only definition Descartes can provide is this: *x is alive if and only if x is alive*. Clearly, this is not what MacKenzie had in mind; a tautologous definition is not an informative one. But this is precisely what's at stake: life cannot be further defined, and Descartes' inability to provide a definition of life in other terms does not prevent him from having a meaningful notion of it, any more than his inability to define the union in other terms makes it impossible for him to know that mind and body are united. What is crucial is that, tautologous though it may be, this is a definition that Descartes can actually employ: against expectations, appealing to life itself is not out of the question within his system.

Consequently, Descartes is a nonreductionist about life. But (as covered above), he is also an eliminativist about life. This is an odd conclusion to reach. Since eliminativism is generally taken to be a particularly thoroughgoing form of reductionism, eliminativism and nonreductionism about the same thing ought to be mutually incompatible. There is, however, a way to resolve this without accusing Descartes of gross inconsistency, if we understand Descartes as an eliminativist about life in biological contexts, and as a nonreductionist in metaphysical ones. When accounting for the operations of the body, Descartes is fully eliminativist about life, excluding it from playing a functional role in biology. But outside that project, he is free to take a nonreductionist view of the category of 'life'. In this way, there is no problem of incompatibility: eliminativism about life is fully compatible with nonreductionism about life as long as the positions are applied only within separate projects. This is presumably the present-day situation with regard to certain strands of neuroscience and traditional psychology: the first is eliminativist or reductionist about certain things that are treated nonreductively within the other. As long as they belong to different projects with different ontologies and different epistemic aims, there is no problem of incompatibility between them. It is only if we try to collapse one project into the other that a problem arises.

For his part, however, Descartes shows no interest in trying to collapse the two projects. He never attempts to reduce life itself to the terms of his dualist ontology, nor does he ever express the desire to do so. He undoubtedly is interested in attempting to reduce various phenomena associated with life, but not to reduce life itself. We would say he had no interest at all in life itself, if it weren't for his affirmation of the category in the letter to Regius, along with various other non-trivial uses of the term. That he talks about life in the way he does with absolutely no handwringing, with no attempt to explain the apparent contradiction, gives us good reason to think that he was not interested in trying to overcome the incompatibility through the collapsing of separate projects. Given this, it seems reasonable to conclude that Descartes is an eliminativist about life within his natural-philosophical biological project and a nonreductionist about life otherwise.

4 Descartes's nonreductionism and vitalism

Vitalism has a long history of being the bogeyman of the life sciences. Painted as the baseless appeal to a magical life force, it is often treated as the disreputable counterpart of serious biological research. Perhaps the only aspect of Descartes's programme in biology that has retained some mainstream respectability is its apparent use of hard-nosed reductionist mechanism to repudiate the purportedly vitalist philosophies of Aristotle, Galen, and Paracelsus that preceded him. And now I am claiming that Descartes thinks there is such a thing as life in itself, and that it is irreducible into more basic terms. That might seem like a cause for concern over whether this reading ruins the one aspect of Descartes's biology that is well regarded. Does it, in other words, turn him into some kind of vitalist?

If vitalism is understood in its bogeyman form, that concern is easily dismissed. Nowhere does Descartes posit or sanction any non-natural life force. On the contrary, he methodically, repeatedly, and explicitly rejects any cause of vital phenomena that falls outside the properties of his extended substance.[8] It is true that, on my reading, he also has an irreducible notion of life, but it plays no role at all in his biological explanations. This is a long way from the kind of approach that appeals to some vital force to make its biology work. Descartes still excises mysterious forces from the science of biology. His sober materialist position abides, and whatever reputation his biology still has remains intact.

---

[8] See Hutchins 2016a.

272 'EVERYONE KNOWS WHAT LIFE IS'

However, vitalism has rarely taken its bogeyman form. Wolfe provides a useful categorization of its various kinds, distinguishing between what he calls 'substantive' and 'functional' vitalisms (Wolfe 2014b; Wolfe 2017; Wolfe in this volume; Wolfe and Terada 2008). Substantive vitalism is the metaphysical commitment to life as some sort of distinct metaphysical substance. We'd find substantive vitalism in the work of, e.g., Stahl or Driesch, whose talk of *anima* and entelechies most closely resembles the form of vitalism reviled by twentieth-century biologists. Functional vitalism, on the other hand, as found in, e.g. the Montpellier vitalists, makes no metaphysical commitments towards life, but takes life to be a guiding principle in research: functional vitalists study the operations of specifically *living* things—they take the category of living things to be functionally salient in the science—but are not concerned with the question of what life itself is (Wolfe 2017; Wolfe 2014b: 255).

Accordingly, in his chapter in this volume, Wolfe gives the following definition of vitalism:

> a robust definition of vitalism should start with the criterion of opposition between living and non-living entities. That is, if we speak of vitalism it must be to refer to cases in which the thinker in question (theorist, scientist, physician, natural philosopher, etc.) is actively concerned with this opposition. This basic criterion of vitalism applies, whether the vitalist handles the distinction as somehow contingent and a matter of empirical investigation, or 'ontologizes' it as a substantial distinction.   (Wolfe in this volume)

Descartes—at least, Descartes the theorist, scientist, physician, or natural philosopher—is no vitalist on this definition. The distinction between living and non-living itself is never an active concern in his biology.[9]

In what sense is it not active? On the face of it, Descartes's treatment of life might indeed look something like functional vitalism. After all, he accounts for vital phenomena piecemeal, while maintaining an indifference towards the status of life itself. The characterizations of 'life' as either a folk term or an Aristotelian term could certainly be read as what the Montpellier vitalist, Barthez, calls 'personifications' of life, introduced purely for the ease of argument (see Wolfe 2017: 235). There is, however, a significant difference between Descartes's approach and functional vitalism: for Descartes, the notion of life is entirely non-functional, at least within his biological project.

Life is non-functional for Descartes because the category does not serve to drive his research.[10] He is careful to address all the phenomena of the body without reference to life. The questions he deals with are never about how such-and-such a

---

[9] Where Descartes does raise the distinction, he does so just to dismiss it (e.g. *Passions* a. 6).
[10] This is how I interpret my position in Hutchins 2016a in light of the analysis here.

process contributes to *life*, but about how such-and-such a process individually contributes to locomotion, or sensation, or the continuation of the heartbeat, and so on. When Descartes does refer to living and non-living (such as in articles five and six of *The Passions*), it is to point out that death is entirely due to the material breakdown of the body. The difference between being alive and being dead thus comes down to the difference between a broken watch and one that is intact and wound (*Passions* a. 6; ATxi: 330–331). Even if Descartes does have an additional, irreducible notion of life, it has no role in his accounts of the operation of the body. Whatever that notion might be, it is undoubtedly non-functional within his biology.

However, if we take seriously Descartes's affirmation of the existence of the category of 'life', as I have suggested we should, this does imply some metaphysical commitment (unlike the category of self-moving things, that of life is not covered by pre-existing commitments—if it were, it would be reducible). And Descartes is not entirely indifferent to ontology. For example, he tells us, among other things, that 'life' is indeed an existent category. This is not substantival vitalism: there is no special Cartesian substance in which life consists. But it is, nevertheless, something at least vaguely ontological.

I have said that, in his biology, Descartes neither attempts to account for life itself nor uses life as a functional element in his explanations; rather, his interest is in the operations of living things. This is precisely the issue, though: the notion of 'living' rears up again, seemingly quite innocuous, but unshakeably, insidiously indispensable. Descartes is interested in the operations of *living things*, of things that intuitively, and perhaps naturally, form a category of their own—the category of living things. Even if he divorces his treatment of the operations of living things from life itself, he makes no attempt to distance himself from seeing them, and describing them, as living things in the first place. No doubt this is at least somewhat pragmatic: we experience living things in the world, and it is rather difficult to refer to them without invoking *life*, even if only adjectivally. But this pragmatism contains a seed of ontology: as grounded in experience, in the 'ordinary course of life and conversation' (to Elisabeth, 28 June 1643; CSMK: 227; ATiii: 692), there is such a thing as the category of life.

This notion of life as feature of experience is reflected in another kind of vitalism: 'attitudinal' vitalism.[11] The idea comes from Canguilhem, who sees vitalism as 'a permanent exigency of life in the living, the self-identity of life immanent to the living' (Canguilhem 2008: 62). Attitudinal vitalism is the identification of life as an ineliminable presence in our experience—both because we experience ourselves as living and because we experience other things as living.

---

[11] See, e.g., Wolfe 2017 and Wolfe and Etxeberria 2018.

274 'EVERYONE KNOWS WHAT LIFE IS'

This, Canguilhem argues, is reflected in mechanistic science's very attempts to bring life within its explanatory scope. On his understanding, mechanism proposes a world that is devoid of life as such, thereby making the mechanist 'a living being separated from life by science'. The mechanist's response to this separation is to seek to reconcile science with the exigency of life that we can't help experiencing precisely by trying to mechanize the latter—by 'attempting to rejoin life through science' (Canguilhem 2008: 62). As such, 'exigent' life is ineliminable even in the attempt to reduce it to something non-living (i.e. mechanism, in this case).

This is not quite Descartes's attitude. He is, of course, a mechanist,[12] but life as such doesn't seem to raise itself as a problem for Descartes in his mechanization of the natural world. This is very much an exigency of the discipline rather than of vitalism. In other words, while attitudinal vitalism in the Canguilhemian sense is still scientifically functional, Descartes's treatment of life is not. Nevertheless, even if life has no exigency in Descartes's scientific project, that does not mean that it fails to make its demands known elsewhere. This is that unshakeable indispensability of life, through which Descartes apparently can't—and certainly doesn't—avoid referring to living things as *living* things. The attitude towards life remains for Descartes, then, but only outside the biological context. As such, Descartes's treatment of life is at least compatible with attitudinal vitalism, albeit in a scientifically non-functional variant. This gives us the somewhat counterintuitive result that vitalism can be non-biological (in that it can exist outside the life sciences, and in that it can coexist with a non-vitalist biology).

When it comes to vitalism, Descartes is clearly not a vitalist in the bogeyman sense of the term. Given the above, however, we would be hard-pressed not to see Descartes as *some sort* of vitalist. He does have a metaphysical commitment to 'life' as a category (assuming we take him seriously on that count). That commitment is only implicit, and is, presumably, only a weak commitment to an obscure notion of life, one that arises in experience rather than being grounded in the science. It is also a commitment to an entirely non-functional notion. But, it is a commitment nonetheless.

Above, I've emphasized just how little Descartes appeals to the notion of life itself within his biology; this might well seem to amount to an objection to the argument I have offered. If life is irrelevant to Descartes's biology, it is not clear that there is a mandate for pressing the point that he defends a nonreductionist conception of life. My response is this: the very absence of any appeal to life within Descartes's biology is part of what makes such a reading of Descartes compelling. Life is a low-stakes commitment for Descartes. Nothing in his treatment of biological operations depends on its existence or on its precise nature. His inability

---

[12] Not incidentally, Canguilhem takes Descartes to be representative of the mechanist attitude (Canguilhem 2008: 63).

to analyse life in the terms of his dualism poses no problem at all, because, whatever he might say about life, it would have no effect on anything else in his system. This allows him the luxury of making the unapologetic, if casual, metaphysical commitment to life that he does. Thanks to its non-functionality, the claim that 'life' is an existent category is a claim he can afford to affirm. *He can know what life is without being able to define it.*

5 Conclusion

When Koshland notes that 'although everyone knows what life is there is no simple definition of life' (Koshland 2002: 2215), he assumes that there is a (non-simple) definition of life available for the taking, and that this definition will eventually be aessible to science. Descartes, by contrast, makes life utterly indefinable. And yet he tells Regius that 'life' is the category that covers all livings things, and is distinct from but just as real as the category of self-moving things. He repeatedly, and seemingly meaningfully, talks of life, in various contexts.

This is a puzzle so long as we assume that the only real things in the Cartesian world are those that are reducible to the properties of extension or thought—or, epistemically, that the only knowledge we can have is reductive knowledge. But Descartes's use of the primitive notion of the union opens the door to non-reductive knowledge, and perhaps even to real entities that are not grounded in thought or extension.

Although he does not explicitly say so, this appears to be how life works in Descartes's system. It cannot be reduced to, or grounded in, the properties of either of the substances that constitute his ontology, and yet it exists. Understood in this way, Descartes's notion of life does involve an ontological commitment. That commitment is a very low-cost one: unlike the union of mind and body, which plays a crucial role in his system,[13] the notion of life does not work within his natural philosophy. As far as his explanations of the operations of living bodies are concerned, the conception of life as real and irreducible is entirely dispensable.

This might seem a little anticlimactic: Descartes has a metaphysical commitment to life, but it doesn't actually make any difference to anything. It is not the case, however, that life makes no difference across the board. While, by design, it makes no difference to Descartes's explanations of biological phenomena, it does allow him to do justice to the seemingly unavoidable presence of life in the world as we experience it. He is not (quite) so hubristic as to deny this feature of the world outright, simply because it is not explicable within his system. Despite his fervent reductionism and rationalism, Descartes acknowledges that what is

---

[13] See Hutchins 2016c, ch. 4.

276 'EVERYONE KNOWS WHAT LIFE IS'

explicable within a given system is not necessarily coextensive with what exists. In this light, his elimination of life from the biological project is a bracketing-off rather than a full-blown denial.

On this reading, we can make sense of what might initially seem the most puzzling aspect of Descartes's treatment of life: that his use of the term and category is entirely unapologetic, despite its apparent incompatibility with his ontology. This is not, I have suggested, mere negligence on his part. On the contrary, he can legitimately refer to life, because he really does take it to exist, in spite of its indefinability and irreducibility. In this way, Descartes gets access to a notion of life, while still being an eliminativist about life within the confines of his dualism. Without endangering the strict materialism of his biology, he even gets to be a vitalist, of some sort.[14]

---

[14] Prior to the Life and Death conference, earlier versions of this chapter were given at the Israeli Philosophical Association Conference in Jerusalem in 2016, the Ben Gurion University philosophy colloquium, and a small workshop at the University of Turin. I owe thanks to the audiences at all these events, and especially to Dennis Des Chene, Alexander X. Douglas, Christoffer Basse Eriksen, Laura Georgescu, Claudia Matteini, Ohad Nachtomy, Sophie Roux, Paola Rumore, Eric Schliesser, Noa Shein, Alison Simmons, Maarten Van Dyck, Sebastjan Vörös, and Charles T. Wolfe. I'd also like to thank Susan James for her comments on, and her very thorough and careful editing of, the printed version.

14

Affect and Effect

Spinoza on Life

Steph Marston

There is an apparent puzzle in Spinoza's metaphysics regarding those things that, in an everyday sense, we think of as living things. The puzzle arises from what is commonly alluded to as the panpsychism in Spinoza's philosophy, grounded in Spinoza's treatment of mind and body in the early stages of Part 2 of the *Ethics*.[1] Wrapping up his argument with the claim that his account resolves the question of mind-body union, Spinoza states:

> The things we have shown so far are completely general and do not pertain more to man than to other individuals, all of which, though in different degrees, are... animate [*animata*]... Whatever we have said of the idea of the human body must also be said of any thing.   (*E*2p13s)

This suggestion that all things are animate presents an obvious challenge to our ways of speaking of some things as living and of others as not living, since those ways of speaking carry implicit appeal to a binary principle of animation. On that principle, some things—people, animals, plants—share some quality of animation (albeit differently manifested) which others—rocks, books, machines—lack. *E*2p13s seems to tell us that this is not the case, and that animation is universal, varying among entities in degree rather than in being present or absent.

Perhaps it may be thought that the appropriate response to this challenge is interpretive quiescence, whether on the grounds that it is not necessary to draw a line between living and non-living things, or on the grounds that Spinoza does not feel the need to draw such a line. It is certainly the case that the question is not framed explicitly in the *Ethics*. However, differentiation between living and non-living things was a significant matter of dispute in early modern philosophy. Scholastics had followed Aristotle in accounting for the development and behaviours of plants and animals through *psuchē*, rendered in Latin as *anima*, or soul, a principle of internal change. Living things were thus deemed to be different in

---

[1] All references to the *Ethics* are to Spinoza 1985. I abbreviate the title to *E*.

Steph Marston, *Affect and Effect: Spinoza on Life* In: *Life and Death in Early Modern Philosophy*. Edited by: Susan James, Oxford University Press. © Steph Marston 2021. DOI: 10.1093/oso/9780192843616.003.0015

278 AFFECT AND EFFECT

kind from non-living things, which lacked *anima*. Cartesian philosophy, on the other hand, contested the explanatory value of the concept of *anima*, holding that the observable biological processes and actions of living things could be fully accounted for in terms of mechanistic bodily motions. While Spinoza does not address the question directly it is clear that, in ascribing *anima* to all individuals, $E2p13s$ directly opposes Cartesian mechanism and at the same time departs from Scholastic Aristotelianism. I argue in this chapter that, although Spinoza's philosophy holds to a universal principle of animation, it also has the resources to illuminate and give warrant for our everyday distinction between living and non-living things.

My central thesis is that living things bring about a more extensive repertoire of effects than non-living things. That is, while there are effects which are brought about by all entities, living entities bring about additional effects which are different in kind from the effects that are common to all. This more extensive domain of effects comes about only in virtue of living entities forming inadequate ideas and acting on them. The extended repertoire of effects attributable to living entities is therefore not only a matter of phenomenal or observable difference, but also shows that those differences are underwritten by the workings of Spinoza's philosophical system.

As context for my argument I discuss interpretations of Spinoza that seek to situate *consciousness* within his philosophy. Such interpretations seek to establish how far our everyday understanding of which entities are conscious can be accounted for in terms of the philosophical system of the *Ethics*, given that all entities within that system express the attribute of mind. There are therefore clear parallels with my question of how far a distinction between living and non-living things can be upheld within that system. I conclude that these interpretations are ultimately unsuccessful in identifying a metaphysical basis for distinguishing between entities which observably manifest consciousness and those which do not. I note that some of the difficulty in resolving this question arises from a focus on entities as individuals; in questioning whether living and non-living things are differentiated in Spinoza's philosophy, I propose to shift the focus of inquiry from the entities themselves to the effects which they bring about.

The main argument of the chapter then proceeds as follows. I show how varying repertoires of effects map onto everyday observable differences between living and non-living entities and among living entities themselves. I then expand on and clarify the concept of a difference in kind among effects, drawing a distinction between transitive effects which comprise bodily motions and the ideas of such motions, and transformative effects which bring about existential changes, including bringing new entities into being. I argue that transitive effects are common to all entities whereas transformative effects are specific to living entities. I then propose a Spinozistic grounding for this distinction, arguing that living entities bring about transformative effects insofar as their striving to persevere in being requires them to form inadequate ideas and put those ideas to use: this process underlies the observable characteristics by which we distinguish living from non-living things. Thus even though all entities are animate to some degree, as *E*2p13s stipulates, living things bring about a kind of effect which is distinctive in the terms of Spinoza's philosophical system and which is not available to non-living things. This difference underpins and gives warrant for the distinction we make between living and non-living things.

1 Differentiation and consciousness

One line of philosophical inquiry that is pressed by the apparent panpsychism of *E*2p13s is that of whether Spinoza has a theory of consciousness. Nadler (2008) argues that consciousness is effectively an emergent property within Spinoza's system, accompanying complexity of bodily composition. Individuals are conscious if their physical make-up and capacity for being affected attains a certain threshold, beyond which increasingly complex individuals have accordingly greater degrees of consciousness. Garrett (2008) reads Spinoza as articulating a philosophy of incremental naturalism: that the scale of consciousness is comprehensive, beginning at the most rudimentary state of existence and encompassing all entities, including artefacts and entities which are parts of other, larger entities. On this picture, human beings have a higher degree of consciousness than both internal entities such as their own pancreases and entities in the world around them such as plants, single-cell organisms, frying pans and so on. Building on Garrett's insight, Marshall (2014) has proposed that, for Spinoza, consciousness is affectivity: that it is the manifestation of an individual's capacity for experiencing fluctuations in its power in response to encounters with other individuals, which is itself related to the complexity of its bodily composition. The greater this capacity, the greater the degree of consciousness in the individual concerned.

None of these attempts to account for differences in the consciousness of individual modes is entirely successful on its own terms. Nadler's claim that consciousness is associated with a relevant degree of complexity trades on Spinoza's claim at *E*2p13s that individuals capable of being affected in many different ways are capable of a great many things. This does indeed suggest that complexity has a role to play in identifying differences among individuals. However, positing a threshold of complexity as a baseline for consciousness falls short of explaining why consciousness should emerge above it or which entities can be identified as having crossed it. Garrett's incremental naturalism captures the full force of *E*2p13s, but ultimately only re-states the puzzle of universal animation, attributing a hypothetical consciousness to all entities regardless of whether they manifest any suggestion of consciousness in their existence. Like

280 AFFECT AND EFFECT

Nadler, Garrett leaves unanswered the question of how the principle of universal animation in Spinoza's text relates to our everyday attributions of consciousness.

Marshall's appeal to affectivity hinges on the thought that, in Garrett's examples, a frying pan is capable of becoming hot, offering resistance to the food placed in it and so on, but is not capable of feeling fear at the prospect of being heated; a pancreas is capable of secreting hormones in response to relevant fluctuations in blood sugar or protein levels, but it is not capable of rejoicing in its ability to do so. This view has the merit of avoiding implausible attributions of quasi-anthropomorphized mental life to phenomenally inanimate things. However, it does so only by relying on the tacit assumption that if we, as human beings, do not recognize an individual's subjectivity then it has no subjectivity to be recognized. Although it is presumably true that frying pans and pancreases do not experience the same kinds of affective responses as humans, Spinoza does not give us textual warrant for inferring from this dissimilarity that they do not have affective responses of their own. Rather, the stipulation at E2p13s that all things are animated seems to block such an inference.

In response to those seeking a basis for consciousness in Spinoza's philosophy, Marrama (2017) argues that the interpretations cited above are grounded on an anachronistic grasp of what Spinoza means by consciousness. There are no textual grounds for assuming that, when Spinoza talks about consciousness, he has phenomenal consciousness in mind, or is trying to deal with the problem that preoccupies his commentators. Spinoza's own invocations of consciousness are concerned not with the question of which individuals are conscious, but rather with specific conceptions and misconceptions within human thought. Seeking criteria for consciousness in Spinoza's work is unlikely to be productive, since he simply is not working with a twenty-first century conception of the term.[2] According to Marrama, Spinoza himself regards all mental activity, whether conscious or not, as following of necessity from the relation between God and individual modes. In other words, if the stipulation at E2p13s that all things are animate conflicts with our everyday intuition that some individual things are conscious while others are not, then that demonstrates the inadequacy of our ordinary understanding of the world.

I concur with Marrama that Spinoza's own uses of the concept of consciousness are remote from problems about consciousness that dominate contemporary philosophy of mind. However, it does not seem to me that this consideration defuses the question of how the universal animation of E2p13s relates to what we observe in the world. Marrama concludes that it is at least consistent with Spinoza's philosophical constructions to conceive of each individual as 'endowed

---

[2] Balibar (2013) also argues that Spinoza's allusions to consciousness address fundamentally different concerns from those of philosophers in our own time.

with a corresponding mind and relevant consciousness of itself' (Marrama 2017, 523). But it is precisely the questions of what kinds of 'corresponding' minds individuals enjoy, what 'relevant' consciousness they possess, and how these features vary among individuals which are raised by Spinoza's postulation that all things are animate. As I suggested in the introduction to this chapter, it is unsatisfactory to respond that Spinoza is not concerned with distinctions among existent individual things. If his philosophical system has nothing to say about the everyday distinctions we draw between living and non-living things, it ignores a central feature of our human experience. Moreover, Maramma's strategy of simply accepting universal animation may perpetuate another form of anachronism. The stipulation at *E*2p13s, that all individuals are animate in different degrees, derives from Spinoza's own formulation of how mind and body are related and thus directly addresses a question of significant dispute between Scholastic Aristotelians and Cartesians. This should prompt us to further investigation of its role in Spinoza's philosophy.

In what follows, I set aside the question of consciousness in favour of the related but different question of how entities manifest their animation. In other words, rather than assuming *panpsychism* in Spinoza's philosophy, I aim to elucidate his *pananimation*. I consider that the term pananimation gives a more faithful and less theoretically loaded encapsulation of the principle articulated at *E*2p13s. One may say that, while *panpsychism* threatens to confer upon all things a mental life analogous to that with which we humans are familiar from our own experiences, a reading of *pananimation* leaves open the question of just what Spinoza's proposal of animation amounts to for any particular entity. I shall argue, even within Spinoza's commitment to pananimation, there are resources within his philosophy for identifying a genuine difference in kind between living things, or those entities which are observably animate, and non-living things, or those which are not.

I also depart from the interpretations outlined above by shifting the focus of inquiry from the composition of individual entities to their effects. By concentrating on the effects that one individual has on others, and the affections and ideas that are generated in the course of these interactions, I aim to show that Spinoza's philosophical system ultimately gives warrant for our everyday distinction between living and non-living things. Living things, I shall argue, are characterized by the fact that they bring about distinctive kinds of effects which differ fundamentally from the effects they share with non-living things. Furthermore, they are able to bring about these effects in virtue of their capacity for responding to their environment: in being affected by other modes and in forming inadequate ideas of them. Effects are therefore the key to differentiating living from non-living things in Spinoza's universally animated ontology; composition assists our understanding of that differentiation only insofar as it frames the variety and nature of relations available to things of each kind.

282   AFFECT AND EFFECT

2 Transitive and transformative effects

In this section I propose that the distinction between living and non-living things is underwritten in an everyday sense by the view that living things bring about effects of a distinctive kind, which are not brought about by non-living things. First, these effects involve processes of chemical transformation in both the entity bringing about the effect and other entities which it affects and by which it is affected. Second, they are integral to the continued existence of the entity bringing them about. I call these effects of living things *transformative* effects, in contrast to the *transitive* effects brought about by all entities.

According to Spinoza, every individual thing necessarily brings about effects:

> Whatever exists expresses the nature, or essence of God in a certain and determinate way (by P25C), that is, (by P34), whatever exists expresses in a certain and determinate way the power of God, which is the cause of all things. So (by P16), from everything which exists some effect must follow, q.e.d.   (*E*1p36d)

Appeals to these effects occur repeatedly in Parts 3 and 4 of the *Ethics*, where bringing about effects reveals individuals for what they are. We see this, for example, in Spinoza's definition of virtue:

> By virtue and power I understand the same thing, that is (by IIIP7) virtue, insofar as it is related to man, is the very essence, or nature, of man, insofar as he has the power of bringing about [efficiendi] certain things, which can be understood through the laws of his nature alone.   (*E*4d8)

While Spinoza cautions that an effect should not be conflated with the nature of the thing that produces it (*E*3p29), it is clear that effects follow from the things that cause them. While it may be difficult to discern the multiple causes of complex effects, each effect must of necessity have a determinate cause (*E*1p11d) and the causes of each effect must in principle be identifiable.

There is thus no doubt that modes can be differentiated and identified by their effects; but it remains to determine whether some effects are different in kind from others. On my account, the effects brought about by individual modes can be understood as falling into two kinds, the first common to all existent modes and the second confined to the modes we identify in everyday parlance as living things.

As a first step, we need to remind ourselves that all existent modes share in the attributes of both body and mind. In bodily terms they exclude other bodies from the spaces they occupy, displace some of the bodies they encounter, and so on. Nor are these effects confined to the attribute of extension: Spinoza's stipulation that 'the order and connection of ideas is the same as the order and connection of things' (*E2p7*) entails that, *ex hypothesi*, these effects are also realized under the attribute of thought, in the ideas of modes' bodies and bodily encounters. Clearly there is observable variation among modes in their capacities for bringing about these effects, depending on their hardness and softness, size, robustness of composition, and so forth. But these effects can all be glossed as those of motion, rest, inertia, momentum, resistance, in other words, the common effects of bodies. We may say that all modes are capable of bringing about effects on other modes, and of being affected by them, in the communication of bodily motion and rest. I call these *transitive* effects.

So far as concerns communication of bodily motion and rest, therefore, all modes are on an equal footing under Spinoza's pananimation. But this does not count out the possibility of there being effects which go beyond the crudely mechanistic. A motivation for the everyday distinction between living and non-living things is just that which the Aristotelians explained through *psuchē*: that living things do things that non-living things do not, such as breathing, feeding, reproducing and so forth. One challenge for the mechanistic hypothesis is the part played by such processes in the continued existence of the entities in question; another is the changes which living things bring about in their environment. The mechanics required to take in and expel air may be the same for an animal as for an air pump, but there the similarity ends: the animal extracts oxygen from the air and absorbs it into its bloodstream, where the oxygen is used to fuel digestion, movement, growth, and so forth, and the air it expels has a different composition from that which it took in. This is not a matter of the difference between natural things and artefacts. A plant and a crystal may both be perceived as growing, that is as having transitive effects of taking up more space and potentially displacing other entities from that space. In each case, growth requires incorporating other entities by which they are affected into their own being. In the case of the crystal, the entities so incorporated are entities sufficiently similar to it as to be capable of accretion to the surface of the crystal, resulting in expansion of its volume and spatial dimensions. In the case of the plant, by contrast, markedly dissimilar entities such as minerals from the soil must be not only incorporated by the plant but also converted into food, which then makes it possible for the plant to grow through the formation of new cells. Unlike the air pump and the crystal, the animal and the plant must bring about real changes in other entities and in themselves in order to have the distinctive effects they do.

Surface similarities in the effects of living and non-living things, therefore, belie the processes by which those effects come about. On the one hand, both living and non-living things can properly be said to manifest the transitive effects of bodies in motion; and at least some of these effects result from their being affected by other entities. However, living things also seem to bring about a different class of effects, involving engagement with the entities by which they are affected so as to reconfigure them and put them to use. In the rest of the chapter I identify these

284 AFFECT AND EFFECT

real changes as *transformative* effects, and I argue that they provide a basis for differentiating between living and non-living things within Spinoza's philosophical system. In the next section I shall explain how we may understand the transformative effects of living things in Spinozist terms. I argue that transformative effects are necessary to the persisting in being of the entity which brings them about and are inextricable from the web of relations between that entity and others. Thus, they are effects both of a mode's actions and of its capacity for being affected by other modes.

3 Effects, affections, and partial causes

In this section I argue that living things bring about the transformative effects they do by acting in specific and distinctive ways. First, I show that, in order to bring about transformative effects, a mode must be affected by other modes; as such, any mode is only ever a partial cause of its transformative effects. I move on to argue that, nonetheless, transformative effects may be properly attributed to a particular mode on the basis that they are brought about by its particular actions. I support this argument by drawing a contrast with transitive effects, which do not require explanation in terms of the actions or nature of any particular mode.

I have proposed that living things bring about transformative effects in themselves and in other entities, and that in order to do so they must interact with other entities. In response to the presence of other relevant entities a living thing may have effects which result in changes internal to it, external to it, or (usually) both. The everyday distinction between living and non-living things in nature picks out the fact that such processes of interaction are essential to the continued existence of a living thing and not to a non-living thing. In the example in Section 2 the plant which does not take on nutrients and go through the processes of respiration will not merely fail to grow, it will die, that is, cease to be a plant, whereas the crystal which does not accrete further similar molecules will remain just as much a crystal. In the terms of Spinoza's philosophy, all modes are necessarily affected by other modes; modes which are living things, however, depend on being affected by other modes in order to persist in their being.

This means that a mode which is a living thing continues in existence only in virtue of its encounters with other modes: its striving to persevere in being is essentially relational, requiring both that it be affected in specific ways by specific modes and that it responds to being affected in ways which produce the internal effects which it requires to maintain its life and which also produce external effects on other modes. One consequence of the mode needing to be in the right relations with other modes is that the effects it has, both internal and external to it, are effects which it can bring about only in conjunction with other modes.

A worry that one may have at this point is how far such shared effects can translate into any individual mode bringing about an effect. In order to defuse this worry, we may consider some complex effect which is brought about by many modes together, but which could not be brought about by any one of them singly. It seems uncontentious to say in everyday terms that the cause of such a complex effect is the conjunction of the modes involved in bringing it about, and that in the absence of any of these modes, that very effect would not have been brought about. But in Spinozistic terms, such a complex effect cannot be clearly and distinctly understood through the nature of any one of the individual modes involved in bringing it about. A mode which contributes to bringing about a complex effect is only a partial cause of it.

There is no problem in principle in attributing a complex effect to a mode which is only a partial cause of it. Observable effects typically have multiple causes; even if some such causes are attributable to a single mode, most will not be. Applied literally, without regard to the complexity of an effect, a requirement that an effect be understood through a single mode would render much of the world causally inexplicable. But there is no conflict with Spinoza's metaphysical system in saying that a complex effect may comprise effects brought about by many modes; rather, there is an epistemological demand to understand observable phenomena by identifying the constituent effects and causes necessary to produce them. Then a mode without which the complex effect would not have come about may properly be regarded as bringing about that complex effect, albeit as a partial cause of it.

This raises a further question of whether it is possible to differentiate among the ways in which modes are partial causes of some complex effect so as to attribute the effect to a particular mode or modes. In the case of a transformative effect such as photosynthesis, for example, the fact that there are multiple necessary conditions for the process to come about might lead us to say that the carbon dioxide molecules which are converted to oxygen in the process are just as much the causes of photosynthesis as the plant. Identifying partial causes with the complex effects to which they contribute, therefore, will not be sufficient to ground a distinction between living and non-living things. My stronger claim is that in a transformative effect some mode or modes *act* in bringing it about, whereas other modes are partial causes of it only by virtue of being affected. I argue that acting in bringing about transformative effects is a characteristic of living things and not of non-living things.

In order to establish this point, it is useful to revisit what Spinoza says about effects and acting. In the final proposition of Part 1 of the *Ethics*, he concludes:

Nothing exists from whose nature some effect does not follow.   (*E*1p36)

We saw earlier in this section that the existence of living things is intrinsically relational, such that they can only ever be partial causes of effects. But E1p36 requires that if a mode exists, then there is some effect which follows from its nature. Since there is no existent mode which is the adequate cause of any of its complex effects, this supports the contention that being a partial cause does not exclude a mode from being considered as the cause of some effect. It can still be considered as bringing about some effect. In Part 3 of the *Ethics* Spinoza explicates the concept of an effect in terms of an individual's acting or being acted upon:

> I say that we act when something happens, in us or outside us, that is…when something in us or outside us follows from our nature, which can be clearly and distinctly understood through it alone. On the other hand, I say that we are acted on when something happens in us, or something follows from our nature, of which we are only a partial cause. (*E3d2*)

If this definition were taken to suggest that there is a binary distinction between acting and being acted upon,[3] it might seem to threaten my claim that some modes act in being partial causes, since being a partial cause involves being acted upon. But the complexities involved in being a composite individual (*E2pp13–14*) mean that a mode which is an observable thing in the world constantly undergoes things and acts in its encounters with other modes. Further, at *E2p14* Spinoza draws an explicit connection between a mode's capacities for being affected on the one hand and perceiving and forming ideas on the other. A binary reading would also be in tension with *E3p1*, where Spinoza characterizes the mind as both acting and being acted upon. Rather than positing a dichotomy between mutually exclusive states, Spinoza's text suggests that acting and being acted upon are interdependent and reciprocal states of being.

Here I argue that the causes of transformative effects involve multiple modes and that only some of those modes *act* in bringing about the effects in question. I propose that acting in bringing about transformative effects is a defining feature of living things which is not shared by non-living things. We have seen in the case of living things that their persistence in being relies on their interdependence with other entities and that interactions between a living thing and other entities result in transformative effects both within the living thing itself and beyond it. In these interactions, however, different modes play different parts. A living thing is affected by other entities which comprise aspects of its environment: For example, a plant is affected by aspects of its environment such as sunlight, water, oxygen, and soil, and in the course of its striving to persevere in being it must go through various biological processes such as respiration, nutrition, and photosynthesis.

---

[3] Bennett (1984); Kisner (2013); LeBuffe (2010)) seems tacitly or explicitly to presume such a binary distinction.

The plant and the features of its environment are all partial causes of those processes and their outcomes. However, I argue that in the terms of Spinoza's system those processes could not come about without the plant's distinctive contribution: the plant must *act* to form ideas of its environmental features which organizes those features in a particular way. For example, the plant is affected by different kinds of bodies comprising soil; it acts to form ideas of those affections and acts further to form the ideas and corresponding bodily changes by which, say, minerals are absorbed into its body and converted into food and ultimately new cells. This process is not an automatic outcome of any instance when the relevant modes and conditions are present; rather, it is dependent on the receptivity and response of the plant. The plant's acting is therefore integral to bringing about the transformative effects of its biological processes, even though those processes also involve other entities.

We can contrast this picture of the plant's acting to produce effects which are necessary to its persevering in being with the case of transitive effects. I have said that transitive effects are the common effects of bodies in motion, brought about when entities encounter each other, and that all modes have such effects in common. Like transformative effects, transitive effects always involve a mode's being affected by other modes (E2p13sL3). Unlike transformative effects, transitive effects are universal to all modes: they are brought about in virtue of the common properties of bodies, rather than arising from the contribution of any individual mode (E2p13sL2; E2p37). For example, the crystal grows in the situation where it comes into contact with entities of the same ratio of motion and rest: sharing that ratio in common, they cohere automatically (E2p13sL5). This effect can be understood simply in terms of bodies in motion, without the need for further explanation.[4]

Transformative effects, then, are a class of effects that require one or more of the modes of which are their partial causes to act in bringing them about. I suggest that acting in bringing about transformative effects is the distinctive feature of living things within Spinoza's system: non-living things involved in bringing about transformative effects are affected, rather than acting.[5] We can therefore say that a transformative effect in which a living thing acts is properly attributable to that living thing, even though it is only a partial cause of the effect. Thus, living things can be differentiated from non-living things in the terms of Spinoza's philosophical system in being those modes which act as causes of transformative effects.

---

[4] This not to deny that transitive effects are often accompanied by transformative effects—indeed, where living things undergo transitive effects perhaps this is always the case—but their coexistence does not mean they cannot be distinguished.

[5] It is also true that a living thing may be involved as a partial cause in a transformative effect in which it is affected but does not act, like a plant being eaten by a goose, but that does not negate the point that it previously brought about transformative effects of its own.

288 AFFECT AND EFFECT

4 Transformative effects, acting and inadequate ideas

I have argued that there are resources in Spinoza's philosophy to warrant our everyday distinction between living things and non-living things: living things act in being the partial causes of transformative effects, whereas non-living things do not. Thus, a transformative effect can be properly attributed to a living thing having brought it about, rather than being merely a fortuitous conjunction of circumstances. Being such a partial causes involves a mode not only acting on other modes but also being affected by them. My reading of Spinoza has some implications which are perhaps counter-intuitive to Spinoza scholars. Here I show that these novel interpretive claims can be upheld within Spinoza's philosophical system.

First, I have argued that we can attribute transformative effects to living things even where other entities are required for the effect to come about. Attributing an effect in this way to a mode which is a partial cause raises the question of whether that mode is also somehow an adequate cause of the effect. A cause of some effect is adequate if that effect can be clearly and distinctly perceived through that cause (*E*3d1), and is explicitly contrasted with a partial or inadequate cause. Spinoza elaborates this point in terms of acting and undergoing things: a mode is said to act if it is an adequate cause of some effect, such that the effect can be clearly and distinctly understood through that mode alone (*E*3d2). I have argued that modes bring about transformative effects only in virtue of being affected by other modes, but that nonetheless a transformative effect may properly be attributed to a mode which acts in bringing about that effect. I suggest further that this should also prompt us to say that the mode which acts in bringing about a transformative effect is an adequate cause of that effect.

My interpretation hinges on what it means to say that an effect is understood through some particular mode *alone*. I suggest it is incoherent to take this condition as a requirement for the mode's independence of action. In Spinoza's metaphysics only God can be an adequate cause in the sense of acting without being affected; if modes act at all, they do so from within a system of irreducible interdependence, in the context of their encounters with other modes. Rather, I argue that the criterion for being an adequate cause has the force of a counter-factual condition: without that very mode, the effect would not come about. In the previous section, I said that the plant's acting is integral to producing the transformational effects of its biological processes, even though other modes are involved in those effects and are necessary to them. In this sense, the plant's transformational effects follow from its nature and may be clearly and distinctly understood through it alone: in the case where the plant did not act, the effects would not come about. The fact that the plant needs to be affected by other modes in order for it to bring about transformational effects is no obstacle to perceiving it as an adequate cause of them.[6]

My second novel interpretive claim is that when a mode acts to bring about a transformative effect, it is acting in virtue of its inadequate ideas. This is not simply a question of the effect requiring interaction with another mode, since this this is the case for all effects within Spinoza's system. In the case of a transitive effect, the effect of one mode encountering another is determined by the different ratios of motion and rest in the composition of each of the entities involved (E2p13sL3)—that is, by the constitutive adequate ideas common to each mode. In the case of transformative effects, by contrast, a mode responds to encountering another mode by forming its own inadequate ideas of the encounter and the other entity. In forming those inadequate ideas of the encounter the mode both undergoes affections and acts; when it acts, the effects of its acting are the effects of the inadequate ideas it forms. For example, a plant's use of sunlight in photosynthesis requires it to be receptive and responsive to the sunlight *in a particular way*. The light meets the plant; the plant is affected by the light and forms an idea of it. This idea of the sunlight is inadequate: it is sunlight only as the plant perceives it, as a useful feature of its environment. Responding to sunlight by bringing about the effects of photosynthesis depends on the plant's making use of its *inadequate* idea of sunlight as apt for photosynthesis.

Thus, a living thing has just the transformative effects that it does, not through some hypothesized adequate idea constituting its essence or autonomous capability, but through its *inadequate* ideas of its environment and the other entities it encounters. While the transitive effects of encounters among modes merely instantiate the adequate ideas common to bodies, transformative effects may be understood as outcomes of processes through which entities act to form and make creative use of their inadequate ideas.

Transformative effects, then, are not merely those which involve both adequate and inadequate ideas: rather, a living thing's transformative effects rely on the success of its acting to form those inadequate ideas which are required in order for it to persevere in being. Further, the effects in question go beyond its own development, to alter how things stand in the wider world: in the process of photosynthesis, for example, the plant both creates carbohydrate molecules for its own growth and releases oxygen, which enables other living things to persevere in being. So my argument that modes act in virtue of their inadequate ideas cannot be deflected by objecting that the living thing *qua* mode acts only in its own development, of which it is *ex hypothesi* an adequate cause in virtue of its essence, while its external effects are mere accidents. This objection merely

---

[6] The more pressing worry is that perceiving the plant as an adequate cause of its trasformational effects may present an epistemic hazard in the form of a disincentive to improving the adequacy of one's *understanding* by investigating the complexity of how it brings those effects about.

290 AFFECT AND EFFECT

presses the question of how to determine which effects are required for the mode's development.

Further, the fact that numerous entities may be similarly constituted, with correspondingly similar capacities for being affected and similar repertoires of effect does not undermine the thought that the effects brought about by each particular entity are particular to it and attributable to its acting on its inadequate ideas. Rather, apparent similarities in the effects of phenomenally separate entities should be taken as an indication that we are perceiving something in common among them (*E*2p39d) and so act as an epistemic prompt to investigate those effects further, in pursuit of an improved understanding of their similarities to and differences from other effects and of their causes.

5 Transformative effects and pananimation

I have argued that living things bring about transformative effects which are not shared by non-living things and that these can be identified in Spinoza's system as effects brought about by certain modes acting in virtue of the inadequate ideas they form in being affected by other modes. I have further argued that there is no barrier to viewing a mode which is a partial cause of some effect as also being that effect's adequate cause, provided that the effect requires that mode to act in bringing it about. To summarize: the distinctive effects which are characteristic of living things are bound up with their particular capacities for being affected in encounters with other entities, on the one hand, and with their acting to form inadequate ideas of those entities, on the other. The effects of a living thing's inadequate ideas are fundamental both to its striving to persevere in being and, in their impact on its environment, to its relations with other modes. That living things have the transformative effects they do therefore relies on their forming inadequate ideas: rather than being some kind of defect which might ideally be overcome, inadequate ideas are an essential aspect of their existing and acting as those living, changing things.

On my interpretation, Spinoza's philosophy does indeed provide a systematic grounding of our everyday differentiation between living and non-living things, without either appealing to a special metaphysical concept such as *psuchē* or denying our intuitions by casting living things as mere automata. Rather, focusing on the varying repertoires of effects observed among entities shows that some such variations represent not only differences in degree but differences in kind, such as the distinction between modes which act in consequence of forming inadequate ideas and those which do not. This may seem to have the paradoxical result that the pananimation thesis drops out of the explanatory picture altogether. However, this is not the case: the pananimation thesis is a summary of Spinoza's arguments at the opening of Part 2 of the *Ethics*, especially *E*2p10–p13, and those arguments establish the basis for modes being able to act *at all*. So a mode's being able to act in virtue of its inadequate ideas derives from the considerations which underpin the pananimation thesis.

I cannot claim that my reading of Spinoza makes his pananimation any less strange. On pananimation, *every* mode is animate, not only the living things which bring about transformative effects. My reading argues that Spinoza's philosophy has the resources to account for an everyday distinction between living and non-living things *despite* pananimation: in other words, that this is an instance where we can find warrant in Spinoza's system for upholding a perceived difference among the entities which comprise our environment. What we are to make of the animation of non-living things, whether occurring naturally or created as artefact, remains a matter for further inquiry.

15

Vitalism and the Metaphysics of Life
the Discreet Charm of Eighteenth-Century Vitalism

Charles T. Wolfe

1 Introduction

Vitalism is a slippery beast, a contested discursive and doctrinal terrain, perhaps a 'family resemblance' word. To some, particularly in the Anglophone humanities world, vitalism is a doctrine which invokes 'unfathomable life' as 'raw, unverbalized, lived experience' capable of resisting 'the petrification of social forms and personalities...sedimented categories and schema' (Jones 2010, 4). Vitalism is also applied, to name some diverse examples, to Aristotle's *anima*, Hume's account of ideas, the vitality of crowds in movement (Elias Canetti), the apparently animistic power of the electricity grid, food, or trash (Jane Bennett), not to mention confusions with panpsychism or even a closer cousin, vital materialism.[1]

To scholars of early modern philosophy, again particularly in the English-speaking world, vitalism is often taken to be a theory of living matter, or at least, of dynamic, self-organizing matter, and the word is then sometimes loosely used by scholars to refer to the presence of 'mind', rather than 'life' in matter. That is, 'vitalism' is often used to describe the view that matter possesses properties associated with 'minds'; that view, 'panpsychism', has relatively little to do with claims about life, organisms, living bodies, and how any or all of these differ from 'dead' or 'inanimate' matter.

---

[1] This is not a chapter on the (infinite?) catalogue of possible misuses of the term 'vitalism', although it would be an interesting task and would yield some challenging results—what do Aristotle, Harvey, Cavendish, Spinoza, Locke, Leibniz, Hume, Smith, Bergson, Hans Driesch, and Jane Bennett (on her animistic-vitalism of trash see Coole and Frost 2010, 9) have in common? (Granted, I allowed for the possibility of vitalism being a 'family resemblance' term, but that would be a very extended family...). Besides the claims about Aristotle as a vitalist to which I return below, Kawamura mistakenly describes Spinoza's *natura naturans* as 'vitalist' (Kawamura 2014, 216n.); Henry, in an otherwise admirable paper, strangely refers to Leibniz as a vitalist (Henry 1987, 16); Cunningham 2007 draws passing attention to the possible connection between Hume's thought and Montpellier vitalism—but 'vitalism' in Cunningham seems to mean 'a doctrine concerned with the activity of the mind' (more specifically its liveliness): I think 'vivacity' is metaphorically overplayed if it is made into 'vitalism'. I detail other cases, particularly the odd reading of Adam Smith as a vitalist, in Wolfe 2018.

Charles T. Wolfe, *Vitalism and the Metaphysics of Life: the Discreet Charm of Eighteenth-Century Vitalism* In: *Life and Death in Early Modern Philosophy.* Edited by: Susan James, Oxford University Press. © Charles T. Wolfe 2021. DOI: 10.1093/oso/9780192843616.003.0016

An example of this tendency to label as 'vitalist' any early modern philosophical project which is anti-mechanist and asserts some form of animation in matter occurs in the editor's preface to the most recent edition of Henry More's treatise on the immortality of the soul. The editor speaks of the significance of More's 'vitalist philosophy'.[2] Another example is to be found in recent commentary on Cavendish, in which she is referred to as a vitalist but also, sometimes in the same sentence, as a materialist.[3] The passages cited in support of this description are of this sort: 'why should it not be as probable, that God did give matter a self-moving power to her self, as to have made another creature to govern her? For nature is not a babe, or child, to need such a spiritual nurse, to teach her to go, or to move ...' (Cavendish 1664, 2.6). The term 'vitalism' is used here to describe the view that Nature has a self-moving power. Granted, Cavendish also speaks the language of a materialist (stating, e.g., that 'The first cause is matter, the Second is Motion, The third is figure which produceth all natural effects,' and describing the soul as material—albeit 'material self-moving substance'). Yet, in support of the 'vitalist' label she currently bears, she also holds that 'pressure and reaction does not make perception' and precisely adds later in this text (the *Philosophical Letters*) that Nature possesses a self-moving power, and that 'there is no part of Nature that hath not life and knowledge'.[4]

My first critical point regarding terminology, but not just terminology, is that this use of 'vitalism' is not only confusing, but sometimes downright inexact, because it conflates two distinct conceptions of vitalism. We can see these conceptions at work in the above interpretations of Cavendish. Her vitalism is said to lie in her metaphysics of self-organizing matter and in her vision of 'minded' matter (panpsychism). Neither of these commitments significantly involves a notion of 'Life' or bears on problems such as its definition, its importance, or what it is not.

Collapsing 'mind' and 'life' as sources of the self-organizing powers in matter creates a considerable conceptual morass. Specific claims about the nature of organic life and the difference between living and non-living beings (two 'planks' of vitalism, as it were) should not be confused with panpsychism. For the panpsychist, the universe is 'more like a great thought than like a great machine,' as the eminent British physicist James Jeans once put it in 1930. As he went on to

---

[2] A. Jacobs, Preface to More 1659/1987, n.p.

[3] As in the title of Wilkins 2016, or a chapter in Boyle 2018. For further discussion of these cases and the pros and cons of using 'vitalism' there, see Wolfe 2020.

[4] 'The Text to my Natural Sermon,' in Cavendish 1655, A4r; Cavendish 1666/2001, 221; cf. 137; Cavendish 1664, 1.iv, 18; ibid., I.xxx, 98, 99. In chapter 3 of her 2018 study, D. Boyle repeatedly uses the term 'vitalist materialism' to describe Cavendish without ever defining it (to be clear, I learned a lot from Boyle's work, especially her brilliant 'deflationary' touch as regards Cavendish's philosophy of nature and account of gender, which is not reflected in the present essay as it does not deal with Cavendish per se). In his *True Intellectual System of the Universe* (1678), Ralph Cudworth denounced hylozoism for giving life and perception to matter, and thus being atheistic (Cudworth 1678, I.iii, 105; I. iv, 667); it has been argued that his target was Cavendish (cf. James 1999, 229–230).

add, 'Mind no longer appears as an accidental intruder into the realm of matter; we are beginning to suspect that we ought rather to hail it as a creator and governor of the realm of matter' (Jeans 1930, 137). But many accounts of the differences between living and non-living things do not rely on a panpsychist outlook. Granted, one cannot police the usage of terms, and 'life', 'vital', and 'vitalism' could be said to imply a notion of 'mind' or 'consciousness'. But I now want to argue for the historical and conceptual benefits of keeping them apart.

In a useful paper on vitalism and chemistry in the early modern period, Kevin Chang suggests a distinction that helps clarify the terrain we are dealing with. He distinguishes two kinds of vitalist theories: cosmic vitalism and immanent vitalism. What he calls 'cosmic vitalism' aligns with the broad usage I have been pointing to thus far. It tends to blur the divide between 'life' and 'mind' in its presentation of the universe in general as alive, sentient, or conscious. As we have seen, this vision of the universe as a 'living animal' clearly has a place in early modern philosophy. It is exemplified, for instance, in Diderot's description of something like a continuum of sensation in living nature: 'from the elephant to the aphid, from the aphid to the sensing, living molecule, there is not a single point in all of nature that is not experiencing suffering or pleasure',[5] which is tantamount to saying that the universe is alive in its entirety. 'Immanent' vitalism, in Chang's sense, is a more restrictive view, as it applies to the living body rather than to the universe as a whole. Differently put, immanent vitalists, who are distinctly 'modern' in the sense that their characteristic concerns begin to be visible in the post-Cartesian context, notably in figures such as the Halle professor of medicine Georg-Ernst Stahl (1659–1734), are concerned with what makes a living thing, living (versus matter as a whole, or dead matter, or machines, etc.). They are not concerned with defending a view in which literally *everything* is alive.

Indeed, it seems to me that we need to distinguish the vision of matter as self-moving (or perceiving, or suffering, or experiencing pleasure)—i.e. the vision of an animated universe—from more restrictive (and often, medically based or located) claims about the vitality of the living body; in that sense, I take the 'vital' in 'vitalism' to have a strong and perhaps necessary relationship to 'life science'. I think it would be preferable to restrict the term 'vitalist' to claims of the latter kind. But rather than merely insisting that the former, cosmic doctrines cannot be termed 'vitalist', because this term should be reserved for certain interpretations of organic, embodied life, it may prove useful to start with some initial distinctions. Building on these, I shall reflect on the specifically 'organic life'-centred species of vitalism. Closer examination reveals that it is less strictly (or univocally) immanent than Chang's distinction might have it. Notably because

---

[5] *Le Rêve de D'Alembert*, in Diderot 1975–, vol. XVII, 140.

it proves difficult to extricate even the most naturalistic, non-ensouled vitalism from metaphysics *überall*.

2 Cosmic and immanent vitalisms

The ancient sense of cosmic vitalism that is later reworked and reconfigured as panpsychism harks back to Plato's world-soul and the Stoic *pneuma*, and was influentially revived by Ficino in the Renaissance. According to this view, a 'universal spirit' permeates and enlivens 'all things in the geocosmos' (Chang 2011, 324). As we have seen, forms of cosmic vitalism persist into the early modern period. In contrast, forms of immanent vitalism 'presumed a principle of life that was intrinsic to matter,' and 'was very often visualized as a "seed" implanted in the basic unit of the living substance' (ibid.). A well-known instance of this type of view, though one that Chang does not discuss, is Gassendi's Lucretian idea of *semina rerum*.[6] We might see 'immanent vitalism' as a background condition for the specifically embodied or organic vitalism studied within the medical tradition that I shall be concerned with here. Indeed, Chang points to Stahl as an example of an immanent vitalist. Stahl is commonly referred to as an 'animist', as someone whose theory of life and matter 'drew a boundary between the heavens and the earth and between lifeless matter and the living being' (Chang 2011, 328). In his work, the scope of vitalism shifts from the 'geocosmos' to the more restricted arena of organic life.

According to Chang, the conceptual distinction between cosmic and immanent vitalism aligns with a historical shift: 'After Stahl, vitalists never reclaimed the inorganic world as their territory. The vital principle was forever localized in the organism and vitalism confined to the life sciences' (ibid.). Of course, even with this narrower focus, usage can be still be loose, as when people call William Harvey, or later, the eighteenth-century British physician John Hunter, vitalists for holding that 'the blood is life'. Harvey, echoing Leviticus 17.10–14 ('For the life of the flesh is in the blood'), writes 'vita igitur in sanguine consistit' (in the translation of the period, life 'consists in the blood ... because in it the Life and Soule do first dawn, and last set'). William Hunter states that 'the blood has life', 'the blood is endowed with life' and suggests that if people find this idea difficult, it is because 'the mind [is] not accustomed to the idea of a living fluid'.[7] But it is not enough to hold that the blood is life, to be meaningfully termed a vitalist.

---

[6] On atoms, seeds, and *semina rerum* in Gassendi's thought, see LoLordo 2007, 186f.; on the impact of *semina rerum* on early modern matter theory, see Hirai 2005. The question of why notions of vital minima are still present in Stahl and beyond, and how they relate to an immanent vitalism, awaits further study.

[7] Harvey 1651, ex. LI, 303; Hunter 1794/1828, 97.

296 VITALISM AND THE METAPHYSICS OF LIFE

I will say more below about how my distinctions both overlap with, complement, and at times call into question Chang's distinction between cosmic and
immanent vitalism. Briefly put, I accept (and expand on) the concept of an
immanent vitalism, which ultimately becomes a doctrine, or set of possible
doctrines, *located within or in relation to advances in the life sciences*, rather
than a cosmology or a metaphysics of universally living matter. I also agree with
his claim that there is a historical movement from one to the other. But, as I shall
argue, elements of cosmic vitalism are harder to shake off than he allows,
inasmuch as it is harder for vitalism to dispense with metaphysics than it
might seem.

I have suggested that we focus on what Chang calls immanent vitalism and
limit talk of vitalism to talk of living things. But if immanent vitalism arises at a
particular historical period, as Chang proposes, what is its source? Building on
Chang's suggestion on how to localize and define it, I propose that the notion of
immanent vitalism is first and foremost, medical. In the history of medicine and
attendant sciences, 'vitalism' is not just any claim about life or what is alive; rather,
it designates a theory or theories focusing on the (genuinely or seemingly)
irreducible properties of an organism as a whole. This group of theories is opposed
to the mechanist or iatromechanist family of theories, which treat the organism as
a machine. But in locating this kind of vitalism historically, there is a tendency
among historians to oversimplify the context in which it arose. What is often
presented as a straightforward opposition between vitalism and mechanism
should really be seen as a 'triangulation' between these two positions, and a
third, 'animism', which explains the functioning of the organism in terms of
the soul.

Animism, as an early modern medical doctrine, is most commonly associated
with Stahl and his followers.[8] For Stahl, 'it is the soul that is directly responsible for

---

[8] E.g. François Boissier de Sauvages in Montpellier (Martin 1990), although some eighteenth-
century authors (e.g. Barthez 1806, 72) trace the doctrine back to Aristotelian influences in Telesio,
Scaliger, and Sennert. On the influence of Scaliger and Aristotle himself on Stahl, see De Ceglia 2006,
esp. 266–268. This should not lead us to retroactively term Aristotle a vitalist, as some otherwise careful
scholars once did: the eminent historian of Renaissance medicine W. Pagel spoke of 'Aristotle's
conception of the vital principle, the Anima' (Pagel 1944, 147; see also Pagel 1953), perhaps inspiring
the equally prominent historian of early modern medicine M. Grmek to state that 'Aristotle carries out
a vitalist project' (Grmek 1990, 117). That said, in her recent study of Aristotle on generation (Connell
2016), S. Connell has a much more careful way of describing Aristotle as a vitalist: 'soul and form are
causally efficacious and can be immaterial, and thus Aristotle turns out, in this context at least, to be a
vitalist' (Connell 2016, 197). For Connell, differently to much of the emphasis in my analysis, vitalism
means positing 'a fundamental ontological distinction between matter and life', entailing that Aristotle
is a vitalist on her reading, since for him, 'matter is not able to be alive without the presence of soul,
which is the source of life and is irreducible to matter' (218). Part of the intention of the present essay is
to show that the vitalism of a Cavendish (and to some extent, Aristotle *sensu* Connell) should not be
equated with other forms of vitalism, and that the latter forms are neither especially focused on 'soul'
nor especially opposed to materialism, nor necessarily metaphysical (cf. Connell 2016, 233, n. 154:
'Vitalism is a metaphysical rather than a scientific hypothesis since it is unfalsifiable'—something that
Georges Canguilhem would have perhaps endorsed, but also debated: cf. Etxeberria and Wolfe 2018).

corporeal structures'.[9] Stahl explicitly writes in his criticisms of Leibniz, in the 1720 collection known as the *Negotium otiosum*, that he 'protests against' statements which 'absolutely exclude the soul from assuming any power, in any manner or respect, at any place, on vital motions... [T]he appetites of the soul are the authors of vital motions.' In fact, 'it is the soul that makes the lungs breathe, the heart beat, the blood circulate, the stomach digest, the liver secrete'.[10]

As we shall see below, anti-vitalist historiography (notably in the history of medicine, though also as it is subsequently picked up in the history of philosophy) tends to collapse the distinction between animism and vitalism to form a single 'supernaturalist' vitalism, in which an entity such as the soul, or a force such as the vital force, is presented as both explanatory of living processes and somehow 'above' them. To critics of such a view, distinctions such as that between cosmic and immanent vitalism, or between immanent vitalism and animism do not affect its supernaturalism and therefore tend to be ignored. However, soul-based explanations and vitalist explanations should not be treated as interchangeable, whether in terms of their theoretical framework, or in terms of how they were viewed. It is important to bear the triangulation between animism, mechanism, and immanent vitalism in mind when seeking to understand vitalism in its historical context, because Stahlian animism was by no means viewed as interchangeable or even fully compatible with vitalism, by the Montpellier vitalists whom I discuss below. In that sense, Chang's category of 'immanent vitalism' is still too broad, as it encompasses all versions of the view that living organisms are immanently alive, including those that hold that the source of this life, or perhaps the *differentia specifica* that makes such entities alive, is the soul. If immanent vitalism itself is caught in a variety of contexts, oppositions, and potential misdefinitions, and anti-vitalist historiography has a biased view of the situation (insofar as it aligns vitalism with supernaturalism), how should we obtain a clear picture of what vitalism was? Two complementary approaches offer themselves: to restrict ourselves to historical uses of the term, or to ground a careful (if stipulative) definition on these uses. Adopting the latter approach, I next turn to one of the first recorded uses of the term 'vitalism', which indeed is set in the context of the tripartite distinction discussed above.

3 Vitalism contra animism

In what is usually presented as the earliest occurrence of the term, Charles-Louis Dumas (1765–1813), Professor, then Director of the 'École de Santé' at

---

[9] Duchesneau and Smith, 'Introduction,' in Duchesneau and Smith 2016, xvii.

[10] Stahl, Enodation XX, in Duchesneau and Smith 2016, 149; Stahl 1706, §§ 81 and 98 (here, § 98, in Stahl 1859–1864, vol. 2, 347).

298 VITALISM AND THE METAPHYSICS OF LIFE

Montpellier from 1794 on (and Dean of the Montpellier Faculty of Medicine from 1807 onwards),[11] wrote that 'vitalism' was the doctrine of their faculty, and that it should not be confused either with 'spiritualism' (by which he meant animism) or 'materialism'. Materialists explain living phenomena in excessively 'physical' terms, while spiritualists (that is, Stahl and his followers) do so in excessively 'metaphysical' terms (Dumas writes that spiritualists 'relied excessively on the metaphysical sciences', while materialists relied excessively on the 'physical sciences').[12] What about vitalists? Vitalists are

> Physiologists . . . who do not relate all the phenomena of life to matter or the soul, but to an intermediate principle which possesses properties [*facultés*] different from the one and the other, and which regulates, disposes and orders all acts of vitality, without being impelled by the physical impulses of the material body or the moral affections and intellectual foresight of the thinking principle.[13]

Dumas' definition helps avoid confusion between animism (soul-based explanations) and vitalism, and additionally indicates, again contrary to a lot of subsequent scholarship, that the post-Cartesian choice is not just between 'soul' and 'matter'—in a sense that this is the very *raison d'être* of an intelligent vitalism, which is neither a Cavendish-style animate matter theory, nor a Stahlian animism.

At this point we begin to have a sense of vitalism that is both historically robust and analytically helpful. When I referred above to the need to take historical uses of the term seriously, *while also* seeking to articulate a careful (if stipulative) definition based on these uses, I meant something like this: a robust definition of vitalism should start with the criterion of opposition between living and nonliving entities. That is, if we speak of vitalism it must be to refer to cases in which the thinker in question (theorist, scientist, physician, natural philosopher, etc.) is actively concerned with this opposition. This basic criterion of vitalism applies, whether the vitalist handles the distinction as somehow contingent and a matter of empirical investigation, or 'ontologizes' it as a substantial distinction. The first option is exemplified by Claude Bernard's notion of *milieu intérieur* (which he

---

[11] Dumas received his medical degree in Montpellier in 1785, then undertook further studies in Paris. After nearly being appointed to a chair in Paris, he was a professor in the new 'École de Santé' (chair in anatomy and physiology), then its director. He became Dean of the Medical Faculty (and Professor Clinical Medicine) in 1807, Rector of the Académie de Montpellier (1808–1813), and Councilor of the Imperial University in 1812 (Condette 2006, 161).

[12] 'Discours préliminaire,' in Dumas 1800, vol. 1, 66.

[13] Ibid. Williams has reiterated the view that Dumas was the first to use the term 'vitalism', as a way of marking the disciplinary and doctrinal identity of the Montpellier School (Williams 2003, 276). But as Toepfer has noted, 'vitalisme' (the English usage is later, while German usage is closer to the French in time) was used at least twenty years earlier, by the physician Pierre Thouvenel . . . who studied in Montpellier (Thouvenel 1780, 40; cf. Toepfer 2011, 692f.). Thouvenel is discussing the various medical 'sects' of antiquity and their successors in his time; 'vitalism,' which he does not define per se, seems to be equated with Hippocratism, as he distinguishes it from Galenism and 'methodism' (ibid.).

defends on an experimental basis),[14] the second by Stahl's notion of the *anima*, which, even though it is far removed from Cartesian substance dualism, is nevertheless categorically opposed to the world of mere matter (and mechanism), as he argues against Leibniz (for whom 'everything in nature happens mechanically').

This view of vitalism rests on some historically specific premises. Indeed, the criterion I suggest also ends up narrowing the historical scope of vitalism, because the explicit concern with living (organic, biological, medical, or otherwise embodied) entities versus their opposite (matter in general, atoms, dead bodies, etc.) is not a universal, trans-temporal feature of philosophy, *as an oppositional claim*. When Aristotle describes the living body as 'ensouled', he is not worrying about a competitor explanation of the body as a 'mere' machine, whereas when Stahl describes the living body as governed in all parts and processes by the soul, he *is* worrying about such competitor claims. In fact (and this is difficult to prove in factual terms) I strongly suspect the oppositional dimension of the vitalist claim is post-Cartesian, or from the standpoint of the history of science, post-Scientific Revolution. Notably, Cavendish and Diderot, albeit in quite different ways, both reacted explicitly to a certain hegemony of the physico-mechanical sciences (and the experimentalist rhetoric attached to them); in Cavendish's case, targeting the experimental philosophy and defending a variant of cosmic vitalism, and in Diderot's case, claiming (in a more pro-experimentalist way) that the emerging life sciences of his time, including that which was not yet named 'biology', but also chemistry, amounted to a kind of paradigm shift away from the physico-mathematical study of inanimate matter.[15]

I have identified a sense (I believe, a crucial sense) in which vitalism is grounded on a distinction between organisms and dead matter—a distinction which can come in more or less metaphysical forms. A major example of this 'oppositional' concern, if not a piece of avowed vitalism, is the debate between Leibniz and Stahl, as much of their discussion turns on the difference between organisms and mechanisms. Both Leibniz and Stahl agree that organisms are different from mechanisms, and that it is crucial to account for this difference; but they (sharply) disagree as to how this is to be done. In line with his subsequent animism, Stahl appeals to a more substantival concept of the soul as what gives life, while Leibniz places more emphasis on the organizational complexity or composition of

---

[14] Presenting himself as a proper laboratory scientist not tainted by metaphysics (of which vitalism would be a species, in his view), Bernard claimed that 'it didn't matter at all if Harvey or Haller were spiritualists or materialists'—he might have added 'or if Bordeu or Bichat were vitalists'—given that all that matters is their observations and experiments (Bernard 1878, 45). But significantly, the concepts Bernard develops, e.g., most famously, the *miliey intérieur*, are very much distinctively *vital* concepts (see Huneman and Wolfe 2017).

[15] Diderot, *Pensées sur l'interprétation de la nature*, § 4, in Diderot 1975–, vol. IX, 30–31; commentary in Wolfe 2017b. On the situation of 'proto-biology' or biological discourse in the decades prior to the 'naming' of biology as a science in the late eighteenth century, see Wolfe 2019.

300 VITALISM AND THE METAPHYSICS OF LIFE

organisms (an emphasis which has affinities with the later vitalist emphasis on organic *structure*). The same opposition also shapes other debates and discussions, but as with Stahl and Leibniz, theorists offer a range of views about how the two types of theory differ. One important issue which I will discuss below is whether or not the distinction between living and non-living things is necessarily a *metaphysical* one.

Once vitalism comes to be viewed in the terms I've just described, it becomes more manageable. Rather than encompassing the full range of historical and contemporary senses of vitalism (from Aristotle's *anima* to Hume's vision of the mind or Adam Smith's vision of society), the term acquires a more specific sense. In the first place, debates about vitalism come to range over a set of explanatory claims about living beings, whether or not they invoke a 'vital principle' or 'vital force'. Furthermore, within this discourse there are of course a number of distinct approaches. For example, a *medically* driven vitalism has different target explananda than an *embryological* vitalism. (As Georges Canguilhem put it, 'A vitalist, I would suggest, is someone who is led to reflect on the nature of life more because of the contemplation of an egg than because she has handled a hoist or a bellows';[16] but that describes a vitalist fascinated by the processes of generation more than it does a medical vitalist, seeking to understand and explain how the body fends off disease or reacts as an organismic whole rather than a set of molecules or organs).

On the face of things, all these views are instances of what Chang calls immanent vitalism, i.e. a vitalism solely focused on the living body, rather than a discourse on the living cosmos, so that cosmic vitalism seems to have been left behind. But this is not entirely clear, because cosmic vitalist theories of vital or self-organizing matter were presented as metaphysical, while immanent vitalist theories of living organisms were presented as more empirical. But in fact, this distinction is hard to maintain. Metaphysics seeps back into immanent vitalism, bringing with it shades of its cosmic counterpart.

This problem is already evident in Dumas' appeal to an 'intermediate principle which possesses properties different from the one and the other, and which regulates, disposes, and orders all acts of vitality'. If life is neither reduced to matter *per se* nor explained in terms of soul, what is the status of the 'vital

---

[16] Canguilhem 2008, 64; this can easily be turned into 'vital materialism' with a wider focus, as in Diderot's bold statement 'Do you see this egg? It is with this egg that we can overturn all schools of theology' (*Le Rêve de D'Alembert*, in Diderot 1975–, vol. XVII, 103–104). I do not discuss the varieties of 'vital materialism' here (see Wolfe 2017b; on the interplay between vitalism and materialism in the Montpellier context see Wolfe and Terada 2008, Wolfe 2020), but concur with Catherine Wilson's remark that 'The vital materialist might reject the theory of hexameral creation presented in Scripture, affirm epigenesis and the self-organization of living forms in place of generation by preformation and growth, posit "organic molecules" existing alongside those of "brute matter", and regard sentience and thought as emergent phenomena and as manifested widely in nonhuman nature' (Wilson 2016, 1002–1003).

principle' that replaces them? Vitalisms of the immanent kind are often defined as doctrines which explain life in terms of special, metaphysically specified principles or forces. To this extent they seem to be metaphysical. But while this is sometimes true, there are clear exceptions. Whether we speak of strong versus weak vitalism, or of metaphysical versus non-metaphysical vitalism, we should bear in the mind the difference between life understood as a kind of special 'substance' and life as 'relation', that is, as a particular kind of organization. In the versions of Montpellier vitalism that I discuss in Section 4 (particularly Bordeu and Ménuret), what is unique to living things is not specified as soul or vital force (i.e. a special substance), but rather as particular kinds of relations (or structure, or organization, depending on the vocabulary used), with their corresponding functional properties. They view this structural approach as dispensing with the (fruitless, or at least 'not-belonging-to-medicine') debates that figures like Stahl and earlier van Helmont were engaged in. Yet the problem of metaphysics is not easily waved away.

One might ask what or which metaphysics is at issue here. While it is rarely well defined on either side of the divide, one could express the situation this way: if vitalists were reacting to the mechanistic reduction of all material properties including those of the living body to some version of a 'size, shape and motion' ontology, but, *pace* Dumas, did not want to play the animist card and explain Life in terms of the soul, they then were faced with some version of the following choice. They either had to explain vitality (self-preservation, self-maintenance, or regulation, perhaps organismic unity and biological individuality) in terms of a special force or principle that was not present in matter per se, or they could explain it as a particular kind of organization (i.e. structure, or in other words, a particular arrangement of matter with specific functional properties, variously specified as 'sympathy', 'conspiration', 'cohesion', etc.).[17] Let us turn to some concrete instances.

4 Vitalist ontologies and self-criticisms

Various authors in the early modern period and moving into the early eighteenth century, criticized apparently immaterial agents of life, such as Cudworth's plastic natures or More's plastic powers. Significantly, not all of these criticisms came from authors aligned with a 'mechanistic' standpoint (which would amount again to a kind of simple opposition between mechanism and its 'other', where the content of the other view could variously be seen as immaterialism, animism, vitalism, etc.). Corresponding to Dumas' description at the end of the century,

---

[17] Thanks to Susan James for making me be clearer and more explicit on this point.

302 VITALISM AND THE METAPHYSICS OF LIFE

some of these criticisms were *vitalist criticisms*. They also bear witness to a tension internal to what Chang would term immanent vitalism, namely, between more and less metaphysical versions thereof. More metaphysical forms of vitalism would assert the existence of vitality (a vital force, a vital principle, an entelechy, etc.) as 'over and above' the systems of relations of the material, physical world. Less metaphysical vitalisms, like those of Ménuret and Bordeu, which I discuss below, would focus on the types of 'organization' of living matter specific to organisms, and seek to grasp the systemic features of this organization—without relating it back to an underlying substance or force.

The most prominent figure of Montpellier vitalism, Paul-Joseph Barthez (1734–1806), seemed to confirm the idea of vitalism as a doctrine of metaphysically specified vital principles... until he began to produce self-criticisms, specifically targeting the idea of a vital principle. Much less well known, but brilliant and arguably vastly more original, Jean-Joseph Ménuret de Chambaud (1739–1815,[18] often referred to just as Ménuret) entirely dispenses with such entities, as he accounts for vitality in entirely structural terms, with no appeal to a foundational principle (or substance): that is, to be alive is to be organized in a certain manner, thus, to possess a certain structural unity. Similar ideas are put forth by Théophile de Bordeu (1722–1776) as well, who shall I briefly discuss. The question I shall put to the *montpelliérain* texts is: does this form of immanent vitalism rely on metaphysical principles, or not?

Barthez flirted with vital forces in the first edition of his *Nouveaux éléments de la science de l'homme* (1778)[19] but gave up that approach subsequently—at least for the most part. Barthez had initially asserted the existence of an independent vital principle, but withdrew this when he added a chapter to the second edition of his *Nouveaux eléments* entitled 'Skeptical considerations on the nature of the vital principle'.[20] In this revised version, he justifies his usage of the term 'vital principle' (which he finds more convenient, and less specific than the older *enormon* or *impetuum faciens*), and defines it as 'the cause which produces all vital phenomena in the human body' (Barthez 1806, vol. I, 47).[21] Barthez won't pronounce on whether the vital principle is a substance, because, as he shrewdly notes in a chapter entitled 'Does the Vital Principle have an independent

---

[18] Ménuret, who was born in Montélimar in 1739 (and died in Paris in 1815), published mainly under the name Jean-Jacques, for reasons that remain unknown, although his given name was Jean-Joseph; his birth date is usually wrongly given as 1733. Between late 1758 and 1761, when he was aged between nineteen and twenty-two, he contributed a staggering number of medical entries to the *Encyclopédie*, which have only recently been identified as his.

[19] 2nd revised edition, 1806.   [20] Barthez 1806, vol. 1, Chapter III, § xxvi, 82–111.

[21] Barthez does not argue here for this anthropocentrism, which is actually a bit awkward in vitalist terms, but others more inclined to a re-spiritualized reading of the vital principle in the next generation insisted on the relevance of the human soul and the moral dimension of our selfhood... Barthez does add later on that humans are superior to animals due to the 'perfection of their organs and the perfectibility of their intelligence', and explains that the vital principle is 'tightly linked to the organs', while its 'functions' are closely related to 'those of the Soul' (Barthez 1806, vol. I, 60).

existence, or is it just a mode of the human body, by which this body is alive?',
what a substance is, is a matter of considerable disagreement (ibid., chapter III,
§ XXXVI, 97f.).

In a General Remark appended to the set of notes in the second edition of his
Nouveaux éléments, Barthez complained that several prominent critics (he refers
to Blumenbach as a 'journalist') targeted him for 'personifying the vital principle'.
In fact, he claims, he never appealed to this principle as an ontological ground
which could explain other phenomena; rather, he posited it in order to make sense
of new results and observed phenomena.[22] Again, he acknowledged that he had
used the term 'vital principle' in the first edition of the *Nouveaux éléments* (1776),
but protests that he never intended it in the sense of an 'independently existing
entity' (97, n. 18). Indeed, Barthez warned that one should follow an 'invincible
skepticism' (27; Notes, 98, n. 18) or a 'reasonable Pyrrhonism' (226) when it
comes to the vital principle. He only 'personified' this principle, he explained, for
ease of argument (107), for 'one cannot have a priori knowledge of either Matter
or Spirits' (83). Summing up his position in a wonderful phrase, he says: 'I am as
indifferent as could be regarding Ontology considered as the science of entities'
(Notes, 96, n. 17).

Barthez speaks at length of the need to avoid 'substantializing' the vital principle and instead take a sceptical approach to it by treating it, for example, as a
Newtonian unknown. But what does such a sceptical approach amount to?
Contrary to what one might expect, it does not mean taking a demystifying,
deflationary attitude to vital phenomena. Instead, Barthez wants to analyse the
vital principle in terms that are directly vindicated by experience (107). This runs
counter to what became the standard criticism of vitalism, namely, that it was a
metaphysical position, perhaps a metaphysics in biomedical disguise.

It is difficult to decide for or against Barthez here, given the highly interpretive
and contested nature of the territory, but I shall make two remarks, one more
critical, the other more sympathetic.

On the critical side, it is undeniable that Barthez seems 'addicted' to the
language of the vital principle, even when he adds that he is not 'personifying' it
or engaging in Ontology. Moreover, he is representative in this regard. While
some Montpellier vitalists such as Bordeu or Ménuret were more cautious than
Barthez and took care to present the language of vital principles or forces as a kind
of heuristic, others, including Barthez's protégé Jacques Lordat, hypostatized the
vital principle even further. Lordat, for example, explicitly opposed his appeals to
vital principle to the experimentalism of the group of physicians based in Paris,
known as the Paris School (Lordat 1842; Staum 2001, Wolfe 2013).

---

[22] Barthez 1806, vol. I, Notes, 4; the notes added to this edition form a separate section, paginated
separately.

304 VITALISM AND THE METAPHYSICS OF LIFE

On the more charitable side, it seems a bit dogmatic (and reminiscent of certain Darwinians in later centuries) to rule out appeals to an explanatory principle designed to facilitate theoretical unity and cohesion among qualitatively diverse phenomena. The obvious analogy here, endlessly used in this period, is with Newtonian attraction: hadn't the great Newton posited an unknown x which was not itself qualitatively or causally specified, yet which played a key role in the formation of a larger theory covering phenomena as diverse as tides and planetary motion? Why, then, shouldn't other sciences posit 'unknowns' in the same manner? Canguilhem puts the case for this most forcefully:

> Eighteenth-century vitalists are...not impenitent metaphysicians but rather prudent positivists, which is to say, in that period, Newtonians. Vitalism is first of all the rejection of all metaphysical theories of the essence of life. This why most of the vitalists referred to Newton as the model of a scientist concerned with observation and experiment.... Vitalism ultimately means the recognition of life as an original order of phenomena, and thus the recognition of the specificity of biological knowledge.[23]

This is a very strong claim. Applied to the Montpellier school, it captures the outlook of some theorists better than others. It is indeed true that some of the Montpellier vitalists referred a great deal to Newton and aimed to imitate his style of explanation; but this does not mean that there was no trace of metaphysics in their works, as Canguilhem implies. Barthez is an interesting case in point. In the second edition of his work, he goes to great lengths to deny that his initial analysis of the metaphysical principle had a metaphysical flavour. He adds a number of deflationary arguments, as we have seen, and also introduces lengthy (and repetitive) discussions of empiricism, induction, hypothesis and experiment, referring particularly to Bacon and Hume. Yet, as his critics saw, these measures do not entirely erase his metaphysical commitments.

Closer to Canguilhem's ideal of vitalism as rejecting 'all metaphysical theories of the essence of life' is Ménuret. Ménuret's aim is hardly ever to defend some notion of an independent and/or ontologically unique vital force. Rather, his focus is *structural*; his aim is to call attention to an aspect of living things that both mechanists and animists neglected, namely the specifically organic structure of the body:

> In their hands [*sc.* the mechanists], the human body became an extremely composed machine, or better, a workshop of ropes, levers, pulleys and other mechanical instruments. They thought that the general goal of all these springs

---

[23] Canguilhem 1955, 113.

(*ressorts*) was to serve the progressive movement of the blood, the only one which is absolutely necessary to life.... They believed that movement merely obeyed the ordinary laws that apply to all *inorganic* machines, treated the human body geometrically, and rigorously calculated all the various degrees of force required for particular actions, or how much was lost, etc. – but all these calculations, which obviously varied tremendously, shed no light on the *animal economy*. They did not even pay attention to the *organic structure* of the human body which is the source of its main properties.[24]

This is neither a strictly anatomical perspective on organisms, nor one appealing to an immaterial vital principle. Rather, Ménuret is interested in the *articulation of the parts* of an organism, i.e., the nature of the relations between its parts as well as their material properties. His phrase 'organic structure' encompasses a lot, as it is meant to emphasize how vitalist models differ from sheer mechanism, but also Stahlian animism, both of which neglect organic structure for symmetrically opposite reasons. The distinctively structural character of this form of vitalism is also visible in the way figures such as Bordeu and Ménuret discuss the whole-part relations of organisms. Again reflecting the triangulation I described following Dumas' retrospective analysis of the vitalist school, one could say that their vitalism is neither squarely reductionist nor emphatically holist, but combines elements of each, meaning that it is not a 'top-down holism'.

To borrow a distinction from Des Chene, the vitalist appeal to structure is not a rejection of mechanism on metaphysical grounds, but rather as empirically insufficient (Des Chene 2002). And this structural emphasis allows for a closer relationship between mechanist and vitalist approaches than is usually imagined. The structurally minded vitalist and the ... open-minded mechanist might have a lot more in common in their investigation of Life and the properties of living beings than we would think. (One could go even further with this dialectic of mechanist and vitalist approaches to Life and imagine, as Hutchins does, that card-carrying mechanists like Descartes might have vitalistic elements in their systems that cannot be reconciled with their own ontology,[25] so that Descartes can be the ruthless mechanist of renown while still maintaining a notion of life that we might see as a strand of vitalism.)

When I suggest that the holism at work in this form of vitalism is not necessarily a 'top-down' holism, I mean that if we examine their discussions of the 'animal economy', including the prominent status of the bee swarm metaphor (Kleiman-Lafon and Wolfe forthcoming), which emphasize how Life is composed

---

[24] Ménuret, 'Œconomie Animale', *Enc.* XI, 364b, emphasis mine.

[25] Hutchins argues that, somewhat surprisingly, Descartes can allow for knowledge that is reducible to neither thinking nor extended substances, and that he treats life as such an irreducible: as in the case with the mind-body union, 'Cartesian knowledge need not ... bottom out in the terms of his dualist ontology' (Hutchins in this volume).

of a multitude of little 'lives' in interaction rather than just of inanimate parts, we do not see these vitalists beginning with the irreducibility of organismic identity (as some still do with the problem of consciousness). Rather, they are deeply interested in the material properties of the 'parts' (organs, 'lives') and, to be sure, in the higher-level systemic features displayed in their interaction. To use a distinction proposed by David Chalmers, one could see this as a case of weak, rather than strong emergence (Chalmers 2006) and by extension, of weak rather than strong vitalism. We are dealing here with forms of immanent vitalism overall (to use Chang's distinction with which I began), but now with its important internal differentiations. Both weak and strong vitalism are holistic, but strong vitalism is necessarily a top-down holism that will deemphasize the nature of the material properties of the constituents of an organic body, in favour of a vital principle or force, or 'soul' as in Stahl—an entity which controls, governs, or vitalizes the organic body. Weak vitalism does not appeal to such entities, and consequently pays significantly more attention to the nature of the relations between these constituents, including their material properties. As Stephen Gaukroger comments (regarding the eighteenth-century vitalist context), 'one might say that it is because the parts are living that the whole is living, and it is because the living parts are connected in the way they are that the whole is the way it is' (Gaukroger 2010, 400). Ménuret, on his part, explains how a stable inter-action between parts ('lives', i.e. individual organs) is what constitutes health:

> The body should only be considered as an infinite assemblage of small, identical bodies, similarly alive and animated, each possessing a life, an action, a sensibility – [that is] both a specific, particular interaction (*jeu*) and movement, and a common, overall life and sensibility. All parts contribute in their own way to the life of the entire body, and as such they reciprocally correspond to and influence one another.[26]

Granted, the idea of defining 'Life' in terms of smaller 'lives' rather than just ordinary parts has something anti-reductionist (thus holistic) about it; but it is a holism where componential analysis, that is, analysis of the properties of the parts, still plays a role.[27] In that sense, not only is the form of vitalism expressed in the above passages—we could call it weak vitalism—far removed from claims about mysterious vital forces (in other terms, strong emergence); this structural approach to life is also closer to materialism than is often said, if we notice the appeal to a kind of *vital materiality*, including in the desire to not explain life in terms of soul. Thus, while in Stahl it was important that matter is not active

---

[26] Ménuret, 'Pouls', *Enc.* XIII, 240a.
[27] For more concrete cases including the vitalist discussion of the functioning of the glands as a paramount non-mechanist case, see Wolfe 2017a, 2019.

(activity comes from the *anima*), in Ménuret and Bordeu, vitalism is genuinely concerned with the specific *materiality* of specific systems such as the glands. Even Barthez, the theorist of the vital principle, says that the latter principle only exists 'as a faculty attached to the combination of motion and matter, in which a living body consists'.[28]

5 Weak and strong vitalisms: the problem of metaphysics

If cosmic and immanent vitalism were distinguished essentially by their object or scope, that is, with the former projecting vitality across the cosmos and the latter restricting its claims to the nature of the living body, I have suggested in addition that the category of immanent vitalism covers some very different positions. Notably, it includes (this is Chang's first major example of immanent vitalism) Stahl's system, as well as the different variants of Montpellier vitalism. But as we saw above, these are not to be collapsed into one view. We should distinguish further between metaphysically grounded theories such as those of Stahl or the early Barthez, and vitalisms that focus on the organic structure of organisms and the relations between their parts, such as those of Ménuret and Bordeu.[29] This can be framed in terms of strong versus weak vitalism. Weak vitalism, in its focus on structure rather than on a vital substance, is less obviously metaphysically grounded.

Consider the case of Théophile Bordeu[30]—one of the other most prominent figures of the Montpellier school. Just as Barthez had ultimately declared he would not engage in ontological considerations and that one should be sceptical as regards the vital principle, Bordeu in his masterpiece, the *Recherches anatomiques sur la position et la fonction des glandes* (1751), which doubles as a work of medical theory and a vitalist primer, reflects on Stahlian and other possible explanations of the 'self-preserving' force in animals. Here Bordeu seeks to achieve some reflexive distance from 'essentialist' (that is, metaphysical) claims.

---

[28] Barthez 1806, vol. 1, Notes, 100, n. 18; he also quotes La Mettrie approvingly on the relations between life and death (ibid., vol. 2, Notes, 181 n. 34).

[29] It may well be that the latter kind of vitalism goes particularly well with a medical focus, concerned with the relations between the body, its organs, and their parts, whereas a more biological approach, in its focus on the micro-level of vital minima, is more potentially speculative (as can be seen notably in the case of Driesch's entelechies, agents he posited to explain the self-organizing dynamics of the embryo).

[30] Bordeu also served as a fictional character in Diderot's *Rêve de D'Alembert* (1769)—in which he nevertheless appears as a doctor, espousing what we would call vital materialist theories. In addition to various medical works including his important study of the glands, and a work of history of medicine (*Recherches d'histoire de la médecine*, 1764) he was the author of the long entry 'Crise' in the *Encyclopédie* (a topic reflecting the Hippocratic dimension of Montpellier vitalism, in this case the focus on the 'critical phases' of a disease).

308 VITALISM AND THE METAPHYSICS OF LIFE

First, Bordeu explicitly acknowledges that we do not have direct access to such forces:

> It is difficult...to explain oneself, when it comes to speaking of the force which so carefully directs a thousand singular motions in the human body and its parts; what terms should I use to describe them?...I will discuss Stahl's hypothesis elsewhere: he claimed that the soul directed everything in the animal body. Whatever the case may be, I can state that all living parts are directed by an ever-vigilant self-preserving force; does this force belong, in certain respects, to the essence of a part of matter, or is it a necessary attribute of its combinations?[31]

Second, he introduces—quite unusually for this context; I have not seen this done in other medical or medico-theoretical works of this period—the idea that such properties have to be approached through *metaphors*: 'This is again one of these *metaphors* which I must be allowed...I can only suggest a *way* of conceiving things, *metaphorical* expressions, comparisons....'[32] Bordeu is introducing a degree of mediation that distinguishes his theory from other forms of metaphysical vitalism. To say (as Stahl himself does not) that the Stahlian concept of soul is a metaphor is essentially to say that the concept has *functional* value (or not) depending on how well it models phenomena. It is not to make an ontological claim about what sorts of things exist, and their essential properties.

We have seen that theorists who explained the vitality of organisms by appealing to their structure aimed to avoid appealing to a substantial principle that gives organisms life. But they continued to worry about whether they had succeeded. Figures of the period worried about how to ensure that their own interest in vitality would not be viewed as 'metaphysical vitalism'. Why, though, was it important to them to differentiate themselves from vitalists who were committed to the idea that the life of organisms can only be explained by something metaphysically close to a substance?

The question of whether or not vitalism is, or must be a metaphysics is twofold: on the one hand, it is a matter of our own judgement. Does all discussion of a vital force or a vital principle amount to a substantival metaphysics, in which 'life' is a substance, as it were? On the other hand, it is also an issue which the actors themselves debated. That is, it is not just part of some later negative portrayal of vitalism—except it proved a troublesome pudendum to be rid of. Why they were concerned with differentiating themselves from metaphysical vitalism at all, I address below.

We find this anxiety expressed by Albrecht von Haller, one of the dominant figures in eighteenth-century physiology—not himself a vitalist, indeed he took

---

[31] Bordeu 1751, § CVIII, in Bordeu 1818, vol. 1, 163.
[32] Ibid.; I have replaced Bordeu's 'we' with 'I'.

some pains to distinguish his views, notably his theory of sensibility and irritability, from the vitalist theories, but in the end Haller, too, is seeking to describe uniquely *vital* properties. Discussing Francis Glisson, Haller wrote that Glisson's discovery of the property of the irritability of muscular tissue did indeed anticipate discoveries of his own. However, Glisson ended up 'ruling himself out' of legitimate scientific discourse in Haller's view (which was influential), by tying his medical discoveries to a metaphysics of the 'energy of Nature' (Giglioni 2008). Indeed, Glisson, the author of significant medical works, such as *De rachitide* (1650) and *De anatomia hepatis* (1654), also produced a metaphysical treatise on the 'life of nature,' the *Tractatus de natura substantiae energetica, seu de vita naturae ejusque tribus facultatibus perceptiva, appetitiva, motiva* (1672), usually referred to as *De vita naturae*. In this treatise he describes life as immanent to matter: 'life is the intimate and inseparable essence of matter' and 'matter contains within itself the root of life'.[33] In the 'short history' of irritability that Haller appended to his *Dissertation on the Sensible and Irritable Parts of Animals* (1753), he explained that Glisson 'discovered the active force of the elements of our bodies' and 'was the first who invented the word *Irritability*' (Haller [1755] 1935, 42–43). But Haller nevertheless 'rejected the idea of irritability as the bodily manifestation of a universal unsentient power embedded in matter' (Giglioni 2008, 466), as a kind of category mistake. Irritability was neither a property of matter itself, for Haller, nor something implying special extra-physical properties (2014a).

In the passages I have called attention to in Barthez, Bordeu, and above in Haller, the problematic construct we might call 'metaphysical vitalism' is being repeatedly denied in favour of a more heuristic, functional, experimentally focused view (in Haller's case, he is not seeking to distinguish himself from this construct, unlike the montpelliérains, but to draw a clear demarcation line between Glisson's metaphysical vitalism and his own 'experimental, non-metaphysical life science').

One could multiply such examples of one (weakly vitalistic) thinker desperately seeking to tar a predecessor with the brush of (strong) vitalism, in order to make her own investigations into vitality (irritability, homeostasis, metabolism, etc.) seem properly naturalistic and non-metaphysical. If we make use of the distinction between strong and weak vitalism, in which the latter is understood as less metaphysical, or even non-metaphysical, focusing on vital properties inasmuch as they are accessible to experimentation, it is intriguing—and not sufficiently noticed—that the distinction is also present as a tension *internal to vitalism*. In other words, when critics of vitalism accuse it of being a metaphysics of vital forces masquerading as science, or in slightly less strong terms, a form of science excessively freighted with metaphysical concerns, it is important to note that this problem existed *within vitalism* as well.

---

[33] Glisson 1672, § 8; I quote from a draft translation of *De Vita Naturae* by Guido Giglioni, which he was kind enough to share with me.

310   VITALISM AND THE METAPHYSICS OF LIFE

The tension is there, whether purely in philosophical terms, or reflecting a context in which it is precisely the mantle of the legitimate life scientist that is being fought for (like Haller contra Glisson), or even a more internal tension between two physicians (to be precise, a physician and a physician-pathologist, namely Bordeu and Bichat). Thus, I have suggested that vitalism is in fact, not just plural or in need of subtle typologies, but a genuine *Kampfplatz*, a conflict zone. In each of these cases, something like metaphysical vitalism is being opposed, in favour of a more or less explicitly expressed 'weaker' form of vitalism. Some of these figures would reject the label 'vitalist', like Haller, who viewed himself precisely as a prudent Newtonian engaged in rigorous quantitative analysis of properties such as irritability (although some of his partisans, like Charles Bonnet, immediately labelled such properties 'vital principles'[34]); others would accept it but immediately make distinctions.

This problem of whether vitalism had to be a metaphysics or not, and if it was, whether this was too great a cost to bear, stands out as a feature in the nineteenth-century medical discussions of the topic. Thus the Paris doctor Jean Bouillaud, contributing an entry on vitalism to a medical dictionary in 1836, apologized for the presence of metaphysics in his entry: 'I admit that metaphysics is quite out of place in a dictionary of practical medicine and surgery, but how can one write an article on Vitalism without delving at least in part into the dark depths of metaphysics?' (Bouillaud 1836, 759). Bouillaud was at least trying to defend Montpellier vitalism from the standard charge at the time that it was too 'high-falutin', too far removed from clinical (and experimental) medicine. But by the time of Charles Daremberg's extremely influential two-volume *Histoire des sciences médicales* in 1870, the judgement is without appeal: collapsing Stahl's animism and Montpellier vitalism into one supernaturalist doctrine, Daremberg 'has no trouble whatsoever stating that any attempt to explain life by some *entity* outside of the organism itself, appears to [him] to be a primitive conception', a throwback to the earliest, archaic days of medicine.[35]

As we've seen, what Daremberg calls a 'primitive conception' is by no means present in any of the Montpellier vitalists discussed in this essay. I have cited Bordeu, for instance, essentially giving voice to a similar objection to Daremberg's, albeit phrased in less polemical terms. Bordeu (like Ménuret) does not want to appeal to a metaphysically special substance or entity to do justice to what is specific to living bodies. Yet, contrasting directly with the consensus view in the historiography of vitalism I mentioned above (a view which is *also* part of the discussions and problematizations *internal to* medical discourse), we should

---

[34] Bonnet, *Considérations sur les corps organisés* (1762), vol. I, chap. X, in Bonnet 1779, III, 128.
[35] Daremberg 1870, vol. 2, 1022. As late as the 1960s, the historians of medicine Bariéty and Coury are still reproaching vitalism in the life sciences for being a metaphysics: 'here (i.e. in Sauvages and Barthez but also in Stahl, CW), biological phenomena are treated as a particular case of metaphysics' (Bariéty and Coury 1963, 478).

consider a different attitude towards the question, is vitalism a metaphysics (i.e. is vitalism necessarily a doctrine with metaphysical commitments)? This different view is intimated, rather than directly argued for by Canguilhem, in a provocative and important paper entitled, modestly enough, 'Aspects of Vitalism' (Canguilhem 2008: originally a lecture delivered in Paris in the immediate post-war years). He hints that vitalism cannot do without metaphysics, and, as a corollary, that various constructive and fruitful episodes in life science are not possible without this vitalism. Yet Canguilhem carefully distinguishes this from any appeal to some eternal irreducibility of vitality. It is straightforward enough to distinguish between vital matter theory and debates on organism in terms of the former being meta-physical while the latter are apparently empirical; but to locate the delimitation point between Glisson and Haller on irritability is harder, not least since Haller himself in other texts muses on the *vis insita* and other distinctive features of vitality. In addition, there will be vitalist moments which are hard to eradicate (when scientists claim that vitalism has been refuted, it often turns out to be a particular, restrictive case of vitalism that may have been overturned). This way of emphasizing that it is not so easy to dispense with vitalism, and indeed, with vitalism as a metaphysics, is more likely than Canguilhem's alternate (and equally provocative) claim that vitalism is *in esse* the rejection of any metaphysics of life, which I mentioned above (Canguilhem 1955, 113).

6 Conclusion

While 'vitalism' is used in many ways at different times and places (even once we restrict usage somewhat, whether in terms of actual usage of the term and/or of the presence of certain minimal conceptual criteria), the Montpellier vitalists point to a central problem—a problem for them and for subsequent and even contempor-ary theorists. How can one account for the nature of organic life if it seems that both mechanism and animism fail to account for core organic (in fact, organis-mic) properties? This problem has by no means been consigned to the rubbish bin of history (or biology, or indeed philosophy).

I have tried to show that 'vitalism', first, should ideally refer just to theories with an active concern in defining Life, vitality, or organisms and in opposing some or all of these to inanimate matter, machines, pure physics (or whatever the preferred opposition is). Of course, the cultural historian discussing the cult of the naked body in late nineteenth-century Scandinavia may wish to speak of 'vitalism', illustrating my point that it is difficult to police the use of language or even conceptual labels. But if we turn things around, I would ask: don't we need a term to refer to theories at the intersection of the life sciences (typically medicine, biology, physiology, and related disciplines) and philosophy, which are explicitly concerned with organic life? Now, such theories can come in different strengths and with varying commitments; thus, I've argued elsewhere that it is historically inexact to define vitalism as the belief in a supernatural vital force which exists 'over and above' the natural world. Typically, such accusations of vitalism were polemical in nature, as when Descartes declared that Nature is not a goddess (who thought so?) or Francis Crick told an audience of biologists that if any of them were vitalists, it might have been fine in the past but it made them 'cranks' in the present.[36] Such accusations tend to performatively reinforce a certain kind of reductionist conviction (to atomism, to biochemistry, or to genocentrism depending on which period we are talking about) rather than actually 'refuting' an empirical claim.[37]

Second, in this now somewhat narrowed conceptual space for vitalist theories, it might help to distinguish between 'strong' and 'weak' vitalisms (borrowing Chalmers' 2006 distinction between strong and weak emergence). The vitalist who insists that there is a special living substance, or that a science studying living beings is ontologically apart from all other sciences, is a strong vitalist; the vitalist who is interested in the functional (or 'systemic', or 'organizational') properties of certain arrangements of living matter, but resists the temptation to *ontologize* these properties, is a weak vitalist. For example, Claude Bernard, like Albrecht von Haller, professed to dislike the metaphysical excesses of vitalism, but saw his task as the discovery, definition and to some extent quantification of *distinctively vital properties* (notably, what ultimately became known as homeostasis): that seems like weak vitalism.

But such distinctions are neither foolproof nor definitive: for instance, in earlier work I suggested a similar distinction between 'substantival' and 'functional' vitalism, and described Stahl as a paramount case of a substantival (or 'strong') vitalist (Wolfe 2015, 2017a). Yet even Stahl (whose unwavering focus on the soul and consequent reliance on the soul as the basis, fundament and sole explanatory principle leads to his being termed instead an 'animist') could be described in different ways: if we focus on his critique of mechanism and his insistence on the role of the soul in medical explanations, he seems clearly like an emblematic 'strong vitalist', but if we focus on his account of disease, or the relation between chemical and organismic explanations, he seems more like a 'weak vitalist'. In that sense, it is too simple to dismiss attempts to define 'life' as naïve or too metaphysical (as Mayr does: 'These endeavours are rather futile since it is now quite clear that there is no special substance, object, or force that can be identified with life': Mayr 1982, 53). Even if they are not conclusive, attempts to define life (of

---

[36] Descartes, *Le Monde*, AT XI, 36–37; Crick 1966, 99.

[37] I do not examine cases such as Hans Driesch's 'entelechies' and the robust criticism they received in the Vienna Circle, for reasons of historical focus and length. But this case is often used as a kind of *experimentum crucis* marking the death of vitalism, given Driesch's appeal to ontological 'danglers', the entelechies. For a more sympathetic view, see Chen 2018.

which vitalism might be the most dramatic case) they are parts of the biological landscape.

Third, I've suggested that vitalism proper, i.e., a claim which starts from vitality being 'localized in the organism,' with vitalism consequently 'confined to the life sciences' (Chang 2011, 328), or at least confined to a discursive space in which philosophical considerations were also bounded by the life sciences, is not present prior to a certain deflationary project often associated with the Scientific Revolution (even if the latter historiographic category is quite controversial nowadays). Again, it is not that Aristotle or Jean Fernel did not care about life or had no theory thereof. Rather, it is the status of living beings in the physical universe was not a *problem* for them—was not a problematic issue, that cried out for a solution (whether this solution was presented in strictly empirical or more ontologized forms). That is, one of the reasons why it seems strange to describe Aristotle, Campanella, Fernel, or Harvey as vitalists is that the problem-space they inhabit (some scholars will prefer to speak in a post-Kuhnian manner, of 'controversies') is foreign to what we might call the 'Vitalismus-Problem'. The vitalism problem—why are organisms, or living bodies (depending on the formulation) different from the entities described in basic physico-mechanical terms?—is 'not ancient'.[38] Additionally, it is perhaps no coincidence that the name 'vitalism' is explicitly used, in the late eighteenth century, much around the time when 'biology' as a science is named. The fact that 'vitalism' appears at much the same time as 'biology' has not been discussed much so far, if it all.[39]

Lastly, I acknowledge that the approach towards 'metaphysics' in this chapter is not univocal. Initially (Section 1), in the name of greater precision and increased content for the term 'vitalism', I suggested that we not include active matter or panpsychist theories under this heading. By the end (Section 4), I examined some instances in which metaphysics seems unavoidable. And throughout, I've noted cases of attempted exclusion and differentiation *within vitalism* ('she's a metaphysician, I'm not!'), that don't seem to go away. How might these points be reconciled?

First, my desire to discriminate between senses of the term did not imply a kind of strict 'demarcation' between metaphysics (of vital force, soul etc.) and science (as in Legallois' hope to find the nature of life by decapitating rabbits: Cheung 2013). Ironically, such demarcation claims are peppered throughout the texts I have discussed or mentioned: Haller or Bernard do not wait for the modern synthesis of evolutionary theory and genetics to denounce their predecessors for being (strong, metaphysical) vitalists, while they continue to produce analyses which are 'objectively' (but weakly) vitalistic. Second, it then seems hard to forever

---

[38] To use an expression recalling a classic, provocative paper, 'Why the Mind-Body Problem isn't Ancient' (Matson 1966).

[39] I make some preliminary moves in that direction in Wolfe 2019.

314 VITALISM AND THE METAPHYSICS OF LIFE

do without vitalism, and vitalism seems in turn to not be wholly free or separable from metaphysics (unless we restrict ourselves to projects like Ménuret's, perhaps). This doesn't change the fact that such vitalist moments are ultimately destined for self-dissolution, in the sense that the concepts and entities in life science are perpetually being 'de-ontologized': 'By far the most interesting feature of the quest for the defining essence of life, and surely its greatest peculiarity, is that even while focusing attention on the boundary between living and non-living, emphasizing both the clarity and importance of that divide, this quest for life's essence simultaneously works toward its dissolution' (Fox Keller 2002, 292). Yet, even if vitalism is always easily defined in terms of heuristics or other utility (the way it would be in Bordeu and Ménuret), it might be quite difficult to definitively get rid of. Not because it conveys a higher 'truth' or message concerning a special vital substance or, more experientially, some unmediated raw *Erlebnis*, but because it stubbornly resists direct refutation.

Acknowledgements

I would like to thank Kevin Chang, Kathryn Tabb, and especially Susan James for their very helpful comments on earlier versions of this chapter.

Bibliography

Ablondi, Fred. 1995. 'Death According to Descartes: Why the Soul Leaves the Body'. *Iyyun: The Jerusalem Philosophical Quarterly* 44, pp. 47–53.

Ablondi, Fred. 1998. 'Automata, Living and Non-Living: Descartes' Mechanical Biology and His Criteria for Life'. *Biology and Philosophy* (13), pp. 179–186.

Aldobrandini, Tommaso. 1594. *Laertii Diogenis de vitis dogmatis et apophtegmatis eorum qui in philosophia claruerunt, libri X. Thoma Aldobrandino interprete. Cum adnotationibus eiusdem.* Roma: Zanetto.

Aler, Jan. 1965. *Catalogus van de bibliotheek der Vereniging Het Spinozahuis te Rijnsburg.* Leiden: Brill.

Alfieri, Vittorio Enzo. 1936. *Gli atomisti. Frammenti e testimonianze.* Bari: Laterza.

Allison, Henry E. 2011. *Kant's Groundwork for the Metaphysics of Morals: A Commentary.* Oxford: Oxford University Press.

Ameriks, Karl. 2012. 'Kant, Human Nature, and History after Rousseau'. In *Kant's Observations and Remarks: A Critical Guide.* Edited by Susan Meld Shell and Richard L. Velkley. Cambridge: Cambridge University Press, pp. 247–65.

Ameriks, Karl. 2012. *Kant's Elliptical Path.* Oxford: Clarendon Press.

Ames, William. 1642. *The Marrow of Sacred Divinity, Drawne out of the Holy Scripture.* London: H. Overton.

Andrault, Raphaële. 2014. *La vie selon la raison - physiologie et métaphysique chez Spinoza et Leibniz.* Paris: Champion.

Andrault, Raphaële. 2019. 'Spinoza's Missing Physiology'. *Perspectives on Science* 27(2), pp. 214–243.

Antognazza, Maria Rosa. 2014. 'Metaphysical Evil Revisited'. In *New Essays on Leibniz's Theodicy.* Edited by Samuel Newlands and Larry Jorgensen. Oxford: Oxford University Press, pp. 112–134.

Apollinaris, Sidonius. 461–484 CE. *Epistulae* [online]. Available at: <http://www.perseus.tufts.edu/Apollinaris.Epistulae>.

Aquinas, Thomas. 1911. *Summa Theologica.* Translated by the Fathers of the English Dominican Province. London: Burns, Oates, and Washbourne.

Aristotle. 2009. *The Nicomachean Ethics.* Translated by William David Ross. Oxford: Oxford University Press.

Aristotle. 2015. *De anima.* Edited and translated by R. D. Hicks. Cambridge: Cambridge University Press.

Armstrong, Aurelia. 2009. 'Autonomy and the Relational Individual: Spinoza and Feminism'. In *Feminist Interpretations of Benedict Spinoza.* Edited by Moira Gatens. University Park: Pennsylvania State University Press, pp. 43–64.

Aquinas, St Thomas. 1988. *Summa theologiae.* Milan: Editiones Paulinae.

Arnobius of Sicca. IV cent. C.E. *Adversus nationes libri septem.* [online]. Available at: <https://www.thelatinlibrary.com/arnobius/arnobius1.shtml>.

Ashcraft, Richard. 2010. *Locke's Two Treatises of Government.* Oxford: Routledge.

Astell, Mary. 2002. *A Serious Proposal to the Ladies.* Edited by Patricia Springborg. Peterborough: Broadview Press.

316 BIBLIOGRAPHY

Astolfi, Giovanni Felice. 1606. *Delle Vite de' filosofi di Diogene Laerzio, libri X. Ripieni d'istorie giovevoli; soggetti piacevoli, essempi morali, e sentenze gravi. Ridotte nuovamente a l'intero numero, e a l'ordine di quelle di Laerzio stesso, accresciute, e migliorate di molto, da quelle, ch'erano le date fuori nelle passate editioni.* Dal r.p.f. Gio. Felice Astolfi. Venice: Bertoni.

Augustine, Saint, Bishop of Hippo. 1998. *The City of God against the Pagans.* Edited and translated by R. W. Dyson. Cambridge: Cambridge University Press.

Augustinus, Saint, Bishop of Hippo. 2001. *De trinitate.* Lateinisch-Deutsch. Edited and translated by Johann Kreuzer. Hamburg: Meiner.

Augustine, Saint, Bishop of Hippo. 391 CE. *De utilitate credendi ad Honoratum liber unus.* [online]. Available at: <https://www.augustinus.it/latino/utilita_credere/index.htm>.

Augustine, Saint, Bishop of Hippo. 400 CE. *De baptismo contra Donatistas libri septem* [online]. Available at: <https://www.augustinus.it/latino/sul_battesimo/index2.htm>

Augustine, Saint, Bishop of Hippo. c. 411 CE. *Epistola ad Probam* (Ep. 130) [online]. Available at: <https://www.augustinus.it/latino/lettere/lettera_131_testo.htm>.

Augustine, Saint, Bishop of Hippo. 418 CE. *De gratia Christi et de peccato originali libri duo* [online]. Available at: <http://www.augustinus.it/latino/grazia_cristo/index2.htm>.

Bachimius Denstonius, Arnoldus. 1682. *Pan-sophia enchiretica, seu philosophia universalis experimentalis,* Nürnberg: Zieger.

Bacon, Francis.1900. *The Works.* 14 volumes. Edited by James Spedding, Robert Leslie Ellis and Douglas Denon Heath. Boston: Houghton Mifflin.

Bagnoregio, Bonaventure of. 1259. *Itinerarium mentis in Deo* [online]. Available at: <https://www.thelatinlibrary.com/bonaventura.itinerarium.html>.

Balibar, Etienne. 1997. *Spinoza: From Individuality to Transindividuality.* Delft: Euburon.

Balibar, Etienne. 2013, *John Locke and the Invention of Consciousness.* London: Verso.

Bariéty Maurice, Coury Charles. 1963. *Histoire de la médecine.* Paris: Fayard.

Barth, Christian. 2011. 'Bewusstsein bei Descartes'. *Archiv für Geschichte der Philosophie* 93, pp. 162–194.

Barthez, Paul-Joseph. 1806. *Nouveaux éléments de la science de l'homme,* 2nd ed., 2 vols. Paris: Goujon & Brunot.

Bates, William. 1700. *The Works of the Late Reverend and Learned William Bates.* London: J. Robinson.

Baumeister, Friedrich Christian. 1737. *Iusta funebria Gothofr. Gerlachio indicit simulque de exsilio mortis Leibnitiano disserit.* Gorlici: Richter. Reprinted in Id., 1741. *Exercitationes academicæ et scholasticæ.* Lipsiæ et Gorlicii: Richter, pp. 94–102.

Baumgarten, Alexander Gottlieb. 1739. *Metaphysica.* Halæ Magdeburgicæ: Hemmerde.

Bayle, Pierre. 1826. *An Historical and Critical Dictionary, selected and abridged from the Work of Peter Bayle: with a Life of Bayle, Volume II.* London: Hunt and Clark.

Bayle, Pierre. 1969. *Dictionnaire historique et critique. Nouvelle édition.* Reprint of the Paris edition of 1820–1824. Geneva: Slatkine Reprints.

Bayle, Pierre. 2000. *Bayle: Political Writings.* Edited by Sally Jenkinson. Cambridge: Cambridge University Press.

Beauchamp, Tom L. 1976. 'An Analysis of Hume's Essay *On Suicide*'. *Review of Metaphysics* 30 (1), pp. 73–95.

Beauchamp, Tom L. 2005. 'Suicide'. In *The Oxford Companion to Philosophy New Edition.* Edited by Ted Honderich. New York: Oxford University Press, p. 902.

Beck, Lewis White. 1969. *Early German Philosophy; Kant and His Predecessors.* Cambridge, MA: Belknap Press of Harvard University Press.

BIBLIOGRAPHY 317

Beiser, Frederick. 1987. *The Fate of Reason: German Philosophy from Kant to Fichte.* Cambridge, MA: Harvard University Press.

Beiser, Frederick. 1992. 'Kant's Intellectual Development'. In *The Cambridge Companion to Kant.* Edited by Paul Guyer. New York: Cambridge University Press.

Beiser, Frederick. 2002. *German Idealism: The Struggle Against Subjectivism, 1781–1801* Cambridge, MA: Harvard University Press.

Beiser, Frederick. 2010. 'Mathematical Method in Kant, Schelling, and Hegel'. In *Discourse on a New Method: Reinvigorating the Marriage of History and Philosophy of Science.* Edited by Michael Friedman, Mary Domski, and Michael Dickson. Chicago: Open Court.

Beiser, Frederick. 2017. 'The Enlightenment and Idealism'. In *The Cambridge Companion to German Idealism.* Edited by Karl Ameriks. Cambridge: Cambridge University Press, pp. 21–42.

Bennett, Jonathan. 1984. *A Study of Spinoza's Ethics.* Indianapolis: Hackett Publishing Company.

Bernard, Claude. 1878. *Leçons sur les phénomènes de la vie communs aux animaux et aux végétaux.* Paris: J.-B. Baillière.

Berthelot, Marcellin. 1983. *Les origines de l'alchimie.* Bruxelles: Culture et Civilisation.

Betsch, Gerhard, 2005. 'Johann Conrad Creiling (1673–1752) und seine Schule'. In *Mathesis, Naturphilosophie und Arkanwissenschaft im Umkreis Friedrich Christoph Oetingers (1702–1782).* Edited by Sabine Holtz. Stuttgart: Steiner, pp. 43–59.

Bilfinger, Georg Bernhard. 1982. *Dilucidationes philosophicæ de Deo, anima humana, mundo, et generalibus rerum affectionibus.* Hildesheim: Olms.

Blount, Charles and Gildon, Charles. 1695. *The Miscellaneous Works of Charles Blount . . . : To Which Is Prefix'd the Life of the Author.* London.

Bohatec, Josef. 1912. *Die Cartesianische Scholastik.* Leipzig: A. Deichert.

Boehm, Omri. 2014. *Kant's Critique of Spinoza.* Oxford: Oxford University Press.

Bolduc, Carl R. 2015. *Kant et Spinoza: Rencontre paradoxale.* Paris: Éditions du Félin.

Bonnet, Charles. 1779. *Œuvres d'histoire naturelle et de philosophie de Charles Bonnet.* 8 volumes. Neuchâtel: S. Faulche.

de Bordeu, Théophile. 1818. *Œuvres complètes, précédées d'une Notice sur sa vie et ses ouvrages par Monsieur le Chevalier de Richerand.* 2 volumes. Paris: Caille et Ravier.

Bouillaud, Jean. 1836. 'Vitalisme'. In *Dictionnaire de médecine et de chirurgie pratiques.* Volume 15. Edited by Gabriel Andral. Paris: Méquignon-Marvis, J.-B. Baillière, pp. 758–762.

Boureau-Deslandes, André-François. 1712. *Réflexions sur les grands hommes qui sont morts en plaisantant.* Amsterdam, pp. 3–4.

Boyle, Deborah. 2018. *The Well-Ordered Universe: The Philosophy of Margaret Cavendish.* Oxford: Oxford University Press.

Broadie, Sarah. 2001. 'Soul and Body in Plato and Descartes'. *Proceedings of the Aristotelian Society* 101 (1), pp. 296–308.

Brooks, G. P., and Aalto, S. K. 1981. 'The Rise and Fall of Moral Algebra: Francis Hutcheson and the Mathematization of Psychology'. *Journal of the History of the Behavioral Sciences* 17 (3), pp. 343–56.

Brown, Deborah J. 2014. 'The Sixth Meditation: Descartes and the Embodied Self'. In *The Cambridge Companion to Descartes' Meditations.* Edited by David Cunning, Cambridge: Cambridge University Press, pp. 240–257.

Brown, Deborah J. and Normore, Calvin G. 2019. *Descartes and the Ontology of Everyday Life.* Oxford: Oxford University Press.

318 BIBLIOGRAPHY

Brown, Stuart. 1995. 'Leibniz and the Classical Tradition.' *International Journal of the Classical Tradition* 2, pp. 68–89.

Brown, Stuart. 1998. 'Some Occult Influences on Leibniz's Monadology'. In *Leibniz, Mysticism and Religion*. Edited by Allison P. Coudert, Richard H. Popkin, and Gordon M. Weiner. Dordrecht: Springer, pp. 1–21.

Brown, Stuart. 1998. 'Soul, Body and Natural Immortality'. *The Monist* 81, pp. 573–90.

Brownrig, Ralph. 1661. *Fourty Sermons*. London: T. Roycroft.

Burton, Robert. 1989. *The Anatomy of Melancholy. Volume One*. Edited by Thomas C. Faulkner, Nicolas K. Kiessling and Rhonda L. Blair. Oxford: Clarendon Press.

Cahn, Zilla Gabrielle. 1998. *Suicide in French Thought from Montesquieu to Cioran*. New York: Peter Lang.

Callanan, John J. 2013. *Kant's Groundwork of the Metaphysics of Morals: An Edinburgh Philosophical Guide*. Edinburgh: Edinburgh University Press.

Callanan, John J. 2014. 'Mendelssohn and Kant on Mathematics and Metaphysics'. *Kant Yearbook* 6 (1), pp. 1–22.

Callanan, John J. 2019. 'Kant on Misology and the Natural Dialectic'. *Philosophers Imprint* 19 (47), pp. 1–22.

Camerarius, Elias. 1721. *Bigæ hypothesium Leibnitianarum, quarum prima est de peste certo avertenda altera de morte in exilium acta (du bannissement de la mort) modestam pensitationem*. Tubingæ: Sigmund.

Campos, Andre S. 2010. 'The Individuality of the State in Spinoza's Political Philosophy'. *Archiv für Geschichte der Philosophie* 92 (1), pp. 1–38.

Canguilhem, Georges. 1977. *La formation du concept de réflexe aux XVIIe et XVIIIe siècles*. Paris: Vrin.

Canguilhem, Georges. 2008. *Knowledge of Life*. Edited by Paola Marrati and Todd Meyers. Translated by Stefanos Geroulanos and Daniela Ginsburg. New York: Fordham University Press.

Canz, Israel Gottlieb. 1996. *Meditationes philosophicæ* (1750). Hildesheim: Olms.

Carson, Emily. 1999. 'Kant on the Method of Mathematics'. *Journal of the History of Philosophy* 37 (4), pp. 629–52.

Carson, Emily. 2004. 'Metaphysics, Mathematics and the Distinction between the Sensible and the Intelligible in Kant's Inaugural Dissertation'. *Journal of the History of Philosophy* 42 (2), pp. 165–94.

Casertano, Giovanni. 1984. 'Pleasure, Desire and Happiness in Democritus.' In *Proceedings of the First International Congress of Democritus*. Volume I. Xanthi: Bouloukos, pp. 347–353.

Cassiodorus, F.M. Aurelius. 1865. *Opera omnia in duos tomos distributa*. Edited by Johannes Garetius. Paris: J.P. Migne

Cassirer, Ernst. 1951. *The Philosophy of the Enlightenment*. Translated by Fritz C. A. Koelln and James P. Pettegrove. Princeton: Princeton University Press.

Cassirer, Ernst.. 1983. *Kant's Life and Thought*. Translated by James Haden. New Haven: Yale University Press.

Cavendish, Margaret. 1655. *Philosophical and Physical Opinions*. London: Martin and Allestrye.

Cavendish, Margaret. 1664. *Philosophical Letters, or, Modest reflections upon some opinions in natural philosophy maintained by several famous and learned authors of this age, expressed by way of letters*. London.

Cavendish, Margaret. 1666. *Observations upon Experimental Philosophy*. London: A. Maxwell.

Cavendish, Margaret. 2001. *Observations upon Experimental Philosophy*. Edited by Eileen O'Neill. Cambridge: Cambridge University Press.

Cavendish, Margaret. 2003. 'The Description of a New World Called the Blazing World'. In *Margaret Cavendish, Political Writings*. Edited by Susan James. Cambridge: Cambridge University Press.

Chalmers, David. 2006. 'Strong and Weak Emergence'. In *The Re-emergence of Emergence: The Emergentist Hypothesis from Science to Religion*. Edited by Philip Clayton & Paul Davies. Oxford: Oxford University Press, pp. 244–256.

Chang, Kevin Ku-Ming. 2011. 'Alchemy as Studies of Life and Matter: Reconsidering the Place of Vitalism in Early Modern Chemistry'. *Isis* 102 (2): pp. 322–329.

Charron, Pierre. 1601. *Of Wisdom*. Translated by Samson Lennard. London: Luke Fawne.

Chen, Bohang. 2018. 'A Non-Metaphysical Evaluation of Vitalism in the Early Twentieth Century'. *History and Philosophy of the Life Sciences* 40 (3).

Cheung, Tobias. 2013. 'Limits of Life and Death: Legallois's Decapitation Experiments'. *Journal of the History of Biology* 46, pp. 283–313.

Chitwood, Ava. 2004. *Death by Philosophy. The Biographical Tradition in the Life and Death of the Archaic Philosophers Empedocles, Heraclitus, and Democritus*. Ann Arbor: University of Michigan Press.

Cholbi, Michael. 2000. 'Kant and the Irrationality of Suicide'. *History of Philosophy Quarterly* 17 (2), pp. 159–76.

Choron, Jacques. 1973. 'Death and Immortality'. In *Dictionary of the History of Ideas*. Volume 1. Edited by Philip P. Wiener. New York: Scribner's Sons, pp. 634–46.

Cicero, Marcus Tullius. 1927. *Tusculan Disputations*. Translated by J. E. King. Cambridge, MA: Harvard University Press.

Cicero, Marcus Tullius. 1951. *De natura deorum* I, 43 120. Translated by Harris Rackham. London: Heinemann; Cambridge, MA: Harvard University Press.

Cicero, Marcus Tullius. 1960. *Tusculanae disputationes* I, 11 22. Translated by John E. King. London: Heinemann; Cambridge, MA: Harvard University press.

Cicero, Marcus Tullius. 1991. *On Duties*. Edited by Miriam T. Griffin and E. M. Atkins. Cambridge: Cambridge University Press.

Cicero, Marcus Tullius. 44-43 BC. *Philippicae* [online]. Available at: <http://www.thelatinlibrary.com/cicero/phil2.shtml>.

Cicero, Marcus Tullius. 44 BC. *De officiis ad Marcum filium libri tres* [online]. Available at: <https://www.thelatinlibrary.com/cicero/off.shtml>.

Clarke, Desmond. 1997. 'Introduction'. In La Forge, Louis de. *Treatise on the Human Mind*. Edited and translated by Desmond M. Clarke. Dordrecht: Kluwer, pp. xiii–xxv.

Clarke, Desmond (editor and translator). 2013. *The Equality of the Sexes: Three Feminist Texts of the Seventeenth Century*. Oxford: Oxford University Press.

Clarke, Desmond. 2016. *French Philosophy, 1572-1675*. Oxford: Oxford University Press.

Clauberg, Johannes. 1691. *Opera omnia philosophica*. Amsterdam: Blaeu.

Cleland, Carol E. and Chyba, Christopher F. 2002. 'Defining "Life"'. *Origins of Life and Evolution of the Biosphere* 32 (4), pp. 387–393.

Condette, Jean-François. 2006. 'Dumas, Charles-Louis'. In Condette, Jean-François. *Les recteurs d'académie en France de 1808 à 1940. Dictionnaire biographique*, Tome II. Paris: Institut national de recherche pédagogique, p. 161.

Condillac, Étienne Bonnot de. 1984. *Traité des sensations*. Paris: Fayard.

Connell, Sophia. 2016. *Aristotle on Female Animals: A Study of the Generation of Animals*. Cambridge: Cambridge University Press.

320 BIBLIOGRAPHY

Coole, Diana, and Frost, Samantha. 2010. 'Introducing the New Materialisms'. In *New Materialisms: Ontology, Agency, and Politics*. Edited by Diana Coole and Samantha Frost. Durham: Duke University Press, pp. 1–43.

Cottingham, John. 1985. 'Cartesian Trialism'. *Mind* 94, pp. 218–230.

Cranston, Maurice. 1957. *John Locke. A Biography*. London: Macmillan.

Creiling, Johann Conrad. 1722. *Principia philosophiæ autore G.G. Leibnitio, à § 40 ad finem*. Tubingæ: Sigmund.

Crick, Francis. 1966. *Of Molecules and Men*. Seattle: University of Washington Press.

Critchley, Simon. 2009. *The Book of Dead Philosophers*. London: Granta.

Crocker, Lester G. 1952. 'The Discussion of Suicide in the Eighteenth Century'. *Journal of the History of Ideas* 13 (1), pp. 47–72.

Crone, Daniel M. 1996. 'Historical Attitudes Toward Suicide'. *Duquesne Law Review* 35 (7), pp. 7–42.

Cunningham, Andrew. 2007. 'Hume's Vitalism and Its Implications'. *British Journal for the History of Philosophy* 15 (1), pp. 59–73.

Cudworth, Ralph. 1964. *The True Intellectual System of the Universe: The First Part* (1678) Stuttgart-Bad Cannstatt: Frommann.

Cyprianus, Tashius Caecilius. III cent. CE. *Epistulae* [online]. Available at: <https://archive.org/stream/corpusscriptoru16wissgoog#page/n639/mode/2up>

Daremberg, Charles. 1870. *Histoire des sciences médicales*. 2 volumes. Paris: Baillière.

Debus, Allen George. 1997. 'La médecine chimique.' In *Histoire de la pensée médicale en Occident*. Volume 2. Edited by Mirko D. Grmek. Paris: Le Seuil, pp. 37–59.

De Ceglia, Francesco Paolo. 2006. 'Soul Power: Georg Ernst Stahl and the Debate on Generation'. In *The Problem of Animal Generation in Early Modern Philosophy*. Edited by Justin E.H. Smith. Cambridge: Cambridge University Press, pp. 262–284.

Des Chene, Dennis. 2002. 'Life after Descartes'. Unpublished presentation at HOPOS.

Deleuze, Gilles. 1992. *Expressionism in Philosophy: Spinoza*. Translated by Martin Joughin. New York: Zone Books.

Deleuze, Gilles. 2001. *Spinoza: Practical Philosophy*. Translated by Robert Hurley. San Francisco: City Lights Publishers.

Della Rocca, Michael. 1995. *Representation and the Mind-Body Problem in Spinoza*. New York: Oxford University Press.

Della Rocca, Michael. 2008. *Spinoza*. London: Routledge.

Descartes, René. 1996. *Œuvres*. 11 volumes. Edited by Charles Adam and Paul Tannery. Paris: Vrin.

Descartes, René. 1984–91. *The Philosophical Writings of Descartes*. 3 volumes. Edited and translated by John Cottingham, Robert Stoothof Dugald Murdoch and Anthony Kenny. Cambridge: Cambridge University Press.

Descartes, René. 1998. *Descartes: The World and Other Writings*. Edited and translated by Stephen Gaukroger. Cambridge: Cambridge University Press.

Descartes, René. 2009. *Tutte le lettere 1619-1650*. Edited by Giulia Belgioioso. Milan: Bompiani.

Descartes, René. 2015. *The Passions of the Soul and Other Late Philosophical Writings*. Translated by Michael Moriarty. Oxford: Oxford University Press.

Des Maizeaux, Pierre. 1716. 'Explication d'un passage d'Hippocrate, dans le Livre de la Diete, et du sentiment de Melisse et de Parmenide, sur la Durée des Substances etc.: pour servir de Réponse à un endroit du nouveau système de Mr. Leibnitz, de la Nature et de la Communication des Substances, ou de l'Harmonie préétablie'. *Histoire Critique de la République des Lettres, tant Ancienne que Moderne* 11, pp. 52–72.

BIBLIOGRAPHY 321

Des Maizeaux, Pierre. 1716. 'Nouvelle Explication du Passage d'Hippocrate dont il est parlé dans le II. Article de ce Volume. Par Mr. Des Maizeaux. A Mr. Jean Masson'. *Histoire Critique de la République des Lettres, tant Ancienne que Moderne* 11, pp. 290–7.

Des Maizeaux, Pierre. 1720a. 'Lettre de M. Des Maizeaux à M. l'Abbé Conti; Contenant l'explication d'un passage d'Hippocrate...A Kensington le 21 d'Août 1718'. In *Recueil de diverses pièces, sur la philosophie, la religion naturelle, l'histoire, les mathématiques, etc. par Mrs. Leibniz, Clarke, Newton, et autres Autheurs célèbres.* Volume 2. Amsterdam: Duvillard et Changuion, pp. 362–81.

Des Maizeaux, Pierre (ed.). 1720b. *Recueil de diverses pièces, sur la philosophie, la religion naturelle, l'histoire, les mathématiques, etc. par Mrs. Leibniz, Clarke, Newton, et autres Autheurs célèbres.* 2 volumes. Amsterdam: Duvillard et Changuion.

Detlefsen, Karen. 2014. 'Biology and Theology in Malebranche's Theory of Organic Creation'. In *The Life Sciences in Early Modern Philosophy.* Edited by Ohad Nachtomy and Justin E. H. Smith. Princeton: Princeton University Press.

Detlefsen, Karen. 2016. 'Descartes on the Theory of Life and Methodology in the Life Sciences'. In *Early Modern Medicine and Natural Philosophy.* Edited by Peter Distelzweig, Benjamin Goldberg and Evan Ragland. Berlin: Springer.

Diderot, Denis. 1955–1970. *Correspondance.* Edited by Georges Roth & Jean Varloot. Paris: Minuit.

Diderot, Denis. 1975. *Œuvres complètes.* Edited by Hans Dieckmann, Jacques Proust and Jean Varloot. Paris: Hermann.

Diderot, Denis. 'Tree.' Translated by Ann Marie Thornton. In *The Encyclopedia of Diderot and d'Alembert*, Collaborative Translation Project, University of Michigan [online]. Available at: <https://quod.lib.umich.edu/cgi/t/text/text-idx?c=did;cc=did;rgn=main;view=text;idno=did2222.0001.751>

Donne, John. 1648. *Biathanatos. A Declaration of that Paradoxe, or Thesis, That Self-Homicide is not so Naturally Sin, that it May Never be Otherwise.* London: Humphrey Moseley.

Donne, John. 1839. *Works.* 6 volumes. London: J. W. Parker.

Douglas, Alexander X. 2015. *Spinoza and Dutch Cartesianism.* Oxford: Oxford University Press.

Duchesneau, François. 1998. *Les modèles du vivant de Descartes à Leibniz.* Paris: Vrin.

Duchesneau, François. 2016. *The Leibniz-Stahl Controversy.* Edited and translated by Justin E. H. Smith. New Haven: Yale University Press.

Dumas, Charles-Louis. 1800. *Principes de physiologie, ou introduction à la science expérimentale, philosophique et médicale de l'homme vivant.* 2 volumes. Paris: Crapelet.

Epicurus. 1926. *The Extant Remains.* With short critical apparatus, translation, and notes by Cyril Bailey. Oxford: Clarendon Press.

Erasmus, Desiderius. 2015. *The Praise of Folly.* Translated by Hoyt Hopewell Hudson. Princeton: Princeton University Press.

Etxeberria, Arantza and Wolfe, Charles T. 2018. 'Canguilhem and the Logic of Life'. *Transversal: International Journal for the Historiography of Science* 4, pp. 47–63.

Faubert, Michelle. 2015. 'Romantic Suicide, Contagion, and Rousseau's Julie'. In *Romanticism, Rousseau, Switzerland: New Prospects.* Edited by Angela Esterhammer, Diane Piccitto and Patrick Vincent. London: Palgrave Macmillan, pp. 38–53.

Favaretti Camposampiero, Matteo. Forthcoming. 'Immortal Animals, Subtle Bodies, or Separated Souls: The Afterlife in Leibniz, Wolff, and Their Followers'.

Feldman, Fred. 1978. *Introductory Ethics.* Englewood Cliffs: Prentice-Hall.

BIBLIOGRAPHY

Fénelon, François. 1848–1852, *Abrégé de la vie des plus illustres philosophes*. In *Œuvres complètes de Fénelon*. Volume 7. Paris: Méquignon junior & J. Leroux.

Flenderus, Johannes. 1731. *Phosphorus Philosophicus Novissimus, seu Logica Contracta Claubergiana Illustrata Commentario Logico-Metaphysico*. Amsterdam: Jansson-Waesburg.

Fortunatus, Venantius Honorius C. 1862. *Opera omnia*. Vol. 88 of *Patrologia Latina*. Parisiis: J. P. Migne.

Foulcher, Jane. 2015. *Reclaiming Humility: Four Studies in the Monastic Tradition*. Collegeville: Liturgical Press.

Fox Keller, Evelyn. 2002. *Making Sense of Life*: *Explaining Biological Development with Models, Metaphors, and Machines*. Cambridge, MA: Harvard University Press.

Fraenkel, Carlos. 2006. "Maimonides' God and Spinoza's Deus Sive Natura'. *Journal of the History of Philosophy* 44 (2), pp. 169–215.

Frey, R. G. 1999. 'Hume on Suicide'. *Journal of Medicine and Philosophy* 24 (4), pp. 336–351.

Frick, Karl. 1960. 'Der Tübinger Alchemist und Professor der Mathematik Johann Conrad Creiling (1673-1752)'. *Sudhoffs Archiv für Geschichte der Medizin und der Naturwissenschaften* 44, pp. 223–8.

Gabhart, Mitchell. 1999. 'Spinoza on Self-Preservation and Self-Destruction'. *Journal of the History of Philosophy* 37 (4), pp. 613–628.

Galvin, Richard. 2009. 'The Universal Law Formulas'. In *The Blackwell Guide to Kant's Ethics*. Edited by Thomas E. Hill. Chichester: Wiley-Blackwell, pp. 52–82.

Garber, Daniel. 2001. 'Descartes on Knowledge and Certainty'. In *Descartes Embodied*. Cambridge: Cambridge University Press, pp. 111–129.

Garber, Daniel. 2005. "A Free Man Thinks of Nothing Less Than of Death': Spinoza on the Eternity of the Mind'. In *Spinoza on the Eternity of the Mind*. Edited by Christia Mercer. Oxford University Press, pp. 103–118.

Garrett, Don. 1994. 'Spinoza's Theory of Metaphysical Individuation.' In *Individuation in Early Modern Philosophy*. Edited by Jorge Gracia and Kenneth Barber. Albany: State University of New York Press. pp. 73–101.

Garrett, Don. 2018. *Nature and Necessity in Spinoza's Philosophy*. New York City: Oxford University Press.

Gaukroger, Stephen. 2010. *The Collapse of Mechanism and the Rise of Sensibility: Science and the Shaping of Modernity, 1680–1760*. Oxford: Oxford University Press.

Geiger, Ido. 2010. 'What Is the Use of the Universal Law Formula of the Categorical Imperative?' *British Journal for the History of Philosophy* 18 (2), pp. 271–295.

Gerhard, Johann. 1777. *Loci theologici*, Tome XVII. Tubingæ: Cotta.

Geulincx, Arnold. 1892. *Opera Philosophica*. The Hague: Martinus Nijhoff.

Giglioni, Guido. 2008. 'What Ever Happened to Francis Glisson? Albrecht Haller and the Fate of Eighteenth-Century Irritability'. *Science in Context* 21, pp. 465–493.

Glisson, Francis. 1672. *Tractatus de natura substantiae energetica, seu de vita naturae ejusque tribus facultatibus perceptiva, appetitiva, motiva*. London: Flesher.

G. Gori and M.F. Spallanzani. 2012. "Commentatio mortis". *Le morti dei filosofi in epoca moderna*, special issue of the *Rivista di storia della filosofia*, No 1.

Gournay, Marie le Jars de. 2002a. *De l'égalité des hommes et des femmes* (1622/1641). In *Oeuvres Complètes*. Edited by J-C Arnould. Paris: Honoré-Champion.

Gournay, Marie le Jars de. 2002b. *Apology for the Woman Writing and other works*. Edited and translated by R. Hillman and C. Quesnel. Chicago: University of Chicago Press.

BIBLIOGRAPHY 323

Gori, Giambattista and Spallanzani, Mariafranca (editors). 2012. *"Commentatio mortis". Le morti dei filosofi in epoca moderna*. A special issue of the *Rivista di storia della filosofia* 1.

Goudriaaen, Aza. 2016. 'Descartes, Cartesianism, and Early Modern Theology'. In *The Oxford Handbook of Early Modern Theology, 1600-1800*. Edited by Ulrich L. Lehner, Richard A. Muller and A. G. Roeber. Oxford: Oxford University Press, pp. 533–549.

Grey, John. 2017. 'Reply to Nadler: Spinoza and the Metaphysics of Suicide'. *British Journal for the History of Philosophy* 25 (2), pp. 380–388.

Grigoropoulou, Vasiliki. 2012. 'Descartes's Physics vs. Fear of Death? An Endless *Translatio* of Thoughts and Bodies'. In *Translatio Studiorum: Ancient, Medieval and Modern Bearers of Intellectual History*. Edited by Marco Sgarbi. Leiden: Brill, pp. 177–195.

Grmek, Mirko. 1990. 'La conception mécaniste de la vie'. In Grmek, Mirko. *La Première révolution biologique*. Paris: Payot, pp. 115–139.

Hadot, Pierre. 1995. *Philosophy as a Way of Life*. Edited by Arnold I. Davidson. Translated by Michael Chase. Oxford: Blackwell.

Hale, Matthew. 1805. *Works, Moral and Religious*. 2 volumes. London: R. Wilks.

Hall, Thomas S. 1970. 'Descartes' Physiological Method: Position, Principles, Examples'. *Journal of the History of Biology* 3 (1), pp. 53–79.

Haller, A. von. [1755] 1936. *A Dissertation on the Sensible and Irritable Parts of Animals*, introduction by O. Temkin, Baltimore: The Johns Hopkins Press.

Hansch, Michael Gottlieb. 1728. *Godefridi Guilielmi Leibnitii Principia philosophiæ, more geometrico demonstrata: cum excerptis ex epistolis philosophi et scholiis quibusdam ex historia philosophica*. Francofurti et Lipsiæ: Monath.

Harrison, John and Laslett, Peter. 1971. *The Library of John Locke*. Oxford: Clarendon Press.

Harrison, Timothy. 2020. *Coming to: Consciousness and Natality in Early Modern England*. Chicago: University of Chicago Press.

Harvey William. 1651. *Exercitationes de Generatione Animalium*. London: Pulleyn.

Hatfield, Gary. 1986. 'The Senses and the Fleshless Eye: The Meditations as Cognitive Exercises'. In *Essays on Descartes' Meditations*. Edited by Amélie Oksenberg Rorty. Berkeley: University of California Press, pp. 45–79.

Hazard, Paul. 1965. *European Thought in the Eighteenth Century*. London: Penguin.

Healy, Róisín. 2006. 'Suicide in Early Modern and Modern Europe'. *The Historical Journal* 49 (3), pp. 903–919.

Heller-Roazen, Daniel. 2007. *The Inner Touch: Archeology of a Sensation*. New York: Zone Books.

Henrich, Dieter. 1992. *Aesthetic Judgment and the Moral Image of the World: Studies in Kant*. Stanford: Stanford University Press.

Henry, John. 1987. 'Medicine and Pneumatology: Henry More, Richard Baxter, and Francis Glisson's *Treatise on the Energetic Nature of Substance*'. *Medical History* 31, pp. 15–40.

Henry, Patrick. 1984. 'The Dialectic of Suicide in Montaigne's 'Coustume de l'Isle de Cea''. *The Modern Language Review* 79 (2), pp. 278–89.

Hintikka, Jaakko. 1967. 'Kant on the Mathematical Method'. *The Monist* 51 (3), pp. 352–75.

Hippocrate. 1973. *Oeuvres complètes, traduction nouvelle avec le texte grec en regard*. Edited and translated by Émile Littré. Reprint of the Paris 1839 edition, 9 volumes. Amsterdam: Hakkert.

Hippocrates. 1990. *Pseudepigraphic Writings*. Edited and translated by Wesley D. Smith. Leiden: Brill.

Hirai, Hiro. 2005. *Le concept de semence dans les théories de la matière à la Renaissance de Ficin à Gassendi*. Turnhout: Brepols.

324 BIBLIOGRAPHY

Hobbes, Thomas. 1994. *Leviathan*. Edited by Edwin Curley. Indianapolis: Hackett Publishing.

Hobbes, Thomas. 1996. *Leviathan*. Edited by Richard. Tuck. Cambridge: Cambridge University Press.

Holden, Thomas. 2005. 'Religion and Moral Prohibition in Hume's *Of Suicide*'. *Hume Studies* 31 (2), pp. 189–210.

Holden, Thomas. 2012. *Spectres of False Divinity: Hume's Moral Atheism*. New York: Oxford University Press.

Hooker, Richard. 1676. *Of the Lawes of Ecclesiastical Polity*. London: R. White.

Hooker, Richard. 1888 (7th ed). *Of the Laws of Ecclesiastical Polity*, in *The Works of that Learned and Judicious Divine Mr. Richard Hooker with an Account of His Life and Death by Isaac Walton*. 3 vols. Oxford: Clarendon Press.

Horace, Quintus Flaccus. 1604. *Opera omnia*. Edited by Theodore Marcilius. Paris: B. Macaeum.

Horace, Quintus Flaccus. 1640. *Poemata. Scholijs siue annotationibus, instar commentarii illustrata*. Edited by John Bond. Lugduni: Dunkerus.

Hume, David. 1980. 'Of Suicide'. In *Dialogues Concerning Natural Religion and the posthumous essays Of the Immortality of the Soul and Of Suicide*. Edited by Richard H. Popkin. Indianapolis: Hackett, pp. 97–105.

Hume, David. 1985. *Essays: Moral, Political and Literary*. Edited by Eugene F. Miller. Indianapolis: Liberty Fund.

Hume, David. 2006a. *An Enquiry Concerning Human Understanding*. Edited by Tom L. Beauchamp. New York: Oxford University Press.

Hume, David. 2006b. *An Enquiry Concerning the Principles of Morals*. Edited by Tom L. Beauchamp. New York: Oxford University Press.

Hume, David. 2008. *Selected Essays*. Edited by Stephen Copley and Andrew Edgar. Oxford: Oxford University Press.

Hume, David. 2009. *A Dissertation on the Passions; The Natural History of Religion*. Edited by Tom L. Beauchamp. New York: Oxford University Press.

Hume, David. 2011a. *A Treatise of Human Nature*. Edited by David Fate Norton e Mary J. Norton. New York: Oxford University Press.

Hume, David 2011b. *The Letters of David Hume II*. Edited by J. Y. T. Greig. New York: Oxford University Press.

Huneman, Philippe and Wolfe, Charles T. 2017. 'Man-Machines and Embodiment: From Cartesian Physiology to Claude Bernard's 'Living Machine''. In *Embodiment*. Edited by Justin E. H. Smith. Oxford: Oxford University Press, pp. 257–297.

Hunter, John. 1828. *A Treatise on the Blood, Inflammation and Gun-shot Wounds* (1794). London: Sherwood, Gilbert & Piper.

Hutcheson, Francis. 2004. *An Inquiry into the Original of Our Ideas of Beauty and Virtue* (1726). Edited by Wolfgang Leidhold. Indianapolis: Liberty Fund.

Hutchins, Barnaby R. 2015. 'Descartes, Corpuscles and Reductionism: Mechanism and Systems in Descartes' Physiology'. *The Philosophical Quarterly* 65 (261), pp. 669–689.

Hutchins, Barnaby R. 2016a. 'Descartes and the Dissolution of life'. *The Southern Journal of Philosophy* 54 (2), pp. 155–173.

Hutchins, Barnaby R. 2016b. 'Does Descartes Have a Principle of Life? Hierarchy and Interdependence in Descartes's Physiology'. *Perspectives on Science* 24 (6), pp. 744–769.

Hutchins, Barnaby R. 2016c. 'Obscurity and Confusion: Nonreductionism in Descartes's Biology and Philosophy'. PhD thesis.

James, Susan. 1999. 'The Philosophical Innovations of Margaret Cavendish'. *British Journal for the History of Philosophy* 7 (2), pp. 219–244.

James, Susan. 2011. 'Creating Rational Understanding: Spinoza as a Social Epistemologist'. *Aristotelian Society Supplementary Volume* 85 (1), pp. 181–199.

James, Susan. 2012. *Spinoza on Philosophy, Religion, and Politics: The Theologico-Political Treatise*. Oxford: Oxford University Press.

James, Susan. 2020. *Spinoza on Learning to Live Together*. Oxford; Oxford University Press.

Jaquet, Chantal. 2003. 'Le Mal de mort chez Spinoza, et pourquoi il n'y faut point songer'. In *Fortitude et servitude: Lectures de l'Éthique IV de Spinoza*. Edited by Chantal Jaquet, Pascal Sévérac and Ariel Suhamy. Paris: Kimé, pp. 147–162.

Jeans, James. 1930. *The Mysterious Universe*. Cambridge: Cambridge University Press.

Jehasse, Jean. 1980. 'Démocrite et la renaissance de la critique.' In *Études seiziémistes offertes à V.L. Saulnier*. Geneva: Droz, pp. 41–64.

Jonas, Hans. 1965. 'Spinoza and the Theory of Organism'. *Journal of the History of Philosophy* 3 (1), pp. 43–57.

Jones, Donna V. 2010. *The Racial Discourses of Life Philosophy: Négritude, Vitalism, and Modernity*. New York: Columbia University Press.

Jones, Matthew. 2006. *The Good Life in the Scientific Revolution. Descartes, Pascal, Leibniz and the Cultivation of Virtue*. Chicago: Chicago University Press.

Joukovsky, Françoise. 1969. 'Quelques sources épicuriennes au XVIe siècle'. *Bibliothèque d'Humanisme et Renaissance* 31 (1), pp. 7–25.

Kant, Immanuel. 1900–12. *Kant's Gesammelte Schriften*. Herausgegeben von der Königlich Preussischen Akademie der Wissenschaften, Erste Abteilung: Werke. Berlin: Reimer.

Kant, Immanuel. 1998. *Critique of Pure Reason*. Translated and edited by Paul Guyer and Allen W. Wood. Cambridge: Cambridge University Press.

Kant, Immanuel. 2011. *Groundwork of the Metaphysics of Morals* (1786). Edited by Jens Timmermann. Translated by Jens Timmermann and Mary Gregor. Cambridge: Cambridge University Press.

Kant, Immanuel. 2015. *Critique of Practical Reason*. Translated and edited by Mary Gregor, with a revised introduction by Andrews Reath. Cambridge: Cambridge University Press.

Kawamura, Fumie. 2014. *Diderot et la chimie: science, pensée et écriture*. Paris: Classiques Garnier.

Kelly, Christopher. 2017. 'Rousseau and the Pursuit of Happiness'. In *Rousseau and Dignity: Art Serving Happiness*. Edited by Julia V. Douthwaite. Notre Dame, Indiana: University of Notre Dame Press, pp. 116–31.

Kerger, Martin, 1663. *De fermentatione liber physicus-medicus*. Wittebergæ: Borckard.

King, Peter. 1830. *The Life of John Locke: With Extracts from His Correspondence, Journals and Common-place Books*. 2 volumes. London: H. Colburn and R. Bentley.

Kisner, Matthew. 2010. 'Reconsidering Spinoza's Free Man: The Model of Human Nature'. In *Oxford Studies in Early Modern Philosophy Volume V*. Edited by Daniel Garber and Steven Nadler. Oxford: Oxford University Press, pp. 91–114.

Kisner, Matthew J. 2013. *Spinoza on Human Freedom: Reason, Autonomy And The Good Life*. Cambridge: Cambridge University Press.

Kleiman-Lafon, Sylvie and Wolfe, Charles T. Forthcoming. 'Unsystematic Vitality: From Early Modern Beeswarms to Contemporary Swarm Intelligence'. In *Active Materials*. Edited by Peter Fratzl, Michael Friedman, Karin Krauthausen and Wolfgang Schäffner. Berlin: De Gruyter.

326 BIBLIOGRAPHY

Klein, Julie R. 2014. "'Something of It Remains': Spinoza and Gersonides on Intellectual Eternity'. In *Spinoza and Jewish Philosophy*. Edited by Steven Nadler. Cambridge: Cambridge University Press, pp. 177–203.

Klein, Julie R. 2019. 'Freedom, Action, and Motivation in Spinoza's Ethics'. In *Materializing Spinoza's Account of Human Freedom*. Edited by Noa Naaman-Zauderer. New York: Routledge, pp. 152–173.

Korsgaard, Christine M. 1996. *Creating the Kingdom of Ends*. Cambridge: Cambridge University Press.

Koshland, Daniel E. 2002. 'The Seven Pillars of Life'. *Science* 295 (5563), pp. 2215–2216.

Kraye, Jill. 1988. 'Moral Philosophy'. In *The Cambridge History of Renaissance Philosophy*. Edited by Charles B. Schmitt; Quentin Skinner, Eckhard Kessler and Jill Kraye. Cambridge: Cambridge University Press, pp. 301–386.

Kuehn, Manfred. 2001. *Kant: A Biography*. Cambridge: Cambridge University Press.

Lactantius, Lucius Caecilius Firmianus. 1886. 'The Divine Institutes'. In *Ante-Nicene Fathers. Volume 7: Lactantius, Venantius, Asterius, Victorinus, Dionysius, Apostolic Teaching and Constitutions, 2 Clement, Early Liturgies*. Edited by A. Cleveland Coxe, James Donaldson and Alexander Roberts. New York: Christian Literature Publishing Co., pp. 9–258.

Lærke, Mogens. 2014. 'Spinoza's Language'. *Journal of the History of Philosophy* 52 (3), pp. 519–547.

Laërtius, Diogenes. 1925. *Lives of Eminent Philosophers*. 2 volumes. Translated by Robert D. Hicks. Cambridge, MA: Harvard University Press.

Laërtius, Diogenes. 1593. *De vitis, dogmatis & apophthegmatis clarorum philosophorum libri X, [...] Is. Casauboni Notae ad lib. Diogenis, multo auctiores et emendatiores*, H. Stephanus.

Laërtius, Diogenes. 1664. *De vitiis dogmatis et apophthegmatis eorum qui in philosophia claruerunt libri X, Thoma Aldobrandino interprete [...]*, Londini, Pulleyn.

La Forge, Louis de. 1974. *Oeuvres Philosophiques avec une étude bio-bibliographique*. Edited by Pierre Clair. Paris: PUF.

La Forge, Louis de. 1997. *Treatise on the Human Mind*. Edited and translated by Desmond M. Clarke. Dordrecht: Kluwer.

Laks, André. 2016. *Early Greek Philosophy. Volume VII: Later Ionian and Athenian Thinkers. Part 2: The Atomists*. Edited and translated by André Laks. Cambridge, MA: Harvard University Press.

Lana, Italo. 1951. 'L'etica di Democrito.' *Rivista di filosofia* 42, pp. 13–29.

LeBuffe, Michael. 2010. *From Bondage to Freedom: Spinoza On Human Excellence*. New York: Oxford University Press.

Le Grand, Antoine. 1705. *An Entire Body of Philosophy According to the Principles of the Famous Renate Des Cartes*. London: Samuel Roycroft.

Leibniz, Gottfried Wilhelm. 1715. 'Eloge critique des Oeuvres de Milord Shaftesbury'. *Histoire Critique de la République des Lettres, tant Ancienne que Moderne* 10, pp. 306–327.

Leibniz, Gottfried Wilhelm. 1718. 'Principes de la nature et de la grace fondez en raison, par feu M. le Baron de Leibnitz'. *L'Europe Savante* (November 1718), pp. 101–123.

Leibniz, Gottfried Wilhelm. 1720a. *Lehr-Sätze über die Monadologie*. Translated by Heinrich Köhler. Franckfurth und Leipzig: Meyers.

Leibniz, Gottfried Wilhelm. 1720b. 'Lettre de M. Leibniz à M. Des Maizeaux, contenant quelques Éclaircissements sur l'*Explication* précédente, et sur d'autres endroits du Système de l'*Harmonie Préétablie*, etc. Hanover ce 8. Juillet 1711.' In *Recueil de diverses pièces, sur la philosophie, la religion naturelle, l'histoire, les mathématiques, etc. par Mrs. Leibniz, Clarke, Newton, et autres Autheurs célèbres*, volume 2. Edited by Pierre Des Maizeaux. Amsterdam: Duvillard et Changuion, pp. 382–388.

Leibniz, Gottfried Wilhelm. 1721. 'Principia philosophiæ, autore G.G. Leibnitio.' *Actorum Eruditorum Supplementa* 7, pp. 500–514.

Leibniz, Gottfried Wilhelm. 1923. *Sämtliche Schriften und Briefe*. Berlin: Akademie Verlag.

Leibniz, Gottfried Wilhelm. 1978. *Die philosophischen Schriften*. 7 volumes. Edited by Carl Immanuel Gerhardt. Hildesheim: Olms.

Leibniz, Gottfried Wilhelm, 1985. *Theodicy*. Translated by E. M. Huggard. La Salle: Open Court.

Leibniz, Gottfried Wilhelm. 1989a. *Philosophical Essays*. Translated by Roger Ariew and Daniel Garber. Indianapolis: Hackett.

Leibniz, Gottfried Wilhelm. 1989b. *Philosophical Papers and Letters*. Edited and translated by Leroy E. Loemker, 2nd ed. Dordrecht: Kluwer.

Leibniz, Gottfried Wilhelm. 1996. *Philosophische Schriften*. Edited by Hans Heinz Holz. Frankfurt/Main: Suhrkamp.

Leibniz, Gottfried Wilhelm. 1997. *Leibniz's 'New System' and Associated Contemporary Texts*. Edited and translated by Roger S. Woolhouse and Richard Francks. Oxford: Oxford University Press.

Leibniz, Gottfried Wilhelm. 2011. *Leibniz and the Two Sophies: The Philosophical Correspondence*. Edited and translated by Lloyd Strickland. Toronto: Iter Inc. & the Centre for Reformation and Renaissance Studies.

Leibniz, Gottfried Wilhelm and Wolff, Christian. 1963. *Briefwechsel zwischen Leibniz und Christian Wolff aus den Handschriften der Koeniglichen Bibliothek zu Hannover* (1860). Edited by Carl Immanuel Gerhardt. Hildesheim: Olms.

Lennon, Thomas. 2013. 'Descartes and Pelagianism'. *Essays in Philosophy* 14 (2), pp. 194–217.

Lessius, Leonardus, S.J. 1617. *De providentia numinis et animi immortalitate libri duo adversus Atheos et Politicos*. Second edition. Antwerp: Balthasar and Joannes Moretus.

Levitin, Dimitri. 2015. *Ancient Wisdom in the Age of the New Science. Histories of Philosophy in England, c. 1640 - 1700*. Cambridge: Cambridge University Press.

Lin, Martin. 2005. 'Memory and Personal Identity in Spinoza'. *Canadian Journal of Philosophy* 35(2), pp. 243–268.

Lind, Vera. 1999. *Selbstmord in der Frühen Neuzeit*. Göttingen: Vandenhoeck & Ruprecht.

Locke, John. 1824. *Works*. 9 volumes. London: Rivington.

Locke, John. 1936. *An Early Draft of Locke's* Essay *together with Excerpts of his Journals*. Edited by Richard I. Aaron and Jocelyn Gibb. Oxford: Clarendon Press.

Locke, John. 1954. *Essays on the Law of Nature and Associated Writings*. Edited by Wolfgang von Leyden. Oxford: Clarendon Press.

Locke, John. 1960. *Two Treatises of Government*. Edited by Peter Laslett. Cambridge: Cambridge University Press.

Locke, John. 1975. *Essay Concerning Human Understanding*. Edited by Paul H. Nidditch. Oxford: Oxford University Press.

Locke, John. *Correspondence*. 1976-1989. Edited by Esmond S. de Beer. 8 volumes. Oxford: Clarendon Press.

Locke, John. 1987. *A Paraphrase and Notes on the Epistles of St Paul*. Edited by Arthur W. Wainright. 2 volumes. Oxford: Oxford University Press.

Locke, John. 1989. *Some Thoughts Concerning Education*. Edited by John W. and Jean S. Yolton. Oxford: Clarendon Press.

328 BIBLIOGRAPHY

Locke, John. 1996. *Some Thoughts Concerning Education*. Indianapolis: Hackett Publishing.

LoLordo, Antonia. 2007. *Pierre Gassendi and the Birth of Early Modern Philosophy*. Cambridge: Cambridge University Press.

Lordat, Jacques. 1842. *Apologie de l'école médicale de Montpellier; en réponse à la lettre écrite par M. Peisse à M. le Professeur Lordat*. Paris: J.-B. Baillière.

Lough, John. 1953. *Locke's Travels in France 1675-1679*. Cambridge: Cambridge University Press.

Lugt, Maaike van der. 2011. 'Neither Ill nor Healthy. The Intermediate State Between Health and Disease in Medieval Literature'. *Quaderni storici* 136, pp. 13–46.

Luria, Salomon. 2016. *Democritus*. Translated by C.W. Taylor [online]. Available at: <https://www.academia.edu/25014428/S.Y_Luria_Demokrit_English_translation_by_C. C.W_Taylor>.

Lusitanus, Amatus. 1635. *Commentarium in Hippocratis Coi Libellum de Alimento*. Florence: Serinartellium.

Lüthy, Christoph. 2000. 'The Fourfold Democritus on the Stage of Early Modern Science'. *Isis* 91 (3), pp. 443–479.

MacDonald, Michael and Murphy, Terence R. 1990. *Sleepless Souls. Suicide in Early Modern England*. Oxford: Oxford University Press.

MacDonald Ross, George. 1982. 'Alchemy and the Development of Leibniz's Metaphysics'. In *Theoria cum praxi. Akten des III. internationalen Leibnizkongresses*. Volume 4. Wiesbaden: Steiner, pp. 40–45.

MacKenzie, Ann Wilbur. 1975. 'A Word About Descartes' Mechanistic Conception of Life'. *Journal of the History of Biology* 8 (1), pp. 1–13.

Makin, Bathshua. 1673. *Essay to Revive the Antient Education of Gentlewomen*. London: J.D.

Malebranche, Nicolas. 1979–92. *Entretiens sur la métaphysique et sur la religion*. In *Œuvres. Volume 2*. Edited by Geneviève Rodis-Lewis and Germain Malbreil. Paris: Gallimard, pp. 649–967.

Malebranche, Nicolas. 1979–92. *Entretiens sur la mort*. In *Œuvres. Volume 2*. Edited by Geneviève Rodis-Lewis and Germain Malbreil. Paris: Gallimard, pp. 969–1040.

Malebranche, Nicolas. 1993. *Treatise on Ethics*. Translated by Craig Walton. Dordrecht: Springer.

Malebranche, Nicolas. 1997. *The Search After Truth*. Edited by Thomas M. Lennon and Paul J. Olscamp. Cambridge: Cambridge University Press.

Mandeville, Bernard. 1988. *The Fable of the Bees*. Edited by Frederick B. Kaye. 2 volumes. Indianapolis: Liberty Fund.

Manning, Gideon. 2019. 'Health in the Early Modern Philosophical Tradition'. In *Health: A History*. Edited by Peter Adamson. Oxford: Oxford University Press, pp. 180–221.

Manton, Thomas. 1873. *The complete works*. 22 volumes. London: James Nisbet.

Markovits, Francine. 2012. 'Une attitude libertine: badiner avec la mort. Boureau-Deslandes et ses *Réflexions sur les grands qui sont morts en plaisantant*'. *Rivista di storia della filosofia LXVII* (1), pp. 19–34.

Martin, Julian. 1990. "Sauvages' Nosology. Medical Enlightenment in Montpellier'. In *The Medical Enlightenment of the Eighteenth Century*. Edited by Andrew Cunningham and Roger French. Cambridge: Cambridge University Press, pp. 111–138.

Matson, Wallace. 1966. 'Why Isn't the Mind-Body Problem Ancient?'. In *Mind, Matter, and Method: Essays in Philosophy and Science in Honor of Herbert Feigl*. Edited by Paul Feyerabend and Grover Maxwell. Minneapolis: University of Minnesota Press, p. 92–102.

BIBLIOGRAPHY   329

Marrama, Oberto. 2017. 'Consciousness, Ideas of Ideas and Animation in Spinoza's Ethics'. *British Journal for the History of Philosophy* 25 (3), pp. 506–525.

Marshall, Eugene. 2014. *The Spiritual Automaton: Spinoza's Science of the Mind*. Oxford: Oxford University Press.

Marshall, John. 1997. *John Locke. Resistance, Religion and Responsibility*. Cambridge: Cambridge University Press.

Masham, Damaris Cudworth. 2004. *A Discourse concerning the Love of God*. In *The Philosophical Works of Damaris, Lady Masham*. Edited by James G. Buickerood. Bristol: Thoemmes Continuum, pp. 11–26.

Mason, Richard. 2007. 'Intelligibility'. In Richard Mason, *Spinoza: Logic, Knowledge and Religion*. Aldershot: Ashgate, pp. 109–122.

Matheron, Alexandre. 1988. *Individu et communauté chez Spinoza*. Paris: Les Éditions de Minuit.

Matheron, Alexandre. 1991. 'Essence, Existence and Power in Ethics 1: the Foundations of Proposition 16'. In *God and Nature: Spinoza's Metaphysics*. Edited by Yirmiyahu Yovel. Leiden: E.J. Brill, pp. 23–34.

Matheron, Alexandre. 1991. 'Physique et ontologie chez Spinoza: l'énigmatique réponse à Tschirnhaus'. *Cahiers Spinoza* 6, pp. 83–109.

Matson, Wallace. 1977. 'Death and Destruction in Spinoza's Ethics'. *Inquiry: An Interdisciplinary Journal of Philosophy* 20 (1–4), pp. 403–417.

Maupertuis, Pierre Louis. 1751. *Essai de Philosophie Morale*. Chez Elie Luzac, fils.

Mayr, Ernst. 1982. *The Growth of Biological Thought. Diversity, Evolution, and Inheritance*. Cambridge, MA: Harvard University Press.

Melanchthon, Philippus. 1834. 'Epistolarum, Praefationum, Consiliorum Liber Primus'. In *Opera quae supersunt omnia. Corpus Reformatorum*. Volume 1. Edited by C.G. Bretshneider. Halis: G. A. Schwethske.

Ménuret de Chambaud, J.-J. 1765. "Pouls (Méd. Econom. anim. Physiol. Séméiot.)." In Denis Diderot and Jean le Rond D'Alembert (eds.) *Encyclopédie ou Dictionnaire raisonné des sciences, des arts et des métiers*, vol. XIII, 205–240. Paris: Briasson.

Mclean, G. R. 2001. 'Hume and the Theistic Objection to Suicide'. *American Philosophical Quarterly* 38 (1), pp. 99–111.

Mendelssohn, Moses. 1997. *Moses Mendelssohn: Philosophical Writings*. Translated by Daniel O. Dahlstrom. Cambridge: Cambridge University Press.

Merrill, K. R. 1999. 'Hume on Suicide'. *History of Philosophy Quarterly* 16 (4), pp. 395–412.

Miller, Jon. 2005. 'Stoics and Spinoza on Suicide'. In *Der Einfluss des Hellenismus auf die Philosophie der Frühen Neuzeit*. Edited by Gábor Boros. Wiesbaden: Harrassowitz Verlag.

Miller, Jon. 2015. *Spinoza and the Stoics*. Cambridge: Cambridge University Press.

Mills, Susan. 2017. 'Death to Death: Descartes, Living Bodies, and the Concept of Death'. *Journal of Philosophy of Life* 7 (2), pp. 338–360.

Milton, John. 1991. 'Paradise Lost'. In *John Milton: A Critical edition of the Major Works*. Edited by Stephen Orgel and Jonathan Goldberg. Oxford: Oxford University Press.

Milton, John. 1644. *Of Education. To Master Samuel Hartlib*. London: Thomas Underhill.

Minois, Georges. 1999. *History of Suicide: Voluntary Death in Western Culture*. Translated by Lydia G. Cochrane. Baltimore: John Hopkins University Press.

Minucius Felix, M. 1885. *Octavius*. In James Donaldson, Alexander Roberts, Arthur Cleveland Coxe (eds.), *Ante-Nicene Fathers*. Volume IV. *Fathers of the Third Century: Tertullian, Part Fourth; Minucius Felix, Commodian, Origen, Parts first and second*. New York: Christian Literature Publishing Co., 173–198.

330 BIBLIOGRAPHY

Monaco, Davide. 2019. 'Individuation and Death in Spinoza's Ethics. The Spanish Poet Case Reconsidered'. *British Journal for the History of Philosophy* 27 (5), pp. 941–958.

Montaigne, Michel de. 1652. *Les Essaiys*. Paris: Courbé.

Montaigne, Michel de. 1845. *The Works of Michel de Montaigne*. Translated by Charles Cotton and edited by William Hazlitt. London: Templeman.

Montaigne, Michel de. 1991. *The Complete Essays*. Translated by M. A. Screech. London: Penguin.

Montaigne, Michel de. 1992. *Les Essais*. 3 volumes. Edited by Pierre Villey and V.-L. Saulnier. Paris: Quadrige/Presses Universitaires de France.

Montaigne, Michel de. 2003. *Essays*. Translated by Michael A. Screech. London: Penguin.

More, Henry. 1987. *The Immortality of the Soul*. Edited by Alexander Jacob. Dordrecht: Nijhoff.

More, Thomas. 2002. *Utopia*. Edited by George M. Logan and Robert M. Adams. Cambridge: Cambridge University Press.

Moreau, Pierre-François. 1994. *Spinoza: l'expérience et l'éternité*. Paris: Presses Universitaires de France - PUF.

Morfino, Vittorio. 2006. 'Spinoza: An Ontology of Relation?'. *Graduate Faculty Philosophy Journal* 27 (1), pp. 103–127.

Moriarty, Michael. 2006. *Fallen Nature, Fallen Selves: Early Modern French Thought II*. Oxford: Oxford University Press.

Moriarty, Michael. 2020. *Pascal: Reasoning and Belief*. Oxford: Oxford University Press.

Morris, Katherine J. 1995. 'Intermingling and Confusion'. *International Journal of Philosophical Studies* 3 (2), pp. 290–306.

Mower, Gordon B. 2013. 'Hume on Suicide'. *The European Legacy* 18 (5), pp. 563–575.

Müller, Georg Heinrich. 1779. *Observationes historico-theologicæ de exilio mortis Leibnitiano, seu de duplici animorum corpore crassiore uno quod deponitur in morte subtili altero quod anima post mortem secum vehere dicitur*. Tubingæ: Reiss.

Murray, Alexander. 2000. *Suicide in the Middle Ages. Volume II: The Curse on Self-Murder*. Oxford: Oxford University Press.

Nachtomy, Ohad and Smith, Justin E. H. 2014. *The Life Sciences in Early Modern Philosophy*. Oxford: Oxford University Press.

Nadler, Steven. 2004. *Spinoza's Heresy: Immortality and the Jewish Mind*. Oxford: Oxford University Press.

Nadler, Steven. 2008. 'Spinoza and Consciousness'. *Mind* 117 (467), pp. 575–601.

Nadler, Steven. 2012. 'Spinoza's Monism and the Reality of the Finite'. In *Spinoza on Monism*. Edited by Philip Goff. New York: Palgrave Macmillan, pp. 233–243.

Nadler, Steven. 2015. 'On Spinoza's 'Free Man''. *Journal of the American Philosophical Association* 1 (1), pp. 103–120.

Nadler, S. 2016. "Spinoza on Lying and Suicide." *British Journal for the History of Philosophy* 24. 2: 257-278.

Nadler, Steven. 2020. *Think Least of Death: Spinoza on How to Live and How to Die*. Princeton: Princeton University Press.

Naudé, Gabriel. 1625, *Apologie pour tous les grands personnages qui ont été faussement soupçonnés de magie*. Paris: chez F. Targa, pp. 271–289.

Obbink, Dirk. 1989. 'The Atheism of Epicurus'. *Greek, Roman and Byzantine Studies* 30 (2), pp. 187–223.

O'Neill, Onora. 1975. *Acting on Principle: An Essay on Kantian Ethics*. New York: Columbia University Press.

BIBLIOGRAPHY 331

Pagel, Walter. 1944. 'William Harvey: Some Neglected Aspects of Medical History'. *Journal of the Warburg and Courtauld Institutes* 7, pp. 144–153.

Pagel, Walter. 1953. 'The reaction to Aristotle in Seventeenth-Century Biological Thought: Campanella,Van Helmont, Glanvill, Charleton, Harvey, Glisson, Descartes'. In *Science, Medicine and History*. Edited by E. Ashworth Underwood. London: Oxford University Press, pp. 489–509.

Pascal, Blaise. 1675. *Pensées de Messieur Pascal sur la religion*. Lyon: Adam Demen.

Pascal, Blaise. 1963. *Œuvres completes*. Edited by Louis Lafuma. Paris: Éditions du Seuil.

Pascal, Blaise. 1998-2000. *Œuvres completes*. 2 volumes. Edited by Michel Le Guern. Paris: Gallimard.

Pascal, Blaise. 2010. *Pensées, opuscules et lettres*. Edited by Philippe Sellier. Paris: Classiques Garnier.

Paterculus, Velleius. 30 CE. *Historiae Romanae ad M. Vinicius libri duo*. [online]. Available at: <https://www.thelatinlibrary.com/vell2.html#104>.

Paton, Herbert J. 1946. *The Categorical Imperative: A Study in Kant's Moral Philosophy*. London: Hutchinson.

Paullini, Christian Franz. 1703. *Disquisitio curiosa an mors naturalis plerumque sit substantia verminosa?* Francofurti et Lipsiæ: Stößeln.

Paullini, Christian Franz. 1692. *Zeit-kürtzender erbaulichen Lust, oder, allerhand außerlesener, rar- und curioser, so nütz- als ergetzlicher, Geist- und Weltlicher, Merckwürdigkeiten erster Theil*. Franckfurth am Mayn: Knochen.

Pelletier, Arnauld. 2016. 'La réception perdue: la monadologie démontrée de Michael Gottlieb Hansch'. *Les études philosophiques* (2016), pp. 475–93.

Pfaff, Christoph Matthäus, 1728. 'Fragmentum epistolæ a cel. D. Christoph. Matthæo Pfaffio...ad doctissimum quendam Virum perscriptæ'. *Acta eruditorum* (March 1728): 125–7.

Pfaff, Christoph Matthäus. 1722. *Schediasma orthodoxum dogmatico-polemico-asceticum de morte naturali*. Tubingæ: Reisii vidua.

Philostratus, 2006. *Apollonius of Tyana, vol. III: Letters of Apollonius. Ancient Testimonia. Eusebius's Reply*. Edited and translated by Christopher P. Jones. Cambridge, MA: Harvard University Press.

Pidoux, Herman. 1853. *Les Vrais principes de la matière médicale et de la thérapeutique*. Paris: Béchet jeune.

Piquer, Andrés. 1762. *Institutiones medicae*. Matriti: Ibarram.

Pinkard, Terry. 2008. *German Philosophy: 1760–1860; the Legacy of Idealism*. Cambridge: Cambridge University Press.

Plato. 1994. *The Collected Dialogues of Plato, Including the Letters*. Edited by E. Hamilton and H. Cairns. Princeton: Princeton University Press.

Plutarch. 1928. *Moralia*. 2 volumes. Translated by F. C. Babbitt. Harvard: Loeb Classical Library.

Plutarch. 2005. *On Sparta*. Edited by Richard Talbert. London: Penguin.

Poiret, Pierre. 1687. *L'œconomie divine, ou système universel et démontré des œuvres et des desseins de Dieu envers les hommes*, 7 volumes. Amsterdam: Wetsein.

Poulain de la Barre, François. 1673. *Discours physique et moral de l'égalité des deux sexes*, Paris: J Dupuis.

Poulain de la Barre, François. 1674. *De l'éducation des dames pour la conduite de l'esprit dans les sciences et dans les mœurs*. Paris: J. Dupuis.

Poulain de la Barre, François. 1675. *De l'excellence des hommes contre l'égalité des sexes*. Paris: J. Dupuis.

332 BIBLIOGRAPHY

Poulain de la Barre, François. 2002. *Three Cartesian Feminist Treatises*. Edited by Marcell Maistre Welch. Translated by Vivien Bosley. Chicago: University of Chicago Press.

Poulain de la Barre, François. 2011. *De l'égalité des deux sexes, de l'éducation des dames, De l'excellence des hommes*. Edited by M.-F. Pellegrin. Paris: Vrin.

Pseudo-Democritus. 2009. *Scritti alchemici. Con il commento di Sinesio*. Edited by Matteo Martelli. Milano-Paris: Arché.

Quantin, Jean Louis. 2009. *The Church of England and Christian Antiquity: The Construction of a Confessional Identity in the 17th century*. Oxford: Oxford University Press.

Ravven, Heidi M. 1998. 'Spinoza's Individualism Reconsidered: Some Lessons from the 'Short Treatise on God, Man, and His Well-Being", *Iyyun: The Jerusalem Philosophical Quarterly* / עיון: רבעון פילוסופי, 47, pp. 265–292.

Reeves, William. 1709. *The Apologies of Justin Martyr, Tertullian and Minucius Felix in defence of the Christian religion with the commonitory of Vincentius Lirinensis translated with a preliminary discourse upon each author. Together with a prefatory dissertation about the right use of the Fathers*. London.

Reich, Klaus. 2001. 'Die Tugend in der Idee: Zur Genese von Kants Ideenlehre'. In Klaus Reich, *Gesammelte Schriften*. Hamburg: Meiner, pp. 306–313.

Renz, Ursula. 2003. 'Klar, aber nicht deutlich. Descartes' Schmerzbeispiele vor dem Hintergrund seiner Philosophie'. *Studia philosophica* 62, pp. 149–166.

Renz, Ursula. 2018. *The Explainability of Experience. Realism and Subjectivity in Spinoza's Theory of the Human Mind*. Oxford: Oxford University Press.

Renz, Ursula. 2019. 'Spinozist Cognitive Psychology: Spinoza's Concept of the Imagination'. In *Konzepte der Einbildungskraft in der Philosophie, den Wissenschaften und den Künsten des 18. Jahrhunderts. Udo Thiel zum 65. Geburtstag*. Edited by Rudolf Meer, Giuseppe Motta and Gideon Stiening. Berlin: De Gruyter, pp. 9–24.

Renz, Ursula. Forthcoming. "Spinoza's Epistemology". In: *Cambridge Companion to Spinoza*. Edited by Don Garrett. Cambridge: Cambridge University Press.

Revius, Jacobus. 2002. *A Theological Examination of Cartesian Philosophy: Early Criticisms*. Edited by Aza Goudriaaen. Leiden: Brill.

Richardot, Anne. 2000. 'Un philosophe au purgatoire des Lumières: Démocrite'. *Dix-huitième siècle* 32, pp. 197–212

Richardot, Anne. 2002. *Le rire des Lumières*. Paris: Champion.

Rorty, Amelie Oksenberg. 1987. 'The Two Faces of Spinoza'. *Review of Metaphysics* 41 (2), pp. 299–316.

Rousseau, Jean-Jacques. 1979. *Emile: Or, On Education*. Translated by Allan Bloom. New York: Basic Books.

Rousseau, Jean-Jacques. 1997. *Julie or the New Heloise. Letters of Two Lovers Who Live in a Small Town at the Foot of the Alps*. Translated by Philip Stewart and Jean Vaché. Hanover: University Press of New England.

Rousseau, Jean-Jacques. 2009. *Discourse Concerning the Origins of Inequality*. Translated by Franklin Philip. Oxford: Oxford University Press.

Rousseau, Jean-Jacques. 2010. *Emile or On Education*. Translated by Christopher Kelly and Allan Bloom. Hanover: University Press of New England.

Ruiz-Mirazo, Kepa, Peretó, Juli and Moreno, Alvaro. 2004. 'A Universal Definition of Life: Autonomy and Open-Ended Evolution'. *Origins of Life and Evolution of the Biosphere* 34 (3), pp. 323–346.

BIBLIOGRAPHY 333

Ruler, Han van. 2007. 'Le Sage et l'Amour de Dieu. Conceptions philosophiques de la béatitude d'Érasme à Spinoza'. In *Spinoza et la Renaissance*. Edited by Saverio Ansaldi. Paris: Presses de l'Université Paris-Sorbonne, pp. 57–80.

Ruler, Han van. 2008. 'Substituting Aristotle: Platonic Themes in Dutch Cartesianism'. In *Platonism at the Origins of Modernity*. Edited by Douglas Hedley and Sarah Hutton. Dordrecht: Springer, pp. 159–175.

Sacksteder, William. 1977. 'Spinoza on Part and Whole: The Worm's Eye View'. *Southwestern Journal of Philosophy* 8 (3), pp. 139–159.

Sacksteder, William. 1985. 'Simple Wholes and Complex Parts: Limiting Principles in Spinoza'. *Philosophy and Phenomenological Research* 45 (3), pp. 393–406.

Saint-Paul, Eustache de. 1609. *Summa philosophiae quadripartita, de rebus dialecticis, moralibus, physicis et metaphysicis*. 2 volumes. Paris: Charles Chastellain.

Salem, Jean. 1996a. 'La fortune de Démocrite'. *Revue philosophique de la France et de l'Étranger* 186 (1), pp. 55–74.

Salem, Jean. 1996b. *La légende de Démocrite*. Paris: Kimé.

Salem, Jean. 2002. *Démocrite. Grain de poussière dans un rayon de soleil*. Paris: Vrin.

Sanderson, Robert. 1841. *Sermons*. 2 volumes. London: T. Arnold.

Savile, Anthony. 2002. 'Leibniz, Composite Substances and the Persistence of Living Things'. In *Individuals, Essence and Identity. Themes of Analytic Metaphysics*. Edited by Andrea Bottani, Massimiliano Carrara and Pierdaniele Giaretta. Dordrecht: Kluwer, pp. 355–67.

Savini, Massimiliano. 2006. 'L'insertion du cartésianisme en logique: la *Logica vetus et nova* de Johannes Clauberg'. *Revue de métaphysique et de morale* 49, pp. 73–88.

Savini, Massimiliano. 2011. *Johannes Clauberg: Methodus Cartesiana et Ontologie*. Paris: Vrin.

Schmaltz, Tad. 2016. *Early Modern Cartesianisms: Dutch and French Constructions*. Oxford: Oxford University Press.

Schmitter, Amy. 2018. 'Cartesian Prejudice: Gender, Education, and Authority in Poulain de la Barre'. *Philosophy Compass* 13 (12), pp. 1–12.

Schneewind, J. B. 1998. *The Invention of Autonomy. A History of Modern Moral Philosophy*. Cambridge: Cambridge University Press.

Schonecker, Dieter, and Allen Wood. 2015. *Immanuel Kant's Groundwork for the Metaphysics of Morals: A Commentary*. Cambridge, MA: Harvard University Press.

Schönfeld, Martin. 2000. *The Philosophy of the Young Kant : The Precritical Project*. Oxford: Oxford University Press.

Schurman, Anna Maria van. 1641. *Dissertatio De Ingenii Muliebris ad Doctrinam et meliores Litteras aptitudine*. Leiden: Elsevier.

Schurig, Martin. 1731. *Syllepsilogia historico-medica hoc est conceptionis muliebris consideratio physico-medico-forensis*, Dresdæ et Lipsiæ: Hekel.

Scodel, Joshua. 2002. *Excess and the Mean in Early Modern English Literature*. Princeton: Princeton University Press.

Screech, Michael A. 1985. 'Good Madness in Christendom'. In *The Anatomy of Madness: Essays in the History of Psychiatry*. Volume 1. Edited by William F. Bynum, Roy Porter and Michael Shepherd. London: Tavistock, pp. 25–39.

Seneca, Lucius Annaeus. 1917-25. *Epistles* [*Ad Lucilium Epistulae Morales*]. 3 volumes. Edited and translated by Richard M. Gummere. Cambridge, MA: Harvard University Press.

Seneca, Lucius Annaeus. 2015. *Letters on Ethics*. Translated by Margaret Graver and A. A. Long. Chicago: University of Chicago Press.

334 BIBLIOGRAPHY

Shaftesbury, Anthony Ashley Cooper. 1711. *Characteristicks of Men, Manners, Opinions, Times*. 3 volumes. London: Darby.

Shaftesbury, Anthony Ashley Cooper. 1999. *Characteristics of Men, Manners, Opinions, Times*. Edited by Lawrence E. Klein. Cambridge: Cambridge University Press.

Shagan, Ethan H. 2012. *The Rule of Moderation*. Cambridge: Cambridge University Press.

Sharp, Hasana. 2011. *Spinoza and the Politics of Renaturalization*. Chicago: University of Chicago Press.

Sharp, Hasana. 2017. 'Spinoza's Commonwealth and the Anthropomorphic Illusion'. *Philosophy Today* 61 (4), pp. 833–846.

Shein, Noa. 2015. 'Causation and Determinate Existence of Finite Modes in Spinoza'. *Archiv für Geschichte der Philosophie* 97 (3), pp. 334–357.

Shell, Susan Meld. 2009. *Kant and the Limits of Autonomy*. Cambridge, MA: Harvard University Press.

Silhon, Jean de. 1991. *Les Deux Vérités, l'une de Dieu et de sa providence, l'autre de l'immortalité de l'âme*. Edited by Jean Robert Armogathe. Paris: Arthème Fayard.

Simmons, Alison. 2011. 'Re-Humanizing Descartes'. *Philosophic Exchange* 41 (1), pp. 1–20.

Simmons, Alison. 2012. 'Cartesian Consciousness Reconsidered'. *Philosophers Imprint* 12 (2) pp. 1–21.

Simmons, Alison. 2013. 'Consciousness: The Philosopher's Leatherman Tool'. Paper presented at the NYU History of Consciousness Conference, November 2013. Unpublished Manuscript.

Simmons, Alison. 2017. 'Mind-Body Union and the Limits of Cartesian Metaphysics'. *Philosophers' Imprint* 17 (14), pp. 1–36.

Simon, Jean Robert. 1964. *Robert Burton (1577–1640) et l'Anatomie de la Mélancolie*. Paris: Didier.

Smith, John. 1660. *Selected Discourses*. London: J. Flesher.

Smith, Justin E. H. 2011. *Divine Machines: Leibniz and the Sciences of Life*. Princeton: Princeton University Press.

Smith, Justin. 2013. 'Heat, Action, Perception: Models of Living Beings in German Medical Cartesianism'. In *Cartesian Empiricisms*. Edited by Mihnea Dobre and Tammy Nyden. Dordrecht: Springer, pp. 105–123.

Specht, Rainer. 1966. *Commercium mentis et corporis: Über Kausalvorstellungen im Cartesianismus*. Stuttgart-Bad Cannstatt: Fromann-Holzboog.

Spinoza, Benedict de. 1925. *Opera*. Edited by Carl Gebhardt. 4 volumes. Heidelberg: Winter.

Spinoza, Benedict de. 1985. *The Collected Works of Spinoza Volume 1*. Edited and translated by Edwin Curley. Princeton: Princeton University Press.

Spinoza, Benedict de. 1999. *Œuvres, III: Tractatus theologico-politicus/Traité théologico-politique*. Texte établi par Fokke Akkerman, traduction et notes par Jacqueline Lagrée et Pierre-François Moreau. Paris: Presses Universitaires de France.

Spinoza, Benedict de. 2016. *The Collected Works of Spinoza Volume 2*. Edited and translated by Edwin Curley. Princeton: Princeton University Press.

Spinoza, Benedict de. 2020. *Œuvres, IV: Ethica/Éthique*. Texte établi par Fokke Akkerman et Piet Steenbakkers, traduction par Pierre-François Moreau, introduction et notes par Pierre-François Moreau et Piet Steenbakkers, avec annexes par Fabrice Audié, André Charrak et Pierre-François Moreau. Paris: Presses Universitaires de France.

Sprott, S. E. 1961. *The English Debate on Suicide. From Donne to Hume*. La Salle: Open Court.

Spruit, Leen. 1999. 'Johannes Clauberg on Perceptual Knowledge'. In *Johannes Clauberg (1622-1665) and Cartesian Philosophy in the Seventeenth Century*. Edited by Theo Verbeek. Dordrecht: Kluwer, pp. 75–93.

Spruit, Leen, and Pina Totaro (eds). 2011. *The Vatican Manuscript of Spinoza's Ethica*. Leiden/Boston: Brill.

Stahl, Georg-Ernst. 1706. *Disquisitio de mecanismi et organismi diversitate*. Halle.

Stahl, Georg-Ernst. 1859-1864. *Œuvres médico-philosophiques et pratiques*. 6 volumes. Translated by T. Blondin. Edited by L. Boyer. Paris: J.-B. Baillière.

Starobinski, Jean. 1984. 'Démocrite parle. L'utopie mélancolique de Robert Burton.' *Les Débats* 29, pp. 49–72.

Statius, Publius Papinius. *Silvae* [online]. Available at: <https://www.thelatinlibrary.com/statius/silvae5.shtml>.

Staum, Martin S. 2001. 'Review: Constructing Paris Medicine'. *Journal of Interdisciplinary History* 31 (4), pp. 641–642.

Steenbakkers, Piet, Jetze Touber, and Jeroen van de Ven. 2011. 'A Clandestine Notebook (1678–79) on Spinoza, Beverland, Politics, the Bible and Sex'. *Lias: Journal of Early Modern Intellectual Culture and its Sources* 38 (2), pp. 225–365.

Steenbakkers, Piet. 2013. *Over de dood van Spinoza, en Spinoza over de dood*. Voorschoten: Uitgeverij Spinozahuis.

Steenbakkers, Piet. 2018a. Review article: 'Edwin Curley (ed., tr.), *The Collected Works of Spinoza*, Volume II'. *Notre Dame Philosophical Reviews* [online]. Available at: <https://ndpr.nd.edu/news/the-collected-works-of-spinoza-volume-ii/>.

Steenbakkers, Piet. 2018b. [In Japanese] 'Supinoza ni totte ikiru ni ataisuru Ningen-teki na Sei towa donoyna mono ka' [Spinoza on a Human Life Worth Living]. Translated by Takeshi Ohno. *Spinozana: Spinoza Kyokai Review* 16, pp. 57–78.

Steenbakkers, Piet. Forthcoming 2021. 'Parallel Masterpieces: Intertextuality in Spinoza's Ethics and Theological-Political Treatise'. In *Spinoza: Reason, Religion, Politics: The Relation between the Ethics and the Tractatus Theologico-Politicus*. Edited by Dan Garber, Mogens Laerke, Pina Totaro and Pierre-François Moreau. Oxford: Oxford University Press.

Stencil, Eric. 2013. 'Antoine Arnauld'. *Internet Encyclopedia of Philosophy* [online]. Available at: <https://iep.utm.edu/aarnauld>.

Stoffell, Brian. 1991. 'Hobbes on Self-Preservation and Suicide'. *Hobbes Studies* 4 (1), pp. 26–33.

Strazzoni, Andrea. 2013. 'A Logic to End Controversies: The Genesis of Clauberg's *Logica Vetus et Nova*'. *Journal of Early Modern Studies* 2 (2), pp. 123–149.

Tarcov, Nathan. 2014. 'Machiavelli's Critique of Religion'. *Social Research: An International Quarterly* 81 (1), pp. 193–216.

Tertullianus, Q. Septimius Florentius. (a) 198-204 CE. *De Baptismo liber* [online]. Aailable at: http://www.tertullian.org/articles/evans_bapt/evans_bapt_text_trans.htm

Tertullianus, Q. Septimius Florentius. (b) 198-204 CE. *De paenitentia*. 21 May 2020. http://www.tertullian.org/latin/de_paenitentia.htm

Tertullianus, Q. Septimius Florentius. (c) 198-204 CE. *Adversus Marcionem*. 21 May 2020. https://www.thelatinlibrary.com/tertullian/tertullian.marcionem1.shtml.

Tertullianus, Q. Septimius Florentius. c. 213 CE. *De virginibus velandis* [online]. Available at: http://www.tertullian.org/latin/de_virginibus_velandis.htm.

Te Winkel, Jan. 1914. *Catalogus van de boekerij der Vereeniging Het Spinozahuis*. The Hague: Belinfante.

336 BIBLIOGRAPHY

Thiel, Udo. 2011. *The Early Modern Subject. Self-Consciousness and Personal Identity from Descartes to Hume*. Oxford: Oxford University Press.

Thouvenel, Pierre. 1780. *Mémoire chimique et médicinal sur la nature, les usages et les effets de l'air et des airs, des aliments et des médicaments relativement à l'économie animale*. Paris: Didot le jeune.

Tierney, Thomas F. 2006. 'Suicidal Thoughts: Hobbes, Foucault and the Right to Die'. *Philosophy & Social Criticism* 32 (5), pp. 601–38.

Timmermann, Jens. 2007. *Kants' Groundwork of the Metaphysics of Morals: A Commentary*. Cambridge: Cambridge University Press.

Timmermann, Jens. 2009. *Kant's Groundwork of the Metaphysics of Morals: A Critical Guide*. Cambridge: Cambridge University Press.

Toepfer, Georg. 2011. 'Vitalismus'. In Toepfer, Georg. *Historisches Wörterbuch der Biologie. Geschichte und Theorie der biologischen Grundbegriffe*. Volume 3. Stuttgart: J.B. Metzler Verlag, pp. 692–710.

Traherne, Thomas. 2005-18. *The Works of Thomas Traherne*. 8 volumes. Edited by Jan Ross. Cambridge: D. S. Brewer.

Trevisani, Francesco. 2011. *Descartes in Deutschland: die Rezeption des Cartesianismus in den Hochschulen Nordwestdeutschlands*. Münster: LIT-Verlag.

Tucker, Ericka. 2020. 'Power, Freedom, and Relational Autonomy'. In *Spinoza and Relational Autonomy*. Edited by Aurelia Armstrong, Keith Green and Andrea Sangiacomo. Edinburgh: Edinburgh University Press, pp. 149–163.

Uleman, Jennifer. 2016. 'No King and No Torture: Kant on Suicide and Law'. *Kantian Review* 21 (1), pp. 77–100.

Verbeek, Theo. 1992. *Descartes and the Dutch: Early Reactions to Cartesian Philosophy, 1637-1650*. Carbondale: Southern Illinois University Press.

Verbeek, Theo. 1999a. 'Johannes Clauberg: A Bio-Bibliographical Sketch'. In *Johannes Clauberg (1622-1665) and Cartesian Philosophy in the Seventeenth Century*. Edited by Theo Verbeek. Dordrecht: Kluwer, pp. 181–199.

Verbeek, Theo. 1999b. 'Clauberg et les Principes de Descartes'. In *Johannes Clauberg (1622-1665) and Cartesian Philosophy in the Seventeenth Century*. Edited by Theo Verbeek. Dordrecht: Kluwer, pp. 113–122.

Velkley, Richard L. 1989. *Freedom and the End of Reason: On the Moral Foundation of Kant's Critical Philosophy*. Chicago:University of Chicago Press.

Viljanen, Valtteri. 2011. *Spinoza's Geometry of Power*. Cambridge: Cambridge University Press.

Waller, Jason. 2009. 'Spinoza on the Incoherence of Self-Destruction'. *British Journal for the History of Philosophy* 17 (3), pp. 487–503.

Walther, Manfred, and Michael Czelinski. 2006. *Die Lebensgeschichte Spinozas*, vol. I: *Lebensbeschreibungen und Dokumente*, vol. II: *Kommentar*. Second, expanded and entirely revised edition of Jakob Freudenthal's Lebensgeschichte, 1899. Stuttgart-Bad Canstatt: frommann-holzboog.

Ward, Keith. 1972. *The Development of Kant's View of Ethics*. New York: Humanities Press.

Warda, Arthur. 1922. *Immanuel Kants Bücher*. Berlin: Verlag Von Martin Breslauer.

Wilkins, Emma. 2016. "Exploding' Immaterial Substances: Margaret Cavendish's Vitalist-Materialist Critique of Spirits'. *British Journal for the History of Philosophy* 24 (5), pp. 858–877.

Wilkins, John. 1682. *Sermons Preached upon Several Occasions*. London: Th. Bassett.

Williams, Elizabeth A. 2003. *A Cultural History of Medical Vitalism in Enlightenment Montpellier*. Aldershot: Ashgate.

Wilson, Catherine. 2016. 'Hume and vital materialism'. *British Journal for the History of Philosophy* 24 (5), pp. 1002–1021.

Wilson, Catherine. 2017a. 'The Living Individual: Leibniz and Buffon'. *Studia Leibnitiana Supplementa* 39.

Wilson, Catherine, 2017b. 'The Building Forces of Nature and Kant's Teleology of the Living'. In *Kant and the Laws of Nature*. Edited by Michela Massimi and Angela Breitenbach. Cambridge: Cambridge University Press.

Winckler, Johann Heinrich. 1742. *Institutiones philosophiæ universæ*. Lipsiæ: Fritsch.

Wolfe, Charles T. 2013. 'Vitalism and the Resistance to Experimentation on Life in the Eighteenth Century'. *Journal of the History of Biology* 46, pp. 255–282.

Wolfe, Charles T. 2014a. 'Sensibility as Vital Force or as Property of Matter in Mid-Eighteenth-Century Debates'. In *The Discourse of Sensibility. The Knowing Body in the Enlightenment*. Edited by Henry M. Lloyd. Dordrecht: Springer, pp. 147–170.

Wolfe, Charles T. 2014b. 'On the Role of Newtonian Analogies in Eighteenth-Century Life Science: Vitalism and Provisionally Inexplicable Explicative Devices'. In *Newton and Empiricism*. Edited by Zwi Biener and Eric Schliesser. Oxford: Oxford University Press, pp. 223–261.

Wolfe, Charles T. 2015. 'Il fascino discreto del vitalismo settecentesco e le sue riproposizioni'. In *Il libro della natura*. Volume 1: *Scienze e filosofia da Copernico a Darwin*. Edited by Paolo Pecere. Rome: Carocci, pp. 273–299.

Wolfe, Charles T. 2017a. 'Models of Organic Organization in Montpellier Vitalism'. *Early Science and Medicine* 22, pp. 229–252.

Wolfe, Charles T. 2017b. 'Varieties of Vital Materialism'. In *The New Politics of Materialism. History, Philosophy, Science*. Edited by Sarah Ellenzweig and John Zammito. London: Routledge, pp. 44–65.

Wolfe, Charles T. 2018. 'Adam Smith, Vitalist?'. *Journal of Scottish Philosophy* 16(3), pp. 264–271.

Wolfe, Charles T. 2019. *La philosophie de la biologie avant la biologie : une histoire du vitalisme*. Paris: Classiques Garnier.

Wolfe, Charles T. 2020. 'Vitalism in early modern medical and philosophical thought'. In *Encyclopedia of Early Modern Philosophy and the Sciences*. Edited by Dana Jalobeanu and Charles T. Wolfe. Cham: Springer.

Wolfe, Charles T. and Etxeberria, Arantza. 2018. 'Canguilhem and the Logic of Life'. *Transversal: International Journal for the Historiography of Science* 4, pp. 47–63.

Wolfe, Charles T. and Terada, Motoichi. 2008. 'The Animal Economy as Object and Program in Montpellier Vitalism'. *Science in Context* 21 (4), pp. 537–579.

Wood, Allen W. 1999. *Kant's Ethical Thought*. Cambridge: Cambridge University Press.

Woolhouse, Roger. 2007. *Locke: A Biography*. Cambridge: Cambridge University Press.

Wootton, David. 2018. *Power, Pleasure, and Profit: Insatiable Appetites from Machiavelli to Madison*. Cambridge, MA: Harvard University Press.

Yolton, Jean S. (editor). 2000. *John Locke as Translator*. Oxford: Voltaire Foundation.

Youpa, Andrew. 2003. 'Spinozistic Self-Preservation'. *Southern Journal of Philosophy* 41 (3), pp. 477–490.

Youpa, Andrew. 2010. 'Spinoza's Model of Human Nature'. *Journal of the History of Philosophy* 48 (1), pp. 61–76.

Zahavi, Dan. 2007. 'The Heidelberg School and the Limits of Reflection'. In *Consciousness: From Perception to Reflection in the History of Philosophy*. Edited by Sara Heinämaa, Vili Lähteenmaki and Pauliina Remes. Dordrecht: Springer, pp. 267–285.

338 BIBLIOGRAPHY

Zammito, John H. 2002. *Kant, Herder, and the Birth of Anthropology*. Chicago: University of Chicago Press.

Zeppi, Stelio. 1971. 'Significato e posizione storica dell'etica di Democrito'. In *Atti dell'Accademia delle Scienze di Torino*, Classe di Scienze morali, storiche e filologiche. CV, pp. 499–540.

Zhuravlev, Yuri N. and Avetisov, Vladik A. 2006. 'The Definition of Life in the Context of Its Origin'. *Biogeosciences* 3 (3), pp. 281–291.

Index

For the benefit of digital users, table entries that span two pages (e.g., 52–53) may, on occasion, appear on only one of those pages.

Aalto, S. K. 247
Aaron, Richard I. 98–100, 102–3
Ablondi, Fred 163, 263–4
Adam, Charles 40
afterlife
 atheism, and 11
 belief in 40, 49–50
 existence of 59
 expectation of 5–6, 47, 49–52, 59
 experience of 59–62
 fear of 9–10
 no fear of 201
 non-existence of 45–6
 philosophical foretaste of 175–6
 pleasure in 5–6, 9–10, 59–62, 174–5
 pleasures of 9–10
 rejection of 194–5
 religion, and 50–1
 society in 62
 soul, and 43
 see also immortality
Akkerman, Fokke 191
Aldobrandini, Tommaso 204
Aler, Jan 188–9
Alfieri, Vittorio Enzo 198–201
Allison, Henry E. 240–2, 244
Ambrose of Camaldoli see Traversari, Ambrogio
Ameriks, Karl 239–40, 252–3
Ames, William 87
Andrault, Raphaële 128
animate things, inanimate things distinguished
 from 14–16, 277–91
anthropology, suicide and 248
Antognazza, Maria Rosa 219
Aquinas, Thomas 12–13, 41, 53–4, 86–7, 92, 99,
 211–14, 217, 224–5
Aristophanes 191
Aristotle 22, 33–4, 44, 47–8, 62–3, 68, 87–9, 94,
 96–7, 102, 159–60, 191, 200–1, 265, 271,
 280–1, 292, 296–7, 299–300, 313
Aristoxenus 198
Armstrong, Aurelia 151
Arnauld, Antoine 4, 11–14

Arnobius 85–6
asceticism
 pleasure, and 122–3
 sense of 157
 Spinoza's critique of 127
Asclepiades 199–200
Ashcraft, Richard 96
Astell, Mary 8–9, 106–8, 120–4
Astolfi, Giovanni Felice 204
atheism
 accusations of 11, 181, 192–5, 253
 afterlife, and 11
 death as punishment for 192, 196
 mediocrity, and 102
Athenaeus 199–200, 205–8
atomism 68–9, 200, 202–4, 311–12
Augustine 26–9, 62–3, 85–7, 94, 105, 212–13,
 217, 223
Aulus Gellius 198
Avetisov, Vladik A. 265

Bacon, Francis 91, 94, 304
Bailey, Cyril 193–4
Balibar, Etienne 150–1, 280
Bariéty Maurice 310–11
Barrow, Isaac 94–5
Barthez, Paul Joseph 272, 296–7, 302–4, 306–7, 309
Bates, William 88
Baumeister, Friedrich Christian 65–6
Baumgarten, Alexander Gottlieb 66
Bayle, Pierre 11–12, 207–8, 223–5, 249–50, 259
Beauchamp, Tom L. 211–12, 227, 231
Beck, Lewis White 239–40
Beiser, Frederick 239–40, 252
Bennett, Jane 292
Bennett, Jonathan 127, 286
Bergson, Henri 292
Bernard, Claude 298–9, 312–14
Berthelot, Marcellin 199–200
Bichat, Marie François Xavier 298–9, 310
biology
 Cartesian 15, 270–6, 278
 mathematics, and 299

340 INDEX

biology (*cont.*)
  perspective of 2–3
  transformative effects of biological
    processes 278, 286–9
  vitalism, and 299, 301, 304, 311–13
Blount, Charles 248
Blumenbach, Johann Friedrich 303
body
  conjunction with mind 25–6, 30–1, 157–68,
    266–8, 270, 275, 277
  death of 50–1, 128, 142, 163
  distinction from mind 49
  life of 133–41, 145–6, 163
  notion of 267–8
  relation with mind 134, 280–1
  separation from mind 10–11, 168–80
  soul and 22, 30, 32, 47–8, 73–4, 82, 102–3,
    163–4
Boehm, Omri 188
Bohatec, Josef 159–60
Boissier de Sauvages, François 296–7
Bolduc, Carl R. 188
Bolus of Mendes 199–200
Bonnet, Charles 310
Bordeu, Theophile 298–302, 305–11, 313–14
Bouillaud, Jean 310
Boureau-Deslandes, André-François 205–8
Boyle, Deborah 293
Broadie, Sarah 161–2
Brooks, G. P. 247
Brown, Deborah J. 268–9
Brown, Stuart 65–6, 68–73
Brownrigg, Ralph 97
Brutus 12
Buffon, Georges-Louis Leclerc, Comte de 2–3
Burgh, Albert 192
Burman, Ross 160–1
Burton, Robert 11–12, 205, 216–17

Caecilius 104
Caelius Aurelianus 199–200
Cage, John 136
Cahn, Zilla Gabrielle 211
Callanan, John 13–14
Callanan, John J. 239–60
Camerarius, Elias 66–8, 71–2
Campanella, Tomaso 313
Camposampiero, Matteo Favaretti 6–7, 64–82
Canetti, Elias 292
Canguilhem, Georges 273–4, 300, 304, 310–11
Canz, Israel Gottlieb 66
Carson, Emily 252
cartesianism *see* Descartes, René
Casaubon, Isaac 204

Casertano, Giovanni 200
Caspar, Ernst Christophe 66
Cassiodorus 85–6
Cassirer, Ernst 239–40, 242–3, 249–50, 252–3
Cato, Marcus Portius 214, 244–6
Cavendish, Margaret 1–2, 15–16, 292–3, 299
Chalmers, David 305–6, 312
Chang, Kevin 294–7, 300–2, 305–7, 314
Charles II, King 87–8
Charron, Pierre 8
Chen, Bohang 311–12
Chene, Dennis Des 276
Cheung, Tobias 313–14
Chitwood, Ava 197
Cholbi, Michael 242–3
Choron, Jacques 65–6
Christianity
  afterlife, and 9–11, 40
  death, and 82
  immortality, concept of 65–6
  knowledge of God 176
  lifespan, notion of 1–2
  mediocrity, and 87
  resurrection, conception of 65–6
  sin, conception of 71–2
  suicide, and 12, 213–17
Christina, Queen of Sweden 53
Chyba, Christopher F. 265
Cicero, Marcus Tullius 10, 85–7, 188–9, 191,
    193, 244
Cioran, Emil 211
Clarke, Desmond 11, 14, 40–2, 106–7, 116–17
Clauberg, Johannes 10–11, 157
Cleland, Carol E. 265
Colerus, Johannes 195–6
Collins, Antony 85–6
Condette, Jean-François 297–8
Condillac, Étienne Bonnot de 4–5
Connell, Sophia 296–7
consciousness
  Descarte's definition of thought, and 22–5
  epistemic self-relation, as 20–2
  feeling alive 3–5, 19–20
  individual 4–5
  life of the soul, and 25–9
  meaning of 3–4
  phenomenology of 4
  source of knowledge, as 35–6
  Spinoza's response to Descartes 26–36
  Spinoza's theory of 279–81
Conway, Anne 1–2
Coste, Pierre 66–7
Cottingham, Eric 276
Cottingham, John 268

INDEX 341

Cotton, Charles 208
Coury Charles 310–11
Cranston, Maurice 98–9
Crick, Francis 311–12
Critchley, Simon 197
Crocker, Lester G. 211, 222, 243
Crone, Daniel M. 211, 220
Cudworth, Damaris 101–2
Cudworth, Ralph 75–6, 293, 301–2
Cunningham, A. 292
Curley, Edwin 125, 139, 144
Cyprian 85–6
Czelinski, Michael 195

d'Ablancourt, Nicolas Perrot 92
Daremberg, Charles 310–11
Darius, King of Persia 201–2
Darwin, Charles 304
De Ceglia, Francesco Paolo 296–7
de Gournay, Marie 106–7, 112–13
de la Forge, Loius 1–2, 4, 11–16, 28–9, 33, 158–9, 162–4, 166–7
de La Mothe Le Vaye, François 40
de Raey, Johannes 159–60, 177–80
de Saint-Paul, Eustache 40–1
death
   banishment of see Leibnizian banishment of death
   Christian philosophical perspectives on 39–40
   contrast with life 106
   Democritus's death, accounts of 197
   exemplary deaths 11–12
   external cause, by 141–4
   good death, notion of 11
   learning to die 10–12
   meditatio mortis 157–80
   mind, of the 145–8
   philosophers' deaths, accounts of 197
   punishment for atheism, as 192, 196
   sin, and 71–2
   Spinoza's meditations 125–9, 148–53
   Spinoza's model of good death 192–6
   see also immortality; suicide
Debus, Allen George 200–1
Deleuze, Gilles 128–9, 137, 152–3
Della Rocca, Michael 127, 132, 151
Democritus 11–12, 67–8, 70–1, 197–208
Demosthenes 191
Des Chene, D. 305
Des Maizeaux, Pierre 64–5, 67–73
Descartes, René 1–4, 22–33, 35, 40–2, 47–56, 59, 62–3, 107–13, 117, 121–4, 129, 157–80, 218–21, 225–6, 263–76, 305, 311–12
Desiderius Erasmus Roterodamus see Erasmus

despair
   ignorance, and 137
   pride, and 97
   science, and 91
   suicide, and 13–14
Desprez, G. 100
Detlefsen, Karen 263–4
di Biase. Giuliana 7–8, 85–105
Diderot, Denis 1–2, 294, 299–300, 307
Diels, Hermann 199–201
Digby, Sir Kenelm 52–3
Donne, John 88, 94–5, 98, 212–13, 216
Douglas, Alexander X. 177–8, 276
Driesch, Hans 292, 311–12
dualism 24–31, 35, 268–70, 274–6
Duchesneau, François 296–7
Dumas, Charles-Louis 297–8, 300–2, 305
duty
   artificial duties, concept of 228–9
   God, to 211–12, 227–8, 230–1, 233
   intellectual 89–92, 95–6, 98
   natural duties, concept of 228–9
   performance of 229
   self, to 222, 232–3, 241, 257
   society, to 12–13, 214, 220–2, 224–5, 227–8, 230–1
   suicide, and 228–9

ecstasy
   pleasure, and 10, 157
   separation of mind from body, and 157
   state of 161–2, 164, 166, 168–9
education
   learning to die 10–12
   learning to live 7–10, 111–13, 124
   see also learning to live
   perspective of 2
   prejudice against women's 8, 116–20, 122–3
   see also knowledge
eleatism 68–9
eliminativism 265, 270–1
Elisabeth, Princess Palatine of Bohemia 5–6, 51–3, 112, 267–8
Elmenhorst, Gevehartus 92
Ennius, Quintus 191
Epicurus 193–4, 201, 244
epistemology
   Cartesian 29, 264
   consciousness, and 20–2, 35
   epistemological demand to understand 285
   immortality, and 62–3
   perspective of 2
   Spinoza 33
   suicide, and 246

342 INDEX

equality and inequality, sexual 116–20
Erasmus 12–13, 92, 161–2, 212–16, 225–6
Eriksen, Christoffer Basse 276
Estienne, Henry 204
eternal life *see* immortality
ethics, perspective of 2
Etxeberria, Arantza 273, 296–7
existence, life as power of 129–33

Faubert, Michelle 255–6
Feldman, Fred 241–2
Fénelon, François 204
Fernel, Jean 313
Ficino, Marsilio 158, 161–2
Filleau de la Chaise, Nicolas 100
Flenderus, Johannes 163–4
Foulcher, Jane 86–7
Fox Keller, Evelyn 313–14
Fraenkel, Carlos 130
Frey, R. G. 227, 231

Gabhart, Mitchell 127
Galen 216–17, 271, 298
Galvin, Richard 241
Garber, Daniel 127, 263
Garrett, Don 132, 136, 151, 279–80
Garve, Christian 244
Gassendi, Pierre 13, 40, 109–10, 122–3, 295
Gaukroger, Stephen 305–6
Geiger, Ido 257
gender, inequality of the sexes 116–20
Georgescu, Laura 276
Geulincx, Arnold 163–4, 176–7
Gibb, Jocelyn 98–100, 102–3
Giglioni, Guido 308–9
Gildon, Charles ('Lindamour') 248–9, 255–6
Glazemaker, Jan Hendriksz 190
Glisson, Francis 308–11
God
  duty to 230–1
  ignorance of 92–3
  knowledge of 176
  purpose for pleasure 47
Goethe, Johann Wolfgang von 13–14, 255–6
good life
  effort to live a 96
  health of the body, and 179
  notion of 1
  reason, and 99
  Spinoza's model of 182–92, 194–5
Goudriaaen, Aza 174–5
Grenville, Denis 89–90, 95–7
Grey, John 127

Grigoropoulou, Vasiliki 158
Grmek, Mirko 296–7

habit *see* learning to live
Hale, Sir Matthew 97
Hall, Thomas S. 263–4
Haller, Albrecht von 308–14
Hansch, Theodor 67–8
Hänsch, Theodor 66
Harrison, John 85–6, 92, 98–100
Harrison, Timothy 4–5
Hartlib, Samuel 106
Harvey William 292, 295, 313
Hatfield, Gary 172
Hazard, Paul 239
Hazlitt, William Carew 208
Healy, Róisín 211–12
Heller-Roazen, Daniel 5
Henrich, Dieter 252–3
Henry, John 244–5, 292
Heraclides of Pontus 199–200
Heraclitus 197–8
Hermippus of Smyrna 198–200
Hintikka, Jaakko 252
Hipparchus 198–9
Hippocrates 68, 201–3, 216–17, 298
Hirai, Hiro 295
Hobbes, Thomas 9–10, 13, 87–8, 252–3
Holden, Thomas 227, 230
Hooker, Richard 87
Horace 85–7
Howe, John 94–5
Hume, David 7–8, 12–13, 211–12, 222, 224–38, 292, 300, 304
Huneman, Philippe 298–9
Hunter, John 295
Hunter, William 295
Hutcheson, Francis 244, 246–8, 252–3
Hutchins, Barnaby 14–15, 163, 263–76, 305
Huygens, Christian 49–50, 53–4

ignorance
  consequences of 137
  despair, and 137
  God, of 92–3
  immortality, and 82
  knowledge, and 89–90, 93–4
  mediocrity, and 88
  state of 89–90, 92–3, 95–6, 98–9, 111–12, 139, 151–2, 189–90
  superstition, and 232
  use of 206–7
immortality
  arguments for 43–7

INDEX 343

Christian philosophical perspectives on 39–40
conceptions of 65–6
de Saint-Paul on 40–1
de Silhon on 41–7
Descartes on 47–54
ignorance, and 82
immortalism *see* Leibnizian banishment of
death 6–7
Lessius on 41–7
Malebranche on 57–63
Pascal on 55–6
proofs of 40
question of 5–7
see also afterlife
inanimate things, animate things distinguished
from 14–16, 277–91
intellectual mediocrity 88–96, 100–1, 104

Jacobs, A. 293
James, Susan 1–16, 152–3, 260, 293, 301, 314
Jaquet, Chantal 194
Jaworzyn, Michael 10, 157–80
Jeans, James 293–4
Jehasse, Jean 197–8
Jerusalem, Karl Wilhelm 255–6
Johann Friedrich, Duke of Brunswick-
Calenberg 72–3
John Philoponus 200–1
Jonas, Hans 128
Jones, Donna V. 292
Joukovsky, Françoise 204
Judaism, afterlife and 11
Julian, Roman Emperor 201–2

Kant, Immanuel 2–3, 13–14, 186–9, 239–60
Kawamura, Fumie 292
Kelly, Christopher 249–50, 260
Kenny, Anthony 276
King, Hugh Fortescue Locke 89–92, 99–100
Kircher, Athanasius 73
Kisner, Matthew 286
Kisner, Matthew J. 127
Kleiman-Lafon, Sylvie 305–6
Klein, Julie R. 125–53
Klein, Julius 9–10
knowledge
consciousness as source of 35–6
God, of 176
ignorance, and 89–90, 93–4
morality, of 88
nonreductionist knowledge of life 269–76,
see also education
Korsgaard, Christine M. 241–2
Koshland Jr, Daniel 264–5, 275

Kranz, Walther 200–1
Kraye, Jill 175–6
Kuehn, Manfred 244, 252
Kühn, Richard 313

La Mothe Le Vayer, François de 40, 259
Lactantius 87, 92–4
Lærke, Mogens 129, 132
Laërtius, Diogenes 11–12, 198–9, 201, 203–8
Laks, André 198–200, 202–3
Lana, Italo 202
Laslett, Peter 85–6, 92, 98–100
Le Grand, Antoine 163–4
Le Moyne, Pierre 223
learning to die 10–12
learning to live
conceptual approaches to 7–10
education, role of 111–13, 124
habit, role of 113–16
introduction to 106–8
prejudice, influence of 116–20
unlearning bad habits 120–4
will, role of 108–10, 124
LeBuffe, Michael 286
Legallois, César Julien Jean 313–14
Leibniz, Gottfried Wilhelm 1–3, 5–7, 12–13,
64–73, 159–60, 219–21, 225–6, 250–1, 292,
296–7, 299–300
Leibnizian banishment of death
death and generation 80–2
early controversies 67–71
historical significance of 82
history of Leibnizian immortalism 66–7
introduction to 64–6
philosophers associated with 71–6
puzzle of identity through death 76–80
Lennon, Thomas 174–5
Lentulus, Cyriacus 157, 159–60
Lessing, Gotthold Ephraim 255–6
Lessius, Leonard 40–3, 45–8, 50–1, 53, 55–6, 59,
62–3
liberty
native liberty, concept of 228–9
philosophy as restorer of 232
suicide, and 228–9
life
bodies, of 133–41, 145–6, 163
Cartesian theory of 263–76
contrast with death 106
after death *see* immortality
distinction between animate and inanimate
things 14–16, 277–91
effects, affections, and partial causes 284–7
eternal *see* immortality

344 INDEX

life (*cont.*)
  extent of 1
  feeling alive *see* consciousness
  good life *see* good life
  indefinability of 264–9, 275–6
  irreducibility of 266–9
  Kant's model of good life 186–9
  love of 244–7
  mediocrity, state of *see* mediocrity
  mind, of the 145–8
  non-functional notion of 274–5
  nonreductionist knowledge, and 269–76
  pananimation 281, 283, 290–1
  power of existence (*potentia*), as 129–33
  Spinoza's meditations 125–9, 148–53
  Spinoza's model of good life 182–91, 196
  transitive and transformative effects 282–4,
    288–91
  vitalism, and 264, 271–4,
  see also biology; learning to live
life sciences
  early modern natural philosophy, and 2–3
  perspective of 2
  philosophy, and 14
  scientific naturalism, and 19
  vitalism, and 271, 274, 294–6, 299,
    309–14
  see also biology; psychology
lifespan
  allotted 222
  beginning 1–2
  end 222
  notion of 1–2
Lima, Teresa Tato 227–38
Lin, Martin 135–6, 145–6
Lind, Vera 216–17
Lindamour *see* Gildon, Charles
Locke, John 4–5, 7–9, 12–13, 35, 85–107,
  113–16, 120–1, 220–1, 225, 292
LoLordo, Antonia 295
Lordat, Jacques 303
Lough, John 98–9
Lucretia 12
Lucretius 214, 295
Ludolf, Hiob 73
Ludwig, Bernd 259–60
Luria, Salomon 198–202
Lusitanus, Amatus 97
Lüthy, Christoph 197–8

MacDonald, Michael 211–12
MacDonald Ross, George 72–3
Machiavelli, Nicolo 42
MacKenzie, Ann Wilbur 263–4, 270

Maimonides (Moses ben Maimon) 130
Makin, Bathsua 106–7
Malebranche, Nicolas 1–2, 5–6, 12–13, 40,
  57–63, 221–2
Mandeville, Bernard 244–8
Manning, Gideon 178–9
Manton, Thomas 88
Maramma, Daniele 280–1
Marcilius, Theodore 85–6
Marcus Aurelius 204
Markovits, Francine 206
Marshall, Eugene 98–9, 279–80
Marston, Steph 14–15, 277–91
Marvell, Andrew 50–1
Mason, Richard 188
Masson, Émile 67
mathematics
  biology, and 299
  morality, and 13–14, 104, 243–4, 247–50
  perspective of 2
  philosophy, and 243–4, 252–4, 256–60
  value of 111–13
Matheron, Alexandre 132, 135–6
Matson, Wallace 127, 313
Matteini, Claudia 276
Maupertuis, Pierre Loius 13–14, 249–52,
  254, 258
Maupertuis, Pierre Louis 243–4
Mayr, E. 312–13
Mazarin, Jules Mazarin, Cardinal 41–2
Mclean, G. R. 227
mediocrity
  atheism, and 102
  development of Locke's ideas on 95–101
  further development of Locke's ideas on
    104–5
  ignorance, and 88
  intellectual 88–96, 100–1, 104
  life as state of 85–8
  moral excellence, and 101–3, 105
meditatio mortis 157–80
Melanchthon, Philip 87
Melissus 68
Ménage, Gilles 204
Mendelssohn, Moses 243–4, 248–51, 255–6
Ménuret de Chambaud, Jean-Joseph 300–2,
  304–7, 310–11, 313–14
Merrill, Kenneth R. 236–7
Mersenne, Marin 40, 49, 54
metaphysics
  distinction between animate and inanimate
    things 15–16, 277
  feeling alive 4
  perspective of 2

INDEX 345

Miller, Jon 127, 182–3
Milton, John 4–5, 106
mind
  conjunction with body 25–6, 30–1, 157–68,
    266–8, 270, 275, 277
  distinction from body 49
  life and death of 145–8
  notion of 267–8
  relation with body 134, 280–1
  separation from body 10–11, 168–80
Minois, Georges 214
Minucius Felix 92–3
Monaco, Davide 143–4
monadology 67, 75, 77–8
Montaigne, Michel de 12–13, 39–40, 58, 94, 101,
  208, 212–13, 215–17, 219–20, 225, 244–7
Montesquieu, Charles-Louis de Secondat, Baron
  de La Brède et de 211
Moore, G. E. 31–2
morality
  conformity with 236
  deontological conception of 252
  Enlightenment scientific morality as to
    suicide 247–50
  explanatory and motivational dimensions
    of 244, 246, 252–3
  knowledge of 88
  learning about 104
  mathematics, and 13–14, 104, 243–4, 247–50
  mediocrity and moral excellence 101–3, 105
  natural philosophy, and 177–8
  a priori grounds of 247
  reason, and 252–3
  subjective principles of 247
  suicide, of 13, 211–12, 227–8, 231, 233, 236–7
  truth, and 47
  virtue, and 8–9, 40–1, 87
More, Henry 5–6, 8, 48, 293, 301–2
More, Thomas 12, 212–16, 225
Moreau, Pierre-François 136
Moreno, Alvaro 265
Morfino, Vittorio 150
Moriarty, Michael 5–6, 39–62
Morris, Katherine J. 174
Murdoch, Dugald 276
Murphy, Terence R. 211–12
Murray, Alexander 216–17
mysticism, immortalism and 74–5

Nachtomy, Ohad 276
Nadler, Steven 127, 132, 185, 279–80
natural philosophy
  Cartesian 47–8, 263, 275
  immortality, and 47–8, 51

  learning, and 106–7
  life sciences, and 2–3
  mediocrity, and 104
  morality, and 177–8
naturalism
  immortalism, and 74–5
  incremental 279–80
  scientific 19
Naudé, Gabriel 206–7
Nedham, Marchamont 87–8
Newton, Isaac 304, 310
Nicholas of Cusa 94
Nicole, Pierre 88, 98–101
Nizolius, Marius 188–9
nominalism 140–1
Normore, Calvin G. 268–9

Obbink, Dirk 193–4
O'Neill, Onora 240–1

Pagel, Walter 296–7
pain, pleasure and 13–14, 46, 233, 247–51,
  258–9, 294
pananimation 281, 283, 290–1
panpsychism
  dualism, and 34
  immortalism, and 73–5
  Spinoza's theory of life, in 277, 279, 281
  vitalism, and 292–5, 313
Paracelsus 271
Parmenides 68, 70–1
Pascal, Blaise 40, 42, 55–7, 62–3, 88, 98–101, 105
Paton, Herbert J. 241–2
Paul, St 94–5, 105
Paullini, Christianus Franciscus 72–3
Pelagius 10–11, 94, 158, 174–8
Pelletier, Arnauld 67–8
Peretó, Juli 265
Petronius 39–40
Pfaff, Christophe Matthäus 71–3
philology, immortalism and 69–70
philosophy *see* natural philosophy
Pinkard, Terry 239–40
Piquer, Andrés 97
Plato 70–1, 94, 158, 161–2, 176, 181, 186, 188–9,
  191, 193, 198, 295
pleasure
  absence of 114, 214
  afterlife 5–6, 9–10, 59–62, 174–5
  asceticism, and 122–3
  born for 50
  control, and 8–9
  ecstasy, and 157
  experience of 294

346 INDEX

pleasure (*cont.*)
  futile 56
  God's purpose for 47
  habitual 122–4
  pain, and 13–14, 46, 233, 247–51, 258–9, 294
  praise of 127
  pursuit of good, and 123–4
  sensory 5–6, 161
  suicide, and 214
  virtue, and 47, 233, 245
Plutarch 102, 250–1
Poiret, Pierre 71–3
potentia see existence
Poulain de la Barre, François 8–9, 106–8,
  116–22
preformationism 81
prejudice
  force of 31–2, 124, 206–7, 230–1
  against women 8, 116–20, 122–3
pride, despair and 97
Pseudo-Democritus *see* Bolus of Mendes
psychology
  life as psychological feature of a thing 34
  perspective of 2
  suicide, and 239–40, 243, 246–8
Pythagoras 74–5

Quantin, Jean Louis 92

Rabelais, François 161–2
Ramus, Petrus 87
rationalism *see* reason
Ravven, Heidi M. 150
reason
  learning to live, and 112–13
  morality, and 252–3
  suicide, and 243, 254–5
reductionism, irreducibility of life 269–76
Regius, Henricus 263–4, 269, 275
Reich, Klaus 188
reincarnation, conceptions of 65–6
religion
  afterlife, and 50–1
  perspective of 2
  suicide, and 13
  see also Christianity; God; Judaism
Renz, Ursula 3–4, 19–36, 131, 134–5
resurrection, conception of 65–6
Revius, Jacobus 92, 157, 159–60, 174–6, 178
Rhodiginus, Lodovicus Caelius 207–8
Richardot, Anne 197–8
Richlieu, Armand Jean du Plessis, Duke of
  Richelieu, Cardinal 41–2
Rorty, Amelie O. 142–3, 148–9

Rousseau, Jean-Jacques 1–2, 13–14, 117–18, 188,
  222, 225, 239, 242–5, 252–7, 260
Roux, Sophie 276
Ruiz-Mirazo, Kepa 265
Rumore, Paola 276

Sacksteder, William 149
Salem, Jean 197–8, 200–1
Sanderson, Robert 87
Santos-Campos, Andre 135–6
Savile, Anthony 65–6
Savini, Massimiliano 170, 178–9
Scaliger, Julius Caesar 296–7
Schaff, Philip 93
Schiavo, Piero 11–12, 197–208
Schmaltz, Tad 159–60
Schmitter, Amy 116–17
Schneewind, J. B. 211–12
scholasticism
  Aristotelian 159–60
  Cartesian 158–60
Schonecker, Dieter 241–2
Schönfeld, Martin 252
Schurman, Anna Maria van 106–7, 110
science
  despair, and 91
  exclusion of women from 117–18
  mechanistic 273, 299
  metaphysics, and 313–14
  philosophy, and 104
  reason, and 243, 247
  value of 111–12
  see also biology; life sciences
Scodel, Joshua 87–8
Screech, Michael A. 161–2, 175–6
self, love of 244–7
Seneca, Lucius Annaeus 12, 39–40, 145–6,
  161–2, 214–16
Sennert, Daniel 296–7
sentimentalism, suicide and 13–14, 255–6
Sextus Empiricus 94
sexual inequality 116–20
Shaftesbury, Anthony Ashley Cooper, the third
  Earl of 1–2, 4, 35, 66–8
Shagan, Ethan H. 86–7
Shapiro, Lisa 8–9, 106–24
Sharp, Hasana 135–6, 150
Shein, Noa 150
Shell, Susan Meld 252–3
Sherlock, William 85–6
Sidonius Apollinaris 85–6
Silhon, Jean de 40–8, 50–1, 53–6, 59, 62–3
Simmons, Alice 4
Simmons, Alison 160–1, 268

Simon, Jean Robert 205
sin, death and 71–2
Smith, Adam 237–8
Smith, John 102–3
Smith, Justin 163, 179, 296–7
society
  afterlife, in 62
  duty to 12–13, 214, 220–2, 224–5, 227–8, 230–1
Socrates 11, 39–40, 193, 198
Sophie Charlotte, Queen of Mecklenburg-Strelitz 64–5, 72–3
Sophocles 191
soul
  afterlife, and 43
  body, and 22, 30, 32, 47–8, 73–4, 82, 102–3, 163–4
  consciousness and life of 25–9
  Platonic theory of 65–6
Specht, Rainer 157
Spinoza, Baruch 1–2, 4–5, 9–11, 14–16, 29–36, 70–1, 125–53, 181–96, 218, 253, 277–92
Sprott, S. E. 211
Spruit, Leen 159–60, 168–70, 172, 190
Stahl, Georg-Ernst 294–300, 305–8, 310, 312–13
Stanley, Thomas 204–5
Starobinski, Jean 197–8
Statius 85–6
Staum, Martin S. 303
Steenbakkers, Piet 11–12, 182, 192, 195–6
stoicism
  immortality, and 53–4
  mediocrity, and 87
  Spinoza and 182–3
  suicide, and 214
Stoothoff, Robert 276
Strahan, William 237–8
Strazzioni, Andrea 159–60
subjectivism, suicide and 243–4
suicide
  Christianity, and 12
  descriptions of 12
  despair, and 13–14
  duty, and 228–9
  duty to God and to society, and 230–1
  early modern philosophy, and 211–13, 217–26
  Enlightenment scientific morality 247–50
  Hume's *Of Suicide* 227–38
  Kant's *Groundwork* 239–60
  liberty 228–9
  limits of philosophical reasoning 234–8
  love of life and of self 244–7
  medieval Christianity, and 213–17
  moral permissibility of 12–13

  morality of 13, 211–12, 227–8, 231, 233, 236–7
  negative magnitudes of feeling 250–2
  question of 12–14
  religion, and 13
  Renaissance, and 213–17
  Rousseau on 252–6
  self, and 233
  sentimentalism, and 13–14
superstition, ignorance and 232

Tabb, Kathryn 314
Tannery, Paul 40
Tarcov, Nathan 42
Tato Lima, Theresa 13–14
Taylor, C. C. W. 198
Te Winkel, Jan 188–9
Telesio, Bernardino 296–7
Terada, Motoichi 272, 300
Tertullian 85–6
theism, immortality and 39–40
Thiel, Udo 4–5
thought, consciousness and 22–5
Thouvenel, Pierre 298
Tigellinus 39–40
Timmermann, Jens 241–2
Toepfer, Georg 298
Toland, John 64–5, 72–3
Totaro, Pina 190
Traherne, Thomas 4–5
Traversari, Ambrogio 203–4
Tredennick, Hugh 193
Trevisani, Francesco 159–60, 178–9
Tropper, Sarah 12–13, 211–26
truth, morality and 47
Tucker, Ericka 151

Uleman, Jennifer 242–3

van Gent, Pieter 190
van Helmont, Jan Baptist 300–1
van Ruler, Han 175–6
van Velthuysen, Lambert 181
Velkley, Richard L. 252–3
Velleius Paterculus 85–6
Venantius Fortunatus 85–6
Verbeek, Theo 159–60, 177–8
Viljanen, Valtteri 132, 151
virtue
  moral 8–9, 40–1, 87
  pleasure, and 47, 233, 245
vitalism
  animism, and 297–301
  cosmic 15–16, 294–7, 299–300, 307

348 INDEX

vitalism (*cont.*)
  criticisms of 301–7
  distinction between life and death 15–16
  immanent 15–16, 294–7, 300–2, 305–6
  indefinability of life 271–4
  introduction to 292–5
  life sciences, and 271, 274, 294–6, 299, 309–14
  metaphysics, as 307–11
  panpsychism, and 292–5, 313
  problems in defining 311–14

Wager, Walter H. 56
Walther, Manfred 195
Ward, Keith 252
Ward, Samuel 87
Warda, Arthur 249–50
Wilkins, Emma 293
Wilkins, John 97
will, operation of 108–10, 124

Williams, Elizabeth A. 298
Wilson, Catherine 300
Wolfe, Charles T 14–16
Wolfe, Charles T. 272–3, 292–314
Wolff, Christian 6, 64–6
women, prejudice against 8, 116–20, 122–3
Wood, Allen W. 241–2
Woolhouse, Roger 98–9
Wootton, David 249–50, 260

Xenophanes 249–50

Yolton, Jean S. 98–9
Youpa, Andrew 127, 135–6, 146–7

Zammito, John H. 252–3
Zeppi, Stelio 201
Zhuravlev, Yuri N. 265
Zorn, John 136